Acclaim for RICHARD ELLIS's

IMAGINING ATLANTIS

"Impressive.... An important volume in the library of Atlantis literature."
—*San Francisco Chronicle*

"Quite a read.... Engaging."
—*The Hartford Courant*

"Truly charming, funny, and assiduous.... Ellis' spirit of non-judgmental inquisitiveness [is] above and beyond the call of duty."
—*Newsday*

"Richard Ellis takes us on a fascinating ride, throwing in lessons in archaeology, history, geology, mythology and art."
—*Fort Worth Star-Telegram*

"[Ellis] shows that, true or not, the very idea of Atlantis is humanly necessary, soothing some yen that all of us have . . . for mysteries that hover always, like a mirage, just beyond the verge of explanation."
—*The News & Observer* [Raleigh]

"In tracing both the scientific pursuit . . . and numerous unscientific flights of fancy, Ellis gracefully imparts much about the history of archaeology and cartography, and the perennial yearning for lost worlds and romantic adventure."
—*Outside*

RICHARD ELLIS

IMAGINING ATLANTIS

Richard Ellis is the author of seven previous books, including *The Book of Whales, Dolphins and Porpoises, Monsters of the Sea,* and *Deep Atlantic.* He is also a celebrated marine artist whose paintings have been exhibited in museums and galleries around the world, and has written and illustrated articles for numerous magazines, including *Audubon, Reader's Digest, National Geographic,* and *Scientific American.* He lives in New York City.

IMAGINING

ATLANTIS

RICHARD ELLIS

VINTAGE BOOKS

A DIVISION OF RANDOM HOUSE, INC.

NEW YORK

IMAGINING
ATLANTIS

FIRST VINTAGE BOOKS EDITION, AUGUST 1999

Copyright © 1998 by Richard Ellis

All rights reserved under International and Pan-American
Copyright Conventions. Published in the United States by
Vintage Books, a division of Random House, Inc., New York, and
simultaneously in Canada by Random House of Canada Limited,
Toronto. Originally published in hardcover in the United States
by Alfred A. Knopf, Inc., New York, in 1998.

Vintage Books and colophon are registered trademarks of
Random House, Inc.

The Library of Congress has cataloged the Alfred A. Knopf edition
as follows:
Ellis, Richard,
Imagining Atlantis / by Richard Ellis. — 1st ed.
p. cm.
Includes bibliographical references and index.
ISBN 0-679-44602-8
1. Atlantis. I. Title.
GN751.E55   1998
001.94—dc21   97-48432
CIP

Vintage ISBN: 0-375-70582-1

Author photograph © David Ellis
Book design by Cassandra Pappas

www.vintagebooks.com

Printed in the United States of America
10   9   8   7   6   5   4   3   2   1

CONTENTS

PREFACE

THERE IS something marvelously organic—and unexpected—about the way one book grows out of another. In 1980, when I had submitted the manuscript and illustrations for a comprehensive book on the cetaceans of the world, Ash Green, my wise editor (then as now), recommended that I break it up into two parts. The first became *The Book of Whales,* and two years later, after a lot of revisions, *Dolphins and Porpoises* appeared. *Monsters of the Sea* grew out of my inability to incorporate the entire Atlantic Ocean into a single book; when I tried to add sea monsters to this unmanageable hodgepodge, I ended up quitting the Atlantic and detouring into a study of giant cephalopods, sea serpents, mermaids, man-eating sharks, and ship-sinking whales. But then, having found a way to return to the back-burner "Atlantic" project, I (figuratively) descended into the depths, brought up *Deep Atlantic,* and wrote about sea-floor spreading, submersible exploration, hydrothermal vents, and the weird and wonderful creatures of the abyss. I was once again trying to encompass everything that had to do with my putative subject, and for no better reason than to be able to answer the common question "Are you going to include Atlantis?" I began a search for information on the Lost Continent. There was more about Atlantis than I had imagined possible, but it had no legitimate place in a book about the geology, exploration, and natural history of the depths. So I turned in the manuscript and the drawings for *Deep Atlantic,* and encouraged by the steadfast support of the people at Knopf, I sallied forth in search of Atlantis.

In one way, the search for the Lost City was easy; it seems that almost everybody, from Plato to Francis Bacon, from Jules Verne and Arthur Conan Doyle to Edgar Cayce and Charles Berlitz, had something to say on the subject. Even Indiana Jones had an opinion. But it was not so easy to ascertain exactly what "the subject" actually was. Was it a prehistorical myth whose origins are lost? Was it somehow related to the 1500 B.C. eruption of an Aegean volcanic island whose repercussions might have destroyed an entire civilization? Did it have to do with pre-Columbians? Ancient Egyptians? Extraterrestrials? Where was I to look for the information? Archaeological journals? The *Bulletin of Volcanology? Bulfinch's Mythology?*

Atlantis has been the subject of so many stories, fables, novels, and movies that it was obvious there was not going to be a single answer. Was there ever a real Atlantis, or has it been a metaphor or symbol for so many things that its reality is forever buried, like Herculaneum, under the accumulated debris of centuries of speculation?

Another, even more important question is "Why bother?" Thousands of books have already been written about Atlantis. In his less than laudatory review of Peter James's 1995 *The Sunken Kingdom: The Atlantis Mystery Solved,* Nigel Spivey wrote, "To witness a soul sucked into the maw of Atlantis would be horrible, if it were not a volunteered folly. There is no universal edict requiring such martyrs. Still they come forward, brimming with the usual hubris of solution and resolution." Unlike James (who thought he had solved the mystery by placing Atlantis in Anatolia), I offer no new or revolutionary explanation. Rather, I believe that Plato wrote the story for his own reasons— which reasons we might be able to guess at—and that those who followed him either embellished an already rich and complex tale with enough complications to make their interpretations crumble like the fabled city itself or approached it from such peculiar vantage points that their creativeness, contumaciousness, or gullibility requires some sort of acknowledgment. Atlantis is such an abundant field for study, that even if we never find a single Atlantean artifact, a long-lost hieroglyphic inscription, or any geological evidence of a sunken landmass, the legend of the Lost Continent will perdure in the human consciousness.

Many may think that this book contains too many quotes and excerpts from other books. I plead guilty to overciting, but with extenuating circumstances. I believe that most later versions of the Atlantis story are misguided, exaggerated, or just plain incorrect, and that it would be insufficient to say that "Ignatius Donnelly is an old humbug" or "Charles Berlitz is irresponsible" without offering evidence to support such assertions. To get a sense of the nature of Atlantean research, I think it is necessary to read what Charles Pellegrino actually wrote, or what Robert Ferro and Michael Grumley thought they were doing when they sailed to Bimini.

As in the past, I could not conduct this search on my own, so like Mr. Jorrocks, I went off in all directions, aided and abetted by people who did not always realize they were being helpful. When I learned that there was an organization called the Thera Institute in London, I wrote to it, and Deborah Stratford gave me a wealth of information on the excavations and history of the volcano on Santorini. She also provided me with the necessary contacts on Crete and Santorini. I journeyed to Crete to inspect the archaeologized remains of the Minoan civilization at Knossos, Hagia Triada, and Phaistos, and then I went across the Aegean to see what was left of Thera and to visit Akrotiri, the site of Professor Christos Doumas's ongoing (and fascinating) dig. At Akrotiri, Doumas was kind enough to spare time from his busy schedule to take us behind (and around and under) the scenes and explain what he was doing and why. Lena Levidis showed us around the Conference Center in Thera and dispensed valuable information on the symposia that have produced so much information on the history of Thera and the Aegean world. It is instructive to visit archaeological sites, but you cannot read the rocks and shards without a guidebook, and for guidebooks to almost everything, I returned to the library at the American Museum of Natural History. I found more than I could use on volcanoes, archaeology, deep-sea exploration, and oceanography, and again, my arcane investigations were inspired and supported by Nina Root, the AMNH librarian. When I needed materials on mythology, ancient history, and traditional and nontraditional literature, I went to the New York Society Library, a great and largely unheralded resource. Appropriately, some of my research was conducted across the Atlantic, by the indefatigable Erica Wagner Gilbert, who dug out some of the more obscure biographical information on the classical scholars listed in the Appendix. For the information on Harold Edgerton's investigations of the sunken Greek city of Helice, I want to thank Liz Andrews and Jeffrey Mifflin of the MIT Archives in Cambridge. Clark Lee Merriam of the Cousteau Society made the text of *A la recherche de L'Atlantide* available, and my brother David helped me with the translation.

In the past, I researched my books in the traditional fashion: I frequented libraries and bookstores, read magazines and journals, wrote letters, and, whenever appropriate or possible, visited locations where I might find material, people, or experiences related to the subject at hand. But now, at least for some of us, the world of research has changed dramatically. Without leaving my desk, I can access scientific or historical journals, call up pictures of volcanoes, chat with mystics, contact archaeologists in the field and see what they are doing. The new research tool, of course, is the Internet, and while I make no claims to have mastered its intricacies (indeed, I can barely claim to know how to find anything), I am constantly astonished by the passageways that can be opened with a keystroke.

One story must suffice, since this is a book about Atlantis, not about technology. I read in *Science* (June 14, 1996) that some doctors had equated the Plague of Athens (430–425 B.C.) with the Ebola virus. The *Science* article referred to a medical journal called *Emerging Infectious Diseases,* so I typed that into my Web browser, and there was the journal, on my screen. I printed out the article, and when the list of references appeared, I looked for those, too. One of them was Thucydides' *History of the Peloponnesian War,* so I accessed that and found his description of the symptoms. (See pp. 244–46 for the results of this Web surfing.) I think this resource will change the way research is done, and will certainly change the way sources are acknowledged.

I know how to cite a book or a journal, or even an unpublished personal communication ("pers. comm."), but I don't know how to cite a Web site or identify the anonymous author of an opinion that came over the Net. In those cases where I have received useful information through a Web site or from E-mail, I have tried to acknowledge the author in a traditional fashion. But if one of the purposes of a bibliography is to permit another person to check your data or consult a particular work for himself, how can anyone else find messages that were sent to me two years ago from Crete or Cambridge? I have attempted to incorporate such information as efficaciously and honestly as possible, but some stray, undocumentable factoids may have crept into the manuscript. I accept full responsibility for any errors, cyber- and otherwise, that appear in this book.

Library research is not a team effort; even though librarians can help you to find things, you have to interpret them on your own. But traveling abroad to ancient volcanic and archaeological sites is better done with someone else, and although one does the actual research and writing alone, it helps to have a friend upon whom you can try some of your more ridiculous ideas, and whose tolerance for such foolishness is almost infinite. Stephanie Guest again came along for the ride, and except for the spider bite in Santorini, she braved the dangers of traveling with (and living with) an obsessive-compulsive—at least on the subjects of these books.

IMAGINING

ATLANTIS

INTRODUCTION

To write the universally readable book on Atlantis would require something more than wide scientific knowledge. It would require something of the inspired guesswork of Columbus, something of the insolence and swagger of the picaroon who pursues his way through *Don Quixote* and the works of Smollett no less arduously for being a figure of fun, and also, not least, a certain reverence for the labours of others in the past, however discredited they may be by contemporary standards of "scientific" Atlantean study. Thus the little tragedy of the main body of Atlantean literature is that it falls between two stools. On the one hand the scholars interested in the subject have not the necessary range of imaginative perception; and on the other the amateurs have not the power of marshalling the facts and drawing the right conclusions from them—a power which ensures that the words of the more erudite persons shall at least meet with respect, if not enthusiasm.

—JAMES BRAMWELL
Lost Atlantis, 1938

IN THIS BOOK, I intend to review many of the ideas that have been suggested for the existence and location of Atlantis. The literature is a rich garden of possibilities, with a history that ranges from Plato, who lived some two and a half thousand years ago, to writers who have published their theories within the past couple of years. When one is reading this vast body of literature, it is inevitable that one's own biases creep in. I could not look at Plato's carefully prepared account in the same way that I read Ignatius Donnelly's hodgepodge of anthropology, archaeology, and fairy story; I could not compare the well-reasoned theory that the myth of Atlantis is connected with the downfall of Minoan Crete with Edgar Cayce's clairvoyant prediction that a fifty-thousand-year-old Atlantis would rise again in the Caribbean in 1968.

The story of Atlantis has long fascinated oceanographers, historians, archaeologists, geographers, explorers, psychics—anyone with a taste for the more intriguing mysteries of human history. In *Atlantis: Fact or Fiction?*, Edwin Ramage, a professor of classical studies at the University of Indiana, writes that "it is difficult to know how many books have been written about Atlantis over this long period of time [since Plato originally wrote about it]. A reasonable round number seems to be 2,000, though estimates range as high as 10,000." (In a 1992 promotion for Eberhard Zangger's *Flood from Heaven,* we read that "estimates range as high as 20,000," but this seems somewhat hyperbolic.) There is no shortage of theories about its rise and fall, ranging in verisimilitude from the identification of Atlantis with North America to Atlantis flying out of the ocean and becoming the moon. In 1922, Karl Georg Zschaetzsch published *Atlantis: Die Urheimat der Arier* (The Homeland of the Aryan), in which he told the story of a blond, blue-eyed race of vegetarian Atlanteans, the only survivors of the collision of the earth with a comet. Zschaetzsch—who claimed that his name proved that he was a descendant of Zeus—attributed virtually every known myth to the "racial memory" of the Atlanteans, from Romulus and Remus to the Christmas star.

I believe that the story of Atlantis has been influenced by many contributors over the thousands of years since it was first broached, and indeed, many of these influences may be lodged in our collective unconscious. Almost every culture contains a story, myth, or legend of the flood-related disappearance of a corrupt civilization. Over the years, various historians (as well as antihistorians, archaeologists, popular writers, occultists, and scuba divers) have tried to tie the story up in a neat package, but while some have succeeded better than others, the mystery still remains unsolved. We will probably never know precisely what inspired Plato to describe "the island of Atlantis that was swallowed up by the sea and vanished" in the dialogues the *Critias* and the *Timaeus,* but conjecture fuels the elaborate studies of legitimate classical historians like A. E. Taylor, Desmond Lee, and J. V. Luce; scientists like Bruce Heezen and Angelos Galanopoulos; and archaeologists of the caliber of Spyridon Marinatos and Sir Arthur Evans. The school of unrestrained conjecture has also given us Ignatius Donnelly, Murry Hope, Rudolf Steiner, Edgar Cayce, Charles Berlitz, and David Zink.

Until Plato's description is validated, or another solution proves to be correct, we will continue to be hard-pressed to separate his legions of successors into appropriate categories of fact or fiction. Moreover, authors who tackle this complicated subject often find themselves in the awkward and unenviable position of somehow having to validate a myth. With only a few exceptions, such as Jules Verne's description of Atlantis in *Twenty Thousand Leagues Under the Sea,* or Conan Doyle's *Maracot Deep,* which are clearly intended to be fiction, much of the Atlantis literature falls into a category that might be called "Atlantean fantasy." (It could be called "science fiction," were that appellation not generally applied to a variety of writing wherein the author makes up almost everything, often including the "science.") In "Atlantean fantasy," the writer begins with some sort of demonstrable actuality—such as the Mid-Atlantic Ridge or the ruins of the Minoan palace at Knossos—and then speculates, often wildly, about how this particular subject might be related to Atlantis. Since many of the proponents of these Atlantean doctrines are respectable scientists, we cannot automatically disregard their theories, but because not one of them—to my mind, anyway—has satisfactorily proven his case, we are left with a bookful of contrasting, and often contradictory, theories. This is the essential nature of "Atlantology," a discipline that combines literature, philosophy, geology, oceanography, archaeology, ancient history, mythology, art history, mysticism, cryptography, and fantasy. There is, as far as I know, no other "science" that employs such a heady mixture and produces such divergent results.

The myth of Atlantis has come down through history as one of the most enduring of all ancient stories. Not a part of any religious cosmography, the story has lasted for thousands of years without benefit of a proselytizing clergy. Where Judeo-Christianity has the Bible, Islam the Koran, and Vedic religions the Upanishads, there is no "religion" based on Atlantean principles, or any sort of a book that might be said to have handed down the wisdom of the ages. It first appears in Plato's dialogue the *Timaeus,* which is itself a philosophical treatise on creation, but Plato was not the founder of a religion. It is a story so powerful that it has lasted solely on the basis of its own merits, passed along, often by word of mouth, for two and a half millennia, and today, in an era characterized by technological marvels like atomic energy and the Internet, the legend of Atlantis still thrives.

Whether its source was extraterrestrial, prehistorical, or imaginary, Atlantis, unique among the Western world's myths, has become a part of our mythohistory. The story of the disappearance of a powerful civilization appears in many forms in many other cultures. Alone among the ancient accounts, Atlantis comes down to us complete, a tale that has survived for three thousand years, woven into chronologies as disparate as Periclean Athens and interplanetary travel.

There is no question that the story of Atlantis originated with Plato, and therefore it is important to examine what he actually wrote. But almost everyone with a theory about Atlantis has done that; Atlantologists have read the dialogues the *Critias* and the *Timaeus* and come up with often irreconcilable propositions. Plato often makes it possible for an author to "prove" that his hypothesis is the correct one; one is able to quote the Greek philosopher—at least on the subject of Atlantis—in such a way as to prove almost anything. Was there really a Lost City? If so, where was it? Did Plato make up the story, or did he base it on historical fact? Which fact or facts? Is some of it true and some of it the product of a vivid imagination?

Plato wrote that Atlantis was "outside the Pillars of Hercules," so when Atlantis is placed in Tunisia or Nigeria, one supposes that the location must have been some sort of a mistake on Plato's part. On the other hand, if someone locates the Lost Continent in the Atlantic Ocean, the suggestion supports Plato's contention and goes a long way toward verifying his story. The idea that Plato was correct, that Atlantis was really an island in the Atlantic Ocean, was first presented (says Bramwell) by a Frenchman named Cadet in 1787, who claimed that the Azores and the Canaries were the remains of the Lost Continent. Others would follow suit; if Plato said it was in the Atlantic Ocean, then that seems a good place to start our search. But did Plato even know the Atlantic Ocean existed?

WHAT PLATO SAID

Our records tell how your city checked a great power which arrogantly advanced from its base in the Atlantic Ocean to attack the cities of Europe and Asia. For in those days the Atlantic was navigable. There was an island opposite the strait which you call . . . the Pillars of Heracles, an island larger than Libya and Asia combined; from it travelers could in those days reach the other islands, and from them the whole opposite continent which surrounds what can truly be called the ocean. For the sea within the strait we are talking about is like a lake with a narrow entrance; the outer ocean is the real ocean and the land which entirely surrounds it is properly termed continent. On this island of Atlantis had arisen a powerful and remarkable dynasty of kings. . . .

—PLATO
Timaeus

I T I S O F C O U R S E impossible to know, or even guess, when men first looked out over the gray Atlantic and thought about crossing it. For eons, men had no idea what lay on the other side, or if indeed there *was* another side. In *The Edges of the Earth in Ancient Thought,* James Romm wrote that "early writers seemed to have assumed, for lack of evidence to the contrary, that Ocean's waters stretched unbounded toward a distant horizon." The prospect of sailing out of sight of the comforting and familiar terra firma must have terrified the earliest sailors, and great credit must be assigned to the first of those brave navigators who ventured toward what must have seemed literally the end of the world. (While the story of Christopher Columbus's men fearing

PLATO, who lived from about 428 to 347 B.C., was entirely responsible for the myth of Atlantis, in the dialogues the *Timaeus* and the *Critias*.

that they were going to sail off the end of the world if they kept going is certainly apocryphal—men have known the earth was round since Ptolemy's second-century calculations—they were unquestionably apprehensive as they sailed steadily toward the setting sun and the unknown.)

To the Greeks, the Pillars of Hercules—the name given to the twin rocks that define the passage we know as the Straits of Gibraltar—represented the gateway from the known Mediterranean to the unknown mysteries beyond. The poet Pindar wrote that the Pillars of Hercules were, almost literally, the end of the world: "Now Theron, approaching the outer limit of his feats of strength, touches the Pillars of Hercules. What lies beyond cannot be approached by wise men or unwise. I shall not try, or I would be a fool."

Before the year 1100 B.C., the Phoenicians, from their outpost at Carthage on the North African coast, had in all probability explored the shores of the Atlantic outside the protection of the Pillars of Hercules, that is, the Straits of Gibraltar. From archaeological evidence, it has been ascertained that the Carthaginians had established a trading post at Essaouira (modern Mogador), about six hundred miles south of Gibraltar on the Atlantic coast of Morocco, some twenty-five hundred years ago.

The first chronicler of an Atlantic voyage was Herodotus, the fifth-century B.C. Greek historian, who also mentions the first known map of the world, a bronze tablet "showing all the seas and rivers" compiled by his predecessor the historian Hecataeus. Also according to Herodotus, Pharaoh Necho II sent a Phoenician expedition to find a route around Africa. It will probably never be known if they completed the circumnavigation, but Herodotus's account (written some one hundred fifty years after the event) suggests that they may have done so:

Accordingly these Phoenicians set out and from the Red Sea sailed into the southern ocean. Whenever autumn came, they went ashore wherever in Africa they chanced to be on their voyage to sow grain in the earth and await the harvest. On reaping the new grain they put again to sea. In this wise, after two years had elapsed, they rounded the Pillars of Heracles and in the third year reached Egypt. Now they told a tale that I personally do not believe (though others may, if they choose), how they had the sun on their right hand as they sailed along the African coast.

Although some analysts of Herodotus have been inclined to question this account, the statement "they had the sun on their right hand," which would refer to the sun's midday position only if the Phoenicians were sailing west while south of the equator, actually supports the claim for authenticity. Naval historian Samuel Eliot Morison believes they succeeded, and called their circumnavigation of Africa from east to west "one of the most remarkable voyages of history." In *Beyond the Pillars of Heracles,* which contains a meticulous analysis of Herodotus's account, the historian Rhys Carpenter wrote, "The curious detail that Herodotus refused to believe this becomes our surest warrant for believing the Phoenician claim that they circumnavigated Africa."

A CENTURY OR SO later, Hanno, the magistrate of Carthage, set out from the Mediterranean and sailed south with "sixty ships of fifty oars each and a body of men and women to the number of thirty thousand," which works out to approximately five hundred persons per ship, an obvious exaggeration. This story can be found in the *Periplous* of Hanno, a Greek translation of an inscribed tablet that has never been found. The narrative tells of the establishment of several colonies along the Atlantic coast of Africa, to safeguard the Carthaginian access to the Canaries and Madeira, the sources of the *Murex* snails that provided the royal purple dye. Hanno passed the Saharan coast, and easily made Cape Bojador, which was to prove such a formidable psychological and physical obstacle to the first Portuguese explorers. The success of this pioneer voyage can be found in Hanno's own narrative, where he describes a tribe that he calls "Ethiopians," various active volcanoes, and also such exotic animals as elephants, hippopotamuses, and "gorillas" (probably chimpanzees—the expedition killed three females and brought the hairy pelts back to Carthage). This coast of Africa would not be seen again by European eyes for another thousand years, when sailors from Portugal would cautiously navigate south around the bulge of Africa, culminating in Bartholomeu Dias's doubling of the Cape of Good Hope in 1488.

In the *Timaeus,* Plato tells us that Solon (630–560 B.C.) reported that the Egyptian priests of Saïs told him the story of a great island that lay in the Atlantic Ocean, just off the Pillars of Hercules.* Its generals mounted an invasion of Greece: "Our records tell [Plato wrote] how your city checked a great power which arrogantly advanced from its base in the Atlantic ocean to attack the cities of Europe and Asia."

The invasion ended not in a military victory for either side but in a double defeat, where the only winner was the force of nature: "*But afterward there occurred violent earthquakes and floods, and in a single day and night of misfortune all your warlike men in a body sank into the earth, and the island of Atlantis in like manner disappeared in the depths of the sea*" (my emphasis). This is the full extent of the original story of the destruction of Atlantis.

With Socrates and Aristotle, Plato is considered one of the authors of the philosophical foundations of Western culture. He was born in 428 B.C., either in Athens or in Aegina, to Ariston and Perictione. We know few details of his life, but after the suicide of his mentor Socrates in 399 B.C., he became disillusioned with Athens and traveled in Greece, Italy, Egypt, and Sicily, and when he returned to Athens, he founded an academy dedicated to the systematic pursuit of philosophical and scientific research. Around 368, when he was forty, Plato was invited to Sicily to educate Dionysius II, but the experiment was a failure and Plato returned to Athens. Rather than adopting the role of "philosopher-king" that Plato had recommended in *The Republic,* Dionysius II became a reckless tyrant. In addition to *The Republic,* the best-known and most influential of the dialogues, Plato wrote the *Timaeus* and the *Critias,* in which the story of Atlantis is first told. Although not dated, the *Timaeus* has long been regarded as one of his last works. In *The Laws,* left unfinished at his death in 347 B.C., he apparently had not completely abandoned the idea of an ideal government, for he recommended the association of a young and high-spirited prince with a wise lawgiver.

---

* The form in which the tale was passed down is one of the more controversial elements in Plato's story. In the *Timaeus,* we read that the story was first heard by Solon, who told it to Dropides and then to Critias (the grandfather of the Critias who is telling the story), who repeated it to his grandchildren when he was an old man. But in the *Critias,* written later, Plato has Critias tell his audience, "My father had his manuscript, which is now in my possession, and I studied it often as a child." If Critias actually had the manuscript, why did he say (in the *Timaeus*), "As soon as we left here yesterday I started telling the story to the others as I remembered it, and when I got back I managed to recall pretty well all of it by thinking it over during the night"?

"The works of Plato," wrote A. E. Taylor in his seminal study of the philosopher's life and thought, "have come down to us absolutely entire and complete." The manuscripts were preserved at the Platonic Academy, and thence in the great library at Alexandria.* Copies of the manuscripts were carefully made from the Middle Ages to the present day, so there is no reason to doubt Plato's authorship.

Plato's dialogues contain the only reference in the whole of ancient literature to the disappearing island of Atlantis, and no further mention is made of this story until other people begin quoting Plato. (Not even Herodotus mentions the story, and he is said to have spoken directly with the priests at Saïs, the very priests who passed the story to Solon.) There are people who take everything he said literally (even though they are unable to locate the missing island), and others who dismiss the whole story as "science fiction." Others categorize it as a fictional account that Plato introduced to demonstrate what an ideal society might be like.

But did Plato make up *everything* about Atlantis? Perhaps not. As with all writers of fiction, he was probably influenced by people and events that he knew, even though he may have modified them beyond recognition. Romm suggests that there was a text circulating in Plato's time that was called *On Marvelous Things Heard,* which contained elements that Plato might have incorporated:

> They say in the sea outside the Pillars of Hercules an unidentified island was discovered by the Carthaginians, many days' sail from shore, which has all kinds of trees, and navigable rivers, and a marvelous variety of other resources. When the Carthaginians began going there often on account of its fruitfulness, and some even emigrated there, the Carthaginian leaders decreed that they would put to death anyone who planned to sail there, and got rid of all those who were living there, lest they spread the word and a crowd gather around them on the island which might gain power and take away the prosperity of the Carthaginians.[†]

---

* The library and museum of Alexandria was established in the city founded by Alexander the Great during the course of his campaigns in Egypt from 334 to 323 B.C. Under Ptolemy I Soter (367–283 B.C.) and Ptolemy II Philadelphus (308–246 B.C.), scholars were encouraged to live and work there, and it was said to house over a million works, including all the Greek classics and translations of works in Assyrian, Persian, Egyptian, Hebrew, and Sanskrit. The library lost some forty thousand volumes in 48 B.C., when it was severely burned in a fire set by Julius Caesar to block Ptolemy XII's fleet, and it was completely destroyed in 686 A.D., when the Arab conquerors of Alexandria burned its contents for fuel.

[†] Although it is included in the Loeb Classical Library's *Complete Works of Aristotle* (in the volume known as *Minor Works*), according to the introduction to the section on *Marvelous Things,* "all authorities are agreed that it is not the work of Aristotle, but is included in this volume as part of the 'corpus' that has come down to us. Most Aristotolean scholars believe it emanated from the Peripatetic School."

Did the Carthaginians actually know of such an island? Probably not, any more than Plato did. Romm quotes Diodorus as suggesting that the Carthaginians wanted to keep the island a secret so they could escape to it if necessary. Furthermore, Diodorus believed that the Pillars of Hercules had been closed in ancient times to prevent "sea monsters" from entering the Mediterranean, and that therefore nobody could get out, Atlantis or not.

Another aspect of Plato's discussion of Atlantis is found in the *Critias,* where he describes the nature of the island's civilization before its destruction. Here we might find some indication of what Plato actually had in mind, for he describes a fanciful civilization, replete with boundless natural riches, "which then lay open to the sun, in marvelous beauty and inexhaustible profusion." The royalty of Atlantis were enormously wealthy ("they possessed wealth such as had never been amassed by any royal line before them"), perhaps because they were able to mine the mineral orichalch, which had a higher value than any other substance except gold. The forests and pastures were exceptionally bountiful, and "the earth bore freely all the aromatic substances it bears today, roots, herbs, bushes and gums exuded by flowers or fruit," and there were two springs, a cold and a warm, and "the supply from both was copious and the natural flavor of their waters remarkable." Man-made structures included temples, gymnasiums, and dockyards, all in excellent order. Since this description fits no known land, and since the plains, the forests, the waters, and the city are so sumptuous, it seems not unreasonable to conclude that Plato was describing a mythical utopia, and that to explain its disappearance, he invented a great natural catastrophe. The area of the Mediterranean in which Plato lived is occasionally subjected to geological misadventures— sometimes on a colossal scale—so it is not surprising that he would have employed such a device. Future Atlantologists would attempt to fit Plato's description into almost every political and geological system known, with varying degrees of success.

Later students of the Atlantis story have pointed out that it is curious that no other ancient historians made reference to Atlantis, except, of course, to quote Plato. In his 1978 essay on the historical perspective regarding Atlantis, J. Rufus Fears wrote, "In the absence of any evidence from the Egyptian sources, the silence of Thucydides, Herodotus, Isocrates, and Aelius Aristedes seems conclusive. Plato's story does not reflect a historical tradition derived from Egypt or Solon or from anywhere or anyone else. It is a poetic invention of Plato." Moreover, its hypothetical location has not always remained just outside the Straits of Gibraltar, but has wandered from the Canary Islands to the

Sahara Desert, Scandinavia, and Palestine, most recently coming to rest on various Aegean islands, especially Santorini and Crete.

I N   O R D E R   T O understand what Plato was describing, it will be necessary to examine the pertinent dialogues in some detail. Fortunately, this exercise has already been undertaken by Sir Desmond Lee, who translated the two dialogues for the Penguin edition, originally published in 1965 and reissued regularly until 1987. (Lee is also the translator of the Penguin edition of *The Republic.*) Other authors, such as Galanopoulos,* employ the dialogues—and quote substantial portions—to demonstrate a particular theory about Atlantis, a subject we will discuss in due course. Lee has no archaeological or historical ax to grind; he does not favor one location over another, although he discusses the various possibilities. In his introduction, he writes: "Socrates [one of the speakers in the *Timaeus*] is anxious to see his ideal society in action, and in reply Critias gives an outline of the Atlantis myth, and suggests that Socrates' ideal society may be found in the Athens of the myth."

Despite an unfortunate inclination on the part of some to rearrange the critical dates to suit their conclusions, Plato clearly wrote that "the citizens whose laws and whose finest achievements I will now briefly describe to you therefore lived nine thousand years ago." (In his explanation of the wandering dates, J. V. Luce wrote, "I shall argue later that the large dimensions of Atlantis and the extreme antiquity of her aggression against Greece are distortions and exaggerations imported by Plato himself into a historical tradition which was garbled before it reached him, and which he failed to identify correctly.")

Unless they arrived from outer space—a possibility that has been suggested—there were no people living nine thousand years before Plato in an elaborate city with groves of fruit trees, hot and cold springs, a racetrack, canals, bridges, tunnels, and an ivory-roofed, silver-covered palace with golden statues.† Rather than a vague description of an ancient metropolis, Plato's account appears to depict an idealized society; the best of all possible

---

* Angelos Galanopoulos was a Greek-born seismologist and a recognized authority on earthquakes and tsunamis. He wrote many papers on these subjects prior to the publication of *Atlantis* in 1969. Edward Bacon was a writer on subjects archaeological who presumably helped with the writing. Therefore, in the discussion of their book, I will refer to Galanopoulos as the author, instead of regularly citing the awkward "Galanopoulos and Bacon."

† For those who would argue that Plato got the dates wrong by an order of magnitude, and where he wrote "nine thousand years ago," he actually meant *nine hundred,* there were no racetracks, canals, bridges, tunnels, or ivory-roofed, silver-covered palaces with golden statues then, either.

worlds from the vantage point of a fourth-century B.C. Greek philosopher. This is especially obvious when one examines the specific measurements he includes in the *Critias.* Other authors have maintained that the inclusion of these precise dimensions proves that Plato was describing a real city, but, of course, it is not necessary to measure something in order to describe its hypothetical dimensions. (In *Twenty Thousand Leagues Under the Sea,* for example, Jules Verne "measured" the *Nautilus* and virtually everything else aboard the fictional vessel. The submarine is exactly 230 feet long and 26 feet wide; its two hulls weigh 1,492.13 tons, etc.) The dimensions given by Plato are so exaggerated that they conform to no possible geographical arrangement, and some of the engineering feats he describes would be impossible even with today's building technology. One is tempted to invoke the words of Pooh-Bah in Gilbert and Sullivan's *Mikado:* "merely corroborative detail, intended to give artistic verisimilitude to an otherwise bald and unconvincing narrative."

The dialogues are by no means restricted to a discussion of Atlantis. The *Timaeus* is by far the longer of the two (the *Critias* seems to have been suspended or interrupted in mid-sentence), and consists of a dialogue between Socrates, Timaeus, Critias, and Hermocrates. Although the Atlantis myth is introduced early on, the majority of the dialogue consists of a multipart discussion of philosophical topics, such as living creatures, the structure and composition of the human soul, sleep and dreams, reason and necessity, the four elements, pleasure and pain, diseases of the mind and body, physical and mental fitness, and the creation of women, birds, animals, reptiles, and fishes. Despite its rambling nature, however, the *Timaeus* plays an extremely important part in the Atlantis story, since it contains the introduction, the explanation of how the tale came to be told.* It is Critias (identified by Desmond Lee as Plato's maternal great-grandfather) who says, "I will tell you; though the story was old when I heard it and the man who told it to me was no longer young." As he tells it: "It was about what might fairly be called the greatest and most noteworthy of all this city's achievements, but because of the lapse of time and the death of those who took part in it, the story has not lasted till our day."

Critias got the story from his grandfather, who got it from his father Dropides. It seems that Solon, one of the wise men and great poets of Athens, had

---

* In his introduction to the Bollingen edition of Plato's *Collected Dialogues,* Huntington Cairns wrote: "Although the *Timaeus* takes the form of a myth, a vision of the physical world, it should not be supposed that it is less profound than the other dialogues. In the *Timaeus* Plato's aim is to reveal order in terms of the world of things. But notwithstanding its mythical form, or perhaps because of it, the *Timaeus* has been one of Plato's most influential dialogues."

traveled around 600 B.C. to Egypt, where a priest told him that his country (Greece) habitually ignored its past, and that there had been a great flood some nine thousand years earlier. "The age of our institutions is given in our sacred records as eight thousand years, and the citizens whose laws and whose finest achievement I will now briefly describe to you therefore lived nine thousand years ago; we will go through their history in detail later on at leisure, when we can consult the records." After establishing the time frame, the priest tells Solon the story of the formation of Atlantis:

> Our records tell how your city checked a great power which arrogantly advanced from its base in the Atlantic Ocean to attack the cities of Europe and Asia. For in those days the Atlantic was navigable. There was an island opposite the strait which you call (or so you say) the Pillars of Heracles, an island larger than Libya and Asia combined; from it travelers could in those days reach the other islands, and from them the whole opposite continent which surrounds what can truly be called the ocean. For the sea within the strait we are talking about is like a lake with a narrow entrance; the outer ocean is the real ocean and the land which entirely surrounds it is properly termed continent. On this island of Atlantis had arisen a powerful and remarkable dynasty of kings, who ruled the whole island, and many other islands as well and parts of the continent; in addition it controlled within the strait, Libya [Africa] up to the borders of Egypt and Europe as far as Tyrrhenia [Italy].

This seems to be a fairly accurate description of the whereabouts of Atlantis, but as we shall see, geography is treated fast and loose by those who want to relocate it into the Aegean. A careful reading of Plato's description locates Atlantis beyond the Pillars of Hercules (the Straits of Gibraltar) in the Atlantic Ocean, which "in those days . . . was navigable." There is a clear distinction drawn between those elements within the strait, that is, in the Mediterranean, such as Egypt and Tyrrhenia, and those without, such as "the other islands" and "the whole opposite continent which surrounds what can truly be called the ocean."

The Egyptian priest continues:

> This dynasty, gathering its whole power together, attempted to enslave, at a single stroke, your country and ours, and all the territory within the strait. It was then, Solon, that the power and courage and strength of your city became clear for all men to see. Her bravery and military skill were outstanding; she led an alliance of the Greeks, and when they deserted her and she was forced

to fight alone, after running into direct peril, she overcame the invaders and celebrated a victory; she rescued those not yet enslaved from the slavery threatening them, and she generously freed all others living within the Pillars of Heracles. At a later time there were earthquakes and floods of extraordinary violence, and in a single dreadful day and night, all your fighting men were swallowed up by the earth, and the island of Atlantis was similarly swallowed up by the sea and vanished; this is why the sea in that area is to this day impassable to navigation, which is hindered by mud just below the surface, the remains of this sunken island.

It is admittedly difficult to interpret a document that is approximately twenty-five hundred years old and has been repeatedly translated from its original language, but Plato's dialogues contain the introduction of the Atlantis myth, and in order to understand it and place the story in some sort of historical (or literary) perspective, we must construe his intentions as well as we are able. Shortly after he describes the island that was swallowed up by the sea, Critias tells the others that "we will transfer the imaginary citizens and city which you described yesterday to the real world, and say that your city is the city of my story and your citizens those historical ancestors of ours whom the priest described. They will fit exactly, and there will be no disharmony if we speak as if they really were the men who lived at that time." Is Plato telling us that the story is fiction, and that he is going to transpose the tale told by the Egyptian priests so that it fits into a different framework? He may be, but then Socrates responds by saying, "Your story is particularly well suited to the present festival . . . and it is a great point in its favor that it is not a fiction but a true history." At this point, we still have no idea if Plato is making up the story of Atlantis, and if he is, what he wants to prove. It is extremely unlikely that one of the world's foremost thinkers would embellish one of his philosophical disquisitions with a story about a city that was swallowed up by the sea unless it served a purpose, and since Plato was particularly interested in ideal societies—see, for example, *The Republic*—it does not seem unrealistic or illogical to interpret the story of the disappearance of Atlantis as a parable, a story to illustrate a moral or religious lesson. And like any good author, he gives us historical references, measurements, and specific persons so as to lend the story the requisite verisimilitude. At this juncture in the dialogues, however, Plato abandons Atlantis and devotes the remainder of the *Timaeus* to lengthy discussions of such non-Atlantean themes as the soul and the reality of the world. Plato does not return to the tantalizing story of Atlantis until the *Critias.*

In this dialogue, he picks up the theme almost immediately. Critias says,

"I'm sure my audience will think I have discharged my task with reasonable credit if I can remember adequately and repeat the story which the priests told Solon and he brought home with him."

> We must first remind ourselves that in all nine thousand years have elapsed since the declaration of war between those who lived outside and all those who lived inside the Pillars of Heracles. . . . The leadership and conduct of the war were on the one side in the hands of our city, on the other, in the hands of the kings of Atlantis. At this time, as we said, Atlantis was an island larger than Libya and Asia put together, though it was subsequently overwhelmed by earthquakes and is the source of the impenetrable mud which prevents the free passage of those who sail out of the straits into the open sea. [A similar passage appears in the *Timaeus*.]

Since the Greek capital is the city-state that was invaded by the Atlanteans (and since the dialogues are taking place between Athenians), it is necessary for the author to describe the Greek city as it existed those nine thousand years earlier:

> Most of the classes of citizen were concerned with manufacture and agriculture. The military class lived apart, having been from the beginning separated from the others by godlike men. . . . They had no private property but regarded their possession as common to all. . . . And indeed what we said then about our territory is true and plausible enough; for in those days its boundaries were drawn at the Isthmus, and on the mainland side at the Cithaeron and Parnes range coming down to the sea between Oropus on the right and the Asopus river on the left. And the soil was more fertile than that of any other country and so could maintain a large army exempt from the calls of agricultural labor.

But in the ensuing nine thousand years, the soil washed away in "many great floods," and "you are left . . . with something rather like the skeleton of a body wasted by disease; the rich, soft soil has all run away leaving the land nothing but skin and bone." In the war that followed, Athens was one of the combatants, and the other was Atlantis. As described by Critias,

> it had mineral resources from which were mined both solid materials [e.g., rock and marble] and metals, including one metal which survives today only in name, but was then mined in quantities in a number of localities on the island, orichalch, in those days the most valuable metal except gold. There was

a plentiful supply of timber for structural purposes, and every kind of animal domesticated and wild, among them numerous elephants. For there was plenty of grazing for this largest and most voracious of beasts, as well as creatures whose habitat is marsh, swamp and river, mountain or plain. Besides all this, the earth bore freely all the aromatic substances it bears today, roots, herbs, bushes and gums exuded by flowers or fruit. There were cultivated crops, cereals which provide our staple diet . . . there were the fruits of trees, hard to store but providing the drink and food and oil which give us pleasure and relaxation and which we serve after supper as a welcome refreshment to the weary when appetite is satisfied. . . .

In the *Critias,* much of the discussion of Atlantis is devoted to matters of political and legal authority, degeneration and punishment, and military service, but subsequent authors looking for the Lost City concentrated on Plato's descriptions of the physical "evidence"—the land and the cities. The city (only one is mentioned) is dominated by a sumptuous palace "whose size and beauty were astonishing to see." There follows a description of the city, which, since it is the heart of the resurrected Atlantis, will be incorporated at some length:

> They began [the construction of the city] by digging a canal three hundred feet wide, a hundred feet deep, and fifty stades* long from the sea to the outermost ring, this making it accessible from the sea like a harbor; and they made the entrance to it large enough to admit the largest ships. At the bridges they made channels through the rings of land which separated those of water, large enough to admit the passage of a single trireme, and roofed over to make an underground tunnel; for the rims of the rings were of some height above sea-level. The largest of the rings, to which there was access from the sea, was three stades in breadth and the ring of land within it the same. Of the second pair the ring of water was two stades in breadth, and the ring of land again equal to it, while the ring of water running immediately round the central island was a stade across. The diameter of the island on which the palace was situated was five stades. It and the rings and bridges (which were a hundred feet broad) were enclosed by a stone wall all round, with towers and gates guarding the bridges on either side where they crossed the water. The stone for them, which was white, black, and yellow, they cut out of the central island and the outer and inner rings of land, and in the process excavated a pair of hollow docks with roofs of rock. Some of their buildings were of a single

---

* A stade (also stadium) was a Greek unit of measure that equaled one-eighth of a mile, or what we sometimes refer to today as a furlong. The Greeks built stadia, foot-racing courses that were one-eighth of a mile in length, hence our sports arenas of that name.

color, in others they mixed different colored stone to divert the eye and afford them appropriate pleasure. And they covered the whole circuit of the outermost wall with a veneer of bronze, and fused tin over the inner wall and orichalch gleaming like fire over the walls of the acropolis itself.

It is these rings, tunnels, and docks that the Atlantean archaeologists are seeking, and not the palace, which is described as "surrounded by a golden wall through which entry was forbidden, as it was the palace where the family of the ten kings was conceived and begotten. . . . There was a temple of Poseidon himself, a stade in length, three hundred feet wide, and proportionate in height, though somewhat outlandish in appearance. The outside of it was covered all over with silver, except for the figures on the pediment, which were covered with gold. Inside, the roof was ivory picked out with gold, silver and orichalch, and the walls, pillars and floor were covered with orichalch." Also, each of the ring-islands contained various temples for various gods and "many gardens for exercise," and "on the middle of the larger island there was a special course for horse racing. . . . Finally, there were dockyards full of triremes and their equipment, all in good shape."

The island of Atlantis rose precipitously above sea level (according to Critias) and was surrounded by a flat plain that was itself surrounded by high mountains. The plain was "rectangular in shape and measured three thousand stades in length and at its midpoint two thousand stades in breadth from the coast." * Because the Atlanteans wanted their plain to be even-sided, "any defects in its shape were corrected by means of a ditch dug round it. The depth and breadth and length of this may sound incredible for an artificial structure when compared with others of a similar kind, but I must give them as I heard them. The depth was a hundred feet, the width a stade, and the length, since it was dug right round the plain, was ten thousand stades." (The technology required to dig a 100-foot-deep ditch that was 600 feet wide and 11,000 miles long is not divulged.) A complex arrangement of channels was cut into the ground to drain the ditch, to float objects to the sea, and "to transport seasonal produce by boat."

In the beginning of the *Timaeus,* after discussing an ideal society, Socrates says that he "would be glad to hear of some account of it engaging in transac-

---

* At 607 feet to a stade, this works out to a plain that is 344 miles (1,821,000 feet) long and 229 miles (1,214,000 feet) wide. This plain would therefore be 78,776 square miles in area, considerably larger than modern Greece itself, which totals 51,146 square miles, including all the islands.

tions with other states, waging war successfully and showing in the process all the qualities one would expect from its system of education and training, both in action and negotiation with its rivals." It is in this context that the story of Atlantis is introduced. We learn of its size and its riches, but its downfall—called its "degeneration" by Plato—is not detailed, because Hermocrates' contribution on this subject is missing. (Plato may have been planning to add another dialogue, the *Hermocrates.*) The *Timaeus* ends with Zeus convening an assembly of gods he is about to address on the subject of "punishment," but before any of the details can be given, the section cuts off.[*]

In his review of the Atlantean literature, J. V. Luce tries to establish the veracity of Plato's story by referring to Ignatius Donnelly, whom he describes as "a man of parts—idealist, novelist, Congressman, and assiduous researcher, not merely in pre-history, but also in the field of Shakespearean scholarship." (Most serious students of Atlantis now regard Donnelly as a humbug, and his "Shakespearean scholarship" consisted of trying to show that Shakespeare's plays were actually written by Francis Bacon.[†] Donnelly's ideas about Atlantis are discussed on pp. 38–44.) Ultimately, Luce dismisses Donnelly's theory as "fundamentally unsatisfactory . . . because its account of the origin and diffusion of higher civilization is completely at variance with what is now the accepted outline picture based on the archaeology of the Middle East," but then he brings in Lewis Spence, Donnelly's loyal disciple, calling his work "more moderate and plausible." Spence wrote that "a great continent [Atlantis] formerly occupied the whole or the major part of the North Atlantic region," and that it disintegrated into two island continents, one of which completely disappeared around 10,000 B.C., and the other of which (known as Antilia) "still persists fragmentally as the West Indian Islands." For Plato's location of Atlantis, Luce concedes that it "had to be enlarged to the point where there was no room left for it within the straits. [Because of its large size,] it had to go outside into the boundless ocean which bore the name of Atlas."

Desmond Lee separates the responses to Plato's Atlantis into three categories: the *crazy,* the *geological,* and the *historical.* Into the first of these categories he places such luminaries as Ignatius Donnelly, who wrote *Atlantis: The Ante-*

[*] Most scholars assume that the dialogue ends where it does because Plato was interrupted or turned to something else, but in *Lost Atlantis,* James Bramwell suggests that "Plato was still in full possession of his faculties and anxious as ever to leave no loose ends, yet *unable* to go on because he realized that he had reached an impasse."

[†] Sir Francis Bacon will reappear in our discussions of Atlantis; he also wrote an essay called *The New Atlantis,* which was published in 1627 and was one of the earliest examples (in English) of the use of Plato's Atlantis as a setting for fiction.

diluvian World in 1882. Donnelly described a continent that sank exactly where Plato said it did, in the Atlantic outside the Straits of Gibralter, but otherwise, his book is a compilation of improbable affiliations of largely unrelated events. In *Lost Atlantis,* J. V. Luce summed up Donnelly's thesis:

> There was once a land connection between Europe and America; ergo Atlantis. Primitive and cultured people all over the world have Deluge legends; ergo Atlantis. Peruvian and Mexican civilizations were as advanced as anything in the old world; ergo Atlantis. Having accepted all this, one is in no mood for "Genesis contains a history of Atlantis," or "The Carians of Homer are the same as the Caribs of the West Indies."

Except for the location of the Lost Continent, however, Donnelly's book—which has gone through some fifty editions and is still in print—has very little to do with Plato.

Lee's second category of responses to the question "Did Plato invent Atlantis?" is the *geological,* which he defines as "producing the scientific evidence for the existence of an Atlantic continent at some earlier phase in the earth's history." This refers to those who would take Plato literally and place Atlantis offshore in the Atlantic Ocean. Lee succinctly dismisses these possibilities as follows:

> There never was an Atlantic landbridge since the arrival of man in the world: there is no sunken landmass in the Atlantic; the Atlantic Ocean must have existed in its present form for at least a million years. In fact, it is a geophysical impossibility for an Atlantis of Plato's dimensions to have existed in the Atlantic.

There is also what Edwin Ramage refers to as the "debris theory." According to this, some of the islands scattered throughout the Atlantic are the remains of the Lost Continent. These islands include the Canaries, the Madeiras, and, of course, the Azores, but some Atlantean scholars managed to extend Atlantis all the way across the Atlantic Ocean, eventually concluding that it was really America. Adding to the confusion was an entire atlas of missing Atlantic islands that were referred to as "flyaway islands" by Samuel Eliot Morison. (Donald Johnson wrote an entire book on the subject, called *Phantom Islands of the Atlantic.*) Morison is careful to list only those phantom islands that appeared on legitimate maps; he writes, "We must also consider the habits of the map-makers. They have always disliked open spaces. In the Middle Ages they peopled unknown interiors with storied cities and Oriental potentates, and peppered the Atlantic with imaginary islands." Among these imaginary islands—which were not only not Atlantis but nonexistent as well—were Frislanda (which was probably the Faeroes) and, of course, one of the favorites of Atlantologists, the Azores.

I N   1 4 2 7 the pilot Diogo de Silves, possibly on a return voyage from Madeira, reached the islands that would eventually be named the Azores, but it was Gonçalo Velho Cabral who is credited with the official discovery of the islands in 1431. Velho first claimed Santa Maria, then São Miguel, Terceira ("third"), São Jorge, Graciosa, Pico, and Fayal. The seven islands were named the Ilhas dos Açores ("Isles of Hawks"), and within a year, the Portuguese had settled in. While searching for the nonexistent island of Antilia, Diogo de Tieve discovered the remaining two islands in 1452.

Also known as the "Isle of the Seven Cities," Antilia was probably the most notorious of the nonexistent Atlantic islands. It appeared on maps as early as 1452, and later on Martin Behaim's 1492 globe, which depicted the world as Columbus knew it. Columbus thought that Antilia (i.e., "island opposite," meaning opposite Portugal, or possibly opposite the Pillars of Hercules) was part of "the great island of Cipangu," and headed directly for it on his first voyage. Although the island never appeared, the name Sete Cidades can be found today on Atlantic maps; it is the name of a village on the Azorean island of São Miguel. But, of course, none of this was known to Plato; the Atlantic Ocean was largely a mystery to the ancient Greeks.

In his discussion of the various Atlantis theories, Desmond Lee wrote, "We must remember Plato's purpose—to describe a rich, powerful and technologically advanced society to serve as an opponent of his ideal Athens. He had a fertile imagination and in Atlantis produced the first work of science fiction. And (using that description in its widest sense) he certainly started something." In his conclusion, where he divides his responses into a case for the prosecution (wherein Atlantis is entirely fictional) and a case for the defense (where some parts of the story are rooted in historical fact), J. V. Luce tells us (for the prosecution) that

> when Plato was asked by Dionysius I to write something for a literary "festival" in Syracuse, he planned the trilogy *Timaeus-Critias-Hermocrates* with a West Greek coloring. The major fact in West Greek life was the power of Carthage, which controlled much of the Mediterranean and the coasts of the islands

west to Gibraltar and out onto the Atlantic. This gave Plato the idea of inventing an ancient "Atlantic" power, and bringing it into conflict with the prehistoric Greeks. He decided to treat this fiction on an epic scale, describing in
detail the numbers and resources of the protagonists, and introducing the
usual divine machinery of Zeus and the other gods. The fiction bears all the
marks of the "noble lie"—a device recommended in the *Republic* as useful for
propaganda purposes in the interests of national solidarity. . . . This piece of
pseudo-history was also useful for moral purposes. . . . He could praise his
own ancestors for their outstanding courage and leadership in his fictitious
crisis.

For the defense, however, Luce makes a stronger case. He relates the story
of the Egyptian trade with Keftiu (Crete), which was suddenly cut off by a
great cataclysm whose effects were communicated by refugees and sailors.
Solon heard a somewhat garbled story about this disaster, which came down
to Plato, who realized the dramatic possibilities of the tale. "He gilded the
palace architecture," wrote Luce, "with touches of oriental splendor from his
readings in Herodotus and Ctesias. He filled the upland pastures with herds of
African elephants.* . . . Above all, he made Atlantis very large, and put it far
back in time and far away in space." Four years before Luce, Desmond Lee
wrote: "The Egyptians were in touch with Crete and would be likely to hear
something of the Thera catastrophe. . . . Nor does it seem to me in the least
surprising that the story should occur only in Plato. By his own account it had
survived as, so to speak, a bit of family gossip in Critias' family. There was nothing in the Greek mind or memory to connect it with Crete."

When he presents the case for the fictional interpretation of Plato's Atlantis
story, J. V. Luce says:

> The whole thing is as fictional as Lilliput or Brobdingnag. Plato, like Swift, was
> artist enough to embroider some realistic detail on his canvas. He also put in
> the romance of a plausible setting by representing it as a tradition deriving

---

* In 1904, a British paleontologist named Dorothea Bate prowled around the islands of Cyprus and Crete
and discovered the fossil remains of various Pleistocene mammals, including shrews, antelope, deer,
hippopotamuses, and elephants. She could not explain their presence there, but Donald Johnson (1978,
1980) observed that some of these mammals—particularly deer, hippos, and elephants—are excellent
swimmers, capable of colonizing new territories by swimming to them. The elephants of Crete (and
Malta, Sardinia, Cyprus, Rhodes, and Delos) were dwarf species, standing no more than two feet high,
and not the towering recent pachyderms of Africa and Asia. Earlier theories had these animals walking
to the islands by crossing land bridges from the mainland, but Johnson's studies of swimming elephants
strongly suggest that they arrived by water. In a 1986 article, Paul Sondaar suggested that the elephants
of the Aegean islands might have lived concurrently with the first human settlers there, some seven
thousand years ago, and that at least on the island of Tilos, ivory was used by Neolithic peoples.

from Egypt, where historical records were much more ancient than anything in Greece. But can we really suppose that this tale, with its strong Hellenic interest, survived all those years at Saïs, and was never apparently noted or acquired by anyone else except Solon, who very conveniently happened to be an ancestor of Plato himself?

Luce then counters his own "case for the prosecution" with a defense that demonstrates that Plato's story of Atlantis is "a startlingly accurate sketch of the Minoan empire in the sixteenth century B.C." He produces a detailed chronology to show how Plato might have heard the story of the palaces on Crete, but his account is so full of subjunctive qualifiers such as "might have heard" and "may have seemed to him" that it cannot be taken seriously. And finally, with nothing resembling evidence to support such an excercise, he describes the process whereby Plato wrote the story:

> His imagination got to work on the details. He gilded the palace architecture with touches of oriental splendor from his readings in Herodotus and Ctesias. He filled the upland pastures with herds of African elephants. The square allotments and the great irrigation ditches owe much to Egypt (which he had seen) and Babylon (which he had not). The great naval arsenal could be an idealized version of Syracuse, with a touch of Carthage. Unconsciously perhaps, he may have introduced something of the luxury of Homer's Phaecia, itself in part a memory of Minoan Crete.

Like Desmond Lee, J. V. Luce is a respected classical scholar. (Among his other academic honors, he was a lecturer in Greek at Glasgow University; senior tutor at Trinity College, Dublin; and visiting professor in classics at Trinity College, Hartford, Connecticut.) Academic credentials, however impressive, do not automatically validate a theory. (If they did, we might just as easily accept Velikovsky's idea that the planet Venus came close to Earth and caused the disappearance of Atlantis.) A careful reading of Luce's treatise—the book is entitled *Lost Atlantis: New Light on an Old Legend*—does not prove his case. It is filled with conjecture and distortion of facts, designed, like the fictions of Ignatius Donnelly and Charles Berlitz, to validate the hypothesis that the author set out to prove in the first place. Perhaps the most irresponsible part of Luce's "defense" is a fabicated "cross-examination" of Plato, where the philosopher says, "I always felt that the Atlantean story, strange though it was, could be basically true, and no mere fiction. Some of the details had an authentic ring about them. . . ."

In 1933, W. A. Heidel wrote "A Suggestion Concerning Plato's Atlantis." His rationale for writing about what he calls "this hackneyed theme" was that he had "a new suggestion, though incapable of proof, [that] is at least reasonable and in accord with the context of Plato's thought." According to Heidel, there are no Egyptian accounts of Atlantis or the Athenians, so by introducing his story with a tale told to Solon by the Egyptian priests, Plato "as clearly as possible indicates the fictitious character of the narrative." He recounts an intricate story told by Herodotus involving Sesostris, an Egyptian king who subdued the Scythians, which contains this sentence: "This king, said the priests, set out with a fleet of long ships from the Arabian Gulf and subdued all the dwellers by the Red (Arabian) Sea, till as he sailed he came to a sea which was too shallow for his vessels." Thus, says Heidel, the unnavigable body of water that Plato says is the Atlantic is actually the mouth of the Indus River, and the battle between the Athenians and the Atlanteans is a description of the expeditionary force of Darius's general Scylax as he attempted to invade India. Although Heidel readily admits that his theory is "hardly susceptible of demonstration," he does make a valid point when he concludes his essay with, "Certainly it is more reasonable to look for the answer in Greek history and geography than in the latest findings of modern geology." (And Heidel was writing some years before Spyridon Marinatos's 1939 suggestion that the explosion of Thera had destroyed the Minoan civilization on Crete.)

Another approach, called by its author the "prehistorical," depends upon information only recently available to researchers. In *Plato Prehistorian,* Mary Settegast writes:

> The Thera hypothesis was formed before seafarers were discovered in the Late Paleolithic Aegean, and before the magnitude of the loss of Greek lands to the post-glacial seas was fully known. The extent of the mid-to-late nineteenth millennium spread of arrowheads was not yet recognized; the date of Jericho's fortifications had not been moved back to the last half of the ninth millennium; and the depth and complexity of the Magdalenian culture, whose location in time and space closely parallels that of the European holdings of Plato's Atlantic Empire, was still to be demonstrated.

Settegast recognizes that tenth-millennium man was still living in caves, hunting and gathering his food; and that the horse-racing, seafaring, technologically adept Atlanteans would have lived—if Plato's dates are to be believed—"more than three thousand years before the appearance of domestic plants and animals in the archaeological record of Greece." (Edwin Ramage said much the same thing in his essay "Ancient and Modern Perspectives" when he wrote, "At that time [9500 B.C.] Greece was in the late Paleolithic period and man was still living in caves or rock shelters and was hunting and gathering his food.") But they may have been seafarers as well. The discovery of worked obsidian in the Franchthi Cave on the Peloponnese, however, suggests that Paleolithic men managed to venture out into the Aegean, since the source of this obsidian was the island of Melos, one hundred sea miles to the southeast. The melting of the ice sheet (the Würm glaciation) from 16,000 B.C. to around 13,000 B.C. substantially altered the coastlines of ancient Greece. Rising waters covered much of the land that had earlier connected now-isolated islands, and even the Peloponnese was much more a part of the mainland than it is now (Van Andel and Schackelton 1982). What does this mean with respect to Plato's Atlantis? Maybe nothing, but on the other hand, Settegast believes that this rise in sea level may have resulted in the inundation of the land referred to by Plato (*Critias*) when he wrote, "You are left, as with little islands, with something rather like the skeleton of a body wasted by disease. . . ."

Examination of the cave paintings suggests that the Magdalenians had domesticated the horse (there are also bone engravings that seem to show a harness or a bridle), so to Settegast, the idea of "horse-racing" in Atlantis no longer seems quite so far-fetched. As for the remainder of the Magdalenian art (most of which has not been found), she asks if it would be possible that the "controlling center" was "the home base of the Atlantean governors, from whom the art of Europe was receiving its uniform direction and style."

THERE ARE any number of authors who have chosen to analyze the dialogues and find that careful inspection reveals so many inconsistencies that the story must be a fable. For example, in *Lost Atlantis*, James Bramwell writes:

> The fake in Plato's case should be apparent from the fact that the "papers of Solon," which are represented as family heirlooms, have never been heard of by anybody outside the family. Also, there is a suspicious contradiction in his account of the transmission of the Solon story. In *Critias* Critias says: "His actual papers were once in my father's hands, and are in my own to this day." But elsewhere he tells his audience that he has been reflecting all night to try and remember the story he heard in his youth. . . . Now why, if he had the MS., did he have to rely on his memory?

In 1841, long before anyone had tried to locate Atlantis in Crete, Bimini, North Africa, or Germany, the nineteenth-century French classicist T. Henri Martin published *Etudes sur le Timée de Platon* (Studies on the Timaeus of Plato), in which he made seven points that he believed demolished the idea that Plato was describing a real place: (1) Plato's story is fiction. (2) It has an Egyptian, not a Greek origin. (3) The Egyptian priests made up the story for their own political advantage. (4) If Atlantis did exist, it was in the Atlantic where Plato said it was, not in Africa, Germany, America, or Palestine. (5) It is impossible to believe that the disappearance of an island of the size described by Plato would not have altered the geography of the world, but as far as we know, Africa, Europe, and Asia are more or less where they always were. (6) There was no continent running along the edge of Oceanus and no shallows where an island used to be. (7) We had better stop looking for Atlantis; it is just "Utopia."

Whether he wrote historical fact or science fiction, Plato is unquestionably the most important author in the Atlantis canon. Without his dialogues, there would be no connections to draw between the Minoan civilization and the Lost City. There would be no searches in the Mediterranean, the Atlantic, the Baltic, or the Caribbean. Ignatius Donnelly might have remained in Congress; Lewis Spence would have had to call his quarterly something else; but Edgar Cayce might have imagined Atlantis anyway, since he claimed never to have read Plato. But without Plato, there would be no Atlantis.

WHO WRITES OF ATLANTIS?

LIKE QUEEQUEG'S HOMELAND of "Kokovoko" in *Moby-Dick*, Atlantis "is not drawn on any map"; nor will you find it in any compilation of Greek mythology. It is sui generis, an island unto itself, a chimeric place that takes whatever form its describer wishes to give it. It can be a great city that sank into the sea, or a continent that was destroyed by an errant asteroid. It can be a city in the Aegean, or an outpost in the Sahara Desert. It can be a submerged island in the North Atlantic, or a community high on the slopes of California's Mount Shasta. It has appeared in historical studies, projections of the future, archaeological monographs, philosophical discourses, geological tracts, astronomical treatises, science fiction novels, sea stories, studies of ancient hieroglyphics, travel books, psychic revelations, poems, movies, and comic books, and there are countless crackpot explanations about what and where it *really* was.

As we shall see, some writers produced what was clearly fiction, but what are we to make of some of those who wrote about Atlantis a few years after Plato? In his treatise *On Meteorology*, Plato's student Aristotle (384–322 B.C.) says that the sea outside the Pillars of Hercules is shallow because of mud, echoing his teacher's description, but he also says that Atlantis does not exist. The philosopher Crantor, who lived somewhat later than Aristotle, wrote the first known commentary on Plato's dialogues, in which he accepted the story of Atlantis without qualification. Pliny the Elder, describing the formation of the Atlantic, speaks of great formations of land being swept away "where the

Atlantic Ocean is now—if we believe Plato." By the time of Christ, Atlantis had taken its place as a quasi-official island somewhere beyond the Pillars of Hercules. Around 30 B.C., the Roman historian Diodorus Siculus completed his forty-volume *World History,* in which he discussed the battle between the Amazons and the Atlanteans, "who dwelt in a prosperous country and inhabited great cities." (Of this battle, Ramage says, "For Diodorus . . . it is no longer a case of whether Atlantis ever existed or not, but of how to relate its inhabitants to the other mythological peoples that lived out here at the end of the world. Most of what Diodorus says has to be taken as sheer embroidery.")

In his *Life of Solon,* written a century later, Plutarch gives the previously anonymous Egyptian priest of Saïs a name (Sonchis), and Solon is described as studying with him at Heliopolis. Plutarch writes, "He heard the story of the lost Atlantis, and tried to introduce it in a poetical form to the Greeks." Later in *Solon,* Plutarch writes:

> Plato, ambitious to elaborate and adorn the subject of the lost Atlantis, as if it were the soil of a fair state unoccupied, but appropriately his by virtue of some kinship with Solon, began the work by laying out great porches, enclosures, and courtyards, such as no story, tale or poesy ever had before. Therefore the greater our delight in what he actually wrote, the greater our distress in view of what he left undone. For as the Olympieium in the city of Athens, so the tale of lost Atlantis in the wisdom of Plato is the only one among many beautiful works to remain unfinished.

It appears from Plutarch's description of Plato's "lost Atlantis" story (or fable) that Plato had embellished the story told to him by Solon, fabricating those very elements (great porches, enclosures, courtyards) that make the story read more like fantasy than fact. Later on, Plutarch wrote, "Now Solon, after beginning his great work on the story or fable of the lost Atlantis, which, as he had heard from the learned men of Saïs, particularly concerned the Athenians, abandoned it, not for lack of leisure, as Plato says, but rather because of his old age, fearing the magnitude of the task."

Some two hundred years after Christ, the Roman scholar Aelian (170–230 A.D.) wrote *De natura animalium,** in which he discussed an animal called the "sea

---

* Aelian's seventeen-book collection, *On the Characteristics of Animals,* was published in three volumes in 1959 by the Loeb Classical Library, Harvard University Press. It is described as a "mixed collection of facts and beliefs concerning the habits of animals taken from Greek authors with some personal observation, and having as their chief object entertainment. Fact, fancy, legend, stories and gossip all play their part in a narrative which has, of set purpose, no arrangement. If there is any ethical motive, it is that the virtues of untaught yet reasoning animals can be a lesson to thoughtless and selfish mankind."

ram" ("which many have heard tell but few know the natural history"), said to be found in the straits between Corsica and Sardinia. "The head of the male sea ram," wrote Aelian, "is bound with a white band, like the diadem, one might say, of Lysimachus or Antigonus or some other Macedonian king. . . . Dwellers by the ocean tell the story that the ancient kings of Atlantis who traced their descent from Poseidon, wore head-bands of the skin of male sea rams, as a sign of authority. The queens likewise wore fillets of the female sea ram. . . ." Aelian also supplied Theopompus's description of the vast continent, "beyond the boundary of this world . . . with huge animals and men twice the stature of ours." (Other than Aelian's transcript, all of Theopompus's works have been lost.) Of this story, Aelian wrote, "Those who consider Theopompus of Chios as a trustworthy writer may believe this story. For my part, in this story and in several others, I can only see the writer of fairy tales."

After Plato had introduced the concept of a utopian society that vanished, other authors picked up the theme. Their interpretations sometimes differed from the legend of the Greeks, where the dissolute inhabitants of a flourishing civilization were punished by the cataclysmic destruction of their city. Atlantis was also used as a structure for fictionalizing an ideal modus vivendi, as in *The New Atlantis,* an essay published posthumously in 1627, a year after the death of its author, the English statesman, scientist, and philosopher Francis Bacon. Like many of the Atlantis stories that followed, it concerns some travelers blown off course (they are on their way from Peru to China and Japan) who fetch up on a previously undiscovered shore on an island in the South Sea. (In seventeenth-century England, the little-known Pacific Ocean was often referred to as the South Sea; Balboa had viewed its vast expanses one hundred fourteen years earlier, and Sir Francis Drake had crossed it in the *Golden Hind* in 1579, only forty-seven years before the publication of Bacon's essay.) At the suggestion of St. Bartholomew, the ancestors on the island—which is known in their tongue as "Bensalem"—had built an ark and thus avoided the flood, and settled on this island, where they flourished for "an age or more."

There is no question that Bacon had read Plato, since his *New Atlantis* contains many specific references to the Greek philosopher, articulated by the "Governor," who explains Bensalem to the newcomers. He tells them "of the magnificent temple, palace, city, and hill, and the manifold streams of goodly navigable rivers" and how "within less than the space of one hundred years the Great Atlantis was utterly lost and destroyed; not by a great earthquake, as your man [Plato] saith, but by a particular deluge or inundation, these countries having at this day far greater rivers and far higher mountains to pour

Sir Francis Bacon, author of *The New Atlantis*, published in 1627 — a fable about a lost island in the Pacific

down waters than any part of the Old World." The "Great Atlantis"—having been flooded and drained—is now America.* The "New Atlantis" of Bacon's study is the island of Bensalem, where the travelers have landed.

The inhabitants of Bensalem are completely self-sufficient, since their island is "5,600 miles in circuit, and of rare fertility of soil in the greatest part thereof," and they practice productive commerce and trade with neighboring islands in the South Sea. Some nineteen hundred years earlier, the king of Bensalem had ordained that every twelve years two ships were to set out to collect information "especially of the sciences, arts, manufactures and inventions of all the world, and to bring unto us books, instruments, and patterns in every kind. . . ." With this information, the people of Bensalem managed to construct a futuristic city with towers a half mile high ("which we use for insulation, refrigeration, conservations," and for a clear view of the weather); fresh- and saltwater lakes; artificial wells and fountains; great and spacious houses, "chambers of health, where we qualify the air as we

---

* "Marvel you not," says the Governor, "at the thin population of America, nor at the rudeness and ignorance of the people; for you must account your inhabitants of America as a young people, younger a thousand years at the least than the rest of the world, for that there was so much time between the universal Flood and their particular inundation. For the poor remnant of human seed which remained in their mountains peopled the country again slowly, by little and little, and being simple and savage people (not like Noah and his sons, which was the chief family of the earth), they were not able to leave letters, arts and civility to their propriety; and having likewise in their mountainous habitations been used (in respect of the extreme cold of those regions) to clothe themselves with the skins of tigers, bears, and great hairy goats; when after they came down into the valley, and found the intolerable heats which are there, and knew no means of lighter apparel, they were forced to begin the custom of going naked, which continueth at this day."

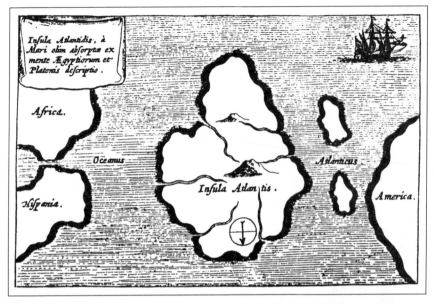

Insula Atlantidis, à
Mari olim absorpta ex
mente Ægyptiorum et
Platonis descriptio.

Africa.

Oceanus

Hyspania.

Atlanticus.

Insula Atlantis.

America.

ATLANTIS LOCATED IN the Atlantic, as shown in the 1665 *Mundus Subterraneus* by Athanasius Kircher

think good and proper for the cure of divers diseases"; parks and enclosures for all sorts of beasts and birds; "dispensatories or shops of medicines; and divers mechanical arts which you have not; and stuffs made by them, as papers, linens, silks, tissues, dainty works of feathers of wonderful luster; precious stones of all kinds"; "instruments of music and harmonies which you have not"; engine houses, mathematical houses, and "houses of deceits of the senses, where we represent all manner of juggling, false apparitions, impostures and illusions, and their fallacies." After explaining the wonders of this ancient but advanced civilization, the king presses two thousand ducats upon the English representative who was alone chosen to hear of Bensalem's wonders, and says, "God bless thee, my son, and God bless this relation which I have made, I give thee leave to publish it, for the good of other nations, for here we are in God's bosom, a land unknown." In what is perhaps the greatest tribute to Plato, Bacon's narrative finishes—as does the dialogue *Critias*—without an ending. Bacon's *New Atlantis* closes with the words "The rest was not perfected." By the seventeenth century, Atlantis was revived and embedded in the European consciousness.

SINCE BACON, there have been more revivals of the Atlantis scenario than "the glittering serpent" would ever have believed possible. Of the more respectable theories, the one with the most current support is the Minoan. For this reason, I have devoted a substantial portion of this study to a discussion of early Cretan civilization. Of all the proposed sites of Atlantis, only Crete and Santorini can be visited and the evidence evaluated by the casual observer. One can see the vast crater where a great island once stood, and the dusty rubble that marks the location of the palaces and houses of the Minoan empire. Even if Minoan Crete was not Atlantis—and it probably was not—the Minoan civilization deserves careful study.

It is, of course, only one of a number of possibilities. As T. Henri Martin wrote in the nineteenth century, "Many scholars, setting sail in quest of Atlantis with a more or less heavy cargo of erudition, but without any compass except their imagination and caprice, have voyaged at random. And where have they landed? In fifty different places." James Bramwell, writing in 1938, reduced Martin's fifty places to "eight main hypotheses": Atlantis in America, in North Africa, and in Nigeria; Atlantis as an island in the Atlantic Ocean; Atlantis as Tartessos; Karst's theory of a twofold Atlantis; Gidon's theory of the land subsidences between Ireland and Brittany in the Bronze Age; and the theory that Plato's Atlantis represents a memory of the flooding of the Mediterranean basin. Bramwell details some of these theories, but, unfortunately, with precious little documentation. Some of these Atlantean theorists, like Francis Bacon, are well known, but others, like Frobenius or Karst, are more obscure. L. Sprague de Camp's chapter "Through a Glass Darkly" provides an excellent introduction to some of the more dubious theories of the location of Atlantis.

The idea of Atlantis in America originated with Francis Bacon, who wrote *The New Atlantis* in 1626, shortly after the first Englishmen had crossed the Atlantic to settle in the New World. As for North Africa, its vast expanses of sand seem to have generated any number of Atlantean stories, usually fabricated by Frenchmen who happened to be working there. In 1874, the French archaeologist Félix Berlioux claimed to have found the Lost City at the foot of the mountains in the Moroccan Atlas range, between Casablanca and Agadir. Berlioux's theory was the basis for a novel called *L'Atlantide,* by Pierre Benoît, in which two Frenchmen find the Lost City in the mountains of southern Algeria, where for some reason the men wear the veil while the women do not. The heroine Antinéa keeps a pet leopard named Hiram, and she has such power over men that they commit suicide when she discards them. The novel was published in England as *Atlantida,* and in America as *The Queen of Atlantis,* and it was made into a movie three times: in 1921 as a silent film, in 1932 as a German-language talkie, and in Hollywood as *Siren of Atlantis* in 1948.

Claude Roux, another Frenchman, proposed that the Mediterranean coast of northwest Africa was once composed of great shallow lagoons that were extremely fertile and densely populated, but that successive invasions decimated the population until this "Atlantis" became only a memory. (Along with Jean Gattefossé, Roux assembled a seventeen-hundred-item bibliography on Atlantis in 1926.) In 1929, Count Byron Kuhn de Prorok published *Mysterious Sahara,* in which he contended that he had found traces of Atlantis in the desert, including a skeleton that he announced was that of Tin Hinan, the legendary matriarch of the Berbers. (Tin Hinan was also the subject of *L'Atlantide.*) The skeleton turned out to be the remains of a recently deceased Berber dignitary. Paul Borchardt, a geologist, claimed to have found Atlantis in Gabès, Tunisia, when he uncovered an ancient fortress, but it turned out to have been of Roman origin. Also in Tunisia, a German named Albert Herrmann found what he described as ancient irrigation works, which he concluded was a colony of Atlantis that had been located in the eastern Mediterranean but had originated in the German region of Friesland (now part of the Netherlands). Herrmann also decided that Plato's numbers were off by a factor of thirty, and when he shrank the measurements accordingly, his Atlantis fit nicely into a corner of Tunisia. The manipulation of Plato's dates would later develop into an important element in Atlantological research.

Bramwell also discusses "the explorer Leo Frobenius," who claimed to have found Atlantis in the Yoruba country of Nigeria, based on a rather imaginative reading of Plato, where he reinterprets the "flourishing vegetation" as palm trees, bananas, and peppers and manages to get Plato's always difficult elephants onto the right continent. The last of the African-Atlantis theories was propounded in 1930 by Otto Silbermann, who decided that Plato's nine-thousand-year-old story was ridiculous on its face, since any civilization that old would have been forgotten long before the rise of Egypt. He suggested instead that Plato was recounting a Phoenician story describing a war with Libya that took place around 2450 B.C. in the Libyan desert, and like so many of his compatriots, he wrote a book.

Tartessos remains one of the great mysteries of ancient times. In *Beyond the Pillars of Heracles,* Rhys Carpenter presents a detailed study of its history—and the confusion surrounding it. In book I of the *Historia* (which Carpenter prefers to translate as "inquiry" rather than "history"), Herodotus tells us that "the Phocaeans were the first of the Greeks to undertake long sea voyages. It was they who made Adria known, and Tyrrhenia, and Iberia and Tartessos." They hailed from Phocaea, the northernmost of the Ionian cities, on the west coast of Asia Minor, celebrated as a great maritime state. In their great fifty-oared longboats (pentecontes), they arrived at Tartessos "and made themselves agreeable to Arganthonius, the King who had ruled the place for eighty years, and lived to be a hundred and twenty." According to Herodotus's very specific description, "They were driven westward right through the Pillars of Hercules until, by a piece of more than human luck, they succeeded in making Tartessos." "If indeed they were the first Greeks to find it," writes Carpenter, "then they were the first of their race to have seen and passed through the Gibraltar Strait and encounter the Atlantic tides." Carpenter dates the Phocaean explorations from the early seventh century, which means that Herodotus (c. 485–425 B.C.), who related the story first, had to depend upon tales passed down to him. It also means that Plato, who lived from 428 to 347, would have been familiar with Herodotus's stories of the Phocaeans' explorations, and we can therefore safely say that Plato had at least enough knowledge of the Atlantic Ocean to include it in his tale of Atlantis.

In another, unrelated passage, Herodotus discusses the opening of Tartessos to Greek commerce:

> A Samian ship whose captain and owner was a man named Kolaios put in at the island of Platea on his way to Egypt. . . . But as he was putting to sea again with the intent of sailing thither, he was carried off course by an east wind. And because the tempest did not abate, the mariners, thanks to divine guidance, passed out between the Pillars of Hercules and came to Tartessos. Now at this time this was an untouched virgin market, with the result that when they reached home again they made the greatest profit from their cargo of any Greeks about whom we have any reliable information. . . . So the Samians took out a tenth part of the profits, namely six talents, and had a bronze cauldron of Argolic type made, with heads of griffins jutting out around it; and this they dedicated to the temple of the goddess Hera; and under it they set three huge ten-foot figures of men kneeling.

This passage is, as Carpenter writes, "a nest of difficulties." The island of Platea has been identified as lying between Crete and North Africa, but how are we to interpret a storm that was powerful enough to drive a ship eight hundred miles off course and out of the Mediterranean into the Atlantic without mishap?

Many scholars want to show that Tartessos was the biblical "Tarshish," but while the names are similar enough to have caused confusion for two thousand years, the two places are now believed to have been completely different. Tarshish was situated in the eastern Mediterranean; Tartessos was far to the west. Jonah was heading for Tarshish before he had all that trouble with the whale, and in Ezekiel 27:12 we read that "Tarshish was thy merchant by reason of the multitude of all kind of riches; with silver, iron, tin, and lead, they traded in thy fairs." A German historian named Adolf Schulten identified the parallel between Tarshish and Atlantis, pointing out that both were rich in metals and both disappeared. He spent several seasons digging to the north of the estuary of the Guadalquivir, but all he found was a single iron finger ring, with unintelligible letters engraved inside it. The truth, says Carpenter, is that there was no city of Tartessos, but rather, it was the name of the river (now the Guadalquivir) that served the mining commerce of the region. (There is still a mining town on the Río Tinto in southern Spain called Tharsis.) Tarshish, on the other hand, was probably the Greek trading town of Tarsus, only a few miles along the southern coast of Turkey from the Phoenician shoreland, a much more likely destination for Jonah.

Along came Mrs. Ellen Mary Whitshaw,* director of something called the Anglo-Spanish-American School of Archaeology, who claimed to have found evidence of Atlantis in Andalusia, and wrote a book with that title in 1928. In the practice common to Atlantologists, Mrs. Whitshaw uses Plato retroactively to support her findings. She wrote, "My theory, to sum it up concisely, is that Plato's story is corroborated from first to last by what we find here, even to the Atlantean name of his son Gadir, who inherited that part of Poseidon's kingdom which lay beyond the Pillars of Hercules and ruled at Gades, having its echo in the traditional Gadea on the Río Tinto in the jurisdiction of Niebla, an ancient mill under the shadow of a Stone Age fortress, relics of which still stand."

According to Bramwell, the botanist François Gidon maintained that the Atlantis story contains an echo of the land subsidences between Brittany and Ireland, which opened up the English Channel, and that the Atlantis civiliza-

---

* In some discussions of Spanish Atlantis literature, Mrs. Whitshaw is referred to as "Whishaw." This confusion appears to be self-generated, since she signs her preface "according to the ancient custom by which a married woman in Spain retains her maiden name, which is that of both of her parents: *Elena María Williams y Windsor, Viuda de Whishaw (Don Bernardo)*."

tion described by Plato was indeed a Bronze Age civilization. An orientalist named Joseph Karst believed that there was an early Atlantis in the Arabian Sea, and another one in North Africa, "which at that time was still linked to Sicily by a Sicilian-Tunisian land bridge. . . ."

I have in front of me a book called *The Ancient Atlantic.* I don't know who owned the book before; I got it in a used-book store. When I opened it, I found a sheaf of yellowed clippings between the pages, MILD QUAKE IN L.A. and MEXICAN SEXTUPLETS DEAD, and also a map of the Atlantic Ocean floor which had been used in an Alcoa magazine ad ("Come along with Alcoa, as we probe earth's last frontier—and the richest"). The last owner was obviously interested in unusual phenomena—why else buy this book? It was apparently self-published by the author, L. Taylor Hansen. (From the initials, I could not tell if LTH was a man or a woman, but when I found "L. Taylor Hansen: A Sketch" in the index, I turned to page 423 and found a pencil drawing of the author, Lucile Taylor Hansen, dated 1942 and signed "Regaledo.") The colophon page reads, "Printing: Tomorrow River Printers, Amherst, Wisconsin, 54406," and "Binding: National Bookbinding Company, Stevens Point, Wisconsin, 54481," so I think we are safe in assuming that Ms. Hansen lived (or lives) somewhere in the middle of the Badger State.

Ms. Hansen's magnum opus is not your ordinary vanity-press book, hastily assembled and poorly manufactured. It has a proper dust jacket (but, alas, no author biography on the back flap), a reasonable binding of a sort of maroon leatherette, and typography that may not be of the highest quality but is not typewriter type, either. Moreover, *The Ancient Atlantic* is filled with color illustrations (remember, in 1969 they did not have color Xeroxing), a couple of foldout pages, and sixty-five chapters that cover everything from the Atlantis legend to Norse mummies, and include "The March of the Ar-Zawans," "The Loch Ness Monster: A Plesiosaur," "The War Dogs of the Ancients," "The Kerrians or Carians," and "The Round-Headed Landsmen." The book, which is the size of a small coffee table, is a hefty 437 pages long, including the index, and cost me fifteen dollars. There are very few photographs, but there are about two hundred maps and illustrations, apparently drawn by the author, all of which are quite terrible. It is tempting to leaf through this book and poke fun at Ms. Hansen's off-the-wall archaeology, but that is not my intention. Rather, I have cited this curious book to introduce the vast body of literature that is devoted to the myth of Atlantis, usually written to demonstrate that the myth is true, in one form or another.

LET LUCILE HANSEN introduce one of the first of the Atlantean scholars: the estimable Ignatius Loyola Donnelly. "During the eighties of the
last century," she wrote, "Ignatius Donnelly wrote a book called 'Atlantis and
the Antediluvian World' [*sic*]. It was excellently researched for its day and the
mistakes it made were due to the fact that science had not enough material
to entertain a different viewpoint." One of the most imaginative and influen-

AFTER PLATO, Ignatius Donnelly (1831–1901)
was the most influential figure in the history
of Atlantology.

tial of Atlantean scholars, Donnelly
was born in Philadelphia in 1831.
In the introduction to the 1976 edition of Donnelly's book, E. F. Bleiler
described him as "short, fat, red-
headed . . . ebullient, witty, hard-
working, gifted with remarkable
powers of self-conviction, cheerful
despite repeated misfortune on all
levels of his life. . . ." A lawyer, he
moved to Minnesota in 1856, and
with John Nininger he cofounded a
cultural center called Nininger City
which failed after a year, leaving
Donnelly the town's only resident.
This seemed naturally to lead to
politics, and Donnelly became the
lieutenant governor of Minnesota
and then a member of Congress.
He read voraciously—especially, it
is said, in the Library of Congress—
and published books on a wide variety of subjects. These included three
novels; *Ragnarok: The Age of Fire and
Gravel,* in which he tried to show
that certain gravel deposits were the
result of a near collision between
the earth and a comet (a theme to
be developed some sixty years later
by Immanuel Velikovsky); and sev-

eral books in which he argued that Shakespeare's plays were actually written by Francis Bacon. (He also managed to break the code that proved that Bacon had written the plays of Marlowe and the essays of Montaigne.)

But by far his most successful and popular work was *Atlantis: The Antediluvian World,* published in 1882. The book has gone through some fifty editions in several languages and is still being sold in bookstores. "Since Donnelly's book," wrote Martin Gardner, "an unbelievable number of similar works have appeared, though none has yet surpassed Donnelly's in ingenuity and eloquence." While it is tempting to paraphrase the ingenious and eloquent Ignatius Donnelly, probably the best way to understand the enduring fascination of this book is to quote the thirteen "distinct and novel propositions" with which he begins his disquisition:

1. That there once existed in the Atlantic Ocean, opposite the mouth of the Mediterranean Sea, a large island, which was the remnant of an Atlantic continent, and known to the ancient world as Atlantis.

2. That the description given by Plato is not, as has been long supposed, fable, but veritable history.

3. That Atlantis was the region where man first rose from a state of barbarism to civilization.

4. That it became, in the course of ages, a populous and mighty nation, from whose overflowings the shores of the Gulf of Mexico, the Mississippi River, the Amazon, the Pacific coast of South America, the Mediterranean, the west coast of Europe and Africa, the Baltic, the Black Sea, and the Caspian were populated by civilized nations.

5. That it was the true Antediluvian world; the Garden of Eden; the Garden of the Hesperides—where the Atlantides lived on the River Ocean in the West; the Elysian Fields situated by Homer to the west of the Earth; the Gardens of Alcinous—grandson of Poseidon and son of Nausithous, King of the Phaeacians of the Island of Scheria; the Mesomphalous—or Navel of the Earth, a name given to the Temple at Delphi, which was situated in the crater of an extinct volcano; the Mount Olympus—of the Greeks; the Asgard—of the Eddas; the focus of the traditions of the ancient nations; representing a universal memory of a great land, where early mankind dwelt for ages in peace and happiness.

6. That the gods and goddesses of the ancient Greeks, the Phoenicians, the Hindus, and the Scandinavians were simply the kings, queens, and

heroes of Atlantis; and the acts attributed to them in mythology, a confused recollection of real historical events.

7. That the mythologies of Egypt and Peru represented the original religion of Atlantis, which was sun-worship.

8. That the oldest colony formed by the Atlanteans was probably in
Egypt, whose civilization was a reproduction of that of the Atlantic island.

9. That the implements of the "Bronze Age" of Europe were derived
from Atlantis. The Atlanteans were also the first manufacturers of iron.

10. That the Phoenician alphabet, parent of all European alphabets, was
derived from an Atlantis alphabet, which was also conveyed from Atlantis
to the Mayas of Central America.

11. That Atlantis was the original seat of the Aryan or Indo-European
family of nations, as well as of Semitic peoples, and possibly also of the
Turanian races.

12. That Atlantis perished in a terrible convulsion of nature, in which the
whole island was submerged by the ocean, with nearly all its inhabitants.

13. That a few persons escaped in ships and on rafts, and carried to the
nations east and west the tidings of the appalling catastrophe, which has
survived to our own time in Flood and Deluge legends in the different
nations of the Old and New Worlds.

It is obvious that in Atlantis, Donnelly had found the cause of almost
everything.* Unfortunately, there is neither space nor time for a detailed
analysis of his book, but it speaks more than satisfactorily for itself. He believed
that Plato's story was "a plain and reasonable history of a people who built
temples, ships, and canals, who lived by agriculture and commerce, who in
pursuit of trade, reached out to all the countries around them." (He dismisses
Bacon's *New Atlantis* as "a moral or political lesson in the guise of a fable.")
Readers with an interest in his theories about "The Ibero-Celtic Colonies of
Atlantis," "The Turanian, Semitic, and Aryan Links with Atlantis," or "The

---

* In the foreword to the 1949 edition of Donnelly's *Atlantis*, Edgerton Sykes ("Fellow Royal Geographical
Society, Fellow Royal Central Asian Society, Fellow Royal India Society," etc., etc.) described the author
as "one of the many liberal intellectuals which the Anglo-Saxon world produced in the nineteenth cen-
tury, in what may well have been the last outburst of learning before it was swamped with mediocrity."
An alternative view was expressed by Arthur C. Clarke, who wrote (in his autobiography, *Astounding
Days*), "Donnelly should be the patron saint of the peddlers of UFO/parapsychology mind rot. . . ."

Origin of Our Alphabet" may consult these chapters in the book.

Donnelly's thesis explained the similarities between pre-Columbian and Egyptian civilizations, often by bending facts until they were virtually unrecognizable. In *Atlantis: Fact or Fiction?*, Edwin Ramage wrote: "The propositions . . . hint at the general lack of critical judgment that pervades the book. On nearly every page there is an example of rash assumption, hasty conclusion, circular reasoning, or argument based purely in rhetoric. Many statements of fact are not fact at all, and in his enthusiastic drive to create his Atlantis he reveals a surprising naïveté." Examples of his twisting of "facts" to make a point are legion, but here, one example will suffice. Answering his own question "Where was Olympus?" he says, "It was in Atlantis," and then explains how he came to that conclusion: "Olympus was written by the Greeks 'Olympus.' The letter *a* in Atlantis was sounded by the ancient world broad and full, like the *a* in our words *all* or *altar;* in these words it approximates very closely to the sound of *o.* It is not far to go to convert Atlantis into Oluntos, and this into Olumpos. We may, therefore, suppose that when the Greeks dwelt in 'Olympus,' it was the same as if they said that they dwelt in 'Atlantis.' "

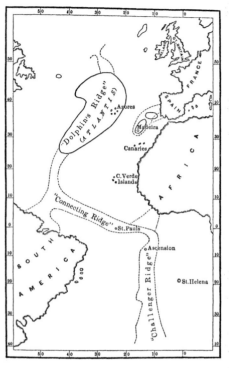

ACCORDING TO Ignatius Donnelly, Atlantis was located more or less where Plato said it was: in the Atlantic Ocean, outside the Pillars of Hercules.

IN RAMAGE'S BOOK (a collection of essays on various aspects of the Atlantean legend), the geologist Dorothy Vitaliano takes Donnelly to task on scientific grounds, which is a little like taking a sledgehammer to a mosquito. She dismisses his above-mentioned proposition 12 by showing that landmasses can sink, but not in a day and a night, and never on the scale attributed by

Plato to Atlantis. She writes that "suddenly and catastrophically submerged areas, usually coastal areas depressed as the result of an earthquake, or in rare cases, a collapsing volcanic island, such as Krakatoa in 1883 or Santorini . . . are seldom larger than a few square miles."*

Ignatius Donnelly's *Atlantis* was published in 1882, the year before Krakatau erupted. We are probably fortunate that he had moved on to other subjects by 1883 (the year of the publication of *Ragnarok*), for the gigantic explosion of Krakatau would surely have provided Donnelly with an abundance of supporting evidence for the possibility of disappearing civilizations. The explosion, which began on August 27, was heard in Australia, over two thousand miles away, and sent a 50-mile-high cloud of volcanic ash into the sky that circled the earth for two years. A 6,000-foot-high mountain was reduced to a caldera 4 miles across with only portions of the rim (now the islets of Rakata, Pulau Sertung, Lang, and Polish Hat) projecting above the surface of the Sunda Straits (see pp. 199–203). He did, however, devote an entire chapter to the question "Was Such a Catastrophe Possible?," in which he wrote that "there is ample geological evidence that at one time the entire area of Great Britain was submerged to the depth of at least seventeen hundred feet," and that "the Canary Islands were probably a part of the original empire of Atlantis." Not only is such a catastrophe possible, but comparable events have occurred time and again throughout history. He mentions the 1775 earthquake at Lisbon ("the point of the European coast closest to Atlantis"), the 1815 eruption of the Javan volcano "Tomboro," and Santorini, of which he wrote:

> The Gulf of Santorin, in the Grecian Archipelago, has been for two thousand years a scene of active volcanic operations. Pliny informs us that in the year 186 B.C. the island of "Old Kaimeni," or the Sacred Isle, was lifted up from the sea; and in A.D. 19 the island of "Thia" (the Divine) made its appearance. In A.D. 1573 another island was created, called "the small sunburnt island." In 1848 a volcanic convulsion of three months' duration created a great shoal; an earthquake destroyed many houses in Thera, and the sulphur and hydrogen issuing from the sea killed 50 persons and 1,000 domestic animals. A recent examina-

---

* It is a little too easy to ridicule the exaggerations and ignorance of Ignatius Donnelly from the secure vantage point of the present, when we have a much more comprehensive understanding of geology and ancient history than was available to him. In the introduction to the 1976 Dover edition of *Atlantis: The Antediluvian World*, E. F. Bleiler wrote, "In Donnelly's day geology was an infant science, and his position, though extreme, was not outside the range of acceptance. Eighteenth- and nineteenth-century geology contained many theories of violent earth action, and the concept of cataclysm was still current during Donnelly's lifetime. . . . Indeed, well into the twentieth century, one can still find reputable geologists writing of land bridges that might break or sink in relatively brief periods."

tion of these islands shows that the whole mass of Santorin has sunk, since its projection from the sea, over 1,200 feet.

"All these facts," he wrote, "would seem to show that the great fires which destroyed Atlantis are still smoldering in the depths of the ocean; that the vast oscillations which carried Plato's continent beneath the sea may again bring it, with all its buried treasures, to the light; and even that the wild imagination of Jules Verne, when he described Captain Nemo, in his diving armor, looking down upon the temples and towers of the lost island, lit by fires of submarine volcanoes, had some groundwork of possibility to build on."*

Although Donnelly's *Atlantis* is a garbled muddle of misunderstood geology, anthropology, mythology, and linguistics, it had twenty-three printings from 1882 to 1890, and a Dover edition was issued in 1976, almost a century after it was written. In the introduction, Bleiler asks, "Why should Dover Publications reprint a book that cannot be taken seriously, a book that is admittedly wrong in all its major conclusions, and can never be rehabilitated?" His answer:

> Donnelly's *Atlantis: The Antediluvian World* is a remarkable tour de force. His enthusiasm vivified what might have been embalmed in a cabinet, and turned it into a book vital for certain temperaments. Donnelly created a vision of a golden past, of soaring adventurers, spreading civilization around the world, of Edens that once existed, were let perish—and should be a lesson to all of us. Strangely enough, there is a moral in Donnelly's Atlantis, just as there was in Plato's: power corrupts. . . .

Did Donnelly pay any attention to his critics and detractors? We will never know, but a careful reading of his book leads to the almost inescapable conclusion that he believed every word he wrote. Certainly a lot of other people did, including the Scottish mythologist Lewis Spence, who published *The Problem of Atlantis* in 1924. (Subsequently, he would produce several more books on this subject, including *The History of Atlantis,* published posthumously in 1968; he died in 1955.) In the introduction to the 1949 "modern revised edition" of Donnelly's book, Spence wrote, "I should like to make it clear that my hypothesis

---

* There are indeed submarine volcanoes "smoldering in the depths of the ocean"; the entire Mid-Atlantic Ridge is a seam of volcanic activity. Although deep-earth convulsions, like earthquakes or volcanoes, occasionally destroy land, more often they create it. A case in point is Iceland, built almost entirely of hardened lava that has welled up from the sea floor. Although people like Donnelly would like to equate the sinking of Atlantis with the Mid-Atlantic Ridge, the Ridge is actually rising rather than sinking.

respecting the existence of an Atlantean culture-complex in certain parts of Europe and America . . . is the direct outcome of Donnelly's method, a mere modern application of it, indeed. . . . If Plato stands at the threshold of our quest, it is the torch of Donnelly which most brightly illuminates our passage along the rough and shadowy highway which we hopefully traverse."

One of history's most dedicated Atlantean scholars, Spence was a newspaperman, a poet, and cofounder of the *Atlantis Quarterly,* a journal devoted to Atlantean and other occult studies. Although Spence would not have us accept the fundamentalist view of Plato's description ("We must remember that it is not by any means incumbent upon us to attempt to justify Plato's account word for word. . . . It is obvious that we are dealing with a great world-memory, of which Plato's story is merely one of the broken and distorted fragments"), he assembles material from many disciplines, among them ethnology, geology, history, biology, and folklore, and then concludes that an entire continent used to bridge Europe and America. (In their 1952 study of the Gulf Stream, Henry Chapin and F. G. Walton Smith said that Spence "has made the most thoroughgoing and serious study of the Atlantis question since Donnelly.") He says the continent sank in the middle of the Atlantic Ocean, leaving as evidence of its existence the Azores, the Canaries, and Madeira in the east, and in the west, where there was another sunken continent called Antilla, now the location of the West Indies.* He further describes the Atlantean inhabitants of the predeluge continent as "Aurignacians or Cro-Magnons . . . exceptionally tall, sons of the gods indeed, the male height averaging from 6 ft. 1 in. to 6 ft. 7 in., although the women were small, the proof of a mixed race." Lest this sort of thing sound like advocacy of a master race, Spence was obsessed with what he believed was a parallel between the fall of Atlantis and the decadence of Europe in the 1940s. In 1942, he published *Will Europe Follow Atlantis?,* in which he argued that all Europe—but especially Nazi Germany—was suffering from great moral decay, and unless they returned to true Christianity, the Germans were going to receive a punishment "of the self-same form meted out to the people of Atlantis."

Spence falls into the protohistorical trap of assuming that since other myths—such as Homer's account of the Trojan War—had proved to be based on fact rather than fiction, therefore Plato's story of Atlantis must also be true.

---

* As "evidence" for this theory, he writes the following: "The soundings taken by vessels dispatched by the various European and American Admiralties served to map out the bed of the Atlantic, and revealed the existence of a great bank occupying a major portion of the whole Atlantic basin. This is covered with volcanic detritus. The irregularities of its surface could not have been produced by submarine agencies, but must have received their present contour while still above water."

He writes, "It is now generally accepted by critics of insight—the others do not matter much—that when a large body of myth crystallizes round one central figure, race, or locality, it is almost certain to enshrine a certain proportion of historical truth capable of extraction from the mass of fabulous material which surrounds it, and when so refined, is worthy of acceptance by the most meticulous of historical purists."

Somehow, Spence manages to demonstrate that Plato's detailed plan of Atlantis is so similar to that of Carthage, and that "a comparison of these resemblances, which include the most unusual features, will leave no doubt in any unbiased mind that the plan of Carthage was substantially the same as that of Atlantis." Unfortunately for Spence's theory, Carthage's "unusual features," consisting of a citadel on a hill (the "Byrsa"), docks, canals, a circular colonnade, and a great seawall, were built long after Plato's Atlantis, even if we afford Spence the benefit of the doubt and assume that Atlantis existed only nine hundred years before Plato, and not the nine thousand years that Plato claims. How to deal with this? Easy: "Plato could not have been aware that this description [of Atlantis] could apply to a future Carthage, therefore it seems probable . . . that Carthage was planned in accordance with ancient Atlantean design which had long been in vogue in North-Western Africa and Western Europe." In the middle of his learned discussion, Spence throws this in: "I must also point out that the passage which speaks of the twenty golden statues of the kings of Atlantis and their wives has a striking parallel in Peruvian history." (In later chapters, he will incorporate intricate elements of Peruvian history, as well as other Mesoamerican cultures, to prove that the history of Atlantis was closely connected with that of Mexico and South America.)

In *The Ocean River,* Chapin and Smith invoke "the French savant Termier" (actually Professor Pierre Termier of Paris, a geological Atlantologist), describing him as "convinced that there is enough geological evidence to put solid ground under the overseas legends." (Spence identifies Termier as "a geologist of the highest standing and authority, Director of Science of the Geological Chart of France.") In 1915, Termier wrote: "Geologically speaking, the Platonic history of Atlantis is highly probable. . . . [I]t is entirely reasonable to believe that long after the opening of the Strait of Gibraltar, certain of these emerged lands still existed, and common among them a marvelous island, separated from the African Continent by a chain of smaller islands."*

---

* Termier believed that a vitreous lava known as tachylite was supposed to dissolve in seawater after fifteen thousand years, but when a hunk of it came up on a broken transatlantic cable in 1898, he examined it and decided that its "porous microcrystalline structure" showed that it had solidified in the air, neatly demonstrating—to his followers, anyway—that there had once been a continent there.

Although "a geologist of the highest standing," Termier could have had only vague knowledge about the Mid-Atlantic Ridge (which was first examined in the late 1940s), so his description of the floor of the Atlantic has to have been based on what was known at the time. Nevertheless, he came surprisingly close to describing what would eventually prove to be a vast undersea mountain range when he postulated two great valleys parallel to the coastlines of Europe and North America, separated by an elevated "middle zone." He believed that the "middle zone" was S-shaped (which it is) and ran from Greenland to 70° south latitude (which it almost does). But then he says that the eastern region of the Atlantic is "a great volcanic zone," and that the bottom of the ocean there is "the most unstable zone on the earth's surface, where at any moment unrecorded submarine cataclysms may be taking place." (And so they are, but they are not dropping the continents into the sea.) In his richly textured prose (Termier's theories were published in 1912 in France, and reproduced in translation in the Smithsonian Institution's *Annual Report* for 1915), Termier said:

> Meanwhile, not only will science, most modern science, not make it a crime for all lovers of beautiful legends to believe in Plato's story of Atlantis, but science herself, through my voice, calls their attention to it. Science herself, taking them by the hand and leading them along the wreck-strewn ocean shore, spreads before their eyes, with thousands of disabled ships, the continents submerged or reduced to remnants, and the isles without number enshrouded in the abyssmal depths.

(Although he does not mention Termier by name, W. D. Matthew of the American Museum of Natural History in New York wrote a brief reply to "some writers" who believed that a land bridge across the Atlantic in former geological times could be equated with Plato's Atlantis. Matthew (writing in 1920) said, "Examination of the story in detail shows that it is a fable, and that the scientific evidence does not lend any support whatsoever to it nor vice versa.")

As the agent that caused the Atlantean continent to disappear into the ocean, Spence invokes continental drift, although he does not actually name it. In his 1924 book, he cites Termier, J. William Dawson, Henry Fairfield Osborn, Alfred Russel Wallace, and Professor Edward Hull ("whose investigations have led him to conclude that the Azores are the peaks of a submerged continent that flourished in the Pleistocene period") as his sources, but he does not mention Alfred Wegener, who first published the theory in 1915. Spence says that more daring speculators believe that beneath the ocean spaces no solid Sal [silica and aluminum] exists at all, and the continental masses float on the liquid Sima [silica and magnesium] much as icebergs in the ocean. If, for any reason, a fissure develops in these floating masses the break may grow until at last two separate bodies appear, which will naturally drift away from each other by degrees. Such a condition, it is thought, accounts for the separation of the American Continent from the Old World.

More often than not, Atlantean scholars manipulate existing science in a convoluted way to prove their specious doctrines, but in this instance, an Atlantean proponent accidentally incorporated a highly speculative (but now accepted) doctrine—that of continental drift—into his arguments. Among the "more daring speculators" was Alfred Wegener, who had published *The Origin of Continents and Oceans* in 1915, to almost universal rejection.

In 1926, at a symposium called by the American Association of Petroleum Geologists, Wegener's theory was widely ridiculed, since it was impossible for anyone to imagine what forces could possibly move entire continents. In his "definitive" study (of 1924), Sir Harold Jeffreys, a British geologist, dismissed the theory of continental drift in these words: "It is quantitatively insufficient and qualitatively inapplicable. It is an explanation which explains nothing we want to explain." In their unfortunate analysis of the Atlantean and continental-drift hypotheses, Chapin and Smith wrote that Wegener's theory was only one possibility, and that "a newer but equally fascinating proposal has recently been advanced by J. P. Rothe, who believes that that the Mid-Atlantic Ridge is really the submerged coastline of Africa and Europe, now sunk beneath the waves. The western basin is thus the true ocean, while the eastern basin is really part of the sunken mainland." If the "eastern basin" is part of the sunken mainland, then part of that submerged continent was very likely to be Atlantis. J. P. Rothe's ideas have faded into oblivion, and Wegener was vindicated—the continents *do* drift around like icebergs, albeit somewhat more slowly—and so far, there is no evidence to indicate that the mysterious island (or continent) of Atlantis disappeared into the Atlantic Ocean.

Chapin and Smith concede that "sub-marine dredging and the firing of explosive charges and the painstaking reading of delicate instruments will bring new evidence to clinch the matter," and finally label the legend "a fascinating myth or fable." But, they write, "perhaps the reverse may come about, and the future thus bring new life to Atlantis in the mind of man." Of course, Chapin and Smith, writing in 1952, did not have the advantage of the discovery of sea-floor spreading, and they believed (following Termier) that the Mid-Atlantic Ridge was "a great 7,000-mile submarine mountain chain from Iceland in the north to Bouvet Island . . . [that] divides the Atlantic Ocean into eastern and western basins." Such an underwater chain exists, but it has now been recognized as a mountainous seam of volcanic action, surrounded on either side by fracture zones, which would make the existence of a submerged continent more than a little implausible, and would substantially detract from the credibility of Donnelly, Spence, and "the French savant Termier."

Many of the early Atlantologists—including Donnelly, Spence, and Termier—liked to use complex scientific arguments to prove the existence of Atlantis. Always the innovator, Donnelly came first, with his chapter "The Flora and Fauna of Atlantis." In addition to a garbled discussion of fossil camels, cave bears, and domesticated animals, Donnelly believed that one of the strongest indicators of Asia and Africa's dependence upon Atlantis thousands of years ago is the presence of the seedless banana. "Is it not more reasonable," he asks, "to suppose that the plantain, or banana, was cultivated by the peoples of Atlantis, and carried to their civilized agricultural colonies to the east and west?" He answers: "It would be a marvel of marvels if *one* nation, on one continent, had cultivated the banana for such a vast period or time until it became seedless . . . but to suppose that two nations could have cultivated the same plant, under the same circumstances, on two different continents, for the same unparalleled lapse of time, is supposing an impossibility." Q.E.D., Atlantis proved by a banana. (Fifty years later, when Lewis Spence wrote about the biological evidence, he said that "the prolonged controversy which raged round the question of the Atlantean origin of the seedless banana . . . seems to me worse than futile. . . . I propose to adhere to the conclusions of tried modern scientists, and to disregard the gropings of the older school as no longer of much avail in our quest.")

ATLANTEAN SCHOLARSHIP often depends on the refutation or denial of previous theories; Atlantis cannot have been in the Bahamas and Mediterranean at the same time. (At one time or another, Atlantis has been located in the Arctic, Nigeria, the Caucasus, the Crimea, North Africa, the Sahara, Malta, Spain, central France, Belgium, the Netherlands, the North Sea, the Bahamas, and various other locations in North and South America.) But Spence pinpoints the actual location of Atlantis—even though he quotes Termier as saying "we must not even consider this problem." Based on a convoluted discussion of Carthage, the stone forts of the Aran Islands, the design of Mexico City, and the Egyptian pyramids, he says, "Dolphin's Ridge, then, I accept as the site of lost Atlantis." Named for the ship *Dolphin* that took soundings in the vicinity, the ridge is a long oval, connected underwater to the Azores, South America, and the "West African island of St. Pauls." (It turns out that Ignatius Donnelly also thought that Dolphin's Ridge was the long-sought location; he wrote, "The Atlantis of Plato may have been confined to the 'Dolphin Ridge' of our map.")

At the conclusion of the preface to *The Problem of Atlantis* (reissued in 1974 as *Atlantis Discovered*), Spence declared, "On the other hand, I think I have brought cogent arguments against the now widely accepted theory that the idea of Atlantis arose out of a memory of the former civilization of Crete." He launches into a spirited devaluation of the story—which first appeared in the British newspapers in 1909—that the palace at Knossos in Crete recently discovered by Sir Arthur Evans was concrete evidence of the existence and location of Atlantis. Spence argues that, rather than the Atlantis legend being based on the downfall of Knossos, the mythology has become confused, and "it is the Cretan civilization that was modeled on that of Atlantis." He defends this argument as follows: "The theory that Crete was a colony of Atlantis is greatly assisted by the circumstance that the Cretans were largely of that Iberian race which undoubtedly emanated from Atlantis." Undoubtedly. "They worshipped a goddess who was connected with the serpent like the Mexican Coatlicue, whom she remarkably resembles in details of costume." In his final argument, Spence enlists the support of Heinrich Schliemann: "And let it be remembered," he crowed, "that the man who justified his dreams of Troy to the confusion of a thousand scoffers entertained as firm a belief in the existence of a submerged Atlantis."

An even more bizarre footnote to the annals of Atlantean scholarship was added by Paul Schliemann, who identified himself as the grandson of the German archaeologist who excavated Troy and Mycenae (see pp. 107–10). He claimed that among his grandfather's papers was a note instructing the reader to break open the "owl-headed vase" that contained certain documents relating to Atlantis. Breaking it open, Paul Schliemann found bits of pottery, objects made of fossilized bone, and a silvery coin. In October 1912, in the *New York American,* young Schliemann told the story he called "How I Found the Lost Atlantis, the Source of All Civilization," in which he described his worldwide search for the evidence mentioned by Heinrich, which took him to Egypt (where he found coins like the one in the vase, made of an alloy

PAUL SCHLIEMANN, who claimed to be Heinrich Schliemann's grandson, said that he found evidence of Atlantis in his grandfather's papers, including this map, which was published in the *New York American* on October 20, 1912.

of platinum, aluminum, and silver), Central America (where he found another owl vase), and West Africa. In his article, Paul Schliemann included the startling revelation that a Mayan text and a Tibetan manuscript both told the story of a cataclysm in a country called Mu, and, even more sensationally, that he had actual Atlantean artifacts in his possession. Schliemann claimed that all this material unequivocally proved the existence of Atlantis—which he said had sunk, leaving only the Azores as the tips of the submerged mountains—and he promised to reveal all in a forthcoming book. (He also identified his grandfather as "excavating at the Lion Gate at Mycenae in Crete," a most unlikely quote, since of all people, Heinrich Schliemann would know that Mycenae was not in Crete.) Neither the book nor Paul Schliemann's "evidence" ever appeared, and under close examination, his references bore a strong resemblance to other published texts, especially those of Ignatius Donnelly.* Most writers repeat this story without taking the trouble to question whether Paul was really Heinrich's grandson, but several dubious investigators have revealed that while Heinrich had a *brother* named Paul, he had no grandson by that name.

With the advent of more sophisticated tools for underwater exploration, one might assume that searchers would be able to see that there is no drowned continent on the bottom of the ocean, but the pull of the legend is so powerful that despite overwhelming evidence to the contrary, we are still getting books purporting to prove the existence of Atlantis. (And such books will continue to appear, since it is impossible, of course, to prove that it does *not* exist.) To write one of these books, the author has to be predisposed to believe not only Plato but the veritable legion of Atlantologists who succeeded him.

Charles Berlitz, the grandson of the founder of the language schools, in 1974 published a book called *The Bermuda Triangle,* in which he discussed the "hundreds of ships and planes, with their crews and passengers, [that] have disappeared without a trace during the last fifty years," and in 1977, he published *Without a Trace,* which is (according to its flap copy) "filled with startling stories of strange occurrences within the Triangle: peculiarities of sea and weather; the appearance of 'ghost ships' and a catalog of vessels which have disappeared from 1800 through 1976; clouds that seem to chase and capture planes; time warps; and the possibility of a doorway in the area leading to another dimension, or even to outer space." In his chapter "Lost Atlantis—Found in the Bermuda Triangle?," Berlitz introduces his idea that the "Triangle," in addition to swallowing ships, has also gobbled up an entire continent. He finds support for this idea in the Bimini explorations of Dr. David Zink, the prophecies of Edgar Cayce, and the research of "Ronald Waddington of Burlington, Canada, a researcher and theorist on the Bermuda Triangle." Waddington—who is quoted at length in *Without a Trace*—theorizes that underwater volcanoes are constantly shooting chunks of radioactive, densely magnetic material into the air, short-circuiting the electrical equipment of passing airplanes and causing them to nose-dive into the ocean. As for ships, "chunks of this radioactive material could shoot to the surface with the velocity of a hydrogen bomb and home in on the steel hulls of ships like the magnetic head of a torpedo. . . ."

---

* Circumstantial evidence of Paul Schliemann's dependence on Donnelly can be seen in his designation of the "owl-headed vase." In Heinrich Schliemann's *Troy and Its Remains* (1875), the two vases are described as "a terra-cotta vase with a helmeted image of the Iliac Athena," and "a Trojan terra-cotta vase with an ornament like the Greek *lambda.*" In Donnelly's *Atlantis: The Antediluvian World* (1882), the same illustrations are reproduced, only now they are both labeled "owl-headed vases."

Berlitz acknowledges that "Waddington's suggestions predicate no link between Atlantis and the present occurrences in the Bermuda Triangle, [but] the
series of reactions he describes might, nevertheless, have endured as a by-
product of the catastrophe that caused the Atlantean lands to sink beneath the
ocean." Berlitz was evidently so entranced with the mystery of Atlantis that he
wrote another book about it, *Atlantis: The Eighth Continent*.

On the endpaper maps, which consist of a drawing of the eastern Atlantic
basin drained of water, Berlitz sets the tone for this exposé: "On this modern
map of the Atlantic Ocean Floor we can see that oceanic islands such as the
Azores, Madeira, and the Canaries are connected to great submerged plateaus,
some of them in the very area that this sunken land was supposed to be, as if
they were the mountaintops of Atlantis, the eighth continent." The map
shows no such thing; it simply shows the seamounts that characterize this
region of the Atlantic and the abyssal plain between the Canaries and Madeira.
There is nothing on Berlitz's map that looks anything like a plateau or a missing continent. But by the time we get to the introduction, Berlitz (who lists
Ignatius Donnelly and Lewis Spence in his bibliography) is in full cry: "A civilization developed in these huge islands and spread, through conquest and col-
onization, throughout the Atlantic Basin and farther to the islands and coasts
of the Mediterranean. Thousands of years before the beginnings of history in
Egypt and Mesopotamia, this civilization disappeared into the Atlantic Ocean,
leaving only isolated colonies on the surrounding continents which grew into
the civilizations that we consider the beginnings of history."

Berlitz covers all the possible locations discussed by earlier authors, including Tunisia, Heligoland (a German pastor named Jürgen Spanuth located
Atlantis in the North Sea off Germany), Yucatán, Bolivia, Morocco, Nigeria,
Arabia, Brazil, Antarctica, the Indian Ocean, the Sahara Desert, and "other
parts of Europe and Asia," but in the end, although he cannot locate it exactly,
he says that the very number of possible sites "may also be considered as an
indication of the common culture of a previous civilization, whose great stone
remains on all continents (except Australia and Antarctica—and perhaps
there too when further explorations are made) tend to resemble one another
in construction and astronomical orientation." In other words, the prolifera-
tion of reports, none of them more dependable than the others, suggests to
Berlitz that Atlantis must have existed, even if we are not sure where it might
have been. And as for Thera, he dismisses it as a legitimate possibility and says
it was "simply one more victim of natural disasters in the Mediterranean and
is not in name or description connected with the Atlantis of Plato and other

commentators." (Anyway, he says, Thera is too small to have been occupied by the number of people Plato said lived in Atlantis.)

For skeptics who require documentation, Berlitz provides a story that he says is "well reported in a ship's log and also in the press." In March 1882, the British merchant vessel *Jesmond,* Captain Robson commanding, was sailing from Messina, Sicily, to New Orleans with a cargo of dried fruit. A couple of hundred miles west of Madeira, the ship encountered muddy water and enormous shoals of dead fish. They sighted smoke coming from an island where no island was supposed to be, dropped their anchor, and went ashore on an island that had "no vegetation, no trees, no sandy beaches . . . [and was] bare of all life as if it had just risen from the ocean." What do you do when you land on an uninhabited, barren island in the middle of the Atlantic Ocean? Why, naturally, you begin to dig. The crew uncovered massive walls, and then "bronze swords, rings, mallets, carvings of heads and figures of birds and animals, and two vases or jars with fragments of bone, one cranium almost entire . . . and what appeared to be a mummy enclosed in a stone case." Captain Robson loaded all this booty aboard the *Jesmond* and continued his voyage. Berlitz does not say whether he off-loaded his cargo at New Orleans, but he does tell us that Robson intended to present the stuff to the British Museum. Alas, the log of the *Jesmond* was destroyed in the Blitz of 1940, and the artifacts never showed up at the museum. Berlitz thinks they may still be there, "filed in the capacious attics and basements common to all great museums."

Beyond the unfortunate loss of the *Jesmond*'s log, there are more than a few problems with Berlitz's approach to his subject. First is the wholesale inclusion of statements and data without attribution. Ordinarily, attributions are identified by including the name of the author and the work in the sentence, as in, "as Conan Doyle said in *The Maracot Deep. . . .*" Another method involves footnotes or notes in the back of the book identifying the source of the information, neither of which device is employed here. (Another mechanism, used primarily in scientific publications, is the use of parenthetical citations, e.g., "(Verne 1870)," which follow a quote and enable the reader to check the source of a particular quote and, if necessary, verify it.) In Berlitz's *Atlantis,* we are given all sorts of "facts" used to make a particular point, but without the possibility of knowing who was responsible for the statement in the first place, or, indeed, if anyone other than Berlitz himself was the actual source.

In his chapter entitled "The Great Islands Under the Sea," Berlitz outdoes himself in non- or misattributed statements. The entire book is filled with such useless data, but a couple of examples will serve as demonstrations: To explain the presence of "architectural remains" on the sea floor, Berlitz refers to "pictures taken from the *Anton Bruun* research vessel for the purpose of photographing bottom fish in the Nazca Trench off Peru in 1965," where "a chance photograph showed massive stone columns and walls on the mud bottom at a depth of one and a half miles." In fact, there is no such thing as the "Nazca Trench," but off Peru, the Peru-Chile Trench is some 10,000 feet deep. In 1965, if such a sighting had somehow been made, it probably would have been published somewhere. But Berlitz does not say how he knows about it, and moves right on to the next sentence, which is about the submersible *Archimède* that encountered a "flight of giant stone steps at a depth of 1,400 feet off the Bahamas."

Berlitz introduces the theory of continental drift and somehow contorts it to verify the existence of Atlantis. He has oceanographer Maurice Ewing discuss beach sand on the floor of the ocean, and he quotes him as saying, "Either the land must have sunk two or three miles or the sea must have been two or three miles lower than now." Ewing did say this (in a 1949 *National Geographic* article on the Mid-Atlantic Ridge), but he followed it immediately with, "*There is no reason to believe that this mighty underwater mass of mountains is connected in any way with the legendary lost Atlantis which Plato described as having sunk beneath the waves*" (my emphasis). Berlitz then presents "Dr. R. Malaise" (but gives no supporting reference in the bibliography), who found the "remains of land-grown plants in cores taken two miles down in the Mid-Atlantic Ridge." Ignoring the information that would refute such a statement, Berlitz then goes on to say that "the theory of the vertical movement of tectonic plates and its modification of the continental-drift theory has brought about a reassessment of the possibility that Atlantis once really existed as lands in the Atlantic Ocean." His conclusion—that the various seamounts off the Azores prove the existence of a sunken continent—is not supported by any of his quotes, but the quotes and conclusions are mostly fabrications and distortions, anyway.*

Berlitz's comprehension of biology and zoogeography is so wrongheaded that it beggars understanding. For example, he wrote that there are "two kinds of seals, the monk and the siren, found off the coast of the Azores," from

* Brad Steiger, the author of *Overlords of Atlantis and the Great Pyramid* (1989), disputes Ewing's statements by quoting "Professor Georgly [*sic*] Lindberg of the Soviet Union's Zoological Institute of the Academy of Sciences," who said that there was indeed a North Atlantic continent, presently submerged in 4,500 to 5,000 meters of water. Steiger also identifies Charles Berlitz's elusive "Dr. Malaise" as "Dr. René Malaise of the Riks Museum in Stockholm." Steiger mentions Plato and "Plimy [*sic*]," but the last may be only a typographical error—then again, it may not. Steiger's book also contains discussions of subjects such as "Did the Ancient Egyptians Have Television?," "Undersea UFOs," and "Monsters in Mining Tunnels."

which he infers that "they were among the birds and animals isolated on the ocean islands after the disappearance of their former habitat of continental proportions." In fact, there are monk seals on various islands in the Mediterranean and eastern North Atlantic, but they did not find themselves stranded there when a continent disappeared out from under them. (Seals are good swimmers, and could easily have colonized the islands from other European or African locations.) There is not now, nor has there ever been, a seal known as the "siren"; the only creature that bears this name (because it belongs to the family Sirenidae) is the manatee, a mammal not related to the seals and certainly not found in the Azores. (The closest manatees are found in West Africa.)*

Charles Berlitz's chapter on animal life is obviously derived from Spence's "biological evidence," since it makes just as little sense and, in one instance, lifts a whole paragraph about birds circling around an open area of the sea as if trying to land where there is no land—an obvious indication that there used to be a continent there. Further using animals to verify the existence of Atlantis, Berlitz incorporates a long-winded, irrelevant section on dinosaurs in which he proves—at least to his own satisfaction—that a large-scale catastrophe was responsible for their disappearance, and argues that if such a catastrophe could cause such creatures to vanish, it could certainly eradicate a city. He writes: "Perhaps the combination of fiery shocks from the sky, the resultant shaking of the Earth, and flooding from the sea was the sequence of events that occurred in the prehistoric world that perished."[†]

In his 1950 *Worlds in Collision,* Immanuel Velikovsky (1895–1979) argued that the planet Venus had closely approached Earth as a comet and caused tremendous upheavals on this planet, many of which—like the downfall of Atlantis—are documented in ancient texts. Velikovsky also seems to be among the first to identify Plato's 8,100-year chronological error, and wrote, "There is one too many zeros here." He says that the cause of this mistake is that "numbers that we hear in childhood often grow in our memory, as do dimensions.

---

* Berlitz's discussion of seals and manatees comes from an obviously hasty—and wildly erroneous—reading of Lewis Spence on the same subject. In his chapter "The Biological Evidence," Spence quotes "the Messrs. Sclater . . . who recognize . . . two genera of mammals that are characteristic of the Mesatlantic region, Monachus, the Monk Seal, and the Sirenian Manatus, [whose] ancestors have spread along some coast-line which probably united the Old World and the New at no very distant period."

[†] In *Flim-Flam!,* his 1982 exposé of "psychics, ESP, unicorns and other delusions," James Randi wrote, "It is careless of a man to fail to sufficiently research a subject on which he claims to be an authority. It is irresponsible for him to resist telling the facts when he discovers them. And it is irresponsible and callous for him to continue to misrepresent matters about which he has been informed to the contrary. *J'accuse* Charles Berlitz of these failings."

When revisiting our childhood home, we are surprised at the smallness of the rooms—we had remembered them as much larger." Regardless of this somewhat unproductive interpretation of the compression of time, however, Velikovsky's often bizarre ideas about the history of catastrophe received great publicity. In discussing Velikovsky's ideas, L. Sprague de Camp wrote, "An even madder theory of periodical catastrophes was brought out recently by Immanuel Velikovsky, a Russo-Israeli physician and amateur cosmogonist whose publishers stirred up an extraordinary hoopla in 1950 to sell his book."

It has not been shown that Venus came close enough to Earth to cause "a torrent of large stones coming from the sky, an earthquake, a whirlwind [and] a disturbance in the movement of the earth," but many of the phenomena described by Velikovsky could easily be attributed to large-scale volcanic eruptions. For example, in the Plagues of Egypt, where he ascribes "a thick darkness . . . which may be felt" (Exodus 10:21–22) to "onrushing dust sweeping in from interplanetary space," a more logical interpretation of the darkness would be the ash cloud emitted by a great volcanic eruption, as has been observed many times in recent history.

Velikovsky believed that "the swift shifting of the atmosphere under the impact of the gaseous parts of the comet, the draft of air attracted by the body of the comet, and the rush of the atmosphere resulting from the inertia when the earth stopped rotating or shifted its poles, all contributed to produce hurricanes of enormous velocity and force and of world-wide dimensions." But again, a somewhat more prosaic—albeit immense and terrifying—explanation for this catastrophe can be found in the phenomenology of volcanoes. The *nuée ardente,* or "flaming cloud," produced when a heavier-than-air ash cloud cascades down the slope of an erupting volcano at speeds up to 100 miles an hour, as it did at Mount Pelée in 1902 (see pp. 143–47), seems to be a more likely explanation. As for "rising tides," certainly tsunamis are a more reasonable explanation than "a comet with its head as large as the earth, passing sufficiently close [that] would raise the oceans of the world miles high."

Velikovsky quotes the Popul Vuh,* the Manuscript Cakchiquel, and the

---

* A regular reference for Atlantologists, the Popul Vuh is the Quiche Mayan book of creation. The Mayan civilization flourished until the sixteenth century, and the town of Quiche was located northwest of what is now Guatemala City. Between 1701 and 1703, a friar named Francisco Ximénez came across a Quiche book describing the creation of the world, written in a Roman alphabet. Ximénez translated the book into Spanish, but the translation was not found until 1857, when an Austrian physician named Carl Scherzer found it in the library of the University of San Carlos in Guatemala City. (It is now in the Newberry Library in Chicago.) The Popul Vuh says nothing about the Atlantic Ocean or a lost continent, but it does contain an account of a flood and perhaps a volcanic eruption: "Again there comes

Manuscript Troano, sacred Mayan texts that describe a time when "the earth burst and the lava flowed," and biblical passages where "the mountains shake with the swelling" (Psalm 46:3) and "the earth trembled . . . the mountains melted . . ." (Judges 5:4–5). It takes very little imagination to see that in Job (9:6–7), when "the pillars [of the earth] tremble . . . the sun . . . riseth not and sealeth up the stars," the events being described might easily refer to a volcanic eruption. It is not that Velikovsky does not know of or acknowledge volcanoes; he says, "An entire year after the eruption of Krakatoa . . . in 1883, sunset and sunrise in both hemispheres were very colorful. . . . In 1783, after the eruption of Skaptar-Jökull in Iceland, the world was darkened for months. . . ." He simply does not believe that a single eruption would have been sufficient to cause the massive disruptions he discusses. "If the eruption of a single volcano can darken the atmosphere over the entire globe," he wrote, "a simultaneous and prolonged eruption of thousands of volcanoes would blacken the sky."

And what did all of this have to do with Atlantis? In Plato's *Timaeus,* Velikovsky found a passage that echoed all the other references to the earth standing still, or the sky going black:

> "Your story," says the Egyptian priest to Solon, "of how Phaëthon, child of the sun, harnessed his father's chariot, but was unable to guide it along his father's course and so burnt up things on earth and was himself destroyed by a thunderbolt, is a mythical version of the truth that there is at long intervals a variation in the course of the heavenly bodies and a consequent widespread destruction of things on the earth."

To Velikovsky, this is one more validation of his theory of planetary interference with the earth, and he says that Plato himself has verified it. In *Worlds in Collision,* Velikovsky follows his discussion of Atlantis with a lengthy discourse on the origin of Venus as a comet, as described by various observers—he quotes Alexander von Humboldt as asking, "What optical illusion could give Venus the appearance of a star throwing out smoke?"—and then presents a detailed survey of Venus-worship in ancient literature, from Egyptian, Greek, and Indian; and from the "Indians" of North and South America.

---

a humiliation, destruction, and demolition. The manikins, woodcarvings [the Quiches believed that men were carved from wood, women from reeds] were killed when the heart of the sky devised a flood for them. . . . There came a rain of resin from the sky. . . . They were pounded down to the bones and tendons, smashed and pulverized even to their bones. . . . The earth was blackened because of this; the black rainstorm began, rain all day and rain all night . . . their faces were crushed by things of wood and stone . . ." (from the 1985 Tedlock translation).

At this point, he introduces an entirely new concept: that Mars and Venus collided (hence the title of his book) and "the planet Mars saved the terrestrial globe from a major catastrophe by colliding with Venus." He provides documentation for this revelation from the mythology and folklore of the ancient Greeks—he says that the conflict in the *Iliad* is really between Mars (Ares) and Athene (the planet Venus)—as well as from Toltec mythology, the Tao of Chinese cosmology, the Yuddha of Hindu astronomy, and the Babylonian sword god Nergal.

"One of the most terrifying events in the past of mankind," wrote Velikovsky, "was the conflagration of the world, accompanied by awful apparitions in the sky, quaking of the earth, vomiting of lava by thousands of volcanoes, melting of the ground, boiling of the sea, submersion of continents, a primeval chaos bombarded by flying hot stones, the roaring of the cleft earth, and the loud hissing of tornadoes of cinders." That events of this magnitude could have gone largely unrecorded, he attributes to collective amnesia; people forgot it because it was too terrible to remember: "The memory of the cataclysms was erased, not because of a lack of written traditions, but because some characteristic processes that later caused entire nations, together with literate men, to read into these traditions allegories or metaphors where actually cosmic disturbances were clearly described."*

The possession of scientific credentials does not automatically bestow verisimilitude on one's work, especially if one is working outside one's field of expertise. As Moses Finley asked (in his review of Mavor's *Voyage to Atlantis*), "What is it that prompts scientists capable of precise and rigorous work in their own disciplines to career about in other fields of inquiry, where they lack the knowledge, the tools of analysis, or even common sense?" A case in point is the German scientist Otto Muck, who graduated with a degree in engineering from the Munich College of Advanced Technology in 1921 and worked as a scientist/inventor during World War II, inventing the *Schnorchel* for U-boats and contributing to the development of the V-2 rocket at Peenemünde. Somehow, his studies and experience developing Nazi weapons of war qualified him as an expert on Atlantis, so he wrote *The Secret of Atlantis,* which was published in English in 1978. (He died in 1956.)

---

* Many scientists were outraged by the publicity for Velikovsky's book and its classification as "science" rather than "fiction" by the publishers. The book was ridiculed by the scientific community to such an extent that Albert Einstein (who had also liked Charles Hapgood's theory about polar slippage) took up his defense, but for his right to be heard, not for the theory itself. In an interview given to Bernard Cohen and published in *Scientific American,* Einstein said, "You know, it is not a bad book. No, it isn't really a bad book. The only trouble with it is, it is crazy."

It is a maddeningly inconsistent book, alternating lucid passages with absurd statements such as: "In 1836, strange letters were discovered on the rock of Gávea in South America. One of the rocks was sculpted into an enormous bearded man's head wearing a helmet. . . . Bernard da Sylva Ramos, an amateur Brazilian archaeologist, thinks it likely that the letters are genuinely Phoenician." After writing about the "tragicomic chapter in recent research about Atlantis" ("Olaus Rudbeck rediscovered it in Sweden, Bartoli in Italy, Georg Kaspar Kirchmaier shifted it to South Africa, Sylvan Bailly to Spitsbergen, Delisles de Sales preferred the Caucasian-Armenian highlands, Baer suggested Asia Minor, Balch Crete, Godron, Elgee, and later Count Byron de Prorok were certain it was in the oasis of Hoggar, and Leo Frobenius chose Yorubaland"), Muck introduces his own theory, wilder than any of them. He says that where the Gulf Stream intersects with the Atlantic Ridge, there is a vast submerged island that precisely conforms to Plato's description of Atlantis as "larger than Asia and Libya together." Based on the "mean of eight geological estimates," Muck estimates that this island—which he calls "Barrier Island X"—sank about ten thousand years ago, which also coincides with Plato's description. And since this took place outside the Pillars of Hercules—where the Azores are today—there is no question in Muck's mind: Atlantis has been found.

Otto Muck examines the geological evidence and concludes that Alfred Wegener was right about the fit of South America and Africa, but wrong about North America and Europe. In fact, he says, Wegener was so mistaken about the North Atlantic that there is plenty of room for a whole—albeit small—continent. "Every true cataclysm has a center," writes Muck, and this one is no exception. At a depth of about 23,000 feet near the Puerto Rican Plateau, there are two great impact craters that (says Muck) were caused by the arrival of an asteroid—"worlds in collision" again. When this celestial body smashed into the earth, causing a gigantic rift to open on the floor of the Atlantic, and to the accompaniment of great waves and clouds of asphyxiating gases, a 400,000-square-mile island (approximately the acreage of Peru), inhabited by a red-skinned people, sank into the middle of the Atlantic. To support his thesis, Muck mentions the German *Meteor* expedition, which collected data in the Atlantic in 1925: "Did anyone on the survey ship realize what it was they were hearing?" he asks. "Those highly sensitive microphones . . . were recording something very mysterious, very strange—echoes of a world drowned long ago, echoes from Atlantis. Those sound impulses from a Behm transmitter were the first call for 12,000 years by living men of the forgotten island beneath the waters of the Atlantic." He then resorts to a painstaking examination of Mayan astronomical records, which enables him to "determine the exact day on which Atlantis perished and even the approximate hour when the catastrophe began." On June 5, 8498 B.C., at 8:00 p.m., there occurred "the most terrible event that has ever taken place in all the dramatic history of mankind": the sinking of Atlantis—exactly where and when Plato said it sank, but with some causal modifications that the Greek philosopher might not have understood.

One of the more unusual solutions to the problem of Atlantis was proposed in 1979 by another German, a clergyman named Jürgen Spanuth. He had published an earlier study in 1965 (*Atlantis*), and his later book, called *Atlantis of the North,* "restates the conclusions of my earlier researches and adds the new evidence that has accumulated over more than a decade." Spanuth recognizes that the "key to the riddle of Atlantis" lies not in finding where it might have been, or when it sank into the sea, but, rather, in the identification of the original records that Solon mentions, which he believes are Egyptian temple inscriptions and papyrus texts. To the problem of dating Plato's story, Spanuth provides a most inventive solution, easily on a par with Galanopoulos's downward revision of Plato's numbers by an order of magnitude. Spanuth simply decides that "the Egyptians reckon a month as a year," an adjustment he attributes to Diodorus Siculus. Thus, he writes, "if the 9,000 or 8,000 'years' of the Atlantis story are converted into the moon-months of the Egyptian calendar—a year has 13 months—then we arrive at a period between 1252 and 1175 B.C., precisely the time during which all those events of which the Egyptian priests told Solon did in fact occur."

The Atlanteans, says Spanuth, came not from the Mediterranean but from the North Sea, demonstrable by the presence of figures with horned helmets in the Egyptian "Medinet Habu" inscription which resemble Danish helmets from 1200 B.C.* According to Spanuth's reading, Plato's description of Atlantis could apply to no other location than "the area between Heligoland and the mainland at Eiderstedt." (Heligoland—also spelled "Helgoland"—is an island in the North Sea off the coast of Schleswig-Holstein which has been greatly reduced in area because of wave action and erosion.) In precise detail, Pastor Spanuth points out every correlation between Heligoland and Plato's Atlantis,

---

* Although the evidence is fragmentary and inconclusive, most historians believe that the "Sea Peoples" who invaded Egypt during the reign of Pharaoh Rameses II (1290–1223 B.C.), and again during the reign of his successor, Merenptah (1223–1213 B.C.), came from the north, but they mean northern Anatolia and Greece, not Denmark and Germany.

including the island of Basileia that sank into the sea, the red cliffs, the copper mines, and even the mysterious "orichalc," which Spanuth identifies as amber. (He says that this is another "mistranslation," like the one that substituted "year" for the lunar month.) The impenetrable mud that Plato says "made the sea impassable to navigation" is identified as the sandbanks that were left behind when the island of Basileia disappeared, and although Spanuth writes that the Temple of Poseidon described by Plato "sounds so improbable that one might be tempted to assign it to the realm of fantasy," the "almost incredible wealth of decoration in gold, silver and amber, found in Germanic temples [of pre-Christian times]" demonstrates that Plato was describing a real edifice that had been on Heligoland.

The destruction of Atlantis on Heligoland is attributable to any number of "natural catastrophes," including Halley's comet (which Spanuth identifies as Plato's Phaëthon), assorted earthquakes, tsunamis, and the volcanic eruption of Thera, "which, with the help of the Medinet Habu texts, can be dated to 1220 B.C., and which according to contemporary writings and archaeological evidence took place on a spring day." Spanuth dismisses those who would associate Atlantis with Tartessos, or Crete and Thera, and decides that the victory of the Athenians over the Atlanteans was, to quote Plato, "not a fiction but a true history," and corresponds exactly with historical events of around 1200 B.C. Finally, Spanuth quotes "the philosopher Dr. Kahl-Furthmann," who demonstrated that Homer belonged to the Mycenaean age, and that he lived "at a time when Basileia, the royal island of the Atlanteans, had not yet sunk beneath the waves, but, as the Atlantis document tells us, was carrying on a flourishing trade in amber (orichalc) and other goods." This proves—to Spanuth, anyway—that the *Iliad,* the *Odyssey,* the *Timaeus,* and the *Critias* were all written with the island of Basileia in mind, and therefore "the descriptions of Homer and Plato refer to one and the same island."

Pastor Spanuth concludes his dissertation with a chapter he calls "Mistaken Attempts at Dating and Location." Avoiding the temptation to place the author in his own chapter, let us examine the "mistakes." First comes Thera, of course. Despite mentions of Marinatos, Galanopoulos, Mavor, J. V. Luce, and even Jacques Cousteau (who was going to participate in a "1.8 million-dollar large-scale diving expedition, financed by the Greek government"), Spanuth says that "those who would look for Basileia in the depths of the crater of Thera have fallen victims to a gross logical error." This error seems to be that Atlantis, a port city, already existed in the crater *before the great explosion* (Spanuth's emphasis), when the crater did not exist. Then there is Tartessos, proposed by his countryman Aldolf Schulten. Spanuth eliminates this possibility by showing that the 500 B.C. destruction of Tartessos by the Carthaginians can hardly account for the 1200 B.C. disappearance of Basileia, and besides, Tartessos is really Gadir, present-day Cádiz, which is still there, large as life. He says (correctly) that Atlantis is also not near the Azores or the Canaries, because "they . . . are formed from volcanic rock that welled up from below. There was never any continent of Atlantis there." Although it has nothing to do with anybody's theory about Atlantis, Spanuth introduces Pytheas of Massilia* at this point, evidently to reinforce his contention that Plato's "orichalc" was really amber, and that the Greek explorer actually visited the island of Basileia.

Jürgen Spanuth's lengthy and detailed study is the quintessential Atlantis document; it employs intricate connections, complicated "evidence," lengthy documentation, and a hefty bibliography to "prove" exactly what the author believed to be true before he began the research. Germanic in its attention to detail, *Atlantis of the North* does not differ substantially from those studies that would situate the Lost Continent in the Aegean, the Caribbean, or the North Atlantic.

Bruce Rux, who describes himself as a "playwright and writer [who] researches and dramatizes historical events," has written a book called *Architects of the Underworld: Unriddling Atlantis, Anomalies of Mars, and the Mystery of the Sphinx.* "By painstakingly following the paper trails," says the jacket copy, "that connect such apparently unrelated and unexplained events as crop circles, alien abductions, extraterrestrial activities, and other modern-day mysteries, the author uncovers a legacy of misinformation, denial, and official silence from government organizations." Even though the title promises to "unriddle" Atlantis, the book treats the subject in a most perfunctory fashion, classifying it with other myths, which are "all the same myth from great antiquity, becoming individually corrupted in various ways over the ensuing centuries."

---

* Pytheas was a fourth-century B.C. Greek traveler who was the first of the Greeks to visit the British Isles and the North Atlantic coast of Europe. Around 325 B.C., he sailed from Massilia (present-day Marseilles) through the Pillars of Hercules and into the Atlantic, making his first landfall at the Phoenician city of Gades. Following the shoreline, he sailed around Brittany and reached Bolerium (Land's End, Cornwall), where he visited the famous Cornish tin mines. He rounded the westernmost point of Britain and headed north through the Irish Sea, supposedly intent on discovering whether "Albion" was an island or part of the European mainland. Pytheas's story includes a six-day voyage to "Thule," whose location is one of the most controversial issues in Atlantic geographical history. He may have actually sailed there, or he may simply have heard about it from the Britons, but whatever the source, the stories include accurate information on the climate and conditions of some northerly isle. From a place that may have been Pentland Firth in the Orkneys, he sailed to "the northernmost inhabited island," and while it cannot be identified with certainty, it is believed to be either Iceland or an island off the Norwegian coast in the vicinity of the Trondheim Fjord.

According to Rux, there are riddles and codes in history which can be understood only by those who have the key or the perception to understand them. "Atlantis," he writes, "need not be a Greek island that sunk into the Atlantic Ocean. . . . If we take into account that we may very well be dealing with a spacefaring race, then space itself might have been thought of by them as an 'ocean,' and planets as 'islands.' " He then comes to the conclusion that some mythologies—such as the Sumerian—describe outer space as an ocean, which somehow proves that Atlantis is the underworld. The riddle is solved:

> Together with white, red is one of the colors of the striped barber pole, traditionally a place of surgery and healing, its spiral design a hangover [sic] from the caduceus of Hermes. The same colors today belong to the most famous charitable organization in the world, the Red Cross. Red and white are also the colors of "The Land of the Rising Sun," Japan. Red and white are also the colors of Santa's costume, like the Underworld god, a lord of plenty, even with the old name of the Devil, "Nick." The Valkyries wore only red in combat and white in Valhalla, and were famous for their phenomenally white arms. Red, white and black—the colors of Egypt—are still the predominant rock colors in the Canary Islands, and were said by Plato in the *Critias* to be the primary stone color of stone construction in Atlantis, a land which itself "flashed with the red light of orichalcum."*

---

* In my copy of the *Critias,* the stone used for the buildings of Atlantis was "white, black, and yellow," but "they covered the whole circuit of the outermost wall with a veneer of bronze, and fused tin over the inner wall and orichalch gleaming like fire over the walls of the acropolis itself." Anybody who explains Atlantis by invoking Santa Claus and the Japanese flag must be onto some big conspiracy indeed.

ATLANTIS OF THE MYSTICS

I T IS OBVIOUS that there is no end of theories concerning the location and origin of Atlantis. Erudite, provocative books have been written that unequivocally "prove" that it was in the Bahamas, northern Germany, Spain, North Africa, Turkey, or the Aegean. But there is another category of Atlantology, where, disregarding such amenities as history, geography, or archaeology, mystics or psychics claim to "know" about Atlantis. There is virtually no end to the number of books written by the fraternity of the paranormal—Edgar Cayce learned of a fifty-thousand-year-old Atlantis that was described to him by people who had dreamed about it—and to discuss many of them would be to ascribe to them a credibility that most of them do not deserve. Nevertheless, the subject of Atlantis appears regularly in the "Occult" or "New Age" section of bookstores, and therefore we cannot ignore this phenomenon altogether.

As an example of this genre, let us look at *Atlantis: Myth or Reality?* (1991), by Murry Hope, who, in the course of her discussion, refers to many of her psychical predecessors. (At the outset, Ms. Hope identifies herself as someone who "was born with what is broadly termed the 'psychic faculty,' " but she says that she has "endeavored to confine speculations and impressions gained via ESP or other psi-related practices to the final three chapters.")

Early in the book, she reproduces the "abridged translation [of Plato's *Critias* and *Timaeus*] that has been bequeathed to us by that most revered of Atlantean scholars, Ignatius Donnelly." Using Donnelly's abridged translation as her text, Hope launches into an attack on those who might doubt the existence of Atlantis as Plato described it, and at one point suggests that the reason why the *Critias* ends abruptly is that Plato actually finished it, "but some person or persons unknown saw fit to remove the explanation."

Citing her friend Ian Wright, who has "obtained through a combination of normal scientific procedures and psychometry" an idea of where Atlantis was or wasn't, Hope lists the possibilities—and debunks them one by one. Thera (Santorini) is only a possibility if we recognize that "the Minoan civilization was founded on the teachings of Atlantean colonists who arrived in the Aegean several thousand years earlier." Also, Tartessos was "a colony, if not an actual part, of Atlantis"; Tunisia has "cities of Roman origin"; West Africa and East Africa were from "a much later period than that suggested by Plato"; in the North Sea, "the Atland of the Fresians actually went down around 5000 B.C."; North America was "hardly 'sunken,' being very much in evidence today!"; Yucatán was not Atlantis at all, but "part of the greater land mass that stretched across to the Pacific Ocean, which has been given the name of Mu (the Motherland?)"; Brazil ("Mu perhaps"); and finally, Lemuria.

"Lemuria" sounds as if it ought to be the land of the lemurs, and it is. The name was coined by English zoologist Philip Sclater in the 1870s to explain the distribution of lemurs (primitive primates, now found only in Madagascar) via a hypothetical Indo-Madagascan land bridge. Ernst Haeckel suggested that the sunken land bridge might be the original home of man, but the name was appropriated by Madame Helena Petrovna Blavatsky (1831–1891), a Russian occultist living in New York City, who claimed to be receiving letters (later proven to have been written by herself) from her Hindu "master," Koot Hoomi. These letters included elaborate discussions of the seven "Root Races" of man, such as the apelike, hermaphroditic Lemurians, whose downfall was caused by their discovery of sex; the primitive Hyperboreans, who lived in a mystical land in the Far North; the advanced Atlanteans (the Fourth Root Race); and ourselves, the Fifth Root Race.

Madame Blavatsky was very serious about Atlantis; she believed that the oceanographic results of the *Challenger* expedition (1873–76) verified its existence. She was not likely to receive much support from the scientists, however, because she believed that Atlantis (and Lemuria) began to sink several million years ago, and completed their descent 850,000 years ago. Indeed, she believed (or wrote) that where Plato wrote that Atlantis disappeared 9,000 years ago, he actually meant 900,000 years ago.

MADAME HELENA BLAVATSKY, a Russian Spiritualist who arrived in New York in 1871 claiming she had been told all about Atlantis and Lemuria by a (dead) Tibetan mahatma named Koot Hoomi

Maybe Atlantis was in Antarctica. Hope "finds this hypothesis quite logical," since, she says, there are a number of maps that have been copied and recopied from charts that go back thousands of years, several of which show Antarctica as being ice-free. In 1995, a couple with the almost Atlantean name of Flem-Ath published *When the Sky Fell: In Search of Atlantis,* which opens with this statement from Colin Wilson: "The thesis of this book is so simple and yet so startling that it will almost certainly earn Rand and Rose Flem-Ath a permanent place in the history of the earth sciences. It can be summarized in seven words: Antarctica is the lost continent of Atlantis." The Flem-Aths based their findings on the work of Charles Hapgood, a New Hampshire history and science teacher who corresponded extensively with Albert Einstein, who contributed the foreword to Hapgood's *Earth's Shifting Crust.* Einstein wrote:

I frequently receive communications from people who wish to consult me concerning their unpublished ideas. It goes without saying that these ideas are very seldom possessed of scientific validity. The very first communication, however, that I received from Mr. Hapgood electrified me. His idea is original, of great simplicity, and—if it continues to prove itself—of great importance to everything that is related to the history of the earth's surface.

Have the Flem-Aths rewritten geology as we know it? Not exactly. It appears that Hapgood's idea—that the crust of the earth slides intact around a solid core—was presented in 1955 to a group of scientists at the American Museum of Natural History in New York, who found that he had greatly overestimated the speed with which the earth's tectonic plates moved; and in *The Path of the*

Pole, published in 1970, he revised his theory that an imbalance of the Antarctic ice sheet affected the spin of the earth and caused the poles to alter their positions. (Hapgood also wrote *Maps of the Ancient Sea Kings: Evidence of an Advanced Civilization in the Ice Age,* which suggests that he hadn't completely given up the idea of prehistoric civilizations.)

In their reading of (and correspondence with) Hapgood, the Flem-Aths conclude that Atlantis really existed, exactly as Plato described it, except that it had nothing to do with the Atlantic Ocean, or, for that matter, with the Pillars of Hercules, since these were only vague terms to the ancient Greeks and were not meant to be taken literally. The Flem-Aths wrote, "The original meanings of the Greek terms 'Atlantic Ocean' and 'Pillars of Hercules' have been consistently misunderstood. These mistakes, as we have seen, restricted the search for Atlantis to either the North Atlantic Ocean or the Mediterranean Sea. But Atlantis was in the 'real ocean,' the 'World Ocean,' of oceanographers," with the Antarctic smack in the middle of it. This is demonstrated on their maps, one of which shows that the Arabs had accurately mapped North America in 1559. (The information for this map, which is known as the Hadji Ahmed map, was provided, say the Flem-Aths, by the Atlanteans, who didn't want to live in North America because it was too cold.) The Hadji Ahmed map, and several others, including the Piri Reis map of 1513, which shows not only North America but Antarctica as well, have been borrowed from their mentor's *Maps of the Ancient Sea Kings.* The Flem-Aths believe that the ice sheet slid right over the fabled Lost City, and that it is still there. "We could use only the most sophisticated, least intrusive, instruments to peer beneath the ice," they conclude. "If evidence of a civilization is found, a surgical probe could be made. We would hold our breath as we waited to glimpse the ancient city locked in ice." (The Flem-Aths do not mention the sub-Antarctic volcanic island called Deception; it is a collapsed caldera not unlike Santorini in the Aegean, and an obvious candidate for an Atlantean connection.)

If Atlantis is not under the Antarctic ice, how about the Sahara Desert? "The Sahara was once part of an ocean that later became a lake and then a verdant area fit for human habitation. . . ." To support this statement, Murry Hope invokes Charles Berlitz, who wrote that photographs taken from the space shuttle *Columbia* showed that there were buried rivers in the great African desert.

To the question of whether Atlantis was, as Plato described it, in the Atlantic Ocean, Hope devotes an entire chapter. First she quotes Ignatius Donnelly, who said that "there was ample evidence from the sea-bed to suggest that Plato's island does lie submerged in the Atlantic, and that the islands of the Azores were formerly the peaks of its highest mountains." Then she totally misinterprets continental drift, reading it to mean that even when the west coast of Europe and the east coast of North America were conjoined, there was a large space in the Atlantic Ocean which had previously been occupied by Atlantis. She quotes Berlitz's story of the *Jesmond,* a ship that is supposed to have landed on Atlantis in 1882 (see p. 53), and concludes her discussion of the Atlantic by saying that there "must have been a single source of enlightenment somewhere in the far past from which all knowledge of sacred geometry, mathematics, and metaphysics originated, or a centre on the planet's surface that radiated subtle energies that could still be recognized and utilized by the initiated."

In the chapter "Asteroids, Moons, and Axis Tilts," Murry Hope quotes Otto Muck and several Russian authorities who believe that the earth was struck by a giant asteroid with such force that its axial rotation was affected, two great holes in the ocean floor were created, and concurrently, Atlantis was destroyed. There follow discussions about a vapor cloud produced by this impact condensing into the moon, Mayan and African Bushman legends about there originally having been *two* moons, and finally, the question of "Mu," the Pacific parallel of Atlantis and another "lost continent."

In *Lost Continents,* L. Sprague de Camp discusses this "other" lost land, and while we are not particularly concerned with Atlantis's Pacific analogue, the story is worth consideration, if only because it is an example of the "reasoning" that produces some of the more bizarre conceits of Atlantology. In Madrid in 1864, Abbé Charles-Etienne Brasseur discovered a copy of a translation of the *Relación de las cosas de Yucatán,* a book compiled in the mid-seventeenth century by Diego de Landa, a Spanish monk who had come with the conquistadores. The *Relación* contained Landa's interpretation of the Mayan alphabet, and Brasseur decided that two of the symbols stood for "M" and "U," and that therefore, the volcanic eruption described by Landa referred to the lost continent of "Mu." Dr. Augustus Le Plongeon (1826–1908), a physician and archaeologist of Mayan ruins, took Brasseur's rather modest suggestions and expanded them to the point where he fabricated an entire civilization, delineated in his major work, *Queen Móo and the Egyptian Sphinx.* (Queen Móo had fled to Egypt as her continent was sinking, and there built the sphinx as a memorial to her brothers Coh and Aac.)

This proposal was taken up by "Colonel" James Churchward, who published *The Lost Continent of Mu* in 1926. ("Mu" is merely an abbreviated version of

Lemuria.) Churchward wrote that Mu was a "great rich land . . . intersected and watered by many broad, slow-running streams and rivers, which wound their sinuous ways in fantastic curves and bends round the wooded hills and through the fertile plains." Mu had 64 million inhabitants, and fifty thousand years ago they developed a civilization that was far superior to ours. By decoding "Chinese and Japanese records," Churchward also decided that the statues on Easter Island had been made by Lemurians. Perhaps the strangest incarnation of Lemuria is Mount Shasta, on the California-Oregon border, which—as reported in 1932 by a reporter named Edward Lanser, who said he saw them with a telescope—is supposed to have a colony of Lemurians living on its slopes.

Next Hope writes about "Cycles, Time Scales, and Dates," in which we learn that the earth's history is divided into various periodic cycles, and astrological and mystical ages which incorporate the destruction of Atlantis. This chapter concludes with a discussion of "spiritual amnesia," which means that "Atlantis was indeed a reality, the knowledge of which lies deep within the human collective unconscious, into which we are, at times, permitted to delve." According to Hope, the peoples of Atlantis came in three varieties: tall, white-haired, bearded men ("the bringers of law, science, and medicine); red-skinned people with Aztec features; and shorter people with fair skins and hazel eyes. She further informs us that many of the "red" Indians were not dark; "many of the Menominee, Dakota, Mandan, and Zuni tribes were fair, with auburn hair and blue eyes." We also learn that the DNA collected from seven-thousand-year-old bodies preserved in a salt spring in Florida has been shown to have been of Lemurian or Gondwanian origin and "the unidentified strain, Atlantean."

Alongside a map that shows the capital city of Atlantis, with the various rings, channels, tunnels, and bridges that were described in detail by Plato, Hope tells us that one definition of the word "paradise" in her dictionary is "from the Avestan *pairi-daēza,* circumvallation, walled-in park; in other words, some kind of a circular enclosure." Is that far from Plato's "rings of land which separated those of water"? Not only are the two similar in their circumvallations, but it seems possible that Atlantis was really Pairi-daēza. Ignatius Donnelly has made a thorough study of Atlantean linguistics, which Hope says shows an "impressive catalogue of similarities" among English, Chinese, and Chaldean characters. (Charles Berlitz's comparison of English, Amerindian, and Euro-Asian-African also shows how closely affiliated these civilizations actually were.) This proves to Hope "that at some time in the dim and distant past, mankind shared a single language, which became split into different dialects and ultimately altered over long periods of time following cataclysms when people found themselves living in isolated pockets away from the original collective of which they had once formed an integral part." Some of these people formed colonies of Atlantis. Egypt, Greece, Sumeria, and North America are also on this list ("I have always maintained that Atlantis was at one time joined to the North American continent," writes Hope), and, of course, given the Mayan, Aztec, Toltec, and Quiche connections, a sizable piece of the Lost Continent must have been located somewhere in Central or South America. Other regions that are listed as having been colonized by Atlantean missionaries are Africa, the Canary Islands, Ireland, Wales, and Scandinavia. How much of the Atlantean heritage has filtered through to us today? Quite a lot, says Hope, noting that the pyramids and other monoliths, including the nuraghe towers of Sardinia, the chullpa towers of pre-Inca Peru, and even (according to Donnelly) the round stone temples of Ireland, are all evidence of Atlantean influences.

As she promised, Murry Hope saves her discussions of the paranormal for the last three chapters. In the 1890s, Colonel William Scott-Elliot joined the Theosophical Society (founded by Madame Blavatsky and Henry Steele Olcott in 1875), which holds that the Aryans are the "Fifth Race," but that the Atlanteans, who lived a million years ago, are the Fourth. (They were preceded by the Third Race, the Lemurians, some of whom were fifteen feet tall, had eyes so far apart they could see sideways, and heels that stuck out so far that they could walk backward as easily as forward.)

A follower of Madame Blavatsky was Rudolf Steiner (1861–1925), who formed his own spiritual movement, which he called "Anthroposophy," from the Greek words for "man" and "wisdom." In *Cosmic Memory: Prehistory of Earth and Man*, Steiner wrote that "the so-called Atlantean Continent still existed between America and Europe. . . . Today, this forms the floor of the Atlantic Ocean." He cites Scott-Elliot as the source of this information, but as for what follows, Steiner writes, "Today I am still obliged to remain silent about the sources of the information given here. One who knows anything at all about such sources will understand why this has to be so." Steiner died without revealing his sources, but he nonetheless managed to give more than six thousand lectures (which have been collected into three hundred books) on everything from Lemuria to biodynamic agriculture. The "prehistory of Earth and man" was revealed through the Ashaka Chronicle, wherein the Atlanteans could tune into the collective unconscious, which contained recollections of everything that has ever taken place. In Steiner's voluminous writings, he also tells us that Atlantean airships were designed to fly in a much denser atmosphere and would be inoperable in today's thin skies. He also maintained that human bodies, as well as rocks and minerals, were much softer in Lemurian and Atlantean times.

Also included in Hope's chapter entitled "Torch-Bearing Collectives" are the Rosicrucians, the Atlanteans, and Edgar Cayce.

Hope's penultimate chapter is called "Akashic Anomalies," which introduces "the visionary experiences of only a few better-known personalities from the world of psychism and occultism. . . ." Several British psychics are discussed, including Dion Fortune, who saw Atlantis in a vision when she was four years old (and sometime later wrote *The Sea Priestess,* a novel about Morgan le Fay, the princess of Atlantis), and Gareth Knight, "the well-known occultist, Qabalist, and Tarot specialist," who learned of Atlantis from Dion Fortune, but long after Fortune had died. Knight was able to describe the Atlanteans, some of whom were seven feet tall, with "bodies more porous than ours are today." In *A Case for Reincarnation,* Christine Hartley states her belief "that Atlantis fell because her mental faculties outstripped her spiritual achievement. . . ." Fanny Craddock wrote up her Atlantean adventures in the form of novels, but they were, says Hope, "Ms. Craddock's own experiences." Then there is Daphne Viggers, who wrote *Atlantis Rising,* about her astral experiences, and Brad Steiger, who wrote a book of the same name, only his was mostly about other people's psychic experiences. (Steiger also wrote *Overlords of Atlantis and the Great Pyramid.*) Not everyone who has had Atlantean experiences is British; Frank Alper, "who has an enormous following in the United States" and founded the Arizona Metaphysical Society in 1974, "is one of a crop of popular American channellers whose contact goes by the name of Adamis." Alper refers to Mu and the ancient Atlantean landmass as having been destroyed by cataclysms around 85,000 B.C., and according to him, 7,223 years later, ships from alien worlds landed on the coast of Florida to resettle Atlantis beneath the sea.

Edgar Cayce was born in Hopkinton, Kentucky, in March 1877. He hoped to become a preacher, but he had to leave school in the seventh grade because of a throat ailment that reduced his voice to a whisper. A friend offered to cure him by putting him into a hypnotic trance, and in this state, Cayce spoke in a clear, unimpeded voice. Based on this experience, he acquired two personalities, "waking" and "sleeping." According to his son Hugh (writing in *Edgar Cayce on Atlantis*),* "by sleeping with his head on his schoolbooks, he developed

---

* Edgar Cayce had two sons, Edgar Evans Cayce and Hugh Lynn Casey. Edgar Evans wrote *Edgar Cayce on Atlantis,* and his brother Hugh wrote the preface. To avoid confusion in this chapter, Edgar Evans Cayce will be referred to as "Edgar Evans."

a form of photographic memory which helped him advance rapidly in the country school." At the age of twenty-one, he was stricken with a paralysis of the throat muscles, and putting himself into a hypnotic sleep, he prescribed his own medication, which cured him. Cayce (pronounced "Casey") applied this technique to other patients: lying on his back with his feet facing north, he required only their name and address to be able to diagnose their disorders and recommend osteopathic and homeopathic cures. Known as "the sleeping prophet," Cayce was said to be "the greatest mystic America has ever known" and claimed to be able to see every person's "aura" and diagnose people's ailments based on the color of the energy cloud that surrounded them. Cayce did not actually write his ideas down, but dictated his pronouncements, observations, and theories to various stenographers over a period of forty-three years. When he died in 1945, he left more than fourteen thousand stenographic transcriptions of the telepathic-clairvoyant statements he had given to eight thousand different people. These are maintained at the Association for Research and Enlightenment in Virginia Beach, Virginia, an active organization dedicated to the dissemination of Cayce's teachings.

Cayce could "see" into the past and describe complex events that had not been recorded by conventional historians. He was also able to predict the future. In his later years, he predicted the destruction of Los Angeles, San Francisco, and New York; the democratization of Red China; the sliding of much of Japan into the sea; and the end of Communism in the Soviet Union. (All these were supposed to take place between 1958 and 1998.)

He also predicted the reemergence of the Lost Continent of Atlantis, which he gathered from the "life readings" he conducted for some sixteen hundred individuals, about half of whom had "incarna-

EDGAR CAYCE (1877–1945), the best-known psychic and clairvoyant in America. In his trances, he received information about the citizens of Atlantis, who, he claimed, had harnessed atomic energy and developed flying machines fifty thousand years ago.

tions in Atlantis." He was a firm believer in reincarnation, about which he said: "Be it true that there is the fact of reincarnation, and that souls that once occupied such an environ [i.e., Atlantis] are entering the earth's sphere and inhabiting individuals in the present, is it any wonder that—if they made such alterations in the affairs of the earth in their day, as to bring destruction upon themselves—if they are entering now, they might make many changes in the affairs of peoples and individuals in the present?" In a trance, Cayce would "hear" of the incarnations of his subjects, and his rendition would be transcribed. These were collected into what Edgar Evans calls "a coherent, non-contradictory series of events," from which he constructed the history of Atlantis, which he presents in his book.

Of the early days of the earth, he is recorded as saying,

> The extreme northern portions were then the southern portions, or the polar regions were then turned to where they occupied more of the tropical and semitropical regions; hence it would be hard to describe the change. The Nile entered into the Atlantic Ocean. What is now the Sahara was an inhabited land and very fertile. What is now the central portion of this country, or the Mississippi basin, was then all in the ocean; only the plateau was existent, or the regions that are now portions of Nevada, Utah, and Arizona formed the greater part of what we now know as the United States. That along the Atlantic seaboard formed the outer portion then, or the lowlands of Atlantis. The Andean, or Pacific coast of South America, occupied then the extreme western portion of Lemuria. . . . You see, with the changes when there came the uprising of the Atlantean land, and the sojourning southward and the turning of the axis, the white and the yellow races came more into that portion of Egypt, India, Persia, and Arabia.

Part of this revised version of the earth was the continent of Atlantis, which he located as follows:

> The position . . . the continent of Atlantis occupied is between the Gulf of Mexico on the one hand and the Mediterranean on the other. Evidences of this lost civilization are to be found in the Pyrenees and Morocco, British Honduras, Yucatán, and America. There are some protruding portions . . . that must have at one time or another been a portion of this great continent. The British West Indies, or the Bahamas, are a portion of same that may be seen in the present. If the geological survey would be made in some of these, especially or notably in Bimini and in the Gulf Stream through this vicinity, these may be even yet determined.

Cayce reported that a great cataclysm had engulfed a technologically advanced civilization somewhere near the Sargasso Sea (or perhaps in the Bahamas) and broke it up into five islands, the three largest of which were Poseidia, Aryan, and Og. He also said that the survivors had fanned out to various locations to bestow their achievements on ancient civilizations, including Egypt. In fact, he claimed that the Atlanteans had buried their most precious documents in the "Hall of Records" under the paws of the Sphinx.* "Poseidia," he wrote, "will be among the first portions of Atlantis to rise again. Expect it in '68 and '69." Cayce's son (and namesake) wrote *Edgar Cayce on Atlantis,* and even he had trouble accepting his father's prediction. Cayce *fils* wrote, "Unless proof of the existence of Atlantis is one day discovered, Edgar Cayce is in a very unenviable position."

No proof was immediately forthcoming, but in the years when Cayce said Atlantis was supposed to appear, several "expeditions" were mounted—usually to Bimini in the Bahamas, where conditions were more conducive to underwater exploration than those in the Sargasso Sea. One of these was undertaken in 1968 by Robert Ferro and Michael Grumley of New Jersey, who entitled their book *Atlantis: The Autobiography of a Search. A Psychic and a Real Journey to Find the Lost Continent as Prophesied by Edgar Cayce.* There are too many books about the Lost Continent to discuss more than a select few, but Ferro and Grumley's is particularly interesting because, by the authors' own admission, they were under the influence of Tarot readers and marijuana (which they wrote is "a key which could unlock certainly previously closed doorways of perception") and the Cayce Institute in Virginia Beach. Thus equipped, they could hardly fail to find the Lost Continent, and in the warm, clear waters of Bimini, they encountered a geometrical pattern of rectangular rocks that they identified as "proof of an ancient civilization that may have been Atlantis."

Like Ferro and Grumley, Dr. David Zink was a devotee of Edgar Cayce's, but unlike his predecessors (including Cayce), he had read Plato. He had also read the 1969 *Voyage to Atlantis* by James Mavor on the possibility of Atlantis being located on the ancient volcano of Thera in the Greek island group known as the Cyclades. "Although I doubted Mavor's claim," wrote Zink, "his serious approach reinforced my conviction that Atlantis was, indeed, a prehis-

---

* In a 1997 television show in which it was claimed that the Sphinx was five thousand years older than the pyramids, and therefore built by a civilization that predated the Egyptians by at least that much, it was suggested that there actually is a hollow chamber under the paws. If this is the case and there are records of Atlantis buried there, then the story of Atlantis—which even Plato says came from the Egyptian priests of Saïs—might just be true.

toric possibility," so off he went to Bimini to see for himself. After the three "Poseidia" expeditions (in 1975, 1976, and 1977) in which he dived over and photographed the stones, he wrote that "Bimini may ultimately be recognized as the major archaeological discovery of this century in the New World." He also quotes Cayce, who had said that "a world conference was held on Atlantis in 50,727 B.C. to deal with the threat of large animals. Sometime afterward, while attempting to kill them with energy from the crystal, the Atlanteans triggered earth changes that reduced Atlantis to five islands."

That large, often rectangular stones exist off Bimini is a fact. It is not uncommon for undersea rock formations in proximity to beach rock to fracture in relatively straight lines, and then again at right angles, creating what appear to be roadways or the remains of buildings. That the Bimini stones are remnants of man-made structures is, at best, questionable, and that they are part

DAVID ZINK, "historian, explorer, lecturer, mountaineer, blue-water sailor, scuba diver and underwater photographer," who led the "Poseidia" expeditions to Bimini in 1975, 1976, and 1977 to search for the sunken city of Atlantis

of Poseidia, Aryan, or Og seems as unlikely as Edgar Cayce's Atlantean world conference of 50,727 B.C. Wherever it might or might not be, Atlantis has not been verified in Bimini. One cannot help but quote seismologist L. Don Leet here: "We might as well send out an archaeological expedition to search for Lewis Carroll's *Wonderland* or Bacon's *New Atlantis* as a submarine to find Plato's *Atlantis.*"

I N   1 9 9 7 , Ptolemy Tompkins published a memoir in *Harper's* magazine ("Lost Atlantis: Nude Scientists, Giant Sharks, Bad Vibes, and Me") in which he recounted his experiences in Bimini in 1975, as a thirteen-year-old accompanying his father, Peter, who was "investigating a group of giant stones that lay in the shallow water several hundred yards off Bimini's northern shore. It was his fond hope that these stones might prove to be the vestiges of the lost continent of Atlantis, and that they were but the first of many such ruins to emerge from the sea after being hidden for some 10,000 years." Peter Tompkins, the author of the best-selling *The Secret Life of Plants,* had learned about the Bimini Road from reading Edgar Cayce, and even though he and David Zink were looking for the same thing at the same time and in the same place, they do not seem to have run into each other. (Zink thanks Peter Tompkins in his book, but he does not say what for.) According to his son's account, Tompkins senior eventually recognized "that the Road was a completely natural formation, down which no lost civilization, naked or clothed, had ever wandered or danced."

ATLANTIS OF THE SCIENTISTS

T HE POST-PLATO LITERATURE on Atlantis would long ago have been relegated to the "Quacks and Lunatics" section of the library if it were limited to these discussions of planetary collisions, owl-headed vases, reincarnation, or bananas. Even though some of these discussions read like unbridled science fiction, they are—as far as we can tell—supposed to be regarded as factual interpretations of available data. But for the respected oceanographers, geologists, engineers, and archaeologists who have also contributed to the contemporary literature, we need a different sort of inquiry, one in which we examine the data as well as the interpretations in the light of science.

"As the hidden lands beneath the sea become better known," asked Rachel Carson in *The Sea Around Us,* "can the submerged masses of the undersea mountains be linked with the fabled 'lost continents'?" In this 1951 prizewinning book, the chapter "Hidden Lands" is about the floor of the ocean, but Carson makes an intriguing suggestion for the location of Atlantis. Taking us far back in time—"to the shadowy beginnings of human life on earth"—she tells of a land that sank "perhaps not with the dramatic suddenness attributed to Atlantis, but well within the time one man could observe." During the Pleistocene Ice Age, when much of the water of the Northern Hemisphere was locked up in the glaciers, the floor of the North Sea emerged and became land. As the glaciers retreated, meltwater floods raised the sea level until the land became an island, which got smaller and smaller until it disappeared beneath the sea. Now a well-known fishing ground, the Dogger Bank is the remains of such a sunken island, about sixty miles off the northeast coast of England. The sunken bank is a huge moraine about 160 miles long and 60 miles wide (nearly as large as Denmark) which rises to within 50 feet of the surface at its shallowest point, averaging 70 feet higher than the surrounding sea floor. As for the men who escaped the sinking, "perhaps in their primitive way they communicated this story to other men, who passed it down to others through the ages, until it became fixed in the memory of the race. . . . And remembering how once the North Sea had been dry land, they reconstructed the story of the Dogger Bank, the lost island." Although it is located only 250 miles from Jürgen Spanuth's "Atlantis of the North," Carson's version has no earthquakes, tsunamis, or volcanic eruptions; no men in Viking helmets, no Egyptian hieroglyphics; just the inexorable rise of the Atlantic as it covers a large—and probably uninhabited—tract of bogland.

In an appendix to *Lost Continents,* L. Sprague de Camp tallied the "interpreters of Plato's Atlantis and their interpretations." Of the 221 interpretations, the most popular categories are "Atlantic Island," with seventy-eight entries, and "Imaginary," with thirty-two. Of course, such a list is skewed in favor of those authors with specific theories; people are less likely to publish a study if it merely echoes Plato's original description. De Camp's book was published in 1954, so he could not have included James Mavor's *Voyage to Atlantis* and Angelos Galanopoulos's *Atlantis: The Truth Behind the Legend.* Both books were written by scholars who attempted to tie the legend of Atlantis to accepted, scientifically verified facts. Of course, given the nature of the subject, they are bound to exaggerate a bit and, occasionally, to manipulate the facts to ensure that they conform to their hypotheses. In both books, the Atlantis legend is connected with the volcanic eruption of Santorini, and both spend a lot of time demonstrating that Plato was probably right, although his timing and geography may have been a little off.

Spyridon Marinatos provided the inducement in 1950. He published an essay he entitled "On the Legend of Atlantis," which was originally published in Greek in the *Cretica Chronicles;* later, his English translation (now called "Some Words About the Legend of Atlantis") was published by the Athens Museum. In this paper, he wrote that Plato's Atlantis legend was, in all likelihood, a synthesis of several diverse historical traditions, including a Middle Kingdom Egyptian legend about a shipwreck on a lost island and a Sumerian recollection of the biblical flood. He said that Plato did not make it all up:

"Plato's imagination could not have conjured up an account so unique and unusual to classical literature," but he strongly contested the idea that Plato's story of Atlantis could have occurred nine thousand years earlier. "We now know," he wrote, "that no Greeks existed then to perform heroic deeds, nor Egyptians to write them down."

It was Angelos Galanopoulos's 1960 paper ("Tsunamis Observed on the Coasts of Greece from Antiquity to the Present Time") that stated that not only Atlantis but also Deucalion's flood ought to be attributed to the Bronze Age eruption of Santorini. He further said that the eruption caused the Plagues of Egypt, the parting of the waters, and the Phaëthon myth, where the sun stops in the heavens.

James Mavor was an oceanographic engineer at the Woods Hole Oceanographic Institution and one of the designers of the submersible *Alvin*. (He was not, however, the "inventor" of the *Alvin*, a notion he seems to have conveyed to John Lear, science editor of the *Saturday Review*.) In 1965 (according to the dust jacket of his book), Mavor "began investigating the riddle of Atlantis. Since that time he has organized two international expeditions to the Aegean, where

JAMES MAVOR, an oceanographic engineer who set out in 1967 to find Plato's Atlantis on the island of Santorini in the Aegean, and who believed he had succeeded

Atlantis was discovered on the volcanic island of Thera." That might be something of an exaggeration, since Atlantis itself has not really been found, but
there is no question that Mavor believed in what he had done. He also believed
in what Galanopoulos had done, because, he says, "my excursions to Thera
have convinced me that the Galanopoulos model of the origins of the Atlantean myth must of necessity anticipate actual physical findings, and that these,
with the aid of shovel, earth-movers, mine railways and cars, cranes, convey-
ors and the like, will be brought forth and housed in museums." This quote
comes from the last page of Mavor's book, so perhaps it would be advanta-
geous to examine what the two men had to say about Atlantis and Thera.

Mavor begins his book with a definitive statement of his thesis:

> It is my belief—and this book will spell out the reasons for that belief—that
> Atlantis did actually, physically exist, not in the Atlantic Ocean, on the grand
> scale of legend, or in the North Sea, the Bahamas, the East Indies, South
> America, Spain, the Indian Ocean, or other parts of the world which have
> been mentioned as its location, but in a lesser, more familiar dimension, in a
> sea utterly familiar to Plato. It is my belief that Atlantis lay in the Aegean itself,
> on one of the islands of the Cyclades, and in a position and under circum-
> stances that would have certainly insured that its destruction, which did in
> fact occur, would be remembered through time to the Greek era, and through
> Plato to us.

Almost immediately, however, Mavor succumbs to the same temptation
that ensnares so many Atlantologists: he says that because people disbelieved
Homer's story of the Trojan War, which Schliemann eventually showed to be at
least partially true, therefore the legend of Atlantis must also be based on fact.
(This is rather like saying that because the coelacanth, a "living fossil," was discovered to exist after it had been presumed extinct for 75 million years, that the
Loch Ness monster should be accorded the same legitimacy.) Only a couple of
days after he arrived in Greece in July 1965, Mavor met Galanopoulos, whom he
describes as "a short, round-faced, heavyset man in his middle fifties, [who]
always seems to exhibit good-humored cheer." Galanopoulos told Mavor his
theories about Atlantis, which included the rather surprising interpretation
that Thera was the center of the Minoan civilization, and Crete its adjunct. (It
was here that Galanopoulos expressed his idea that Plato's dates are off by a factor of ten, which he repeated emphatically in his own work.) Although their
books differ in some particulars and conclusions, the fact that Mavor met and
quotes Galanopoulos at length means that there is substantial overlap in their
works, and it is therefore possible to discuss them simultaneously.

To show that only small land areas can vanish, Galanopoulos mentions the 373 B.C. disappearance of the Corinthian city of Helice, but he said that larger areas—like Atlantis—could be destroyed only by massive subterranean earth movements. "The collapse of Thera," for example, "was a disaster comparable to nuclear war today. Hundreds of thousands of persons could have lost their lives. Cities, ports, and villages on many islands and on the mainland of Greece and Turkey could have been washed away or inundated by torrential rains triggered by a spew of ash. What remained would have been toppled and pounded to rubble by tidal waves. Fleets of ships would have foundered or been hurled miles inland. Cities on the highlands, at least those close to Thera, would have been rocked and torn by earthquakes. And all the while, volcanic ash would have blackened the heavens, turning day into night, with thunder crashing, lightning searing the sky, and the seas becoming clogged with mud."

James Mavor's 1965 visit to Greece was a vacation trip, with his wife and children. The following year, he read Dragoslav Ninkovich and Bruce Heezen's discussion of the Santorini tephra (in which they discussed deep-sea core samples from a wide area of the Mediterranean that contained residue of the 1500 B.C. eruption), and after writing two articles for the Woods Hole magazine *Oceanus* ("A Mighty Bronze Age Volcanic Explosion" and "Volcanoes and History; or, 'Atlantis' Revisted"), he decided to return to Santorini aboard the Woods Hole research vessel *Chain*. With Harold Edgerton of MIT as part of the expedition,* he planned to pick up Galanopoulos and sail into the great caldera of Santorini. In Greece, they would also be joined by Edward Loring, an American living on Santorini. It was Loring who showed them the piece of lava in the form of a monkey's skull which immortalized by Aris Poulianos in his 1972 article for *Archaeology* entitled "The Discovery of the First Known Victim of Thera's Bronze Age Eruption." (Of this find, Emily Vermeule [1967] wrote that "Mavor's monkey-head identification of Atlantis was not taken seriously by scholars, but it generated considerable popular appeal.") Mavor's grand design included the "Helleno-American Multi-Disciplinary Scientific Investigation of Thera and Quest for Lost Atlantis," which probably sounded better to

---

* Harold "Doc" Edgerton, the inventor of high-speed stroboscopic photography and side-scan sonar (among other things), had a long-standing interest in underwater exploration and photography. In 1954 he deployed a remote-controlled underwater camera from Cousteau's *Calypso* in the Mediterranean, obtaining some of the first shots of rare creatures of the depths. In addition to his participation in Mavor's 1966 expedition, he had lent his expertise and equipment to a 1984 expedition to try to capture the Loch Ness monster on film—with, unfortunately, as much success as they had had at Corinth. David Zink wrote that although Edgerton had "expressed interest in joining us on the expedition [to Bimini], at the last minute Dr. Edgerton was unable to come when the U.S. government asked him to attend a conference in the U.S.S.R."

the American press than it did to the Greeks; and despite its impressive title, his project raised no funds whatsoever. He used his advance from the American publishers to finance some of the early investigations, and several members of his "expedition" had to pay their own way to Greece.

After completing their seismological cruise of the caldera, the expedition came ashore to investigate the settlement at Akrotiri. At the conclusion of their two weeks on Thera, they headed for home, only to learn that their exploits had been chronicled, in a somewhat exaggerated form, in newspapers around the world. For example, the *New York Times* of September 4, 1966, ran this headline: MOAT BELIEVED TO BE PART OF ATLANTIS FOUND IN AEGEAN SEA. Mavor felt vindicated by the media coverage, for he wrote, "We left Athens amid the furor of publicity, some of it regrettable and some quite welcome. I no longer felt alone in my enormous task of proving Galanopoulos' theory. The world press had become our ally."

The next year, Spyridon Marinatos, the Greek archaeologist who had introduced the idea that the Minoan civilization of Crete had been destroyed by a volcanic eruption, joined forces with Mavor. (Early in his account of the 1967 expedition, Mavor writes, "Marinatos planned in November [1966] to search for the sunken classical city of Helice, in the Gulf of Corinth, with the help of Doc Edgerton and his underwater devices," and although Mavor writes that Edgerton "reported on the results of his sediment pinging at Helice" and that "there were plans to start excavating the following June," Mavor never mentions this endeavor again. (It is discussed on pp. 242–44 of this book.) Also aboard was Emily Vermeule, a classical scholar from the Museum of Fine Arts in Boston and the author, two years earlier, of the authoritative *Greece in the Bronze Age.* Jacques Cousteau had evinced an interest in Thera, so Mavor, Marinatos, Vermeule, and Edgerton had to work around his schedule. (Galanopoulos and Loring had dropped out for various reasons, but Loring would be back.)

In any event, the expedition arrived on Santorini and headed for Akrotiri. The vulcanologist Ferdinand Fouqué had excavated here in 1866, and then Messrs. Henri Mamet and Henri Gorceix worked under the auspices of the French School at Athens, unearthing storage jars, tools, pottery shards, and frescoes. On May 25, 1967, thirty-three hours after they arrived on the island, the Mavor expedition dug through the ashes and found the brick walls of a house burned on the upper stories. (As Mavor tells it, their fancy magnetometer did not work that well, and it was Marinatos's "archaeologist's instinct" that showed them exactly where to dig.) They found some artifacts—mostly potsherds—but then Marinatos had to leave, and Mavor and Company could not archaeologize without an archaeologist, so they headed for Crete. The

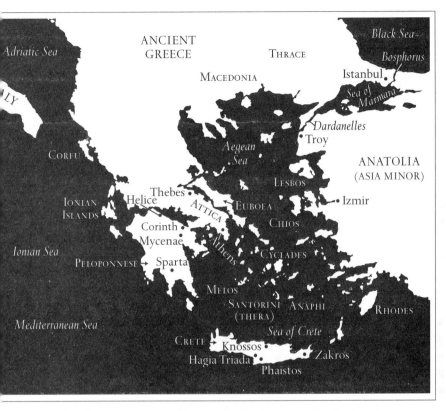

THE GREEK MAINLAND, islands, and bodies of water mentioned in the text

closing of the Suez Canal during the Arab-Israeli war of 1967 prevented Cousteau from bringing his ship *Calypso* to the Mediterranean, so he never joined the expedition. Edgerton, who had hoped to work with Cousteau at Helice, also did not return for the 1967 dig, but he made several unsuccessful attempts to locate the lost Corinthian city.

After a couple of weeks, Marinatos returned to Santorini, and so did the expedition. This time, they excavated seriously and opened no fewer than nine trenches. They found cups, kitchenware, animal bones, shells, and obsidian implements in one trench, and in another, tumbled ashlar blocks, suggesting earthquake damage. They unearthed frescoes that had remained buried for thirty-five hundred years. Beneath a donkey path, in the trench known as "Alvaniti I," they found seven enormous storage jars, intact and with their decorations "as bright as the day they were painted in red, black, and brown."

After Mavor left Greece, Marinatos returned to Akrotiri to continue the excavations. In addition to great numbers of shards, he uncovered a 50-foot-long wall constructed of large stones, which showed a reddish tinge, as if they had been subjected to intense heat. Even though it was buried deep in ash, the wall lay on top of more ash, showing that it had been built after an eruption had blanketed Akrotiri. They demonstrated conclusively that the residents of Thera had returned after an earthquake and rebuilt their settlement. "In my view," wrote Mavor, "we had confirmed much of Galanopoulos' theory that Thera was the metropolis of Atlantis, a heavily populated cult center having wealth and culture the equal of Crete." (A more detailed discussion of the excavations at Akrotiri appears on pp. 170–87.)

When Mavor returned to America, the media picked up on his accomplishments, particularly those that mentioned the Lost City of Atlantis. Mavor and Emily Vermeule gave a press conference at the Museum of Fine Arts in Boston in which they claimed to have found Atlantis, and while they consistently gave credit to Marinatos as the primary archaeologist of the expedition, the American press chose to spotlight the American contributions, and in magazines like *Time* and *Newsweek,* Marinatos was hardly mentioned. Worse, it appeared as if Mavor was about to buy up half the island to continue "his" dig. In *Time,* for example, he was quoted as saying that he was planning to "buy the land over the interred city, and begin a ten-year, $1,000,000 excavation." Not surprisingly, this upset Marinatos, and he not only severed contact with the Americans but arranged to have their archaeological permits rescinded. As quoted by Mavor, Marinatos was concerned that the only thing people were interested in was the Lost City. "Atlantis, Atlantis," he is reported to have said. "All want to know if this is Atlantis. I only say that these palaces could be also as important as Knossos in Crete. There are 2,300 years since Plato wrote. I used to think that Atlantis could be only a concept of Platonic perfection of the government of a state."*

Mavor, however, was convinced that he (and Marinatos) had found Atlantis. "I have suggested," he wrote, "that the Atlantis myth is the central one of a great body of related myth pertaining to the great Thera destruction, the Minoans and their sea empire, the Mycenaean Greeks and their conflict

---

* In Marinatos's 1972 *National Geographic* article ("Thera: Key to the Riddle of Minos"), he does not mention Mavor—or anyone else besides Greek workers, for that matter—and credits the excavations to "our archaeological team from Greece's Department of Antiquities." Marinatos was obviously so upset by his treatment at the hands of the Americans and the American press that he decided to forsake them altogether.

with the Minoans, and the origin of the Aegean peoples." In 1967, when "a Minoan palace" was discovered at Akrotiri (by Marinatos, although it is now Mavor's turn to be churlish, and he does not mention him), this proved to Mavor that "royalty had lived on Thera . . . because Thera was a strategic center of maritime commerce and a cult center, as Plato said of the metropolis of Atlantis." We can probably assume that the prologue of a book, even though it appears at the beginning, was probably one of the last things written. It is therefore instructive to conclude this discussion of *Voyage to Atlantis* with the last paragraph of Mavor's prologue:

> But, in addition to learning of these discoveries, the reader will be introduced to something just as intriguing—a new way of looking at history. The theory that led me to search for Atlantis—*and find it*—casts a whole new light on the interpretation of mythic events. Perhaps the most startling discovery I made was not Atlantis itself, but the realization that Atlantis had lain exposed for centuries, for all to see, if they but knew what to look for.*

Eighteen years after *Voyage to Atlantis,* Mavor published an article in the Woods Hole magazine *Oceanus* in which he elaborated on the theory that the demise of Atlantis might have been brought about by an event even more catastrophic than a mere earthquake and volcanic eruption. By 1984, it had been proposed (Alvarez et al. 1982) that the great Cretaceous-Tertiary extinctions had been caused by the impact of a comet with the earth some 65 million years ago, and the specter of "catastrophism" was raised. As defined by Mavor, "catastrophe theory seeks to explain boundaries and other discontinuities in the cultural, biological, or geological record left in the soils and rocks of the earth's crust. The causes of such circumstances may be either terrestrial or extraterrestrial events, or both, sometimes of a rare or short-lived nature." If a comet or asteroid could wipe out the dinosaurs, think of what it could do to the city of Atlantis.

Other researchers quoted by Mavor support the idea of the extraterrestrial demise of Atlantis, including Otto Muck, who speculated that an asteroid landed off Puerto Rico around 8500 B.C. and set off a chain reaction that caused the Azorean continent to sink, leaving only the mountaintops exposed as the islands we know today. (Immanuel Velikovsky had suggested a similar scenario

---

* Of Mavor's book, Marinatos wrote, "Another book, under the self-confiding title 'Voyage to Atlantis,' was published during this same year, 1969. Its author is Mr. J. Mavor, an expert in electrology. From the psychological point of view it may prove interesting to some scholars." In the seven volumes that Marinatos wrote from 1968 to 1976 about the excavations at Thera, he never mentions Mavor's name.

in *Worlds in Collision* in 1950.) Victor Clube of Oxford and Bill Napier of the Royal Edinburgh Observatory argued that comets have often passed close to earth, causing major convulsions like earthquakes, fires, and floods, and Mavor suggests that "a number of near-eastern myths describe events that may be separate from but contemporaneous with the eruption and collapse of Thera." He lists "the myths of combat between Zeus and Typhon, the Hurrian Song of Ullikummi, the Admonitions of an Egyptian Sage, the Plagues of Egypt . . . the Greek deluge of Deukalion, apparently of the second millennium B.C., and the floods of Noah, and the Epic of Gilgamesh, apparently in the third millennium B.C., may refer to a series of devastating astronomical events." Mavor wrote, "There are indeed many accounts of disasters that appear to have been contemporary, as if a single cataclysmic event occurred about 1400 B.C."

While not claiming that an asteroid might have been responsible for the destruction of Atlantis, Mavor does write, "Except for the Minoan-Thera thesis [which Mavor wholeheartedly subscribed to], attempts to locate Atlantis have been based primarily on mythology with weak scientific evidence. However, the comet theory of destruction, which has been around for at least two centuries, has gained substantial credibility. . . ."

In *Atlantis: The Truth Behind the Legend,* Galanopoulos sets out to resolve the questions of Atlantis, and he includes a chapter entitled "Case Proven," in which he writes:

> We have shown that it is not geophysically possible for Atlantis to have been located in the Atlantic; and proved that none of the theories so far advanced to account for its sudden submersion are tenable. We have gone on to indicate that the only logical location must be the Eastern Mediterranean and that the identification of the Pillars of Hercules with the Straits of Gibraltar need not be taken too literally. Finally we have shown that volcanic activity on a really stupendous scale did take place in the Eastern Mediterranean in the middle of the Bronze Age, that this activity was centered on the island of Santorin, and that it resulted in, among other things, the sudden disappearance of the whole centre of an inhabited, small, round island. The case, therefore, for the identification of Santorin with the Ancient Metropolis of Atlantis is extremely strong, and is supported by a considerable amount of corroborative evidence of very great interest.

Galanopoulos published his book in 1969, so his chronology is not that different from that in Mavor's 1966 publication. (Their goals were similar enough for Mavor to have written, "In 1965 I set out to find confirmation of Dr. Galanopoulos' theory of Atlantis.") Angelos Galanopoulos is marginally more generous toward Mavor than Marinatos was; at least he mentions the American in his 1969 book. He says (but not until page 161), "These [1967] excavations were directed by Professor Spyridon Marinatos for the Archaeological Society of Athens, with the collaboration of Mrs. Emily Vermeule, Boston Museum of Fine Arts, and Mr. James Mavor of the Woods Hole Oceanographic Institute [*sic*]. The results of these excavations are known to be of a revolutionary nature although still only at the exploratory stage. What they have revealed seems to be a Bronze Age Pompeii."

It seems to be a prerequisite in a book about Atlantis to start with Plato, and indeed, the first chapter of Galanopoulos's book (a profusely illustrated, coffee-table volume) is devoted to "What Plato Meant and Said." (An appendix reproduces the text of the relevant portions of the *Timaeus* and the *Critias.*) The author then offers an explanation for the discrepancy in dating, a problem that had heretofore stymied most Atlantean scholars: "Working back 9,000 years from the time the Egyptian priests told Solon that Atlantis was preparing to attack Athens and Egypt and the Athenians were gallantly meeting the attack, we arrive at a date of 9600 B.C.—a time, as Professor Marinatos has rightly said, when 'there were neither Egyptians to record the events, nor Greeks to perform the deeds attributed to them.' . . . The date of 9600 B.C. for Atlantis is both incredible and impossible, in detail and in general alike." He says, "The anomaly of the date of Atlantis is at once obvious and clear-cut— and as will appear later, open to a simple solution." It takes him almost a hundred pages to get to the explanation, but it is simply that the date of the submersion of Atlantis is ten times greater than it should be: "When dimensions and dates are given [by Plato] in thousands, they are all ten times too great. This seems to indicate that when Solon was transcribing the Egyptian writings, the word or symbol representing 100 was mistaken for that representing 1,000."

Between the question and the answer is a fascinating compilation of Atlantean lore, in which the author presents (and discounts) the myriad theories about the location of Atlantis, first in the Atlantic Ocean (the Sargasso Sea, the Atlantic Land Bridge, the Mid-Atlantic Ridge, the "east Atlantic Continent"), and then other possible locations, including Tunisia, Tartessos, northwest France, and Heligoland in northern Germany, but shows that none of these could possibly be correct.

One of the more intriguing arguments for the location of Atlantis in the middle of the Atlantic is what Galanopoulos calls "the argument for the nuptial [*sic*] migration of eels." European and American eels (genus *Anguilla*) leave the freshwater streams and rivers of eastern North America and Europe and head for the ocean to breed, but their reproductive habits were a mystery for years. No juvenile eels (known as "elvers") had ever been seen in European waters, leading to some extraordinary speculations about how and where they breed. Aristotle suggested that they were generated out of mud; others believed that the morning dew on the grass was transformed into eels. A very common superstition was that when horsehairs fell into a rain barrel, they produced a horsehair worm, which then turned into an eel. Around 1907, a Danish ichthyologist named Johannes Schmidt finally solved the mystery when he discovered that eels—American and European—travel all the way to the Sargasso Sea to lay their eggs, and then die. The baby eels somehow decide whether to become American or European citizens and return to the inland streams of their birth, taking two or three years to complete the journey, and then begin the process anew, heading back downstream to breed.

What does this have to do with Atlantis? In recounting this hypothesis, Galanopoulos tells us that some Atlantean scholars believe that the eels used to breed in the freshwater streams and rivers of Atlantic Atlantis, but after it sank into the sea, they continued to return to the place where their genetic memory told them it was, i.e., the Sargasso Sea. (Charles Berlitz repeats this story in his *Atlantis,* stating that the eels are indeed returning to an "ancestral breeding ground, a former waterway now covered by the sea, but whose residual vegetation, the seaweed of the Sargasso Sea, still affords the young eels the protection they need for survival.")

Galanopoulos also discusses "planetary collisions," such as Velikovsky's theory that a wandering comet destroyed Atlantis, and after dismissing all other candidates, he says, "The solution, then, of the Atlantis enigma, must be scientific, logical, and consistent. Is such a solution possible?" Before we reach Galanopoulos's answer—which is, of course, Santorini—we must learn about the "geophysical and archaeological aspects," the workings of the earth.

We are given a full tour of the Cycladean island (called "Santorin" by Galanopoulos), followed by an essay on its volcanic history. (Galanopoulos is a seismologist.) He compares the fifteenth-century B.C. Santorini eruption with that of Krakatau (he spells it the old way, Krakatoa), saying that the Indonesian caldera is only eight square miles in surface area, compared to the thirty-two square miles of Santorini, and quotes Hungarian volcanologist Peter Hédervári, who has calculated that the thermal energy produced by Santorini was three times greater than that produced by Krakatau. Comparing the Krakatau eruption and the Chilean earthquake tsunami of 1960 with Santorini, he is able to calculate that "there cannot be a shadow of a doubt that the Santorin eruption was truly prodigious in scale," then quotes his colleague Spyridon Marinatos, who "believes that the coastal settlements of Crete were destroyed by the tsunami which followed the submersion of the central part of Santorin, at a date which he puts at about 1520 B.C."

The commotion raised by the declaration that the Lost Continent had actually been found led to an unprecedented outpouring of Atlantis articles in the popular press. For example, John Lear, in the *Saturday Review,* published "The Volcano That Shaped the Western World" in November 1966. After almost two full pages of quoting Plato (a most unusual element in an eight-page magazine article), Lear launches into a full-scale vindication of Galanopoulos's theories about Atlantis having been Thera. He actually visited Galanopoulos in Greece, and listened to him discourse on the validity of the conclusions of Ninkovich and Heezen regarding the tephra deposits on the floor of the Aegean (see p. 159). Lear then quotes Ninkovich and Heezen at even greater length than he quotes Plato, and writes, "However the still debated details may come to be sorted out in the end, there cannot now be any doubt at all that the Santorini volcano, through its effects on the sensitive and gifted Minoans, was a major force in bringing about the Golden Age of Greece and hence shaping the whole of western culture." Lear also realizes that "if the central plain that Plato said was part of Atlantis was as big as Plato said it was, Atlantis would never fit into the Mediterranean, let alone the Aegean," but this is only a minor discrepancy to Professor Galanopoulos, who told Lear that "the exaggeration of the size of the island which vanished in the sea, and in the time of its occurrence, is quite a usual process due to eleven centuries which lapsed from the time of the collapse up to the epoch of Plato."*

He then "proves" that Galanopoulos is correct by citing various (unidentified) Egyptian texts in which the destruction of Upper Egypt is described in "sacred Egyptian writings of that period [that] tell of a time of prolonged darkness, thunder, flood, plague, and days when the sun was 'in the sky like the moon.' " The Egyptians bemoan the disappearance of their Minoan supplies: "What shall we do for cedar for our mummies, with the produce of which priests are buried, and with the oil of which chiefs are embalmed as far as

---

* Lear explains Galanopoulos's numerical revisions by saying, "From the scholarly point of view, this may seem an inexcusably arbitrary exercise. But the professor pointed out to me that the same sort of error must be compensated for today whenever an Englishman and an American talk in terms of billions. The American means a thousand millions, but the Briton means a million millions. The ancient Greeks had had similar troubles in reading the glyphs of Egypt."

Keftiu?" (By this time, he has identified Keftiu as Crete.) Because "the Biblical name for Crete was Caphtor," writes Lear, "and the Cretans were called Philistines," the Book of Amos seems to relate that the Minoans were driven from Crete at the same time that the Jews made their exodus from Egypt. (Amos 9:7 says, "Have not I brought up Israel out of the land of Egypt? and the Philistines from Caphtor, and the Syrians from Kir?") According to Galanopoulos, the explosion of Thera could have caused a tsunami that made the waters of the Nile Delta recede, thus permitting the safe passage of the escaping Israelites, while the returning waters drowned the pursuing Egyptians. When Lear's article was published, James Mavor was still optimistic about his fund-raising capabilities, and Lear quotes him as saying that he needed $100,000 for a first-rate expedition, which he intended to raise from the National Science Foundation or the Office of Naval Research. We know that shortly thereafter, Mavor's alliance with the Greeks deteriorated, and although he managed to write *Voyage to Atlantis,* his dreams of unearthing the Lost City—like the city itself—remained a fantasy.

In 1967, Emily Vermeule weighed in with "The Promise of Thera: A Bronze Age Pompeii" in the *Atlantic Monthly.* Vermeule summarized the archaeological history of Thera before introducing Spyridon Marinatos, who had published "The Volcanic Destruction of Minoan Crete" almost thirty years earlier. Although he obliquely suggested that there might be a connection between Thera and Plato's Atlantis, Marinatos was more interested in the destruction of the palaces in Crete and Santorini than he was in a vast island that sank into the sea. "In 1960," wrote Vermeule, "word began to get around that Professor Angelos Galanopoulos had found a new way to link Thera with Plato's myth of the Lost Atlantis." His "new way," of course, was the revised number scheme, where every figure that was supposed to be 1,000 was modified to a more manageable (and believable) 100, which brought Plato's story to the sixteenth century B.C., instead of the chronologically impossible 9000 B.C. She repeats his idea that the Exodus might have been affected by the destruction of Thera, with the waters parting because the ocean was flowing back into the magma chamber evacuated by the prodigious explosion of the island, and she also brings in Ninkovich and Heezen, whose cores showed that the explosion had blanketed the Aegean in volcanic ash. Vermeule tells how Mavor "spoke confidently of ample funds" and asked her to join his expedition.

Vermeule went to Santorini to work with her old friend Spyridon Marinatos, and also with James Mavor, "who was perhaps unprepared for being relegated so firmly to the middle background as he came out of the sea onto land." Ten days before the work was scheduled to begin, Mavor confessed that "he had been unable to get any backing at all—no ship, no submarine, no scientists, no equipment, no money." Marinatos took command, and from then on, it was his dig. He uncovered the first buildings, the wine jars and cooking utensils, and, later, the pictures of boxers, monkeys, antelopes, and lilies.

Emily Vermeule participated in the press conferences that followed the return of the Americans, to the accompaniment of headlines that cried LOST ATLANTIS FOUND and OCEANOGRAPHER DISCOVERS ATLANTIS, but, she wrote, "it was a slack and silly season." Marinatos continued to dig at Akrotiri until his death in 1974, and, after Knossos, it has become the most important of all Minoan sites, with wall paintings that surpassed even those of the great palaces of Crete. (It is the only "active" Minoan archaeological site; Knossos, Phaistos, Hagia Triada, and Zakros are now dormant tourist destinations, with their treasures on exhibition in the museums of Herakleion and Athens.)

Of Mavor's claims that he had found Atlantis, Marinatos said, "Attempts to connect the excavation with Atlantis are irresponsible." But Vermeule disagreed. She concluded her article with, "No one can be sorry that Professor Galanopoulos and Mr. Mavor, hunting Atlantis in the Aegean, focused attention on Thera again after so many years. It may even be true that when Thera sank under the sea with roaring and darkness it helped create one of the world's great myths of nostalgia."

Bruce Heezen, not known as a writer for popular magazines, joined the party. He wrote "A Time Clock for History" for the *Saturday Review* (December 6, 1969), in which he discussed the importance of using volcanic ash deposits as a dating device and, as an example, presented his theory (with Dragoslav Ninkovich) that "the Minoan civilization on Crete may have been wrecked by the same ash fall that buried Thera." In 1967, Marinatos, then inspector general for antiquities in Greece, convened the International Scientific Congress on the Volcano of Thera, inviting one hundred forty archaeologists, geologists, seismologists, oceanographers, and other scientists for an interdisciplinary discussion of the implications of Thera for historical studies, to be held at the Archaeological Society of Athens. Many of the scientists (including Heezen) had never visited Thera before, so after the meetings, Marinatos herded everyone aboard the 10,000-ton ship *Knossos* for a cruise. They visited Akrotiri, the site of Marinatos's spectacular finds; the volcanic outcrops in the caldera known as the Kameni Islands; and also Crete, to see the palace that provided such a fitting name for their ship. Putting these assorted scientists together on such an important site was profitable for their various studies, for they were able to discuss their ideas with people they would not ordinarily meet. The actual date of the eruption of Thera was a hotly debated subject, with estimates ranging from 1180 B.C. (archaeologist Leon Pomerance), 1520 B.C. (Marinatos), 1470 B.C. (J. V. Luce), and 1420 B.C. (Heezen). "The volcanic ash," wrote Heezen, "must be related to the pottery styles and the levels at which destruction of the buildings occurred if we are to ascertain whether the destruction of Crete occurred earlier than, contemporaneous with, or later than the ash fall from Thera. Only thus can we decide whether Crete was stricken by ashes, by tsunami, by earthquakes; only so can we say confidently whether there was one continuous ash fall, or several falls separated by hours or days, or several falls separated by many years." But in his article, Heezen had the good sense not to allude to Atlantis.

Cokie and Steven Roberts (identified as "a free-lance journalist and the chief of the New York Times Athens bureau") wrote "Atlantis Recaptured" for the New York Times Magazine of September 5, 1976. Having read Mavor's book (which was published nine years earlier), the Robertses decided to check out Thera for themselves. By this time, Marinatos was dead, so they visited with Christos Doumas, who had been Marinatos's lieutenant and was now director of the Thera excavations. They toured the excavations, marveling at the accomplishments of the archaeologists, which included the almost miraculous restoration of the frescoes. Although the Robertses present a concise picture of the dig at Akrotiri, their article hardly ever mentions Atlantis. The word appears in the title (but with no explanation of what "recaptured" might mean), and in an introductory passage in which the authors gaze out over the crater of Thera and "recall Plato's account of the lost island."

There appears to be no end to the possible explanations for Atlantis. Not only are people prepared to situate the Lost Continent in locations from Nigeria to Antarctica, but there are those who want to insert the disappearance of Atlantis into some other acknowledged event, such as the biblical flood or the explosion of the Santorini volcano. In 1992, a Swiss geoarchaeologist named Eberhard Zangger published a book called The Flood from Heaven, in which he argued that the story is actually an ancient Egyptian account of the Trojan War. If this sounds as unrealistic as The Lost Continent of Mu, it will be sobering to learn that Zangger's efforts in pursuit of this idea were supported by Stanford University and the German Archaeological Institute from 1984 to 1988. The Flood from Heaven is the story of Zangger's attempts to decipher the Atlantis legends using "modern science, legends, and ancient poetry."

Employing the complex tools of geoarchaeology—the geology of ancient sites—Zangger discovered an "unstratified floodplain deposit several feet thick" at Tiryns and also earthquakes that "could have caused a landslide and, once unstable and in motion, the mud was picked up by the stream and dumped at the first obstacle, the limestone knoll of Tiryns." Since the Athenians were at war with the Atlanteans at the time of this catastrophe, it follows that the home of the Atlanteans (Atlantis) must be the same as the home of the great enemy of Mycenaean Greece: the Trojans. Zangger believes that accounts of the conflict between Troy and Mycenae were passed down from the Egyptian priests of Saïs to Critias's great-grandfather, who passed it along to his descendants, who told it to Solon. The story of Atlantis, therefore, is an Egyptian interpretation of the Trojan War.

Zangger locates the Lost City in Anatolia, where the rich and luxurious city would probably have been Troy, not Athens. One of his more interesting (but inconclusive) statements is that the Greeks knew of *two* sets of Pillars of Hercules, one leading into the Mediterranean and the other into the Black Sea. This, of course, would have been the Dardanelles, but aside from a quote from the Roman poet Servius, who lived around 400 A.D. ("We pass through the Pillars of Hercules in the Black Sea as well as in Spain"), there is no reason to move Atlantis from one end of the Mediterranean to the other. Much more important is the realization that Troy was not destroyed by a natural catastrophe but was probably sacked and burned by the invaders. As Peter James says in *The Sunken Kingdom,* "An Atlantis that did not sink beneath the waves is no Atlantis at all."

To respond to the expected responses to his theory, Zangger includes a section entitled "Counterarguments and Shortcomings." Perhaps the most telling of these is his question about why so few of the descriptions of Troy match the characteristics of Atlantis, to which he responds that very few ancient texts can be taken literally "without any adjustments and interpretations," and although "Troy does not match the description of Atlantis in terms of date, location, size, and island character, it does fit virtually the whole of the rest of the story, at least as far as one can judge it, given the incompleteness of the archaeological record." Without a conformity of "date, location, size, and island character," I believe there is no agreement with the Atlantis legend. As L. Sprague de Camp wrote (in *Lost Continents*), "You cannot change all the details of Plato's story and still claim to have Plato's story. That is like saying the legendary King Arthur is 'really' Queen Cleopatra; all you have to do is to change Cleopatra's sex, nationality, period, temperament, moral character, and other details, and the resemblance becomes obvious."

In the foreword to Zangger's book, archaeologist Anthony Snodgrass

wrote that there are "those who believe that the Atlantis legend poses no problem because it is nothing but an imaginative fantasy of Plato's; and those (a
smaller group) who believe that there is a problem, but that they themselves
have already solved it." One of those who believe they have solved the problem
is Peter James, the British archaeologist who wrote *The Sunken Kingdom: The Atlantis Mystery Solved* (1995), in which he argues that Atlantis was actually located
in what is now Turkey, some thirty miles inland from the modern port of
Izmir. According to James, there was a lake on this site that once covered the
city of Sipylus (also known as Zippasla), which was later renamed Tantalus in
honor of the Anatolian king of the same name. The dried-up lake, says James,
is the site of Sipylus, the city that Pausanias said "disappeared into a chasm, and
water gushed out from a crack in the mountain, changing the chasm into Lake
Saloe: you could see the ruins of the city in the lake until the torrent covered
up even the ruins."*

In order to get the story of Sipylus to conform to the Atlantis legend, however, James has to perform some adroit reinterpretations of the basic tenets of
Plato's story, such as deciding that even though Solon said he heard the story
in Egypt, he really meant Anatolia. (Solon is known to have visited Egypt, but
the story of his visit to Croesus, king of Lydia [Anatolia], might be apocryphal.)
But, says James, "it now seems clear that Plato did have a source for the legend
of Atlantis. He freely embellished it, but the core of the story was not of his
own creation. It came from Lydia, where the memory of the sunken kingdom
of Tantalus was preserved until Roman times." The proof of this supposition,
however, "will only come from excavation. . . . We will then also learn
whether it really succumbed to an earthquake as Pausanias, Pliny, and others
describe. The site holds extraordinary promise . . . as the prototype of Plato's
Atlantean royal city."†

In the *Critias*, Plato tells us that the gods divided up the whole earth and
gave Poseidon the island of Atlantis. On this island he found Cleito, the earth-
born daughter of Evenor and his wife Leucippe, and because "she was of mar-

---

* In a footnote to this passage, Peter Levi, the translator of the Penguin Pausanias, wrote, "Pausanias
apparently lived near Mount Sipylos in Asia Minor, just north of Izmir. The city that was swallowed up
seems to have been a popular myth."

† As further "proof" of his thesis, James includes an appendix, entitled "The Bull Cult of Atlantis," in
which he attempts to correlate the bull games of Crete with the bull sacrifices described by Plato (see
p. 98). Unfortunately, rather than explaining anything, he draws a weak parallel between the bull cults
of Troy (as shown on a single Roman coin, where the images are far from distinct) and those of Atlantis,
and concludes (with nothing but supposition to support his claim) "that the 'Atlantean' custom
reported by Plato may be another genuine relic of the civilization of ancient Sipylus."

riageable age when her father and mother died, and Poseidon was attracted by her and had intercourse with her . . . he begot five pairs of male twins, brought them up, and divided the island of Atlantis into ten parts which he divided between them. . . . The eldest, the King, he gave a name from which the whole island and surrounding ocean took their designation of 'Atlantic,' deriving it from Atlas, the first king."

Peter James says that the names of Tantalus and Atlas were derived from the same source—the Greek root *tlaō,* which means "I bear" or "I endure"— and are therefore "mythological equivalents," which means that one can be substituted for the other whenever it happens to be convenient, as in, "If Atlas was the equivalent of Tantalus, then the origin of Atlantis may be found in the kingdom of Tantalus."

James has researched and walked over the area he discusses, but he has not dug there, because he has not received permission from the Turkish authorities. Nevertheless, he is convinced that his readings prove conclusively that the story of the sunken city is not mere folklore (as J. G. Frazer and other scholars believed) but, rather, "the centre of a historically attested and, for a short time, extremely powerful Bronze Age kingdom."*

There is no question that somewhere around 1500 B.C. there was a gigantic volcanic explosion that destroyed most of the island of Thera and caused massive disturbances, including deadly tsunamis. But Plato's description of the downfall of Atlantis ("But afterward there occurred violent earthquakes and floods, and in a single day and night of misfortune all your warlike men in a body sank into the earth, and the island of Atlantis in like manner disappeared in the depths of the sea") is not a very good description of the explosion of Thera and the subsequent devastation in Crete. Thera largely disappeared, but the royal city of Knossos remained somewhat damaged but certainly above sea level, and even above ground.

Without some rather imaginative bending of the facts, there is simply no way to equate the story of the eruption of the volcano at Thera and the collapse of the Minoan civilization with the story of Atlantis. Angelos Galanopoulos tried to insert an assortment of disparate data into the Atlantis puzzle, but there are just too many pieces that do not fit. Based on his readings of Galanopoulos, James Mavor embarked on an expedition to "Atlantis," fully

* In a review of James's book in the December 8, 1995, *Times Literary Supplement,* Nigel Spivey said, "It is a depressing index of authorial myopia that nearly all the objections raised by James against the Thera-Atlantis identification apply to his own hypothesis. The archaeological support for a kingdom of Tantalus is pathetically slight."

prepared to believe. (In his book, he wrote, "My excursions to Thera have convinced me that the Galanopoulos model of the origins of the Atlantean myth must of necessity anticipate actual physical findings. . . .") The book describing his adventures in Crete and Santorini is misleadingly called *Voyage to Atlantis,* and in the book, he claims to have "solved the mystery." But thirty years after Mavor's book was published, only a dedicated minority believes that Atlantis was found in Santorini.

Mavor's book was reviewed in 1969 by Moses I. Finley, a renowned ancient social historian at Cambridge and the author of *The Ancient Greeks, Early Greece: The Bronze and Archaic Ages,* and *Aspects of Antiquity.* Finley believes that "the Atlantis myth was altogether a Platonic invention. It was left to the modern world to treat it as garbled history." Insofar as the comparison with Krakatau is concerned, he says, "I note that Krakatoa did not destroy Java or Sumatra. Agriculture was not seriously hindered by thin ash deposits; recovery in such situations is rapid, except at the explosive center with its thirty-meter deposits. . . . Many parts of Crete were severely damaged by earthquake about 1700 B.C., but the catastrophe was followed not only by immediate rebuilding but also by further growth and expanded resettlement. The Galanopoulos-Mavor doctrine makes an exception of 1450–1400 Crete without bothering to explain why there should have been an exception. . . ."

As for Galanopoulos's rearrangement of numbers and geography, he says:

> All this tinkering with the evidence is nothing compared with the sleight of hand by which Atlantis is dragged from Platonic myth to history, from the Atlantic Ocean to a small island in the Aegean. 1450 B.C. is about 900 years, not 9,000, before the time of Solon. Very easy, says Galanopoulos: either Solon or his Egyptian informants misread the hieroglyphic numerals by a multiple of ten (and so too with the other large numbers in the Platonic tale). The Pillars of Heracles are not the Straits of Gibraltar, but the two promontories at the southern end of the Greek peninsula. Never mind that for every Greek the Pillars of Heracles meant Gibraltar and nothing else, or that Galanopoulos cannot adduce a single text for his alternative.

Probably because of its multilayered character as a myth, a historical reality, and an archaeological dig, Atlantis seems to attract polymaths. Ignatius Donnelly was an urban developer, a politician, a novelist, and a student of volcanology and Shakespeare; Dr. David Zink lists his credentials as "historian, explorer, [and] lecturer"; and Dr. Charles Pellegrino describes himself as an "astrobiologist/paleontologist." He traveled to the Aegean in 1988, interviewed

Christos Doumas at Akrotiri, and in 1991 published *Unearthing Atlantis,* wherein he presents the theory that the mythological Atlantis was really Thera, whose civilization was destroyed by an earthquake and a tidal wave. (He chooses 1628 B.C. as the actual date, but except for some generalizations about Irish peat bogs, the Greenland ice cap, and California pine trees, we are not told how he arrived at that specific year.) For his conclusions, Pellegrino depends largely on the theories of Spyridon Marinatos, who had been dead for fourteen years by the time Pellegrino got to Santorini. Since Pellegrino never actually spoke to the Greek archaeologist, he made up their conversations. "These scenes," wrote Pellegrino, "while they must in a strict sense be considered fictional, are true to his thoughts, philosophies, and published works." He also said:

> Atlantis, some will argue, was a large mountainous continent somewhere in the Atlantic Ocean. But the Atlantis of our dreams and our myths was almost certainly the lost civilization of Minoan Crete. . . . During the summer of 1650 B.C., the city's tall, white buildings still gleamed under the clear hot sky, and in the words of Plato, there grew on the island every variety of plant that is pleasant to the eye and good for food. In the center of the island there stood a volcanic peak. Its long quiet sleep had lasted for thousands of years, and might have lasted for tens of thousands more. But not forever.

For convenience' sake, however, he has Plato move Atlantis outside the Pillars of Hercules:

> Plato's Atlantis was not just an island civilization in the eastern Mediterranean Sea. The Mediterranean was too small, too close to home, too familiar. His audience might not have been impressed by anything so close at hand, and therefore less inclined to read about it. So the island culture swelled to continental gigantism, and was moved somewhere mysterious and very far away, on the other side of Gibraltar, in the uncharted and seemingly endless reaches of the Atlantic Ocean.

Pellegrino—like every Atlantean theorist before him except Cayce, quotes at length from Plato's original description, but because he is so intent upon proving his case, he often gives the dialogues an additional twist. For example, to prove that Atlantis was really Thera, he cites the famous "bull-leaping" murals at Knossos, and then, to confirm that there is a "spine-chilling fidelity [to] Plato's description of a lost civilization," he quotes this passage from Plato:

There were bulls who had the range of the temple of Poseidon; and the ten kings, being left alone in the temple, after they had offered prayers to the god they thought might capture the victim which was acceptable to him, hunted the bulls without weapons, but with staves and nooses; and the bull which they caught they led up to the pillar.

In the *Critias,* the story continues with the bull being sacrificed and a clot of its blood being mixed into the wine, which they drink from golden cups. Pellegrino now cites the famous Vapheio cups—which were almost certainly of Minoan manufacture, but were not found on Crete—as proof that Plato was actually referring to Crete when he described Atlantis. Without question, these cups show a scene very close to the one described by Plato; bulls are shown being captured "without weapons, but with staves and nooses." There is nothing in the Knossos frescoes, however, that relates to bull *sacrifice,* which is the intended outcome of the capture shown in the cups and is also described in the *Critias.*

Pellegrino makes a completely convincing case for the volcanic destruction of Thera, and hardly any case at all for the identification of Thera with Atlantis. Because Marinatos is not available to defend himself, Pellegrino assigns to him the theory that Thera was actually Atlantis. As in: "It was possible, Marinatos decided, that the shape of Thera was one of several grains of truth in Plato's tale. No other island in or near the Mediterranean exhibited Thera's bull's-eye configuration." Did Marinatos really "decide" that? His 1939 discussion of the volcanic destruction of Minoan Crete does not contain a single mention of Atlantis, and in a *National Geographic* article written shortly before his death, he wrote, "Recently, writers have speculated that the explosion of the island of Thera inspired the legend of Atlantis. . . . But legends of a sunken landmass existed throughout the ancient world, and many antedate the explosion of Thera. . . . This legend may well be the common property of many ancient peoples—as is the tradition of a mighty flood."

In *Unearthing Atlantis,* we read of Captain Jacques-Yves Cousteau's 1976 visit to Santorini in which he descended in the "diving saucer." Pellegrino writes that "Cousteau never did find the bottom," but two pages later, we learn that he "found no hint of artifacts from an ancient civilization, but there were artifacts aplenty from our own time: beer cans, soda bottles, the odd sneaker." (In fact, Cousteau says he reached the bottom at about 200 meters.) According to *A la recherche de L'Atlantide* (Searching for Atlantis), Cousteau's divers first descended in diving suits to a "strange underwater world where . . . the green water is eternally stagnant, filled with sulfur and iron sulfate. . . . We cannot see the bottom. We are following the side of the caldera, which abruptly drops into the sea and disappears in the mysterious depths." "In some places," says diver Frédéric Dumas, "the rocks appear to be rusted." They decide to take the diving saucer into the caldera.

Jacques Cousteau and Albert Falco squeezed into the tight interior of the *soucoupe plongéante* and descended into "what was once the heart of a volcano bursting with boiling lava. . . . If by some miracle there were vestiges of Atlantis at the bottom of this crater, we surely would have no chance of finding them; the debris of 35 centuries would have buried them." They see coral, algae, and some sponges, and then, along with some other fishes, they spot a school of *regalacs,* "extremely rare very-deep-water fishes called 'king of the herrings' by the ancient authors. . . . Their long serpentine bodies are laterally flattened, and covered with little brown spots. The odd dorsal fin looks like a Japanese fan. On its head there are plumes made of fin spines, and under the body are two long, threadlike ventral fins. Their very long dorsal fin extends from the nape to the tail."*

Some of Pellegrino's other observations are not supported by any known evidence, such as his description of "tall white buildings," or his picture caption that says, "Some of the homes were even equipped with showers." It appears that he decided to visit Santorini (he claims to have been inspired by oceanographer Robert Ballard during a dive on the submersible *Alvin*) because he suspected that it had something to do with the Lost City of Atlantis. Once he became involved with Christos Doumas (and the shade of Spyridon Marinatos) at Akrotiri, he eschewed Atlantis and concentrated instead on the disappearance of Thera. Although his book is called *Unearthing Atlantis,* it touches only tangentially on the Atlantis myth.

Some three years after the appearance of *Unearthing Atlantis,* Pellegrino produced *Return to Sodom and Gomorrah,* a book that purports to "solve the Bible's ancient mysteries through archaeological discovery." Much of this book does not concern Atlantis (or Thera, for that matter), but Spyridon and Nanno Marinatos play critical roles in Pellegrino's scenario. Harold Edgerton appears, scanning the floor of the Aegean to demonstrate that the explosion of Thera

---

* From this description, there seems to be no question that the divers saw a school of oarfish, *Regalecus glesne.* The oarfish is actually one of the rarest and most mysterious fishes in the world, and because of its length (as long as twenty-five feet) and the bright red "plumes" on its head, it has been held responsible for many "sea serpent" sightings. This appears to be a rare record for the Mediterranean, and the first case I know of where they are described as traveling in schools.

had done more than dig out a volcanic blowhole. It had torn up the entire eastern Mediterranean. There were cracks in the earth radiating out from the island. One of them was more than a hundred miles long. The sound of the thing must have permanently deafened people three hundred miles away, and any surviving with their hearing intact would have heard it again and again, as the noise shot around the world sixteen times.

All of this is conjecture, since Edgerton never scanned the floor of the Aegean (except perhaps at Helice, about which more later), and the cracks in the earth and the deafened people—not to mention a sound that travels around the world sixteen times—are figments of Pellegrino's imagination. According to Pellegrino, the destruction of Thera meant that the Minoan civilization was cut short, and therefore did not have the opportunity to develop television or interstellar travel. Pellegrino says that Marinatos "could not avoid such thoughts" as he pondered a polished quartz lens that had been found at Knossos. (This lens was evidently used to magnify the work surface of the seal-stones so meticulously carved by Minoan craftsmen, and probably had little to do with television.) Again, Pellegrino puts words into the mouth of Marinatos, as he has him lament, "My poor Minoans. If only they had not been living in the wrong corner of the wrong sea when the mountain exploded, the fires roared, the Earth darkened, [and] the waters were poisoned."

Long after Marinatos's untimely death, says Pellegrino, "the pieces started fitting together." Theran ash was discovered in the Nile Delta, the Greenland ice cap showed evidence of the round-the-world ashfall from Santorini, and tree rings in California bristlecone pines and preserved oak trees in Irish peat bogs narrowed the date of the explosion to around 1628 B.C. (It took three years and the publication of another book before Pellegrino provided the information on which he based the very precise date that he uses in *Unearthing Atlantis*.) *Sodom and Gomorrah* contains more conjecture than *Unearthing Atlantis*. For example, Pellegrino writes, "The archaeological evidence suggests, as Plato had said, that some Minoan architects survived the Theran upheaval." It is more than difficult to respond to such an irresponsible statement; Plato never said anything at all about the Minoans (Arthur Evans invented the term two thousand years after Plato died), let alone that some of their "architects survived the Theran upheaval." Over and over, Pellegrino describes "events" that are grounded only in his imaginings. He writes, "When the first Greek and Egyptian ships sailed into the still-smoldering Thera Lagoon, their crews would not have guessed that a mountain had gone up into the atmosphere. To them, a mountain and most of an island were simply missing and presumed sunk at sea, like a lost Atlantis." But Marinatos wrote that while the Egyptians were known trading partners of the Cretans, they "must have learned of an island being submerged and this was Thera, but being so small and insignificant they did not know of it." Pellegrino ties the eruption of Thera to the Plagues of Egypt in Exodus but has nothing whatever to do with Atlantis. Once again, Pellegrino "proves" that Thera erupted with a colossal bang, but with the exception of some gratuitous references to the Lost Continent, he comes no closer than he did the first time to demonstrating that this explosion had anything to do with Plato's Atlantis.

WAS MINOAN CRETE ATLANTIS?

WHAT WAS THIS "Minoan" civilization that so many are so anxious to identify with Atlantis? On the island of Crete, some twenty-five centuries ago, there flourished an extraordinary culture the likes of which had never been seen before. It was rich beyond imagining, creative, artistic, influential, and enormously successful. Its architects designed splendid palaces of great size and complexity; its artists painted the walls with gorgeous frescoes; its craftsmen formed exquisite pottery; its sailors crossed the Aegean to trade with neighboring kingdoms. As unexpectedly and suddenly as it appeared, it disappeared. This civilization was named "Minoan" for King Minos* by Arthur Evans, the archaeologist who excavated the ruins on Crete at the turn of the twentieth

---

* In Greek mythology, Minos was the son of Zeus and Europa, king and legislator of the island of Crete, about which Homer wrote:

> One of the great islands of the world
> in midsea, in the winedark sea, is Krete:
> spacious and rich and populous, with ninety
> cities and a mingling of tongues.
> Akhaians there are found, along with Kretan
> hillmen of the old stock, and Kydonians,
> Dorians in three blood-lines, Pelasgians—
> and one among the ninety towns is Knossos.
> Here lived King Minos whom great Zeus received
> every ninth year in private council.

century. The Minoans appeared mysteriously around 2500 B.C., and approximately a thousand years later disappeared completely.

The moment when human beings colonized Crete is not known, but it is believed that the first settlers were farmers who arrived some eight thousand years ago, by ship from unknown locations to the east. They used stone tools, but obsidian artifacts have also been found, indicating some sort of interaction with the volcanic islands of the Cyclades, perhaps Melos. (Crete itself is a nonvolcanic island, but it has a history of periodic earthquakes.) There is also some indication that there was contact with seafaring Egyptians of the First Dynasty, who were known to have extended their conquests as far as Palestine. They brought with them domestic animals such as cattle, sheep, and goats. These Neolithic agriculturalists lived in mud-brick houses, perhaps supported by beams hewn from trees, and we assume—at least from the lack of evidence—that they had not developed pottery-making. Later on, perhaps around 3000 B.C., they were making ceramic vases, storage jars, and drinking cups, which were often burnished and decorated. Indeed, the changes in pottery styles afford us the opportunity to identify the transition from the Neolithic to the Bronze Age, when the settlers were making vase-shaped bowls on high pedestals—the smaller ones for drinking, and the larger ones presumably for food. It was during this period that jugs with spouts also appeared, the design based on imports from Anatolia or maybe even from Libya. They buried their dead in circular tombs, and although Sinclair Hood (in his 1971 study, *The Minoans*) says that people "always tended to build tombs to resemble houses," the early Cretans lived in squared-off houses, which suggests that "the custom of collective burial in circular tombs was evidently brought to Crete by immigrants or invaders from some region where round huts had been traditional," such as Egypt.

The first-known sculptures of human beings in the round began to appear around 25,000 B.C. One of the earliest of these is the "Venus of Willendorf," a tiny fertility figure found in a cave in Austria. During the period from 17,000 to 9000 B.C., all of Europe, from Russia to the Pyrenees, seems to have experienced a flourishing of cave painting. This period is usually referred to as the "Magdalenian," after La Madeleine cave in the Dordogne. A few Ice Age artifacts, such as carved antler and bone implements, have been dated from approximately 12,000 B.C. Around 8000 B.C., there was a considerable settlement at Jericho in southern Palestine, and excavations in the early 1960s in Turkey revealed the existence of a densely populated settlement at Çatal Hüyük, characterized by mud-walled houses and fertility symbols in the form of bull's heads. Çatal

Hüyük dates from around 5600 B.C.; the dates for the Archaic period of Egyptian art are about 3200 to 2185 B.C. (Coincidentally, the earliest known illustration of an erupting volcano was found on a wall at Çatal Hüyük, as shown by James Mellaart 1967.)

Plato tells us unequivocally that "the citizens whose laws and whose finest achievements I will now briefly describe to you therefore lived nine thousand years ago. . . ." Nine thousand years before Plato was approximately 9500 B.C., and there is no archaeological evidence anywhere to suggest that humans of that time were creating anything but skin clothing, throwing sticks, and arrowheads. In a few locations in France and southern Spain, they were commemorating their accomplishments with surprisingly sophisticated cave paintings. The best-known of these are in Altamira in Spain, Lascaux in southern France, and the recently discovered, spectacular cave named for its discoverer, Jean-Marie Chauvet, at Vallon-Pont-d'Arc (also in southern France), which is believed to date from 30,000 B.C.

On the subject of Plato's description of the advanced civilization of Atlantis, Arthur C. Clarke wrote (in *The Challenge of the Sea*, 1966) that "hundreds of books have been written, and men have devoted their entire lives to unraveling the truth about Atlantis. Unfortunately, most of the literature on the subject is not merely worthless—it is misleading nonsense produced by cranks. . . . Eleven thousand years is a very long time, but there were highly cultured races of mankind twenty or thirty thousand years ago, as is proved by the beautiful cave paintings that have been found in Spain and France."

In an essay published in 1996, Stephen Jay Gould suggests that these artistic accomplishments should not surprise us; the painters are, after all, our ancestors, and do not differ in any substantive way from us—or from Michelangelo or Picasso, for that matter. Earlier students of Paleolithic cave painting, such as Abbé Henri Breuil and André Leroi-Gourhan, assumed that there had to be some sort of a chronological progression from the primitive to the sophisticated, and the fact that the paintings were so old meant that they had to be rudimentary. Gould wrote: "The Cro-Magnon cave painters are us—so why should their mental capacity differ from ours? We don't regard Plato or King Tut as dumb, even though they lived a long time ago." It therefore seems well within the realm of possibility that humans built the fabulous Atlantis that Plato said was built nine thousand years earlier; the only thing missing is a single shred of physical evidence that they did so.*

---

* Gould argues that since Cro-Magnon men were the same as us, there is no reason why their artists would not be capable of producing cave-wall masterpieces. The existence of the paintings at Lascaux and Chauvet certainly bears this out, but it does not mean that thirty thousand years ago men should also

Throughout the Cyclades, from about the third millennium B.C., small marble statues of women (and, occasionally, men) began to appear. The marble, it is believed, was quarried on the islands of Paros and Naxos. In most cases, the naked female figures had their arms crossed over their abdomen, and they are characterized by an elongated neck, an oval face, and a prominent nasal ridge. In his study *The Cyclades in the Bronze Age*, R. L. N. Barber wrote that these figures were "the most attractive of Cycladic products in the Early Bronze Age . . . and continue to be admired as works of art." They were stylistically advanced for the Neolithic period in which they were made (Sinclair Hood describes one white marble figurine from Knossos as "an outstanding experiment in naturalism"), but even so, they clearly demonstrate the level of artistic achievement of Crete and the Cyclades around 2000 B.C. If Aegean craftsmen of 2000 B.C. were fashioning simple but elegant idols, what justification can there possibly be for an interpretation of Plato that suggests that a civilization predating them by seven thousand years was making "a temple of Poseidon himself, a stade in length, three hundred feet wide . . . covered all over with silver, except for the figures on the pediment, which were covered with gold"?

FIVE THOUSAND YEARS AGO, Europeans lived in the Bronze Age, which means that their predominant metal was that alloy of copper and tin. Around 3000 B.C., in one of the greatest revolutions in history, certain Greeks began to replace their stone adzes, axes, and chisels with tools of bronze, an alloy of copper and tin that is much stronger than stone and better able to hold an edge. Metalworking is believed to have been introduced from the East, perhaps from Palestine, and by the third millennium B.C., the inhabitants of Crete and the Cyclades were making bronze tools. (Although the Greek poet Homer was writing about events that occurred before or during the eighth century B.C., he describes warriors with obsolete bronze weapons and helmets decorated with boar's tusks, which actually went out of use before the end of the Bronze Age.) The introduction of iron marked the end of the Bronze Age. Writing took the form of hieroglyphics or cuneiform inscriptions on clay tablets; writing on papyrus was not developed by the Egyptians until around 2500 B.C.

In *The Quest for Theseus,* Anne Ward includes a chapter called "Bronze Age

have been building steam engines or computers. Early artistic endeavor required genius—just as its later counterparts did—but technology (including architecture) needs the progressive, interdependent development of techniques and materials before it can advance.

Crete," in which she discusses life as it was lived during the period before the flowering of the Minoan civilization. She concedes that it is difficult to reconstruct a thirty-five-hundred-year-old culture that left no written records, but examining the meager remains of the art, architecture, and artifacts, she presses on:

> The houses, mostly mudbrick, were sometimes quite well designed individually, but there was no sign of anything that remotely resembled town planning. A haphazard cluster of homes was grouped together in a completely random arrangement, a characteristic which was to persist and become a dominant feature of even the most sophisticated later palaces. . . . The people who lived in these villages were small and slender with dark eyes and hair, typical of the long-skulled Mediterranean type. Human remains are both scarce and fragmentary, but there are signs that towards the end of the Early Bronze Age a new element arrived in Crete. This new people, taller and shorter-skulled, infiltrated in small groups along the coastline with no apparent violence. Indeed, one of the most striking features of Cretan Bronze Age history is the total absence of threat, internal or external, which was probably a powerful contributing factor to the Cretans' cheerful, inquisitive and gregarious nature, not to mention the rapid development of their peaceful evolution.

The Paleolithic period, sometimes referred to as "prehistorical," is usually believed to have ended around 4000 B.C., when the era we call the Neolithic began. The dates, of course, are only conjectural, but the Babylonians and the Sumerians lived in the period from approximately 3500 to 3000 B.C., and the First and Second dynasties of Egypt occurred around 2800 B.C. Zoser, the king of the Fourth Egyptian Dynasty, ruled from 2780 to 2720 B.C., and the great pyramids were built by Cheops, the king of the Fourth Dynasty who ruled from c. 2700 to 2675 B.C. The "Dynasty of the Pharaohs" lasted for almost two thousand years, from 2200 B.C. to 525 B.C., during which time the Egyptians developed hieroglyphic pictograms, and the Minoans in Crete invented the primitive Greek alphabet. Between 1500 and 1000 B.C., Moses is said to have received the Ten Commandments on Mount Sinai. Around 1020 B.C., Saul became the first king of Israel, and was defeated by the Philistines in 1002 B.C. King David succeeded him, and ascended to the throne of the Kingdom of Judah and Israel around the year 1000 B.C., and he was succeeded by his son Solomon in 960. The Neolithic settlements in Crete are dated between 3000 and 2500 B.C., and we believe that the snake and bull were worshiped by the Minoans in Crete at about the same time (2500 to 2000 B.C.) that the Egyptians believed in Isis and Osiris, deities in the cult of resurrection from the dead. Around 1900 B.C., the first palace of Minos was built at Knossos in Crete, and archaeological evidence has revealed that the Minoans had ventilation systems in their multilevel dwellings, as well as bathrooms with running water. The resurrected murals on the walls of Knossos also show that religious rites took place at this time, often associated with a cult of bull worship. As J. L. Caskey, an American archaeologist, wrote, "Human life and society blossomed at the palaces, where, as many have remarked, elegance and delicacy reached levels that had been quite unknown before and were scarcely to be seen again in Europe for three thousand years."

Unlike the contemporaneous Egyptians of the Early and Middle kingdoms, who left answers in the form of hieroglyphic inscriptions, poems, and chronicles, the inhabitants of Crete left only the remains of mysterious edifices, and unanswered, tantalizing questions. Who built the great palace at Knossos, with its gracefully tapered columns, its labyrinthine corridors, its "bull-dancing" frescoes, its wasp-waisted courtesans? Who was the architect of this splendid palace, whose innovations were barely matched by the more "advanced" civilizations of Egypt, Sumer, and the Indus Valley? What happened to annihilate the civilization that had arisen (and so dramatically fallen) on this isolated island in the middle of the Mediterranean? And what does Crete have to do with Atlantis?

CRETE IS the largest of the Greek islands, 152 miles long and 35 miles across at its widest point. There is a mountain ridge that runs nearly the length of the island on its east-west axis. By 1500 B.C., Crete had become the dominant sea power in the eastern and central Mediterranean: a seat of high civilization, with commodious palaces, fine craftsmanship, and writing. It was the first to boast such accomplishments in Europe—the fact that it occurred on an island made it even more extraordinary—and later, the mainland Greeks adapted the Cretan civilization to develop their own.

Among the first excavators to visit the hard, dry soil of Crete was the German businessman Heinrich Schliemann (1822–1890), one of the most celebrated archaeologists of all time. After making his fortune in international trade, Schliemann "retired" to pursue his passion for archaeology. He was an astonishing polyglot, and in addition to his native German, he taught himself English, French, Dutch, Spanish, Italian, Portuguese, Swedish, Polish, Russian, and Greek, ancient and modern. (Of his ancient Greek—which he

HEINRICH SCHLIEMANN BELIEVED that the *Iliad* and the *Odyssey* were true, and, accordingly, looked for the fabled city of Troy where Homer said it was—and found it.

claimed to have mastered in three months—he commented, "I have thrown myself so wholly into the study of Plato that, if he were to receive a letter from me six weeks hence, he would be bound to understand it.") There being no other way to accomplish it, the brilliant, eccentric Schliemann also taught himself archaeology.

The idea that Troy was to be found under the hill of Hissarlik did not originate with Schliemann. It had been proposed some fifty years earlier by a man named Charles MacLaren, who wrote a book about it in 1822—the year Schliemann was born. MacLaren's ideas (published in *A Dissertation on the Topography of the Plains of Troy*) were theoretical and literary, and not at all archeological. Because he believed that Homer's *Iliad* and *Odyssey* were fact rather than poetic legends, Schliemann dug for Troy where he believed Homer (and MacLaren) had located it, in what is now western Turkey. Others felt that it had been located on the site of a village called Bunarbashi, but when Schliemann tried to run around it—as Achilles had done while chasing Hector—he found that it was impossible because the village was situated at the foot of a ridge. He dug instead at Hissarlik, close enough to the coast so that the Homeric heroes could travel back and forth several times daily. In 1872, he confounded the skeptics by finding stone walls, which he described as "six feet thick and of most wonderful construction," and beneath the first layer, more walls. Reasoning that Troy would be at the bottom, he and his crew of one hundred twenty Turkish workers dug ruthlessly, destroying almost everything in their path. (In his haste to get to the bottom, and thus to the earliest settlement, Schliemann raced past the actual Troy, which later archaeologists would identify.) By the following year, having cleared away and destroyed a mountain of invaluable stratigraphic and archaeological evidence, Schliemann hit pay dirt. In the wall of a building he had already designated as Priam's palace, he found a spectacular trove of golden objects: elaborately wrought necklaces and earrings, diadems, cups, ceremonial drinking vessels, weapons, shields—in all, more than ten thousand items. He and his Greek wife Sophia packed the stuff up and smuggled it to his house in Athens, where he kept it on prominent display.* Naturally, he believed that these items dated from the Trojan War (c. 1190 B.C.), but later scholars proved that their date was almost a thousand years earlier.

Schliemann then proceeded to Mycenae, where, again against all expectations, he announced that he had found an even richer treasure: the tomb of King Agamemnon and his wife Clytemnestra. This time, he relied upon the writings of the Greek travel writer Pausanias, who had visited the area around 170 A.D. and had described what he saw there. "Still," he wrote, "there are parts of the ring-wall left, including the gate with the lions standing on it." The "Lion Gate" was visible to Schliemann some seventeen hundred years later, but where later writers had assumed that the graves of Agamemnon and his murdered friends would be found outside the walls of the citadel, Schliemann took Pausanias at his word and looked inside. (Pausanias wrote, "Clytemnestra and Aigisthos were buried a little further from the wall. They were not fit to lie inside, where Agamemnon and the men murdered with him are lying.") He found the graves, which contained another fabulous treasure, including gold breastplates and gold burial masks, one of which was of a bearded prince. Schliemann immediately cabled the king of Greece: "I have gazed upon the face of Agamemnon." They were indeed royal graves, but of richly dressed persons who had lived some four hundred years before Agamemnon, but it hardly mattered. As the pseudonymous C. W. Ceram (actually Kurt W. Marek, a German writer on subjects archaeological) wrote in *Gods, Graves, and Scholars:*

> The important thing was that Schliemann had taken a second great step into
> the lost world of prehistory. Again he had proved Homer's worth as historian.
> He had unearthed treasures—treasures in a strictly archaeological as well as
> material sense—which provided valuable insight into the matrix of our cul-

* Schliemann, who died in Naples in 1890, willed the treasure to his German homeland, and until World War II, it was on exhibit in Berlin's State Museum for Early History. The "Gold of Priam" was hidden for safekeeping when Soviet troops seized the sector of the city where the museum was located; but they apparently found it anyway, since it has now been learned that the treasure was in Moscow's Pushkin Museum for fifty years. Greece and Turkey claim ownership of the treasure (it is Greek in origin, but it was found on what is now Turkish soil), but a German unearthed it and the Russians have it, so its disposition is very much unresolved.

ture. "It is an entirely new and unexpected world," Schliemann wrote, "that I
am discovering in archaeology."*

Pumice from the Aegean island of Santorini was an important element in
the 1866–69 building of the Suez Canal, since this material, known as *pozzulana,*
was needed for the manufacture of water-resistant cement required for the
harbor installations. In 1866, only a few months after the building had commenced, the long-dormant volcano on the island erupted. Among the visitors
who came to observe the eruption was the French volcanologist Ferdinand
Fouqué, who wrote a classic paper on the eruption (*Santorini et ses éruptions*), and
when he interviewed some of the locals, he discovered that they had been col-
lecting small artifacts from the slopes of the volcano for years. He saw some
gold rings and learned that there were two tombs, long since plundered.
Under twenty-six feet of pumice, Fouqué encountered a crypt with a central
pillar made of blocks of lava, a human skeleton, blades made of obsidian, and
pottery shards that were decorated in a style that neither he nor anyone else
was able to identify. He concluded that a volcanic eruption of c. 2000 B.C. had
divided the island into two parts, now known as Thera and Therasia, but the
presence of the gold and potsherds suggested to him that there might be
something of interest buried under the pumice.

Because he was not an archaeologist, Fouqué asked the French Archaeological School at Athens to provide somebody who could perform proper
excavations. They sent Henri Mamet and Henri Gorceix, who dug under a
vineyard and discovered various rooms that contained pottery, tools, lamps,
and a quantity of stored food, including identifiable barley, rye, chickpeas, and
the bones of rabbits, sheep, goats, a dog, a cat, and a donkey. They also found
walls painted with designs of irises and lilies, but many of the paintings were
charred. Messrs. Mamet and Gorceix worried that the fragile walls of this
underground sanctuary would crumble, so they removed the pottery pieces,
which were eventually assembled into more than a hundred vases, decorated
in a completely unfamiliar style. During the last decade of the nineteenth century, a team of German archaeologists led by Baron Hiller von Gaertringen

---

* Schliemann's accomplishments, while indeed sensational and archaeologically significant, were often
exaggerated and glorified by Schliemann himself. In his 1995 *Schliemann of Troy: Treasure and Deceit,* David
Traill of the University of California at Davis revealed many of Schliemann's self-serving exaggerations
and, in some cases, outright fabrications. The specific details about the discovery of Troy and Mycenae—
almost all of it perpetuated by Schliemann—are often incorrect. Because this is not the place to quote
Traill's book and meticulous research, I have repeated the basic outline of Schliemann's accomplishments, with the disclaimer that they did not necessarily happen exactly as Schliemann said they did.

dug in the ruins of ancient Thera at Mesa Vouno (on Santorini), and also made some tentative trenches in the vicinity of Akrotiri.

The French findings on Akrotiri led Schliemann to believe that there might have been an Aegean civilization earlier than the Mycenaean, perhaps in Crete. He made one visit to the island but could not agree on the price of the land he wished to excavate, and left without turning a stone. (In those freebooting archaeological days, diggers often bought the land outright, so everything they found belonged to them.) When Arthur Evans met with Schliemann in Athens in 1883, he was less interested in the Gold of Troy than he was in Greek coins and seals. (Evans was curator of the Ashmolean Museum at Oxford from 1884 to 1909, and went on to become Extraordinary Professor of Prehistoric Archaeology in 1909.) He went to look for the coins and seals on Crete.

Like Schliemann, Arthur John Evans, born in 1851 in Hertfordshire, is credited with one of the most important archaeological discoveries of all time. But unlike Schliemann, who was self-taught, Evans was trained as an archaeologist, and he had already worked in Sicily and Britain. At the age of forty-three, Evans was lured to Crete because of his interest in Greek numismatics. The story is told that he was extremely nearsighted, and a reluctant wearer of glasses. He could see small objects held a few inches from his eyes in extraordinary detail, and the hieroglyphics on the sealstones from Crete were sharp and clear to him. In Crete, he found that nursing mothers wore these inscribed stones, now called *galopetras* ("milk stones"), around their necks to ensure the health of their babies. Evans bought five acres in Crete, and working with D. G. Hogarth and Duncan Mackenzie, on his own land he unearthed the fabulous palace of Knossos. The hill on which it lies turned out to be man-made; it consisted of an accumulation of building levels and occupation extending back some four thousand years before the palace. It was evident that Knossos was an important cultural capital, and because the intricate ground plan of the palace suggested the myth of the Labyrinth associated with the legendary King Minos, Evans bestowed the name "Minoan" on this sophisticated Bronze Age civilization.

In his *History of the Peloponnesian War,* Thucydides wrote, "The first person known to us by tradition as having established a navy is Minos. He made himself master of what is now the Hellenic sea, and ruled over the Cyclades, into most of which he sent the first colonies." Until Evans began his dig on Crete and unearthed a completely unexpected civilization, the tales of King Minos (and the associated legends of Theseus and the Minotaur) were assumed to be part of the rich tapestry of Greek mythology. "Evans promptly announced to the world," wrote Ceram, "that he had found the palace of Minos, son of Zeus, father of Ariadne and Phaedra, master of the Labyrinth, and of the terrible monster, the Minotaur, that it housed."

The name of Theseus is inextricably bound to the lore of Knossos. In the mythology of the Greeks, he was the son of Aethra and Aegeus, who had visited Aethra in the form of a bull. (Poseidon was also supposed to have visited Aethra on the night of the conception of Theseus, so his paternity is in doubt). His exploits, which are similar to those of Hercules, include the slaying of Procrustes (he of the bed) and his adventures on Crete. He volunteered to take the place of one of the young men who was assigned to bring tribute to Minos, but instead of offering himself up for sacrifice to the Minotaur, he set out to slaughter the half-man, half-bull. Ariadne, the daughter of King Minos, fell in love with him and gave him the ball of twine that he played out as he searched the Labyrinth for the Minotaur. Theseus killed the Minotaur, followed the string out of the Labyrinth, and headed for home with Ariadne and her sister Phaedra. He abandoned Ariadne on the island of Naxos, where she was consoled by Dionysus (Bacchus), who gave her a crown of seven stars which became a constellation after her death. In his haste to return home, Theseus forgot to change his sail from black to white, and his father, Aegeus, thinking he was dead, threw himself into the sea, which sea became known as the Aegean.

In *Man, Myth, and Monument,* classical scholar Marianne Nichols wrote that after Theseus had killed the Minotaur and was returning with its head to King Minos, "his patron Poseidon sent a great earthquake that destroyed the palace and its inhabitants, allowing only Theseus and Ariadne to escape unharmed." Even though this "earthquake" is not usually incorporated into the myth of Theseus, Nichols's mention of it adds a tantalizing note to the complex interweaving of the stories of Knossos and Atlantis.

Although the name of Arthur Evans is indelibly associated with the excavation of Knossos, he was not the first archaeologist to dig there. From December 1878 to February 1879, Minos Kalokairinos had made "soundings" at Kephala, in what would eventually be identified as the west wing of the palace of Knossos, and he had collected storage jars (*pithoi*) that he kept in his house and allowed various scholars to examine. In 1881, an American journalist named W. J. Stillman visited the site and reported to the Archaeological Institute of America that he had examined ancient walls made of gigantic blocks of stone, and that they might have been part of the mythological Labyrinth. Three months into the new century, on March 23, 1900, under Evans's nearsighted but watchful eye, the first shovelful of earth was turned at Kephala. It proved to be a triumph for Evans but nearly a disaster for archaeology. In *The Find of a Lifetime,* her biography of Evans, Sylvia Horwitz wrote:

> Evans, one of the pioneers in archaeology, was unfamiliar with all the modern skills of excavation. He did not know today's accepted techniques of making a deep cut through all the strata from the surface down to virgin soil. Of clearing stratum by stratum horizontally. Of leaving standing sections at frequent intervals from the surface down to serve as "control points," whereby one could relate structures or disturbances to their proper strata.

By the second day of his excavations at Knossos, Evans's workers had uncovered the remains of a house with fragments of wall paintings, and the next day they found walls blackened by fire and the rims of upright *pithoi* buried in the rubble. By the end of a week, he had discovered the first tablet with writing on it, and within a few days, hundreds more.* Squinting at the tablets, he recognized two different kinds of inscribed writing, which he named "Linear A" and "Linear B"—about which more later. In April, on the floor of what appeared to be a hall or corridor, a workman uncovered two large fragments of a fresco that depicted a life-size figure carrying a rhyton. In his notes, Evans wrote that it was "by far the most remarkable figure of the Mycenaean Age that has yet come to light." (At this early stage, he had not yet given the name "Minoan" to this ancient civilization.)

On April 13, workmen began to uncover the high back of a carved gypsum chair, located in a chamber that appeared to have had paintings of winged griffins on the walls. Evans decided that the chair was a throne, the room was a throne room, and that its original occupant had been King Minos. He wrote, "The elaborate decoration, the stately aloofness, superior size and elevation of the gypsum seat sufficiently declare it a throne room," and in an article he submitted to the *Times* of London, he wrote:

> Crete was in remote times the home of a highly-developed culture which vanished before the dawn of history. . . . [A]mong the prehistoric cities of Crete, Knossos, the capital of Minos, is indicated by legend as holding the fore-

---

* Arthur Evans himself probably never used a shovel or pick in the excavations at Knossos. Scores of Christian and Muslim Cretan workers, under the supervision of Duncan Mackenzie, did the digging and handled the removal of artifacts. Nevertheless, we will continue to refer to what Evans "found," since it was unquestionably and exclusively his project.

most place. Here the great law-giver promulgated his famous institutions . . .
here was established a maritime empire . . . suppressing piracy, conquering
the islands of the Archipelago, and imposing a tribute on subjected Athens.
Here Daedalos constructed the Labyrinth, the den of the Minotaur, and fashioned the wings—perhaps the sails—with which Icarus took flight over the
Aegean.

Also during that momentous first season, workers unearthed a life-size
bull's head (without the horns), which Evans described as "perhaps the effigy
of the beautiful animal that won the heart of Pasiphaë, or of the equally
famous quadruped that transported Europa to Crete." Evans believed it was
probably associated with the bull games, but other fragments found near
it included rocks, olive branches, and part of a woman's leg, which suggest
a bull hunt. For a sculpture dated around 1600 B.C., it is truly remarkable.
The animal's eyes are wide and its mouth is open, just like those of the bulls

FROM THE TITLE PAGE of the fund-raising-appeal brochure for the "Cretan
Exploration Fund" in 1900. In the photograph, the throne room is being excavated.

on the famous gold cups found at Vapheio (on the Greek mainland near Sparta), which were unquestionably of Cretan origin. (In *The Bull of Minos*, Leonard Cottrell wrote that "they were thought at first to be 'Mycenaean,' but after Evans's Knossian finds they were recognized to be Minoan in style, probably imported from Crete, or alternatively produced on the mainland by Cretan artists.") The two cups, found together in a tholos tomb twenty years before Evans began to dig at Knossos, graphically depicted the activities involved in the capture of wild bulls. On one cup, bulls are being driven into nets slung between two olive trees, and one bull has thrown a would-be captor to the ground while a girl grapples with it in an attempt to save her compatriot. The other cup shows that the Minoans

THE LIFE-SIZE bas-relief of a bull's head found in the north portico of the palace of Knossos. The original is now in the Herakleion Museum; a reconstruction greets modern visitors to Knossos.

were not above subtle subterfuge: they enticed the bull into the nets by using a receptive cow as a lure. As Evans described the scene: "The bull's treacherous companion engages him in amorous converse, to which her raised tail shows the sexual reaction. The extraordinary human expressiveness of the two heads as they turn to each other is very characteristic of the Minoan artistic spirit." The human figures are also magnificently configured in relief, and the man who captures one of the bulls by throwing a loop around its hind leg is probably the finest surviving picture of a Minoan male.

In *The Palaces of Crete,* art historian J. W. Graham described the material of the Minoan palaces as smoothly dressed blocks of limestone, but the provincial buildings were made of unworked gray limestone, plastered over. Houses were usually two stories high, and the palaces consisted of three, with extensive colonnades and broad staircases. There were sophisticated refinements everywhere: a drainage system of terra-cotta pipes at Knossos, walls faced with thin sheets of gypsum (now known as alabaster), light wells, what appear to be

THE GOLD "Vapheio cups" were not found on Crete, but they are obviously Minoan. They depict various scenes of the capture of wild bulls, including this one of a muscular young man throwing a loop around the animal's hind leg.

bathtubs, courtyards, and, certainly the most surprising of all, elaborate wall paintings that depict (we think) the life and times of the Minoans. (Their only written records are in the still-undecipherable Linear A, so we have to rely entirely on the remains of the crumbled walls, broken pottery, and reconstituted frescoes for clues as to how these people lived some thirty-five hundred years ago.*)

Throughout the ruins of Knossos, brightly colored pieces of plaster continued to turn up—fragments of the frescoes with which the Minoans brightened their walls. At first, Evans tried to reassemble the shattered paintings, but it was not long before he decided to reconstruct them. He commissioned Emil Gilliéron, a Swiss artist who had been working at the French Institute of Athens, to repaint the frescoes. It must be borne in mind that this was—until Evans began uncovering it—a completely unknown civilization, so there were

---

* Archaeologists working at the ancient site of Miletus in western Turkey have discovered shards of Minoan pottery, clearly marked with Linear A. Did the Minoans settle there, did they rule a colony there, or did they export their pottery? Like Linear A itself, the questions remain unsolved (Schneider 1996).

no precedents or examples whatsoever indicating what the people looked like, what they wore, or what they might have been portrayed as doing. With his son Edouard, Emil Gilliéron worked for nearly a decade alongside Evans at Knossos. Together they resurrected an entire palaceful of people. In his enthusiasm, Evans (and probably Gilliéron *père et fils* as well) took enormous liberties when filling in the missing pieces, and even today, visitors to the museum at Herakleion in Crete marvel at the reconstructions, where whole figures were completed on the basis of a head, an eye, or a foot. (The reconstructed originals are in Herakleion; the paintings on the walls at Knossos are copies of the reconstructions, containing no Minoan fragments.) One of their more flagrant errors occurred with the "saffron gatherer," where they decided to fill in the missing pieces of a blue-skinned "boy," until a blue *tail* was found, identifying the figure as a monkey.

"Everywhere the bull!" wrote Evans. Its importance as a symbol of fertility and power can be seen in the architecture (where huge stylized horns form an important element); in the artifacts found in the rubble (plaques, cups, and jewelry decorated with bulls); and in the spectacular frescoes that depict the bull-dancing (also called "bull-leaping," or even "bull-fighting"), where acrobats vault over the horns of a charging bull in one of the great mysteries of ancient times.

The "Toreador Fresco" is at the same time the most important and the most enigmatic of all the Minoan wall decorations. Found in fragments on the floor of a room in the east wing off the central court, this fresco was reconstructed by Evans and Gilliéron to show an activity that has defied interpretation since its discovery. It shows three youths, two females (identifiable by their white skin color), and a male (red skin color) who is apparently leaping over a great spotted bull. The women are positioned at either end of the fresco (and at either end of the bull); the one on the left is grasping the horns; the one on the right has her arms outstretched, waiting to catch the "vaulter." The reconstructed fresco is now in the museum in Herakleion, and since a large proportion of the original pieces—particularly the woman on the right, the vaulter, and the bull—are present, it would appear that the reconstruction is fairly accurate. However, even if the fresco had been preserved in its entirety, it would still present an almost impossible mystery. Even Arthur Evans, so quick to provide interpretations based on minimal evidence, was baffled. He traveled to Madrid to see if he could find a connection between Spanish bullfighting and the Minoan frescoes; he even investigated the American rodeo sport of steer-wrestling to see if he could make some comparison. Frustrated and

PROBABLY THE MOST FAMOUS—and certainly the most misunderstood—of all Minoan frescoes, the "bull-leapers" shows three youths performing some sort of ritual acrobatics with a great spotted bull. Exactly what they are doing has never been satisfactorily explained.

unable to resolve the problem, he could only describe the fresco. In *The Palace of Minos,* he wrote:

> In the design . . . the girl acrobat in front seizes the horns of a coursing bull at full gallop, one of which seems to run under her left armpit. The object of her grip . . . clearly seems to be to gain a purchase for a backward somersault over the animal's back, such as is being performed by the boy. The second female performer behind stretches out both her hands as if to catch the flying figure or at least steady him when he comes to earth the right way up.

His successor J. D. S. Pendlebury also tried to solve the mystery, and wrote:

> Another [interpretation] may have been a bull-fight, of which the action is well-known from a later painted panel at Knossos. At this one-sided game, in which girls as well as boys performed, the acrobat or victim stood in front of a charging bull, grasped its horns, and turned a somersault along its back, an athletic feat which seems to be impossible. If the performers were expected to be killed, the ritual would form a human sacrifice, of which there is no other trace on Crete. The bull was certainly a sacred animal, and itself a principal victim of sacrifice.

On a seal found at Priene (in Anatolia, but the seal is undoubtedly Minoan), there is another representation of a bull and a person that is considerably smaller than the "Toreador Fresco" but no less enigmatic. (The fresco is approximately five feet long; the seal is about the size of a thumbnail.) This is the seal that Evans described as "the finest combination of powerful execution with minute detail to be found, perhaps, in the whole range of the Minoan gemengraver's Art." It shows a powerfully muscled bull with its forelegs up on a large rectangular object, and a man who seems to be leaping headfirst onto the animal's head. "The common but hardly possible explanation of this scene," writes James Graham, "is that it shows a man capturing a bull which he had surprised drinking from a tank. Surely no bull would drink in such a fashion, nor would a Minoan artist have so represented him!" Graham (and other authors) noted that the pattern of latticed lines that follow the four sides of the rectangle and also cross it at a diagonal is repeated in only one other known instance: on the rear face of two niches at the north end of the central court. Graham proposes to resolve the mystery of the seal

MINOAN BRONZE SCULPTURE of a bull and an acrobat, found near the town of Rethymnon, on Crete. The figure of the acrobat (whose legs are missing) is attached to the bull by his long hair.

A MINOAN SEALSTONE that shows a bull engaged in an ambiguous act involving a pair of mysteriously disembodied legs above its head, and an equally enigmatic square object decorated with lozenges

by conjuring up a second. He posits that a mysterious two-step platform to nowhere (also in the central court) represents "one of the doubtless numerous maneuvers which were devised to lend variety and interest to the bull games . . . in which the acrobat, cornered, whether intentionally or not, in this blind angle of the court, quickly stepped up on this platform and, at the right moment, as the bull perhaps succeeded in getting his forefeet on the narrow end of the first step, bounded upon its back and thence to the ground behind the bull, safe from his apparent impasse." This seems a rather strained explanation, with a large measure of speculation, but until a better one appears, it will have to do.

Any explication that is developed four thousand years after the fact and relies upon fragmented pieces of evidence can only be conjectural, but it seems a bit of a stretch to see the bull-dancing as a religious demonstration involving wild animals and death-wish acrobats. It is more likely that the enterprise was a sort of circus act, in which the bull was trained—or at least tamed—so that the acrobats could leap over it. They might not always have been successful.* Whatever the significance of the bull or the bull-dancers to the Minoans, their appearance was not restricted to wall paintings. Men (or women) and bulls are represented on seals, on offering cups, and on perhaps the finest extant Cretan bronze, which shows an acrobat vaulting over the back of a bull. There is also a graceful ivory figure of a bull-leaper, dating from about 1600 B.C., but it is even less useful than the frescoes in determining what actually happened, since there is no accompanying bull.

It is difficult to understand those who equate Plato's descriptions of bull capture and sacrifice with the Minoan practice of bull-leaping. In the one instance, the bull is brought to a sacrificial altar and its throat cut; in the other, it is used—very much alive—for what appear to be ceremonial gymnastics. Plato probably included bull sacrifice because it was an important part of ceremonial practice in Greece of the fourth century, and it is therefore likely that he would have included it in his Atlantis story.

Because it was totally unfortified—unusual for a capital in those battlesome days—Knossos required some means of defense, and nautical relics suggest that the island city was protected by a massive fleet. Pottery shards

---

* There are several representations of failed attempts, where the leaper is shown being trampled by the bull or being tossed like a rag doll, as contrasted with the graceful trajectory of a successful leaper. "With a confined space and a slow, clumsy bull," wrote Anne Ward, "it is just conceivable that once in a while an exceptionally skilled acrobat might succeed in performing perhaps the most dangerous circus turn of all time."

IN *Crete and Mycenae,* Spyridon Marinatos calls this ivory figure of an acrobat (probably a bull-leaper) "a small masterpiece," and writes, "The movement, bold pose and working of detail all command admiration. Fingers, fingernails, veins and muscles are modeled or incised with precision. . . ."

showing all sorts of marine creatures—octopuses, sea urchins, starfish, fishes, dolphins—strongly suggest a marine civilization. (The seafaring propensities of the Minoans also made it possible for them to colonize other islands, such as Strongyle [Santorini], seventy-five miles to the north.)

The most spectacular elements in the astonishing architectural history of Crete are the palaces, and the most spectacular of these was Knossos. Built on the hill of Kephala, revealed by archaeologists to have been the site of an earlier Neolithic settlement, the palace was built around 1900 B.C., in the period known as "Middle Minoan IB" in Evans's chronology. It thrived for two centuries, was destroyed, and then was rebuilt; around 1375, when it was in the hands of the Mycenaean conquerors, it was completely and finally demolished.

During the season of 1901, Evans and his coworkers decided that in order to continue digging, they would have to begin an extensive program of supporting the crumbling walls, adding beams and columns where they had identified the remains, and, in general, reconstructing parts of the palace of Knossos, which had lain buried under the hill of Kephala for more than three thousand years. It was a controversial decision, and one for which Evans has received

THE RESTORED "West Bastion" of the north entrance passage at Knossos. Under the overhang is a copy of the relief of the bull shown in the illustration on page 115. The columns, reconstructed by Arthur Evans, have been painted brick red.

much criticism, but it seemed to him that such measures were necessary to keep the whole dig from collapsing or turning to mud in the spring rains. In *The Bull of Minos,* Cottrell says that "unreflecting visitors to Knossos have sometimes criticized Evans for his 'reinforced concrete restoration.' Such criticisms are unintelligent; he had no alternative," and Pendlebury wrote, "Without restoration the Palace would be a meaningless heap of ruins, the more so because the gypsum stone, of which most of the paving slabs as well as the column bases and door-jambs are made, melts like sugar under the action of rain, and would eventually disappear completely."

Now partially uncovered and partially reconstructed, this is actually the second palace of Knossos, built on top of the ruins of its predecessor. It is therefore referred to as the "New Palace." The building is roughly square in plan, approximately 150 meters (almost 500 feet) on a side, with an immense central court. The palace itself covers an area of some 22,000 square meters (26,312 square yards) and is constructed of stone, wood, and clay. (Eventually, the palace would be shown to include more than a thousand rooms.)

The plan, such as it was, appears to consist of multistoried royal apartments, storerooms, religious shrines, great halls, capacious staircases, rooms, and courtyards randomly added to the central court, which is about 50 yards long and half as wide. (It was the mazelike nature of these rooms that inspired Evans to liken it to the Labyrinth.) The rooms were connected by light wells—

small courtyards that allowed light to enter roofed-over areas. This meant
that no section was ever in darkness, no matter how intricate the plan. At
its greatest height, the palace was five stories tall, but the roofs at every level
were flat, which facilitated its organic architectural growth. The upper floors
were supported by wooden columns, wider at the top than at the bottom
and resting on gypsum bases. (It is said that this column design was modeled
on tree trunks once used to support buildings, placed upside down so they
would not take root and sprout again.) Although no columns have survived,
Evans reconstructed the new ones at Knossos on the basis of a fresco fragment
that showed them to be dark red, with a capital that consisted of a two-tiered
cushion decorated with double axes. The walls were made of rubble masonry
or mud brick, framed with horizontal timbers, and plastered.

Plaster walls were a natural surface for wall paintings, and the frescoes
(paint applied directly to wet plaster) at Knossos are among the most spectacular treasures of the ancient world. Early Minoan houses on Crete were also
plastered, and the walls painted red. Then followed repeated ornamental
designs, but by the Middle to Late Minoan periods, from 1700 to 1500 B.C., the
art of fresco painting had reached unprecedented heights. "The style," wrote
Reynold Higgins, "is the first truly naturalistic style to be found in European,
or indeed, in any art." Only a few of the frescoes at Knossos are more than
fragments, but painstaking restoration has provided a suggestion of the
missing elements in these paintings of processionals and ceremonial or religious festivals. There are depictions of flowers, and a full menagerie of lifelike
studies of birds, monkeys, deer, a cat stalking a pheasant, and a leaping deer.
Seafaring people on an island in the Mediterranean would be more than a
little familiar with marine life, and there are various fishes and an occasional
dolphin.

In the light-welled room that he dubbed the "Queen's Megaron," Evans
unearthed low benches ("to be best in keeping with female occupants," he
wrote) and fragments of frescoes that were eventually reconstituted as the
famous "Dolphin Frieze" and the dancer with the flowing hair. The dolphins
(identified as *Stenella caeruleoalba,* the striped dolphin) are gracefully deployed in
a scene that includes several small fishes. Unfortunately, only a few pieces of
this fresco were preserved, so much of the arrangement is conjectural. The
same must be said for the twirling "dancer," whose loose hair seems to be lifted
by her energetic movements, but, of course, we can only guess what the rest of
the fresco looked like. Perhaps it showed a dance like the one described in book
18 of the *Iliad:*

The god depicted a dancing floor like the one that Daedalus designed in the spacious town of Cnossus for Ariadne of the lovely locks. Youths and maidens were dancing on it with their hands on one another's waists, the girls garlanded in fine linen, the men in finely woven tunics showing the faint gleam of oil, and with daggers of gold hanging from their silver belts. Here they ran lightly round, circling as smoothly as the wheel of a potter when he sits and spins it with his hands; and there they ran in lines to meet each other. A large crowd stood round enjoying the dance while a minstrel sang divinely to the lyre and two acrobats, keeping time with his music, cart-wheeled in and out among the people.

THE CELEBRATED "Dolphin Frieze" in the "Queen's Megaron" in the palace of Knossos. These remarkably lifelike animals have been identified as striped dolphins, otherwise known as *Stenella caeruleoalba.* The grille closes off a doorway leading to a staircase to the upper floor.

Or perhaps, as Jacquetta Hawkes suggests, the dancers took drugs. In her discussion of the dancers "whirling at speed," she says, "It is quite likely that, as today [Hawkes's *Dawn of the Gods* was published in 1968], drugs were sometimes taken to encourage a sense of revelation, possession and trance. On one seal the seated goddess is holding three poppy seed-heads, and in a late figurine she is wearing three seed-heads, cut as for the extraction of opium, set in a crown above her forehead. The growing of opium poppies has a very long history in Anatolia."

We know frustratingly little about the other activities of the Minoans. (Our inability to translate the tablets inscribed in Linear A has greatly contributed to our ignorance.) Men and women are depicted in the frescoes, and there are a few small sculptures that have enabled historians and archaeologists to make educated guesses about life in and around the palaces of Crete. As a rule, ordinary people were not the subjects of commemorative creative arts, so what little evidence there is depicts what we assume are royalty or deities. (An exception is the "harvesters' vase" from Hagia Triada, which shows ordinary villagers returning from [or going to] the fields.) A bas-relief of a standing man is known as the "priest-king" (also called the "Prince of the Lilies") because he wears a high crown of lilies and peacock feathers on his head and a necklace of flowers around his neck. In his outstretched left hand, he holds the end of a rope, and we are left to wonder what sort of creature he is leading. A bull? A griffin? A sphinx? That is the way the fragments have been reconstructed, and the "prince" is one of the best-known and best-loved of all Minoan frescoes.

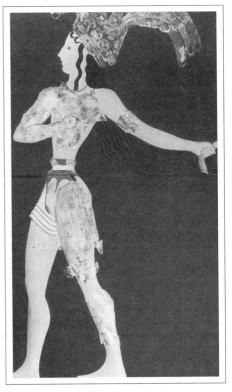

THE "PRIEST-KING" of Knossos, long believed to represent the ideal of Minoan royalty, has been reassessed, and is now thought to consist of parts of three different figures.

Female figures abound, often priestesses or goddesses, but there are also highborn women seen at various rites or sporting events, such as the Knossos fresco that shows a group of gossiping women watching some sort of event—perhaps the bull-dancing. These elaborately coiffed ladies are among the *Parisiennes,* but not even the courtesans of nineteenth-century Paris would have appeared bare-breasted in public, as did the women of Knossos. Whatever their state of dishabille, women played an important role in Minoan Crete, since they appear in wall paintings, vases, and sculpture, and can be seen engaging in virtually all activities, from spectating and dancing to hunting expeditions and bull-leaping. (So far, no women boxers have been found, but there is a sealstone from Knossos that shows a woman [a goddess?] with a sword in hand.) Moreover, Minoan women were beautifully dressed, with elaborate belts that cinched in tiny waists, and heavy, flounced skirts. In many of the frescoes, their hair was intricately styled, with long curls that reached to the shoulders, and shorter curls at the forehead, often held back by a headband or a small, beret-like hat.

By and large, the men of Knossos were dressed more simply than the women, with a short girdle or loincloth that emphasized their lithe, muscular bodies. They are often shown participating in some sport—wrestling, boxing, jumping, running—and, of course, the bull-dancers were often, but not always, male. (The "boxers" and the "fishermen" of Akrotiri are among the most dramatic representations of Minoan youths.)*

One of the strangest interpretations of the palace at Knossos was propounded by a German paleontologist and geologist named H. G. Wunderlich. In his 1974 *The Secret of Crete,* Wunderlich argued that Arthur Evans was completely wrong about the Minoans: the palace was not occupied by Minoan royalty à la the British system, and the villas scattered around were not for nobility descended from the king. The entire complex, he opined, was "a city of the dead; an elaborate necropolis where a powerful cult practiced elaborate burial rites, sacrifices, and ritual games." Although Wunderlich's interpretation is bizarre, he does point out some unusual features of the palace that give one pause. For example, the principal building material was gypsum, a stone so soft and friable that it seems highly unsuitable for a building inhabited by hundreds of people. Also, there were so many windowless rooms; alabaster steps that seem unworn; "bathrooms" with drainage holes but no pipes; and row after row of food-storage vessels, but no kitchen. He further suggests that Linear B will remain undeciphered as long as archaeologists seek a prosaic explanation. "The tablets," he writes, "were shorthand notes given to the dead to take with them into the hereafter. In some cases they were messages to the dead of the mortuary palace. Possibly the Phaistos Disk was one of these telegrams to the 'living dead.' " (In her life of Arthur Evans, Sylvia Horwitz said that Wunderlich's book "showed what problems besides dating an archaeologist can come up against.")

---

* Crete has a real winter, with weather that can be cool, damp, and occasionally very windy, and temperatures that can drop to 40° F. in December, January, and February. To date, no fresco, potsherd, figurine, or seal has shown any Minoan in any sort of cold- or inclement-weather garment. Either the weather has changed considerably in the last three thousand years, or they selectively did their painting, carving, and sculpture to show only spring and summer scenes. Perhaps the Minoans were a lot hardier than we think they were.

MICHAEL VENTRIS, who first realized that the Linear B inscriptions found at Knossos were actually an early form of Greek

Early in the excavations at Knossos, Evans was shown several faience plaques with incised writing on them. Down to the fifteenth century, Crete was occupied by people who wrote a language that is not identifiable, but certainly was not Greek. Cretan writing, a syllabic script known as "Linear A," was inscribed onto clay tablets, vases, and occasionally carved into stone. Evans devoted himself to the translation of Linear A, but he died without breaking the code. ("Ironically," wrote Sylvia Horwitz, "in a lifetime of pursuing his own ends, only one achievement eluded him: the decipherment of Minoan script.") Indeed, many scholars have died without breaking the code, since Linear A is still a complete mystery.*

Sometime around 1400 B.C., this writing was replaced by another, related form, known as "Linear B," which appears almost exclusively on clay tablets. Linear B was also believed to be undecipherable, but in 1952, the British architect and linguist Michael Ventris (working with the classicist John Chadwick) showed that it was actually used to write an early form of Greek (as opposed to Cretan)—a discovery that changed the interpretation of Minoan archaeology. (Ventris, whose genius solved the Linear B conundrum, was killed in 1956 in an automobile accident, when he was thirty-four years old.) Were there Greeks at Knossos before the Cretans? Evidently there were, which meant

---

* In 1909, Evans published volume I of *Scripta Minoa*, containing illustrations of many of the earlier tablets. He kept promising to release more volumes, so that other scholars might have a go at translating or interpreting the inscriptions, but he never did, and, in fact, kept the bulk of the tablets locked up at Youlbury, his house in Oxfordshire. The tablets were not actually published until 1952, nine years after Evans's death.

that the first flowering of Minoan culture, so beloved by Arthur Evans, was actually the earliest stage in the history of Greek art. Most of the tablets written in the Linear B script are, according to Chadwick, "deplorably dull: long lists of names, records of livestock, grain and other produce," but even so, they give us a glimpse into a civilization whose history is very poorly understood, but whose importance cannot be overrated.

A T   H I S   H O M E in Crete (which he called "Villa Ariadne," after the daughter of King Minos), Evans was reading in bed in the evening of June 26, 1926, when he was nearly thrown onto the floor. Objects and books fell from their places as the earth beneath him trembled. He ran out to check his excavations at Knossos. They had been propped up with steel pillars, and remained intact. But then and there the thought occurred to him that the abrupt end of the Minoan civilization had been accomplished by an earthquake. (Evans knew of Fouqué's excavations at Santorini and his theory that the volcanic eruption at Santorini had buried the settlements there.) "Most archaeologists," wrote Ceram in 1951, "do not subscribe to this interpretation. A later day may clear up the mystery."

We do not know what caused the downfall and disappearance of the Minoan civilization, but we do know that a series of earthquakes in Crete wreaked havoc on the palaces, and that the island of Thera blew up, bringing down the Minoan stronghold at Akrotiri. From archaeological evidence, we know that the Mycenaeans invaded Crete after the disaster, and that their civilization, like that of the conquered Minoans, disappeared, leaving only fragmented artifactual evidence of its existence. But we know nothing about the relationship between the civilization of Prepalatial Crete and Mycenae.

Arthur Evans believed that the Minoans not only had conquered the islands of the Aegean but also had invaded the mainland and conquered Mycenae and Tiryns. There is archaeological evidence to support his belief, including obviously Minoan objects found in the shaft graves, such as the gold rings that show goddesses, warriors, or huntsmen, and the silver bull's-head rhyton with a gold rosette on the animal's forehead which closely resembles the steatite rhyton from Knossos. How did the craftsmanship of Crete get to the Peloponnese? We may never know, but "Cretan gold- and bronze-work could have been acquired either by peaceful trading contacts or by looting Minoan settlements," wrote Leonard Cottrell in 1962, "by inducing Cretan craftsmen to work on the mainland or by carrying them off as slaves and obliging them to do so."

A. J. B. Wace, a British archaeologist who worked for many years at Mycenae, took a completely opposing view. He believed that Mycenae had always been politically independent, although he admitted that the earlier Minoan civilization had obviously influenced the Mycenaean. He believed that Mycenaean crafts had a distinctive look, and even suggested that by the middle of the second millennium Mycenae had become more powerful and more commercially successful than Evans's Knossos. Finally, Wace suggested that the Mycenaeans had even conquered Knossos, and had ruled from the throne room from 1450 to 1400 B.C. (The "Mycenaean" derivation of the griffin frescoes in the throne room at Knossos strongly supports this view.) While he was working on his massive, four-volume *Palace of Minos* (1921–36), Evans wrote *The Shaft Graves and Beehive Tombs of Mycenae and Their Interrelation,* in which he claimed that Wace had got his Minoan chronology all wrong. (Although Wace was probably closer to the truth than Evans, his confrontations with the godfather of Minoan archaeology redounded to his detriment. While Evans was alive [he died at the age of ninety in 1941], Wace was not allowed to dig at any site in Greece.)

Palace design is another indication that the two civilizations had developed separately: where the Minoan palace was designed around a large, open central courtyard, the Mycenaean palaces were centered on the megaron, a square interior room that contained the king's throne, and, in the middle of the room, a large circular hearth surrounded by four massive columns. We even have what amounts to an eyewitness description of the megaron at Pylos. In the *Odyssey,* when Nausicaä directs Odysseus to her father Nestor's palace, she says, "Directly you have passed through the courtyard and into the buildings, walk quickly through the great hall [megaron] until you reach my mother, who generally sits in the firelight by the hearth, weaving yarn stained with sea-purple, and forming a delightful picture, with her chair against a pillar and her maids sitting behind. My father's throne is close to hers, and there he sits, drinking his wine like a god."

There are no eyewitness descriptions of Minoan throne rooms—there are no eyewitness descriptions of Minoan *anything*—but we have the excavated palaces themselves, which appear to demonstrate that the precedents for architectural designs came from very different sources. As excavated by the University of Cincinnati archaeologist Carl Blegen (and perhaps described in detail by Homer), the palace at Pylos gives us an idea about the way Mycenaean royalty lived. (No other palace has been reconstructed as extravagantly as Knossos, but meticulous renderings of the palace at Pylos were drawn by Dutch illustrator Piet de Jong, under Blegen's direction.) The palaces were as elaborate and richly ornamented as those in Crete, with painted walls, ceilings, and floors. Where the Minoan palaces were unfortified, the Mycenaeans surrounded theirs with massive circuit walls, built of roughly dressed boulders, with the interstices filled with smaller stones and rubble. The famous Lion Gate is the main entrance to the walled citadel of Mycenae.

H O W E V E R   M I S G U I D E D his motives and erroneous his conclusions, Heinrich Schliemann uncovered the richness of the Mycenaean culture, which had been buried in the earth for almost three thousand years. In addition to the gold treasures that he found at Mycenae, he also revealed evidence of a civilization as sophisticated as the Minoan that it replaced, with great palaces with frescoes and pillared walls, bridges, fortresses, sculpture, paintings of astonishing complexity, pottery, weaving, and records kept in Linear B. The far-ranging Mycenaeans traded pottery and olive oil for copper and tin, from which they forged their bronze weapons.

We look in awe at the accomplishments of the Mycenaeans, but to this day, we do not know what caused the precipitate collapse of their civilization. Did pirates from across the seas invade and conquer? Was it internal strife in the form of revolution? Climatic change, such as a prolonged drought? Did the peasants, starved for food, storm the citadels? Was the collapse of *their* culture an inspiration for the Atlantis story?

In his 1966 *Discontinuity in Greek Civilization,* Rhys Carpenter opines that the downfall of the Mycenaeans was caused not by human intervention but rather by climatic change. He quotes Herodotus, who wrote that after the Trojan War, Crete was so beset by famine and pestilence that it became virtually uninhabitable. He asks, "Could Herodotus by any chance have had access to a true tradition?" Yes indeed: "This, then, is my interpretation of the archaeological evidence coupled with ancient oral tradition: a 'time of trouble' was occasioned by climatic causes that brought persistent drought with its attendant famine to most of mainland Greece; and it was this unlivable condition of their native abode that forced the Mycenaeans to emigrate, ending their century-long prosperity."

The Mycenaeans had penetrated the greater part of the Greek mainland by about 1400 B.C., but some sort of serious troubles befell them by about 1250, when some of the major centers were destroyed by fire. By the end of the thirteenth century B.C., Pylos had burned to the ground. Unlike the Egyptians, who documented and dated virtually all of their activities, the Minoans and

AT THE ASHMOLEAN MUSEUM in Oxford, Sir Arthur Evans rests one hand on a jar decorated with an octopus motif, and the other on a cast of the throne at Knossos.

the Mycenaeans did not appear to engage in such validation, or if they did, we have not encountered it. We know that successive invasions by the Libyans, the Assyrians, and, in 332, Alexander of Macedonia, resulted in the expiration of dynastic Egypt, a civilization that had prospered for almost three millennia, but all we know about the end of the Minoan civilization is that it occurred suddenly. Many of the early archaeologists, like Schliemann and Evans, were the victims of their own egos—they would brook no disagreement whatsoever with their conclusions—but they were also subject to the limitations of contemporaneous archaeological science. The shrines, grave sites, frescoes, sealstones, and funerary offerings are silent on the questions that perplex historians. Indeed, few of the objects in question were intact when found, and

SPYRIDON MARINATOS (1901–1974), the first archaeologist to propose that the Minoan civilization had been
destroyed by the volcano on Santorini

many of them—particularly the frescoes—had crumbled and fallen to the
floor. To reconstruct the frescoes, or, for that matter, to identify the wall from
which they fell, is often exceedingly difficult. Many of them have been imagi-
natively redrawn, based on the most fragmented evidence, and it is therefore
possible that even artifactual evidence can be a subject for controversy, not
only about what it *means* but about what it *is.* (The "saffron gatherer" turned
out to have been a monkey pulling flowers from a pot.)

As early as 1939, Spyridon Marinatos had suggested that the settlements in
Crete (Amnisos, Mallia, Gournia, and Hagia Triada—but not Knossos) were
destroyed by tsunamis, earthquakes, and aerial vibrations originating with the

eruption of Thera around 1450 B.C. World War II and civil unrest in Crete prevented Marinatos from pursuing his theories, but he returned to Santorini in 1958 to investigate the results of the 1956 earthquake that had damaged two thousand houses and killed fifty-three people. In 1956, Professor Marinatos was named director of antiquities and monuments of Greece. He had excavated Minoan buildings at Amnisos and Vathypetro in Crete, and had explored late Bronze Age settlements in Messenia on the mainland. "This island," he wrote of Crete in 1972, "can fire the imagination of any archaeologist. For 1,500 years, beginning about 3000 B.C., Crete and the Cyclades dominated the Mediterranean. Here, indeed, was the birthplace of European civilization." In 1932, as an *ephor* (keeper of antiquities) in Crete, he had unearthed fragments of a fresco at Amnisos, but, he wrote, "what really piqued my interest . . . were the curious positions of several huge stone blocks that had been torn from their foundations and strewn toward the sea. . . . I found a building near the shore with its basement full of pumice. This fact I tentatively ascribed to a huge eruption of Thera, which geologists then thought had occurred around 2000 B.C." When he became visiting professor at the State University at Utrecht in 1937, he took the opportunity to examine the voluminous Dutch material on the explosion of Krakatau in what was then the Dutch East Indies (now Indonesia), and concluded that it blew with "a mere fraction of the destructive force unleashed 3,400 years before by the eruption of Thera." In 1939, Marinatos published "The Volcanic Destruction of Minoan Crete" in the journal *Antiquity,* but even then there were doubters. As Marinatos him-self observed (in his 1972 *National Geographic* article), "The editors added a note pointing out 'that in their opinion the main thesis of this article requires additional support from excavation at selected sites.' " Additional excavations have revealed a civilization of astonishing achievement and complexity, which, because of its uniqueness and mysterious origins, has led any number of people to equate Knossos with the myth of Atlantis. But the continued presence—albeit largely underground—of Knossos has presented almost insurmountable problems for those who have tried to see Knossos as a city that sank into the sea.

THE ARCHAEOLOGIZING OF ancient civilizations is a process not unlike trying to assemble a gigantic jigsaw puzzle with many pieces lost or broken, and in some cases—like that of Knossos—where the complete image of the puzzle, usually printed on the box, is missing. Some of these materials enable us to obtain a fleeting glimpse into ancient life, but more often than not, we cannot accurately interpret what we see. For example, one of the most important single artifacts in all of Minoan archaeology came not from a palace but from the "royal villa" at Hagia Triada (also spelled Aghia Triadha), to the west of Phaistos, excavated by the Italian archaeologist Federico Halbherr in 1910. Located on the protected southern coast of Crete, Hagia Triada was only a short distance from Phaistos, raising the possibility that the villa was occupied by a noble family doing business at the palace. (The ancient name of this location is not known, so it takes its name from the fourteenth-century [A.D.] church near the villa: Hagia Triada means "Holy Trinity" in Greek.)

In a thick-walled tomb just north of the villa, Halbherr found a painted sarcophagus, completely intact, that had been carved from a single block of limestone. Based on the style of the paintings, he dated it from approximately 1450 B.C., before the final destruction of the palace at Knossos. The painted dec-

LIBATION AND OFFERING scene from the Hagia Triada sarcophagus, showing two double-ax columns at the extreme left, with three figures approaching them, two with libation jars (one actually pouring something into a receptacle between the two columns), and, following behind her, another woman carrying a yoke with two more libations. Bringing up the rear is a figure playing a sort of lyre. Facing in the opposite direction are two men, each carrying a small calf, and a third, cradling a funerary boat. At the very right margin, a single armless figure stands, perhaps the mummy or the spirit of the deceased.

orations, on a coating of plaster, were almost as clear and bright as the day they were painted. This coffer is only fifty-two inches long, not long enough for a full-length adult, so the body was probably interred with its legs tucked up, like the bodies placed in the predynastic Egyptian graves, and those of the late Stone and Bronze ages in Western Europe.

The sarcophagus is painted on all four sides, and even the sturdy legs are decorated with a typical Minoan swirl motif. Each end bears a painting of two goddesses in a chariot, one drawn by goats, the other by griffins. On one long side, a trussed bull lies on a table; below the table two goats crouch, presumably awaiting their turn. Directly below the bull's neck, which appears to be pierced by a dagger, is a ceremonial vase to catch the blood seen flowing over the lip of the table. With her back arched regally, a statuesque priestess stands at the bull's tail; a piper stands partially hidden behind the bull; and at the head, another priestess sets her hands upon an altar, identifiable by the libation jug and the basket of fruit above it. Beyond the altar is a tall column, wider at the top than at the bottom, surmounted by an elaborate double ax with a bird (or bird spirit) perched on the top (a motif repeated on the other side), and an altar topped by four pairs of the "horns of consecration," a popular image in Minoan religious symbolism. (There were two—or three—additional figures painted on the left side of this face of the sarcophagus, but the plaster has chipped off, leaving only their feet and the lower parts of their skirts.)

The other side of the Hagia Triada chest contains two double-ax columns at the extreme left, with three figures approaching them, two with libation jars (one actually pouring something into a receptacle between the two columns) and, following behind her, another woman carrying a yoke with two more libations. Bringing up the rear is a figure playing a sort of lyre, whose gender is not evident, because the gown and upper torso are similar to those of the yoke carrier, but the hair is shorter, with a curl in front like the other, obviously male figures, and the skin is rendered in the dark reddish hue that differentiates men from women in comparable Minoan imagery. (The face and hands of the piper on the other side are also reddish.) On the right half of this side, facing in the opposite direction from the two women and the musician, are two men, each carrying a small calf,* and a third, cradling a funerary boat. At the far right margin of this tableau, a single armless figure stands, perhaps the

* In conjunction with the funerary boat, probably intended to be buried with the deceased, it is possible to interpret these two animals not as sacrifices but rather as symbolic sculptures of bulls or even sacred rhytons. Given the Minoans' fluid naturalism in depicting animals, it seems not a little curious that the two "calves" are in identical positions, with their legs stretched fore and aft and, even more unusual, with their tails raised high. A calf—judging from the size, it must be a calf—being carried would not stretch its legs, and it would certainly not hoist its tail.

mummy or the spirit of the deceased, before an altar like those on the obverse, but missing the horns of consecration. It is possible that the sacrifices and libations, along with the musical accompaniment, were ceremonies accompanying the interment of an important personage, but any interpretation is only educated guesswork. As Higgins (1974) wrote of this extraordinary artifact, "These scenes raise many problems, but are evidently concerned with the worship of the dead."

In addition to the discovery of Hagia Triada, Halbherr was responsible for the first excavations of the palace at Phaistos, second in size and splendor only to Knossos. The first palace was built around 1900 B.C., was destroyed by a great earthquake around 1700, and was rebuilt on a more majestic scale than the first one. The palace consists of the usual Minoan complex of rooms, courtyards, storerooms, light wells, and staircases, and a pair of adjoining rooms that have been named the "Queen's Megaron" and the "King's Megaron," with floors of alabaster tiles and frescoed walls. (From the dimensions of the rebuilt palace at Phaistos, it has been possible to calculate that the standard unit of measurement for Cretan architects was 30.36 centimeters, only a fraction of an inch shorter than the standard English foot.) It was here that the famous "Phaistos Disk" was discovered, a clay disk with spirals of hieroglyphics on both sides. Stamped into the three-quarters of an inch-thick clay were human forms, parts of the body, tools, weapons, animals, plants, and even ships. Since the designs were recurring (there are 241 impressions of 41 different types), it was obvious that the same stamps had been used repeatedly. In 1984, a professional cryptographer named Steven Roger Fischer claimed to have broken the code that had baffled archaeologists and linguists since the disk was discovered in 1910. In his 1997 book *Glyphbreaker,* Fischer wrote that the language of the disk is recognized as an ancient Minoan language that is similar to Mycenaean Greek, and contains a call to arms to repel the invading Carians from Anatolia.

Although Knossos seems to have been the capital and the exemplar for most of Cretan architecture, the excavation of several other palaces, such as Zakros, Phaistos, and Mallia, indicate that the Minoans inhabited the entire island. Investigations of sites like these, which have been affected by volcanic eruptions, are usually difficult to locate. (The exception is Akrotiri in Santorini, where potsherds were found on the surface, and where the soil occasionally collapsed under the weight of a passing donkey, indicating hollows beneath.) When buildings collapse and are then covered with ash, there is often very little evidence above the ground. Even such well-documented sites as Pompeii went unexcavated for seventeen centuries. Until Fouqué dug in the ashes of Santorini in 1860, no one even suspected that there was anything

THE "PHAISTOS DISK" is terra-cotta, approximately six inches high and three-quarters of an inch thick. It contains examples of 3,600-year-old Minoan hieroglyphics that were first translated in 1984 by Steven Roger Fischer, a professional cryptographer.

there, and even though Troy was the most famous city in Greek mythology, Heinrich Schliemann did not uncover it until 1876. Until Arthur Evans began to dig at Knossos, a city that had been buried and lost for more than thirty-five hundred years, no one knew that a great city lay smothered in the ashes of the hill of Kephala.

Around the turn of the twentieth century, British archaeologist David Hogarth (1862–1927) discovered a dozen buildings at Zakros, on the coast at the eastern end of Crete. He found clay and stone utensils buried under the ash, and enough artifactual material to suggest that there had been a substantial settlement there. But the British School at Athens, which was sponsoring the part of Evans's excavations that he did not fund himself, decided to concentrate on the spectacular palace at Knossos. Until fairly recently, the only access to Zakros was by foot or muleback over the mountains, or by boat, and sixty years would pass before another archaeologist examined the ruins at the end of the road.

In 1962, Nicholas Platon (whose last name is "Plato" in French) began a methodical excavation at Zakros. "The results," he wrote, "fully justified my expectations. Four large Minoan mansions were found and excavated, as well as two peak sanctuaries [shrines erected on a high point of land] and cemeteries and burial caves of the Minoan and early Greek periods." In 1963, however, results surpassed his expectations, for he uncovered another palace, not as large as Knossos but replete with splendid artifacts, including a bull's-head rhyton like the one found in the queen's throne room at Knossos, and another rhyton that was elaborately inscribed with decorations that show a peak sanctuary. The "sanctuary rhyton" shows a building with columned openings crowned with ceremonial horns—exactly the same shape as the massive, abstract horns at Knossos. Cavorting around the building on the sanctuary rhyton are wild goats with gracefully curving horns, identifying them as the subspecies of goat (*Capra aegagrus cretensis*) that lives only in Crete. (As Platon described it in his 1971 book, *Zakros,* the Cretan wild goat is "almost extinct"; it has probably now disappeared forever.) There appears to have been an emphasis on goats at Zakros, since Platon writes, "It is natural . . . that the goddess in her aspect of Mistress of Animals should have at Zakros wild goats as her attendants. Other evidence of her role as Goddess of Wild Goats is provided by ritual vessels with spouts and handles in the form of a wild goat's head with long, curved horns."

There were also elaborately decorated jugs (often with an octopus motif), and numerous double axes of ivory and bronze that thematically connected this palace with Knossos. Tablets inscribed with the still indecipherable Linear A were also found. Platon describes "daily life at the palace" in some detail, only occasionally mentioning that his descriptions are largely imaginary. Of the envoys to Egypt, he writes, "They must have been very impressive in the meticulous appearance of the participators, their elaborate hairdos with long strands and short curls, the shining belts of precious materials decorated with curvilinear designs, the embroidered kilts, the many attractive jewels. The envoys came from all the palace centers of Crete, and each group must have been distinguished by special characteristics. Many were probably of royal lineage. The references in Egyptian inscriptions to 'The Great Kefti,' the men arriving from the 'Isles of the Green Sea,' indicate the respect given to them." And: "In the palace of Zakros, for the first time on Crete, extensive special installations for the preparation of food were found. . . . [T]he three-legged cooking pots were on the fire. Meats from large and small animals had been carved separately. The nearby larders were full of provisions, and many culinary utensils, ready for use, were found in adjoining storage spaces." There is, of course, no reason to dispute these descriptions, and such scenes may have taken place exactly as he describes them, but remembering that Platon has only crumbled buildings, fractured frescoes, and a collection of broken artifacts to work with, we should be careful not to take his sociology too literally.

As with almost every other popular book in which the volcanic eruption of Thera is mentioned, the Atlantis myth figures prominently in Platon's *Zakros.* In fact, he devotes an entire chapter to it, introducing it with the words, "In the end it was the legend of Atlantis that remained in men's minds, while the ancient Minoan civilization fell out of memory. Now that modern excavation has revealed that civilization, is it true that Crete is Atlantis and Atlantis Crete?" Platon seems to believe that it is:

> The political and social organization of Atlantis offers many analogies to Minoan Crete. The four palace centers so far discovered seem to confirm the coexistence of several kings, among whom the one at Knossos appears to have ranked first among equals (*primus inter pares*). A theocratic political organization like that described for Atlantis would have provided the basis for the so-called *pax Minoica* which was the source of the Creatan *eunomia,* that exemplary condition of civil order under excellent laws.

He concludes the chapter by saying, "There are still other analogies [of Crete to Atlantis], but enough have already been cited to show how faithfully the narrative about the civilization of the Atlanteans reflects the Minoan world which so suddenly and strangely vanished."

It was K. T. Frost, a lecturer at Queen's University in Belfast, who seems to have been the first to make the connection between Minoan Crete and Atlantis. In January 1909, as Arthur Evans was triumphantly excavating the palace at Knossos, Frost submitted an article to the London *Times,* which was published (anonymously) as "The Lost Continent." He wrote:

> As a political and commercial force, therefore, Knossos and its allied cities were swept away just when they seemed strongest and safest. It was as if the whole kingdom had sunk into the sea, as if the tale of Atlantis were true. The parallel is not fortuitous. If the account of Atlantis be compared with the history of Crete and her relationship with Greece and Egypt, it seems almost certain that here we have an echo of the Minoans. . . . The whole description of Atlantis which is given in the *Timaeus* and the *Critias* has features so thoroughly Minoan that even Plato could not have invented so many unsuspected facts.

Frost subsequently wrote a scholarly article for the *Journal of Hellenic Studies* entitled "The *Critias* and Minoan Crete," in which he tried to establish that Plato's Atlantis story relates to the island of Crete, but, of course, since he knew nothing about the eruption of the volcano on Thera, he was unable to identify the force that destroyed the Minoan civilization. Frost was killed in action in the First World War, and his revelations did not appear to make much of an impact on Atlantean scholarship. Arthur Evans, who was busy re-creating an entire civilization based on his excavations at Knossos, seems never to have considered the Atlantis connection, although he attributed the destruction of Knossos in 1500 B.C. to an earthquake and subsequent seismic disturbances, fires, and other conflagrations. In her biography of Evans, Sylvia Horwitz wrote, "Evans, of course, was alive at the time of the Krakatoa eruption, which occurred only yesterday in geological time. He would have been fascinated by what Marinatos found on Thera, destroyed thirty-five hundred years earlier."

Excavations on the volcanic island of Thera were originally performed by Ferdinand Fouqué in 1879, and only six years later, after the spectacular eruption of Krakatau, a Frenchman named Auguste Niçaise drew the first connection between Thera and Plato's Atlantis, in a lecture given in Paris which he called "Les Terres disparues: L'Atlantide, Théra, Krakatau." (K. T. Frost had connected Minoan Crete with the Atlantis legend; Niçaise suggested that the volcanic eruption of Thera might be part of the story.) The story of Atlantis rested on the bottom of the Aegean until 1950, when Spyridon Marinatos published "On the Legend of Atlantis," in which he suggested that Plato had incorporated an Egyptian legend into his dialogues. Ten years later, Angelos Galanopoulos, a Greek seismographer, published a series of articles in which he specifically associated the eruption of Santorini with Atlantis. (It was at this time that Galanopoulos first floated the idea that Plato's "dimensions of lands, channels, trenches around castles, ships and others, had been exaggerated and multiplied by a factor of ten.") In 1969, with Edward Bacon, Galanopoulos published *Atlantis: The Truth Behind the Legend,* the elaborate manifesto of his belief that Atlantis was actually Santorini.

Oceanographers Dragoslav Ninkovich and Bruce Heezen, in their 1965 article about cores from the Aegean sea floor, wrote, "The discovery of the Santorini caldera . . . and the archaeological discoveries on the Minoan civilization, at the beginning of the twentieth century, introduced new data in the interpretation of Atlantis." In 1967, James Mavor of the Woods Hole Oceanographic Institution mounted an expedition to Santorini, where, working (somewhat uneasily) with recognized authorities like Galanopoulos, Marinatos, and Vermeule, he announced that he had indeed found the Lost Continent.

Galanopoulos is the leading proponent of the idea that Atlantis was really

Santorini. However, in order for his theory to work, he has to arrange for some corrections, especially as regards certain numbers. In the epilogue to his book, Galanopoulos writes, "The Atlantis story in Plato is essentially correct in all its points except the date of the submersion of the Ancient Metropolis, which was 900 years and not 9,000 years before Solon, and the dimensions of the plain of the Royal City, which should be 300 x 200 stades and not 3,000 x 2,000 as given in Plato. It may reasonably be deduced that this erroneous factor of ten crept in during the transcription of the Egyptian records. The Ancient Metropolis was the island of Santorin before the submergence of its central part and the plain of the Royal City was the central basin of Crete."* He had to rearrange the dates, because he knew that nine thousand years earlier, there was no such thing as an advanced civilization: "One wild anomaly could perhaps have been allowed," he wrote, "but for Atlantis to have everything—architecture, met-allurgy, writing, agriculture and unborn opponents—between 3,000 and 7,000 years before their time is manifestly absurd."

Pharaoh Thutmose III—known as the "warrior king" for his wide con-quests—ruled Egypt from 1504 to 1450 B.C. In the tomb of Rekhmire, his chief minister, he is shown receiving certain foreigners, known as the "Keftiu." They were long-haired, wasp-waisted, elegant people, wearing short skirts or kilts, and carrying items of tribute that look not unlike those found by Schliemann at Mycenae. One carries a bull's-head rhyton. Evans unearthed frescoes at Knossos which showed virtually the same men, indicating that the Minoans were trading with the Egyptians in the fifteenth century B.C. In the Zakros excavations, Platon also discovered artifacts that looked exactly like those shown in the Rekhmire representations, suggesting "that the absolute chronology has been verified."

Unless we acknowledge that the gods were directly responsible, the destruction of Atlantis requires some sort of geological engine. The earth is susceptible to various natural disasters, including volcanoes, earthquakes, floods, and storms, some of which may occur simultaneously or sequentially. Earthquakes often presage volcanic eruptions; eruptions are often accompa-nied by severe electrical storms. Long before humans as we know them watched in awe, natural forces were at work shaping the planet, and they con-tinue to do so today. The dinosaurs witnessed great volcanic conflagrations,

---

* Responding to this enormous discrepancy in acreage, Luce wrote, "Details like a plain divided into 60,000 equal lots, and surrounded by an irrigation ditch nearly 1,800 km long, are obviously absurd. In any case, how does this square with the generally mountainous character of the island which is empha-sized elsewhere in the account? How did herds of elephants come to be out on an island in the Atlantic?"

and may have been hastened toward extinction by the arrival of a gigantic meteorite that crashed into the earth with an explosion so great that it disrupted climatic conditions for hundreds of years, more than enough time to eliminate their food sources. The tectonic plates of the earth are slowly cruising along atop the lithosphere, shaping the earth's continents, seas, and mountains, but some geological forces can act with such astonishing rapidity that they can change the face of the planet in the wink of a geologist's eye. Nothing on earth can equal the eruption of a volcano for sheer spectacle, as well as potential danger. Volcanoes can add or remove great chunks of land, alter the skies, disrupt growing schedules, destroy man's flimsy structures, and, when Zeus wills it, destroy man himself. No other force on earth reminds us so dramatically of our frailty and impotence in the face of nature's awesome power. Those searching for an early civilization that was destroyed by a great natural cataclysm need look no further than the island of Santorini, only sixty-five miles from Crete.

THE VOLCANO ERUPTS

W E TEND TO think of the Caribbean as a tranquil, turquoise sea dotted with peaceful islands that often serve as vacation destinations. But the Lesser Antilles, stretching for about 450 miles from the Virgin Islands to Venezuela and separating the Caribbean from the Atlantic, are a hotbed of volcanism. That is because these islands mark the place where the North Atlantic Plate subducts beneath the Caribbean Plate, creating a deep trench (the Puerto Rico Trench is the deepest part of the Atlantic Ocean) and causing all kinds of seismic activity. The island chain includes many volcanoes, nine of which have erupted in modern times, and three of which (one on St. Lucia, one on St. Vincent, and one on Guadeloupe) have the same name, La Soufrière, which means "one that gives off sulfurous gases" in French.* The others are Mount Misery on St. Kitts, Hodder's Volcano and Qualibou on St. Lucia, "Kick-'em-Jenny" in the Grenadines, and Mount Pelée on Martinique, one of the most infamous volcanoes in history.

In July 1995, on the island of Montserrat, the volcano known as Soufrière Hills began to erupt, in the first recorded activity of this volcano in historic times. As ash fell on the capital, Plymouth, the city's six thousand people were evacuated to the north end of the island. A new dome formed on the moun-

---

* In 1976, the French government evacuated the entire population of Guadeloupe when it appeared that La Soufrière on that island was about to erupt. The mountain rumbled but remained quiescent, generating only a heated controversy about the wisdom of the evacuation.

tain, and several lava spires formed and collapsed. Throughout 1996, 40,000-foot-high ash clouds towered over the island, earthquakes shook the land, and pyroclastic flows rolled down the mountainside, igniting trees and buildings in their path. By the summer of 1997, ash covered most of the island, seven villages had been destroyed, and nineteen people had been confirmed killed. In August, the British government ordered the complete evacuation of the island. By October 1997 (the date of this writing), earthquakes and explosions were occurring every week.

Mount Pelée is a 4,500-foot-high mountain that looms over the city of St. Pierre, described by the writer Lafcadio Hearn, who lived there from 1887 to 1889, as "the quaintest, queerest, and prettiest withal, among West Indian cities." In February 1902, the inhabitants of the city they called "the Paris of the West Indies" began to notice an odor of sulfur, and in March and April, puffs of steam began to appear at the summit of the roughly symmetrical cone. At the top of Mount Pelée was an ancient crater containing a blue lake known as L'Étang de Palmistes, a popular picnic spot for Pierrotins. Just below the summit was a dry lake called L'Étang Sec. By late April, parts of the city were being showered with a fall of fine gray ash, and the smell was growing stronger. Mrs. Thomas Prentis, the wife of the American consul, wrote to her sister in Massachusetts: "We can see Mount Pelée from the rear windows of our house, and although it is nearly four miles away, we can hear the roar. The city is covered with ashes. The smell of sulphur is so strong that horses on the streets stop and snort. . . . My husband assures me that there is no immediate danger." By May 2, Pelée continued to rumble, explosions occurred in L'Étang Sec, and ash blanketed areas close to the foot of the mountain. Flashing lightning accompanied torrential rains, and the crater began to fill with water. On May 5, the walls of the crater gave way, and an avalanche of hot water, boiling mud, and jungle debris rolled down the mountainside, swept over a sugar mill, and killed the twenty people who had tried to take refuge inside. The detonations could be heard on the island of Guadeloupe, one hundred miles away. On May 7, under a black cloud crackling with lightning, two fiery eruptions glowed like blast furnaces at the summit. Mrs. Prentis wrote that she felt "as if we were standing on the brink of Hell. Every few moments electric flames of blinding intensity were traversing the recesses of black and purple clouds and casting a lurid pallor over the darkness that shrouded the world." On that day, word reached St. Pierre that the volcano La Soufrière on the island of St. Vincent, ninety miles away, was erupting. It did not, as people hoped, relieve the pressure on St. Pierre, but it created its own havoc when its crater lake started bubbling and steaming, releasing great clouds of steam; on May 7, it blew.

Rivers of molten lava flowed down its sides and two thousand people were killed.

At about eight in the morning on May 8, Mount Pelée exploded. An immense crack appeared in the side of the mountain, and two huge black clouds shot out of the summit; one rose straight up to expand and darken the sky, and the other, the terrible *nuée ardente,* roared down the mountain at more than one hundred miles an hour, killing, burning, or asphyxiating everything in its path and demolishing the buildings en route. Three-foot-thick walls of stone and cement were blown down and torn to pieces. No lava poured out of the mountain, but it has been estimated that the temperature of the pyroclastic flow was between 1,300° and 1,800° F., hot enough to soften glass and cause the wooden decks of the ships in the harbor to burst into flames. In *Craters of Fire* (1952), volcanologist Haroun Tazieff described the scene:

> Forty thousand people standing helpless, with the sea at their backs, saw this wall of fire coming straight at them. In three seconds it had reached the villas and the gardens of the fort. In one more second, St. Pierre had disappeared in a burning cloud. The compressed air which the avalanche drove ahead of it flung into the sea, in a solid mass, all that terrified humanity wedged together on the quays. An instant later the water of the harbor was boiling and, in an immense cloud of steam, the ships capsized and were swallowed by the sea, or blazed like torches.

The Comte de Fitz-James, a French traveler who actually saw what Tazieff only imagined, wrote:

> From a boat in the roadstead I witnessed the cataclysm that came upon the city. We saw the shipping destroyed by a breath of fire. We saw the cable ship *Grappler* keel over under the whirlwind, and sink as though drawn down into the waters by some force from below. The *Roraima* was overcome and burned at anchor. The *Roddam* was able to escape like a stricken moth which crawls from a flame that has burned its wings. . . .

The funnel, bridge, and boats of the *Roraima* were swept away, the steel masts were snapped off two feet above their bases, and tons of ash were deposited on the decks. The crews of the burning ships leapt into the boiling sea. After the burning *Roraima* had been abandoned, Assistant Purser Charles Thompson wrote:

> I saw St. Pierre destroyed. The city was blotted out by one great flash of fire. Nearly 40,000 people were killed at once. Of eighteen vessels lying in the roads,

only one, the British steamship *Roddam,* escaped, and she, I hear, lost more than half of those on board.... The spectacle was magnificent. As we approached St. Pierre, we could distinguish the rolling and leaping of red flames that belched from the mountain in huge volumes and gushed high in the sky.

Of the thirty thousand residents of St. Pierre, two survived. One was a shoemaker named Léon Compère-Léandre, who somehow managed to escape the broiling avalanche, and the other was Auguste Ciparis, who was serving time in an underground dungeon. Ciparis (also identified as "Ludger Sylbaris" or "Raoul Sartout") was badly burned, but he survived to become a sideshow attraction in the Ringling Brothers Circus as "The Only Living Object Who Survived the 'Silent City of Death,' Where 40,000 Human Beings Were Suffocated, Burned, or Buried by One Belching Blast of Mont Pelée's Terrible Volcanic Eruption."

President Theodore Roosevelt dispatched the U.S. cruiser *Dixie* with food

NOT A BUILDING was left standing in the town of St. Pierre after the roaring avalanche of superheated ash had rolled down the flank of the volcano.

and medicine for the survivors, but there were only two. Also aboard the *Dixie* to examine and analyze the volcanic eruption and its effects were Edmund Hovey of the American Museum of Natural History, Thomas Jaggar of Harvard University (who would go on to devote the rest of his professional life to volcanology and found the Volcano Observatory in Hawaii), and several other respected geologists. The rescue ship arrived on May 22, two days after Pelée blew up again. The mountain subsided thereafter, but in October, a shaft of solidified lava began to rise from the crater, forced upward by pressure in the mountain. The spine, which came to be known as the "Tower of Pelée," was 500 feet thick at the base and often grew at a rate of 50

IN THE CRATER of Mount Pelée, this 1,020-foot-tall shaft of solidified lava rose at a rate of up to 50 feet a day until it crumbled from its own structural instability.

feet a day. By May 1903, it had risen to a height of 1,020 feet, almost twice as high as the Washington Monument. In September 1903, the obelisk collapsed into a mass of rubble, but while it stood, it served as a grim headstone for the burial of the thirty thousand people who died in the eruption of Mount Pelée.

Greater by far than that which destroyed St. Pierre, one of the most dramatic and terrible eruptions in recorded history took place in the Aegean about thirty-five hundred years ago. A volcano on the island of Thera*

---

* There is much confusion in the geological literature about the name of this island and its volcano. In some recent works, such as Heiken and McCoy (1984), it is referred to as "the well-known caldera of Thira (Santorini)," while Watkins et al. (1978) refer to it as "Santorini (Thera)." Other geologists (e.g., Bond and Sparks 1976) simply call it Santorini. On contemporary maps, there are two large islands (Thera and Therasia) and three smaller ones (Nea Kameni, Palea Kameni, and Aspronisi), and Ninkovich and Heezen resolve the problem by calling it "Thera Island in the Santorini Group." But as to what actually *exploded*, the volcano also has many names (they are the same as those of the island, i.e., Thera, Santorini, etc.), so I will simplify matters by calling the island *Santorini* (as it is known today), and the volcano that erupted in 1450 B.C. *Thera*.

exploded violently, destroying most of the island and covering the remainder with a thick blanket of ash. With a force estimated at some 7,500 megatons, Thera is believed to have been the second-largest explosion in history. (Only the colossal eruption of Tambora in 1815 was larger.) When the volcano blew, around 1500 B.C., there had been a thriving Minoan civilization in Crete, which may have been wiped out by some of the forces—including gigantic waves, seismic shocks, poisonous gases, and ashfalls—caused by the explosion. An alternative explanation for the demise of the Minoan civilization lays the blame at the foot of man. Of this possibility, American archaeologist John Caskey writes, "That the disaster was caused by man is perhaps a little repellent to our sensitivities, but a little—if only a little—easier to comprehend." The Mycenaeans on mainland Greece had grown powerful by then, and were competing with the Minoans for overseas trade. If a gigantic explosion at Thera greatly weakened Crete (perhaps by generating tsunamis that smashed the Cretan fleet on the northern coast of the island), it might have opened the door to an invasion by the Mycenaeans, who burned the other palaces and established themselves at Knossos, which, according to the archaeological evidence, was not burned.

Regardless of what happened to the Minoans in Crete, there is no question about what occurred on the island of Thera. During a series of investigative cruises aboard the research vessel *Vema* in 1956 and 1958, oceanographers Dragoslav Ninkovich and Bruce Heezen collected cores from the floor of the eastern Mediterranean. These cores contained "white, fine-grained wind-transported volcanic ash" that probably came from the eruption of a volcano on the island of Santorini, which blew up somewhere between 1600 and 1450, leaving a huge crater in the ocean floor which Ninkovich and Heezen called "one of the world's largest calderas." Where once there had been an island, there was now what looked like an atoll: a ring of sheer-cliffed islands around a roughly oval lagoon that measures 7 miles from north to south, and 4½ miles from east to west. At its deeper northern end, the lagoon is about six hundred feet deep. (The collapse of the island into the sea may have caused the landslide that in turn triggered the tsunami that swamped Crete—or at least the Cretan ships.) On the island, in the town now known as Akrotiri, there was a Minoan settlement completely buried in the ashes, and not uncovered until thirty-five hundred years later.

In 1967, the Greek archaeologist Spyridon Marinatos found a buried city that contained elaborately painted walls, exquisite pottery, and other evidence of an advanced Minoan outpost on the island. In his 1972 *National Geographic* article, Marinatos wrote, "Parallel legends of a sunken landmass existed throughout the ancient world, and may antedate the explosion of Thera. Such a tradition was known to the Middle Kingdom of Egypt about 2000 B.C. This legend may well be the common property of many ancient peoples—as is the tradition of a mighty flood. Nonetheless, the eruption of Thera could have fathered the legend in its Aegean version: a great civilization wiped out in a flash."

From the air, the island now called Thera, Thira, Santorini, or Santorin (the latter two names derived from St. Irene, the island's patron saint in the Middle Ages) is a squashed, open circle, with two components that seem to

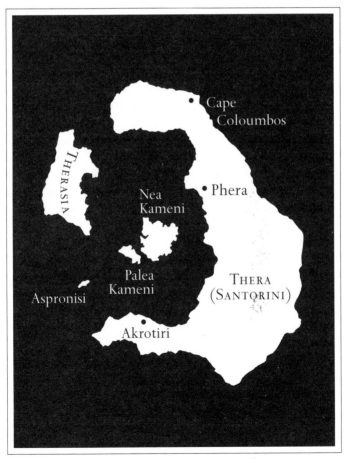

THE ISLANDS OF Thera, Therasia, and the Kamenis, all that remain of the volcano that exploded some twenty-five hundred years ago

have been parts of a single landmass, and three much smaller pieces, two of them in the center of the crescent formed by the two larger elements. A third island pokes out of the water more or less along the circumference of the circle. The inner cliffs of the caldera are composed of layers of hardened lava and pumice, graphically displaying the volcanic history of the island. It is not difficult to imagine this little group of islands as the sunken crater of an extinct volcano, something like Crater Lake in Oregon.

Crater Lake was discovered in 1853 by a man named John Wesley Hillman, who rode his mule up the mountain and, when he reached the top, found himself staring into a gigantic lake. The lake, which is a startling shade of blue, is six miles in diameter and almost half a mile deep at its deepest point. It was formed some sixty-five hundred years ago (around 4600 B.C.), when Mount Mazama, a volcano in the Cascade Range, blew up in an explosion* that destroyed its crown. As the molten magma continued to erupt from the vent and cascade down the slopes, the hollowed-out mountain could no longer support itself, and the remaining summit collapsed into the hole left by the explosion. Although there are no records other than those written on the land itself, we can imagine a gigantic explosion, with a towering cloud of ash and steam, with red-hot lava and huge pieces of rock and mountain blown into the air. Nearly seventeen cubic miles of rock were removed from the mountaintop by the explosion. (The 1980 eruption of Mount St. Helens, which occurred only two hundred miles south of what is left of Mount Mazama, was inaugurated by deep-earth movements in the same range.) In the ensuing millennia, rains filled the caldera of the now-defunct Mount Mazama with water, creating the deepest lake in North America, from which now rises Wizard Island, a cinder cone that is indicative of later volcanic activity.

The evidence for this eruption is easier to find than it is to read, since Mount Mazama still stands, and the ejected matter, now largely overgrown with trees and foliage, can be seen all over the surrounding area. If an explosion of comparable magnitude took place in a volcano that was part of a relatively small island, the evidence would be much more difficult to identify, since an explosion of that kind would probably have blown up the island, and the ejecta would have ended up on distant shores or underwater. Where

---

* The words "explosion" and "eruption" are not synonymous. In the volcanic context, eruption is the inclusive term that refers to a volcanic event, while an explosion can be part of an eruption. The dictionary definition of an explosion is "a sudden rapid violent release of mechanical, chemical, or nuclear energy from a confined region; especially such a release that generates a radially propagating shock wave accompanied by a loud, sharp report, flying debris, heat, light, and fire."

CRATER LAKE in Oregon, formed—as was the caldera of
Thera—when a volcano destroyed the upper portion of a
large mountain. The resemblance to Santorini is striking.

gigantic explosions, such as Tambora, Krakatau, Mount St. Helens, or Mount
Pinatubo, have destroyed mountains in recent history, eyewitnesses have
reported on the extent of the cataclysms, and in the case of the later eruptions,
like St. Helens and Pinatubo, photographers have recorded the events. In the
case of Thera, however, we have to depend on archaeology, geological evidence, speculation, and even, perhaps, on mythology.

IN A 1978 ARTICLE in *Natural History,* seismologists Stephen Sparks and
Haraldur Sigurdsson suggest that the appearance of the island of Thera
(or perhaps it is Crete) in the myth of Jason and the Argonauts "may be the
oldest extant description of a volcanic eruption," and J. V. Luce says that the

myth "may preserve an oblique memory of volcanic phenomena." After acquiring the Golden Fleece, the Argonauts tried to land in Crete, but they encountered a formidable bronze giant named Talos who could heat himself up and kill strangers by enveloping them in a fiery embrace, and who began pelting their ship with rocks. As described by Apollonius Rhodius in the *Argonautica,* the giant was "a descendant of the brazen race that sprang from ash-trees, he had survived into the days of the demigods, and Zeus had given him to Europa to keep watch over Crete by running around the island on his bronze feet three times a day. His body and his limbs were brazen and invulnerable, except at one point: under a sinew by his ankle there was a blood-red vein protected only by a thin skin which to him meant life or death." Medea tells the Argonauts that she will perform her magic to save them, and while lifting a particularly heavy stone, the giant grazes his ankle and "the ichor ran out of him like molten lead." His power drained, the giant collapses with a resounding crash.

"In the volcanic interpretation," wrote Dorothy Vitaliano, "the hurtling rocks would be volcanic bombs, the ankle could be a subsidiary crater, the blood which flowed from the wound could be molten lava (which actually looks metallic rather than red in direct sunlight), the collapse and death of the giant could be the quieting down of the volcano after the eruption, and the red-hot embrace is all too obviously the fate of anyone approaching an erupting volcano too closely."

After the encounter with Talos, the Argonauts sailed well out into the wide Cretan Sea, "and they were frightened, for they had run into that sort of night that people call the Pall of Doom. No star, no moonlight pierced that funereal dark. Black chaos had descended on them from the sky. . . . They could not tell whether they were drifting through Hades or still on the water." Could this be a description of the sky-darkening ash cloud following the eruption of Santorini? Sailing through the "deadly darkness," Jason fetched up at Anaphe, east of Thera, where he sacrificed in sunlight once again.*

Because of its magnitude, the Minoan eruption of Thera is one of the most famous cataclysms in history. Only the eruption of Vesuvius in 79 A.D., in which Pompeii and Herculaneum were destroyed, and Krakatau have received as much attention. In *Legends of the Earth,* Dorothy Vitaliano lists those events in

---

* Would the *Argo* have been swamped by a giant wave if she had been so close to an erupting volcano? Probably not. The only place where the full fury of a tsunami is felt is near or on the shore, so it is possible, as demonstrated at Krakatau, for ships at sea to survive the great waves generated by volcanic explosions. At sea, a tsunami might be experienced only as a slight swell.

which the eruption of Thera has been implicated in one form or another: Jason and the Argonauts, Deucalion's flood, the Deluge, the Plagues of Egypt, the parting of the Red Sea, the myths of Phaëthon and Icarus, the myth of Theseus, and, of course, the collapse of the Minoan civilization and the myth of Atlantis. Originally the province of quacks and mystic historians (because of its association with the Atlantis legend), the Minoan eruption of Thera has become the most intensively studied volcanic event in history.

Based as it has to be on circumstantial evidence, the reconstruction of the island of Thera is largely conjectural. The evidence is geological and archaeological; there are no historical records and no eyewitness accounts. Sparks and Sigurdsson described what it might have looked like to a Minoan sailor in 1500 B.C.:

> A single island occupied the whole area of the present group of five. There would have been a steep volcanic mountain in the island's north, rising to perhaps 3,000 feet above sea level, and a gently sloping plain would have spread across the southern half of the island. The upper slopes of the mountain would have been covered with dark chunks of lava, while the lower slopes were probably covered with vineyards that surrounded the town of Akrotiri on the south coast.

It has long been held that Thera was a single island, probably a low dome, that erupted, exploded, and caused the sinking of the central caldera. "If the Minoan eruption of Santorini was only equal in power to the 1883 eruption of Krakatau," wrote Ninkovich and Heezen in 1965, "the roar of the explosion should have been heard as far as Gibraltar, Scandinavia, the Arabian Sea and central Africa. This area, however, may have been larger. It may be assumed that the roar of the explosion, the aerial vibrations, tsunamis and possibly earthquakes, all originated in the collapse of Strongyle Island, during a relatively brief final stage of the eruption when the tephra, gas and vapours, already ejected, covered the southern Aegean Sea and the eastern Mediterranean with total darkness."

Three layers of tephra have been identified as products of the eruption: the lowest is about 10 feet thick; the second is from 17 to 33 feet thick; and the uppermost layer is from 33 to 100 feet thick. Components of the uppermost layer have been found in deep-sea cores over an area of about 77,000 square miles—a substantially greater area than that covered by the ashfall from the 1883 Krakatau eruption. The tsunami created by the eruption of Krakatau has been estimated at 135 feet high, and it flooded more than three hundred towns and villages, drowning more than thirty-seven thousand people. If, as has been suggested, the eruption of Thera was even more powerful than that of Krakatau, it could conceivably have generated an even larger wave sequence.

According to Mészáros (1978), the tsunami generated by the explosion of Santorini could have reached the island of Cyprus, some seven hundred kilometers (434 miles) away, and "might have penetrated inland with a terrible force. Archaeological excavations revealed that some of the ancient buildings were in fact destroyed by a tsunami in Minoan times." Hungarian seismologists Mészáros and Hédervári visited Ayia Irini in Cyprus in 1974 and found evidence of seaborne pumice on the gently sloping beach. There is not a straight path from Santorini to Cyprus, but a wave would have to pass at a slight angle through a narrow channel between the island of Rhodes and a small island known as Saria at the northern tip of Karpathos. In order to reach Cyprus, the tsunami would have had to be a *reflected* wave, that is, not a direct one. The Greek islands mostly surround Santorini, so there is hardly a straight path from Santorini to anywhere else, except, of course, for Crete, whose 150-mile-long northern coast lies directly to the south, unobstructed by as much as a rock. The only other places that could have been affected by a direct tsunami from Thera are the islands that surround it (Folegandros, Sikinos, Ios, Amorgos, Melos, Anaphe), and those locations in North Africa where the path of the wave would not have been blocked by Crete.

There is such an inconsistency between the volume of tephra from the Minoan eruption and the volume of the caldera—including the depth of the underwater depression in the caldera—that it could not, at least according to Grant Heiken and Floyd McCoy, have been a simple case of a mountain exploding, but "this rather large discrepancy between caldera and tephra volumes could be explained if a caldera or calderas had been present in the volcanic field before the Minoan eruption." In other words, there was an earlier explosion, perhaps one hundred thousand years before the Minoan eruption, leaving a flooded depression (the caldera) within a semicircular island *before* the Minoan eruption. The tephra from the earlier explosion was spread over the mountain and redistributed. This is the only way, wrote Heiken and McCoy, to explain the distribution and stratigraphy of the pyroclastic deposits and lavas, as well as the vast discrepancy between the size of the island before the Minoan eruption and the amount of material around and under the site. The caldera of Thera, at 32 square miles, is considerably larger than that of Crater Lake (26 square miles), and almost four times larger than Krakatau, which strongly suggests that the Santorini explosion was significantly larger than either of the others.*

All that remains today of Thera is a crescent-shaped island in the east; a smaller island now called Therasia, which had been the west coast, and has three little villages on it; and three other tiny spots of land poking out of the sea, known today as the "Burnt Isles": Palea Kameni and Nea Kameni, which are volcanically active to this day, and a tiny rock called Aspronisi. The caldera, now filled in by the Aegean and defined by the shattered remains of the original island, is 6 miles wide and, in places, more than 1,000 feet deep.

The cliffs that ring the caldera are striated with bands of color, ranging from white to cream to brick-red and black. These layers are the products of the millennia of eruptions that created the original volcano, and can be read like a textbook in stratigraphy. The lowest layer is composed of the largest blocks of pumice, their size decreasing in direct proportion to their distance from the original vent. The explosion was of the type known as "plinean" (named for Pliny the Younger's description of the 79 A.D. eruption of Vesuvius that buried Pompeii), in which a huge blast of gas, fragmented lava, pumice, and ash shot into the air from a vent that has been located about a mile west of the present-day capital of Thera.

Blocks of pumice three feet in diameter have been found a mile from the vent, testifying to the immense power of the explosion. (Like Pompeii, Akrotiri was buried under layers of coarsely granulated pumice, with finer ash deposits filtered into the interstices.) When the volcano erupted, seawater poured into the vacancy created by the detonation of the mountain, and was vaporized instantly by the incandescent magma. The fine-grained ash that forms the top layer—the ash known as *pozzolana* and used in the manufacture of cement— was formed when cold seawater and hot magma came into contact, and was minutely fragmented by the intensity of the detonation. The last stages of the eruption, however, were even more violent. The cloud consisting of hot gas and volcanic fragments collapsed under its own weight and became the dreaded *nuée ardente,* the "glowing cloud" that rolled over the land at devastating speeds, perhaps in excess of 100 miles per hour. (It was the *nuée ardente* that

---

* While Santorini may have been the largest eruption in recorded history, larger ones occurred before man contemporaneously recorded them. According to Sparks and Sigurdsson, an eruption that occurred "only" 30,000 to 40,000 years ago was considerably larger and, according to the geological evidence, ejected over 100 cubic miles of ash and covered the area around Naples with enormous masses of mixed gas and solids. They "estimate conservatively that at least one or two eruptions of Santorini's size may occur every thousand years. Thus far, mankind has been lucky that few eruptions of the scale of Santorini have occurred near centers of concentrated population or advanced civilization."

killed thirty thousand people during the 1902 eruption of Mount Pelée.) Like the rest of the island, Akrotiri was buried under 100 feet of ash. When the magma chamber was empty—that is, when the volcano had completely spewed its guts out—the mountain collapsed in on itself, and the present-day lagoon was formed.*

The sequence of deposits in the Minoan eruption, as delineated by Bond and Sparks (1976), is "a plinean pumice fall deposit, interbedded surtseyan-type ash fall and base surge deposits, mud-flow deposits and ignimbrite interbedded with very coarse, well-sorted flood deposits." The "plinean" phase was evidently marked by a high-intensity gas blast, ejecting pyroclastic debris to a height of several miles, where high winds scattered it over a wide area. This phase could have lasted as long as twenty-four hours, judging from similar explosions in recent times. Lava flowed down the slopes of the volcano and into the sea, and when there was no more support for the rim, the caldera collapsed. (The extensive flows of pyroclastic material into the sea might account for the missing volume of ejecta from the explosion: the "discrepancy" identified by Heiken and McCoy.)

Further geological evidence indicates that the Kameni Islands (Nea Kameni and Palea Kameni) appeared in the middle of the caldera around 197 B.C., and there have been subsequent eruptions from the Middle Ages to more recent times, all cataloged in G. C. Georgalas's 1962 list of the active volcanoes of Greece. (The list includes the eruptions of 19, 46, 726, 1570, 1707–11, 1866–70, 1925–26, 1928, 1939–41, 1950, and 1956 A.D.) In 1866, the *Illustrated London News* reported that another island had arisen in "the Bay of Santorin,"[†] between Nea Kameni and Palea Kameni, which was named Mikro Kameni, meaning "Little Burnt Isle." By February 4 of that year, although the new island had cooled on the surface, "the interior was glowing with heat and the atmosphere was illu-

---

* The collapse of the caldera on the uninhabited Galápagos island of Fernandina in June 1968 gave seismologists an opportunity to study a comparable—but considerably smaller—event. Starting with small tremors, earthquake activity increased steadily (or unsteadily, as it were) until June 19, when 200 separate earthquakes were recorded. (In all, 675 quakes accompanied the caldera collapse, 75 of them approaching a magnitude of 5.0 on the Richter scale.) A loud explosion (probably a large earthquake) was heard; and over the island there was a spectacular lightning storm, characterized by bolts of unusual thickness. A volcanic cloud towered 13 miles over the island. In some places, the floor of the caldera collapsed 300 meters (984 feet), but it remained above sea level. However, the lake that had been in the middle of the caldera disappeared. In February 1995, the volcano erupted, producing what Tui de Roy described as "the largest outpouring of lava there this century, an eruption that was to last two and a half months."

† According to this same article, the Bay of Santorin "has long been remarkable for the property its water possesses of cleaning the copper bottoms of vessels by the sulphuric acid produced by submarine gases."

SHOWERS OF ASH rain down on the lagoon of Santorini in 1870 as the volcano begins to rumble.

minated above the fissures while dense masses of smoke and vapour rising from them, and isolated columns of fire, surrounded by vapour, ascended, as it were, from the sea, the flame sometimes appearing to dance along the surface as it ran from end to end of a submarine fissure."

According to Bond and Sparks, "it is the only active volcano in the eastern Mediterranean to have been copiously active in historic times." In addition to its copious activity, all the eruptions of Thera have been classified as "catastrophic" for the inhabitants of the island, with coarse tephra, lapilli, bombs, and blocks being ejected to a distance of two miles from the volcano, and an ashfall that covers the land and the sea. The volcano produces abundant gas, and the rotten-egg smell of hydrogen sulfide is often present. In the Aegean, iron oxides and sulfur can turn the water red and poison marine life, and on land they turn white walls green or rusty red. Tsunamis have followed all historical eruptions of Santorini, causing great damage along the coasts. The gray-white ash, known locally as *pozzolana,* is characteristic of the eruptions of

Santorini, and forms the upper stratum of most of the islands. It is used in the manufacture of hydraulic (water-resistant) cement, which was used extensively in the construction of the Suez Canal from 1859 to 1869. Even today, *pozzolana* is an important element in the island's economy, with annual exports of 2 million tons.

Here is a description of the 1956 eruption by Haroun Tazieff, from his 1964 *When the Earth Trembles*:

> July 9, 1956, in the Cyclades, two shocks of magnitude 7.7 and 7.2, with thirteen minutes between them. The worst damage occurred on the island of Santorin, where the famous volcano grew active again, shooting up incandescent dust and clouds of ash. The earthquake was not volcanic, but tectonic, however, and it was followed by a tsunami which struck the Cyclades, reaching a height of over 80 feet on the shores of Amorgos and Astypalaea, 33 feet at Phaelgandros, 13 at Patmos, and about 6 on the northeast shore of Crete. Thirty boats were sunk; 53 dead, 100 hurt, 500 houses ruined, 1,500 seriously damaged.

This was the most recent event, but on August 11, 1925, there was an eruption of the Kameni Islands which was announced by an explosion that produced a "high, gray, cauliflower column, accompanied by much noise and the ejection of stones, lapilli, and ash—greatly terrifying the inhabitants of Thera" (Henry S. Washington was present on the site from September 13 to 20, and detailed his observations and findings in a paper submitted to the Geological Society of America, dated June 30, 1926). Outpouring lava soon joined the islets of Nea and Mikra Kameni, and by August 23, a lava dome had formed that was 250 feet high, without a crater. Blue, green, yellow, and red flames were seen at the summit, and a succession of violent explosions continued until October 27. The noise of the explosions was deafening, wrote Washington; "at a distance of 500 meters we had to shout to be heard." Almost all of the eruptions were accompanied by the violent ejection of blocks of lava, which varied from fist-sized to baby-sized, and while they appeared black in daylight, at night they were seen to be glowing with a dull red color.

By 1967, as director of the excavations at Akrotiri, Spyridon Marinatos began to turn up a host of evidence for the existence of a highly refined civilization there. From under a blanket of volcanic ash, he uncovered man-sized amphorae, sophisticated plumbing, groundwater conduits, and beautifully frescoed walls, but not a single weapon or skeleton. The absence of human remains and worldly goods suggested to Marinatos that the inhabitants of Akrotiri had had some sort of warning before they abandoned their homes—

unlike the Pompeiians, who were trapped in their houses and probably killed by the explosion of Vesuvius in 79 A.D.

In 1956 and 1958, the research vessel *Vema* was working the eastern Mediterranean, taking cores from the sea floor to see what it was made of. Heezen and Ninkovich of Columbia University's Lamont Geological Observatory examined twenty-one cores from this region and found that tephra from Santorini was present in all of them. They distinguished between "lower tephra" and "upper tephra," which they said came from two distinct eruptions in Santorini, one roughly twenty-five thousand years ago, and the other, in about 1400 B.C.

The tephra layers discovered by Ninkovich and Heezen were but one element in the association of the volcanic eruption of Santorini with the decline of the Minoan civilization; another was the discovery of the Minoan settlement at Akrotiri, on the very island that exploded. However, if the evacuation of Thera occurred in 1490 B.C. and the widespread destruction of Minoan Crete and many other Aegean communities occurred some fifty years later, the eruption itself, no matter how cataclysmic, could not have been responsible for the destruction of the settlements in Crete and at Akrotiri. Excavations at Akrotiri have unearthed no pottery later than the end of the period known as "Minoan IA," which is believed to have concluded in 1500 B.C. It also appears that even though the settlements in Crete were affected by the eruption of Thera, the damage was repaired and they were reinhabited.

The timing problems, however, have elicited a spirited controversy as to what actually happened and when. Excavating a large Minoan house at Pyrgos in south Crete, Gerald Cadogan found volcanic glass shards in the rubble, suggesting that the volcano at Thera erupted more or less simultaneously with the destruction of that building, in the period designated "Late Minoan IB." In the March 1973 issue of the journal *Antiquity,* James Money, an amateur archaeologist and fellow of the Society of Antiquaries of London, suggested that Akrotiri was destroyed by a severe earthquake, then was reoccupied by "squatters," and finally was covered in a thick layer of ash from the main explosion of the volcano. The following year, in the same journal, Christos Doumas, the Greek archaeologist in charge of the dig at Akrotiri, said that it was "unlikely that severe earthquakes were the first in a series of events which constitute the LM IA disaster," but rather that slight tremors gave the occupants time to take necessary precautions and evacuate the city. Furthermore, there were no human or animal remains buried under the ruins, suggesting that "people were not caught unexpectedly by sudden and severe earthquakes," and had enough warning to escape and take their valuables with them. (Most of the artifacts found in the ruins of Akrotiri are pottery; jewelry and objects of art are absent.) The buildings in the town were not damaged enough to have been shaken by powerful earthquakes, and there is evidence that people returned to the village after the quake, presumably to repair the damage. Doumas believes that there were workers repairing the earthquake-damaged buildings (he calls them "re-builders" rather than "squatters") when the volcano began to erupt. Examining the stratigraphic evidence, Doumas concluded that the first layer (that is, the lowest) consisted of medium-sized pumice pellets, followed by a rain of larger pieces and, finally, an enormous quantity of volcanic ash, which formed a deep layer over the entire island, in some places reaching a thickness of five meters (16.4 feet). The collapse of the caldera (and the disappearance of most of the island) occurred at this time, and it probably collapsed rapidly, as it did at Krakatau, over a period of one day or, at most, a few days.

The actual date of the event has also been a subject of much debate. By using "archaeological inference," people like Doumas have dated the eruption around 1500 B.C., and radiocarbon dating of the soils and pumice have given a similar date, but with a deviation of about one hundred fifty years either way. Other methods have also been employed, including the examination of tree rings (dendrochronology) and the analysis of ice cores at distant locations (at least where there is ice to core), such as southern Greenland. In a paper published in *Nature* in 1987, Hammer et al. examined ice layers at the "Dye 3" location in Greenland, where annual layers of snow deposits can be differentiated, and analyzed for dust content and acidity (gas content from volcanic eruptions), thus identifying atmospheric conditions at a particular time. Using this method, Hammer and colleagues were able to date the eruption of Santorini at 1645, with "a standard deviation of ±7 years, and an estimated error limit of ±20 years." Despite all efforts to precisely date the eruption, however, the problem is still unresolved. In his "Summary of the Progress in Volcanology" (in *Thera in the Aegean World III*), Jörg Keller wrote, "But how about the other problem—the calendar age of the eruption? Radiocarbon, ice-core, tree-ring and archaeological correlations—you will agree: fascinating discussions but no definitive answer yet. . . . Shall I make a prediction? Maybe by the next conference, tephrochronology might help again. If ash particles can be found in the ice, if their position is stated, if analytical records exist and are precise enough for correlation with Santorini, or alternatively, with another volcano, then maybe we will know whether a signal in the ice core around 1645 or 1628 B.C., or close to 1500 B.C. can be related to Santorini—I will not make a prediction where it will be!"

In *Volcanoes* (1994), Alwyn Scarth writes, "Thin tree rings indicate poor annual growth which is often attributable to cold weather (which is not necessarily caused by great eruptions). Thin tree rings in bristlecone pines in the southwestern United States were attributed to a cold spell around 1627 B.C., provoked by a dust veil that could have spread from Santorini. Ancient oaks found in the bogs of Northern Ireland also showed small tree-ring growth, caused by a very cold spell around 1628 B.C. But, even if this poor growth were really caused by an eruption, no firm link could be forged with Santorini. Many explosive volcanoes, including a dozen in Kamchatka and the Aleutian arc alone, were better situated and just as likely as Santorini to be the culprit." Even the presence of ash in ice layers cannot be attributed to a specific volcano.

It is not surprising that eruptions thirty-four hundred years ago in Kamchatka went unrecorded, but it has struck some people as odd that an explosion of the magnitude of Thera went completely unrecorded by adjacent—or even distant—cultures. There is plenty of physical evidence of the eruption of Santorini, including tephra in the ice cores, radiocarbon dating, and, of course, the visible stratigraphic history of the island itself, but no one—not the Egyptians, or any other contemporaneous people—recorded anything that would coincide with such a massive geothermal event. The lone voice raising this question belongs to Leon Pomerance, who has written several articles on the subject, including the 1978 "Improbability of a Theran Collapse During the New Kingdom, 1503–1447 B.C."

In this article (published in *Thera and the Aegean World I*), Pomerance points out that for the three hundred years following the postulated date for the explosion of Thera, "there is no observable evidence for the catastrophe that Dr. Dragoslav Ninkovich . . . has now assessed as 14 times that of Krakatau." (Quoted in Behrman's *New World of the Oceans,* Ninkovich said that the eruption of Santorini must have been "around a thousand megatons . . . ten times as powerful as Krakatau in 1883, the biggest known eruption in history.") Pomerance quotes Marinatos's 1939 discussion of the destruction of Minoan Crete, to the effect that "it is impossible to imagine an explosion of the Krakatau-Thera type without tsunamis. It is impossible to ignore the catastrophic power of tsunamis. It is impossible therefore to imagine that Crete and other places in the eastern Aegean escaped terrific damage by the tsunamis around 1500 B.C." Marinatos obviously believed that there *were* tsunamis, but all he can offer as proof is a conjectural comparison with Krakatau:

> The distance between Thera and Crete is only about 62 miles. It is certain, therefore, that the inhabitants in Crete in 1500 B.C. lived through the same

moments of terror as did the inhabitants of Java and Sumatra in 1883. If the
explosion took place during the day, the day was surely turned into night and
much damage was caused by the tremendous vibration of the air. The thunderous roar, too, must have deafened and terrified the Cretans, who had, of
course, no means of knowing what was its cause. Then must have come the
rain of mud and ashes, some cold, some ablaze and burning. Worst of all, however, were the waves which broke over the island, much higher and more
rapid than Krakatau.*

"There is, therefore," wrote Marinatos, "little doubt that waves caused terrible destruction in Crete at that time." "Yet," responds Pomerance, "in the
thirty years [since Marinatos's paper was published] that were to elapse before
the first meeting at Thera in 1969 or subsequently, was Prof. Marinatos ever able
to furnish the slightest evidence of a tsunami assault on the Mediterranean lit-
toral, in answer to the question that I have raised? No proof of archaeological,
geological, economic or social hiatus evidence appears in any of the Thera
monographs. It is perhaps significant that faced with this frustration, he confined his speculations of area-wide damage to the eastern Aegean, a geological
impossibility." †

There is other geological evidence, recorded by the Greek geologists Marinos and Melidonis, but it is so anomalous that it is not at all clear what it is evidence of. On the island of Anaphe, some fifteen miles east of Santorini, they
found layers of pumice in three places: on the western side (facing Santorini)
there was thick-grained pumice 385 yards from the coast and between 150 and
170 feet above sea level. On the northeast coast of the island (facing away from
the volcano), they found deposits that were, respectively, 530 feet and 820 feet
above sea level, both at the head of ravines or valleys. (This naturally brings
to mind the 1958 swash at Lituya Bay, Alaska, where a wave generated by a
colossal landslide drove the water 1,740 feet up the side of the narrow bay.)
Galanopoulos attempts to explain this phenomenon by citing the earthquake-
generated tsunami of May 23, 1960, which began in Chile and created huge

---

* Whether intentional, an error on Marinatos's part, or an error of translation, it is notable that his last
sentence quoted above changes from the subjunctive to the past tense: he discusses "the waves which
broke over the island" as if he knew that they had actually done so.

† In fact, Marinatos did supply "proof" of the tsunami damage, although it too is conjectural. When he
excavated Amnisos, believed to have been the port of Knossos, he found layers of polished pumice stone
where buildings had once stood, and concluded that the buildings had been carried away by the
tsunamis, and that the pumice had come later, carried by the sea from Thera to Crete. He also found
buildings where huge blocks were missing from the walls, and decided that the only force powerful
enough to move blocks that were three by seven feet was a "tremendous natural force—surely the
waves after the eruption."

waves on both sides of the Big Island of Hawaii, but since there are no similar deposits anywhere else in the Aegean, his explanation does not explain very much. Ninkovich and Heezen also believe that tsunamis had to follow an explosion of such magnitude, but of the pumice deposits at Anaphe so often employed to estimate the size of the wave, they wrote, "This is the only suggestion as to the amplitude of the tsunami caused by the Minoan eruption of Santorini." Regardless of the lack of evidence, the Columbia University geologists believed that because the northern coast of Crete was the area most exposed to the tsunami (or tsunamis), and because the Aegean averages 1,000 meters deep between the two islands (with a maximum depth of 1,500 meters), "the whole northern coast of Crete must have been inundated 20–30 min.

THE STRIATED CLIFFS of Thera, photographed from Palea Kameni in the volcanic caldera. The "icing" on top of the cliffs is the village of Phira.

after the collapse of Stronghyli Island. The Minoan tsunami may also have been destructive beyond the Aegean Sea. The most vulnerable areas were the coasts of Tunisia and the low-delta lands of the Nile."

In *Atlantis: The Truth Behind the Legend*, Galanopoulos wrote that a layer of postglacial pumice found some 16 feet above present sea level at Jaffa is evidence that the sea waves produced by the collapse of Strongyle "had a height of more than 22 feet when they reached Jaffa/Tel Aviv, about 562 miles away, [and therefore] we can easily calculate that their height at the starting point would be at least 690 feet." (To this suggestion, Dorothy Vitaliano says that Galanopolous has got the mathematics all wrong, and that besides, the pumice layer at Jaffa did not even come from Santorini.)

Also using Marinos and Melidonis's data, Yokoyama (1978) calculates the original height of the Thera tsunami at 89 meters—292 feet—but says that the source area must remain unknown, as well as the original topography of Thera Island, and that "therefore it is not clear whether the tsunami emerged through the north-western and the south-western openings of the assumed inner bay or from all the peripheral sea-coasts." He believes that the wave was 50 meters (164 feet) high when it arrived at Anaphe 10 minutes after the explosion, and that when it arrived at Jaffa/Tel Aviv, 105 minutes after the explosion, it was 36 feet high.

A more reasonable explanation of the pumice at Anaphe, although less satisfying for advocates of the monster-wave theory, is given in Dorothy Vitaliano's *Legends of the Earth,* where she writes that "such pumice, even at a lower level, would be a remnant of an airborne cover, rather than pumice floated up to such heights by a wave of incredible proportions—nearly four times higher than the highest tsunami run-up ever recorded, which was 210 feet at the southern end of Kamchatka in 1737. In any case, the question is moot, for subsequent investigations have shown that the pumice on Anaphi is from a much older eruption, dated by radiocarbon as sixteen to eighteen thousand years old."

Since virtually all the damage caused by the 1883 explosion of Krakatau was caused by great walls of water, it is indeed problematical that after the explosion of Thera, no wave damage was reported by the Egyptians, and indeed, there was no interruption in commerce between Egypt and Crete, as documented by the datable wall paintings on the tombs of Peumre, Senmut, User Amon, Rekhmire, and Menkheperra-senb, all of the period (1503–1447 B.C.) when the volcano at Thera was supposed to have exploded. Pomerance writes: "If the coasts of Mainland Greece and Crete would have been devastated as they surely would have been by the tsunamis roaring in on the coastal areas within an hour and a half after the great bulk of Thera had collapsed into the caldera, and if the low-lying agricultural plains had been salinated by the sea waters, the calm processional of the Keftiu [Cretans] traveling to Egypt would have been totally impossible. Nor would the recovery of the social fabric of the devastated communities have been possible for hundreds of years later." Having rejected the theories of almost everyone who had written about the volcanic collapse of Thera, Pomerance cannot offer a plausible explanation as to why no one recorded the catastrophe at the accepted moment in time. He has therefore changed the date, suggesting that "the collapse of Thera might have occurred in 1200 B.C."—when no one recorded the catastrophe, either. However, geologists Ninkovich and Heezen wrote that "little of the literature of the Eighteenth Dynasty has been preserved, except, for example, the Triumphant Hymn of Thutmose III, and the Sun-hymn of Ikhnaton, and thus no contemporaneous documents remain to certify whether the eruption of Santorini had an influence on such a sudden change in Egyptian history (the beginning of 'internationalism,' monotheism, and the decline of the Eighteenth Dynasty empire)."

Theirs is such a wide-ranging study, including discussions of core-sampling, archaeology, and mythology, with such disparate sources as Herodotus and Sigmund Freud, that it is not surprising that Ninkovich and Heezen would turn to the Bible for vicarious verification of the eruption of Santorini. Most biblical scholars place the Exodus at the end of the reign of Thutmose III (about 1450 B.C.), and therefore, if Moses and the Israelites were trekking along the Mediterranean coast (the Bible is silent on their actual route) when Santorini exploded, they would have experienced some of the effects of the cataclysm. From Exodus 14:

19. And the angel of God, which went before the camp of Israel, removed and went behind them; and the pillar of the cloud went from before their face, and stood behind them:

20. And it came between the camp of the Egyptians and the camp of Israel; and it was a cloud and darkness to them, but it gave light by night to these: so that the one came not near the other all the night.

21. And Moses stretched out his hand over the sea; and the Lord caused the sea to go back by a strong east wind all that night, and made the sea dry land, and the waters were divided.

22. And the children of Israel went into the midst of the sea upon the dry ground: and the waters were a wall unto them on their right hand, and on their left.

23. And the Egyptians pursued, and went in after them to the midst of the sea, even all Pharaoh's horses, his chariots, and his horsemen.

24. And it came to pass, that in the morning watch the Lord looked unto the host of the Egyptians through the pillar of fire and of the cloud, and troubled the host of the Egyptians,

. . . .

27. And Moses stretched forth his hand over the sea, and the sea returned to its strength when the morning appeared; and the Egyptians fled against it; and the Lord overthrew the Egyptians in the midst of the sea.

28. And the waters returned, and covered the chariots, and the horsemen, and all the host of Pharaoh that came into the sea after them; there remained not so much as one of them.

In his discussion of the geothermal implications of these biblical passages (in *The Great Waves*), Douglas Myles writes, "The reader will know what geological condition is implied by this: either a high-magnitude submarine earthquake involving severe crustal slippage; or a volcanic island in eruption, followed by caldera collapse and invasion of the sea; or both." "Was this an account of a tsunami?" he asks. "More in particular, was it, *could* it have been, those tsunamis which followed the cataclysmic Bronze-Age eruption of Santorini, waves which destroyed in their ports not only the numerous vessels of the Minoan fleet but presumably, virtually all shipping then berthed in east Mediterranean harbors?"

In the Bible, the plagues occur before the Israelites make their exodus, but Galanopoulos suggests that the plagues might actually have been a by-product of the Santorini eruption that occurred before the caldera collapse that caused the terrible tsunami. Some of the ten plagues are easier to reconcile with a volcanic eruption than others. Thunder, fire, and hail (Exodus 9:23–25), and "a thick darkness . . . which may be felt" (Exodus 10:21–22), fit more readily into a seismological explanation than do frogs covering the land (Exodus 8:2–7), dust turned into lice (Exodus 8:16–18), and, perhaps most problematical of all, the death of all the Egyptian firstborn (Exodus 11:5–7).

However difficult the assignment, Myles gives it a game try, and writes that "water into blood" might have been torrential rains discolored by a high content of ferric oxide; "frogs" might have been drawn up into a tornado caused by the intense heat of the eruption; "lice and flies" breed more readily when normally fresh water turns stagnant; when crops fail, starvation causes "boils and blains" in people and the death of livestock; and as for the death of the firstborn, even though he can produce no physical explanation, Myles feels that the importance of firstborn children to the Jews suggests that Moses (the putative author of the second book of the Old Testament) might have made up this "most fearful visitation" in the interests of dramatic value.

Galanopoulos also explains the Plagues of Egypt in terms of the eruption of Santorini, but gives a special twist to the causality:

> Although this explanation is not pressed, it is nevertheless remarkable. The events take place in the same sequence as the natural phenomena which favour the events. The plagues precede the Exodus. The sea-wave which helped the Exodus of the Israelites was produced by the collapse of Santorin; and the collapse occurred after the eruption phenomena which brought

about the plagues. For those who believe that the plagues and the crossing of the waters were miracles of Divine Providence alone, the miracle . . . lies in the timing of the occurrences, the synchronizing of events. Moses is divinely guided to take advantage of the mechanism of occurrences whose manifestation obeys natural laws which are themselves the work of God.

(Galanopoulos also believes that the eruption took place during the summer, when the wind was blowing from the northwest, thus accounting for the tephra distribution found by Ninkovich and Heezen.)

The myth of Deucalion's flood has also been associated with the eruption of Santorini. In Greek mythology, Deucalion, son of Prometheus, was a king of Thessaly. When mankind fell into evil ways, Zeus decided to destroy the world, but Prometheus warned his son and advised him to build a ship and stock it with provisions. It rained for nine straight days and nights, and the waters rose so high that only the top of Mount Parnassus stood above the flood. In the ark, Deucalion and his wife Pyrrha came to rest upon Parnassus, and when the waters subsided, they prayed to Zeus for deliverance. He commanded them to throw "the bones of [their] mother" over their shoulders into the sea, which they interpreted as rocks, the bones of Mother Earth, and the bones turned into men and women. They had a son called Hellen, through whom they became the ancestors of the Greeks—the Hellenes.

The myth of Deucalion bears an obvious resemblance to the story of Noah and the ark, but unlike with Noah, we have documentation for the real Deucalion. A marble pillar (the *Marmor parium,* or "Parian Marble") found on the island of Paros contains a list of the kings of Greece and the major events of their reigns, and Deucalion is listed as having been in power at the same time as Pharaoh Thutmose III, 1504–1450 B.C., which was just around the time of the eruption of Santorini and the exodus of the Israelites. (In the *Timaeus,* Plato has Solon tell the Egyptians the "legend of Deucalion and Pyrrha after the Flood, and how they survived it, and to give the genealogy of their descendants"; and in the *Critias,* he says the Acropolis of Atlantis crumbled "when earthquakes occurred simultaneously with the third of the disastrous floods which preceded the destructive deluge in the time of Deucalion.") Based on the concurrence of these historical events, J. G. Bennett has suggested that the actual date for the explosion on Santorini was 1447 B.C.

In about 1700 B.C., the two largest palaces on Crete—Knossos and Phaistos—were destroyed by fire that may have been initiated by an earthquake, but they were rebuilt, and the period that followed the rebuilding is considered the high point of Minoan civilization. The palaces were built and the frescoes were painted during this period, and from the wall paintings, we assume that the events portrayed—the bull-leaping, for example—took place at that time. Also, metalworking, gem-engraving, and ivory-carving reached heights never attained before or since in Crete. (Since we have no chronology for Minoan civilization, most dating of Cretan stratigraphy and artifactual material is based on the presence of material from other civilizations, where the dates are known. Since the Egyptians kept such good records, when an Egyptian artifact is found at a Minoan settlement, it can be used, but not conclusively, to date the Cretan excavations.)

We have amassed enough data to gain a pretty good idea of *what* happened, but exactly *when* it happened is still a problem. There were at least two earthquakes, one around 1600 B.C. and the next about one hundred years later, that destroyed all the palaces in Crete except Knossos. By 1450, Phaistos, Mallia, and Zakros had been destroyed, mostly by fire, and then abandoned. Did the invading Mycenaeans conquer and burn the other palaces but occupy Knossos? We do know that the Minoan influence waned after 1450, replaced by the Mycenaean presence, but we have no way of telling if the Mycenaeans took advantage of an already crumbled civilization or caused the crumbling themselves. Tablets found at Knossos, written in Linear B, identify some eighty-five settlements in Crete that were under Mycenaean hegemony after 1400. Around 1375, the palace of Knossos was finally destroyed, perhaps by another earthquake. This time, the palace was not rebuilt, and it was not until the thirteenth century A.D. that the site was occupied again.

A N O T H E R   C A T A C L Y S M   H I T   Crete about 1450 B.C., but the nature of this one is in dispute. Was it another earthquake? A tsunami? A massive fire? An invasion? We are not sure what happened in Crete, but we do know what happened in Thera. First an earthquake rumbled the island, and smoke and steam began to issue from the summit of the mountain. Many people abandoned their homes, but others, with no place to go, went back. Shortly thereafter, the mountain exploded. What had been a roughly circular island, perhaps ten miles in diameter, crowned by a towering conical mountain, was transformed by an ear-shattering, earthshaking explosion into a humongous cloud of steam and ash, and then a gigantic hole in the ocean, into which the sea rushed with incredible force. This volcanic eruption, one of the most powerful ever known, not only destroyed most of the island of Thera, but its effects were certainly felt sixty miles away, on the island of Crete, and probably at greater distances throughout the Aegean.*

Somewhere during the period 1600–1400 B.C., the volcano at Santorini erupted, and while there is no question that it destroyed most of the settlements on that island—because it destroyed most of the island—its effect on Crete is the subject of continued argument and speculation. Spyridon Marinatos postulated the connection between Crete and Thera as early as 1939, when his article "The Volcanic Destruction of Minoan Crete" was published in the journal *Antiquity*. Sparks and Sigurdsson (1978) speculated that high-altitude winds carried a cloud of ash toward Crete, and that where the ashfall was thickest, crops were probably smothered and destroyed. "But we doubt," they wrote, "whether such a moderate shower would by itself have been sufficiently catastrophic to destroy an entire civilization."

By 1967, when Marinatos began work on the island of Thera to excavate the settlement that was buried thirty-five hundred years earlier under volcanic ash after the island's violent explosion, the groundwork had already been laid for a theory that associated Thera with Atlantis. When Marinatos uncovered the frescoes that showed sailing ships and dolphins, he was prepared to suggest—somewhat obliquely—that he was digging in the ruins of Atlantis. Without reviewing all of Marinatos's arguments, we shall leave him digging in the ashes (figuratively, that is; he died in 1974), with these words from Elliot Roberts, who wrote a letter to the *Saturday Review* in 1967, commenting on science editor John Lear's article celebrating the Galanopoulos/Mavor 1966 "Atlantis" expedition to Santorini:

> Regarding Atlantis, who can guess rightly where and when it was? Plato spoke of an island in the Atlantic, in front of the Pillars of Hercules, larger than Libya and Africa. While Plato was self-contradictory and of obscure meaning in parts, it does not seem that he was speaking of a small island in the Aegean. Perhaps, nevertheless, Santorini *was* Atlantis; however, I do not think you can support the idea by reference to the submarine configuration. The collapse of vast mountains of earth into a subterranean void (the process of caldera formation) is no ordered process. It is chaotic, and it is inconceivable to me, at least, that any original contours could have been preserved as suggested by Galanopoulos.

* Elliot Roberts, chief of the Geophysics Division of the U.S. Coast and Geodetic Survey, had this to say about the disaster in Santorini: "In opposition to the widely held idea that the Santorini eruption destroyed the Minoan civilization, permit me to suggest a plausible alternative: A great tectonic earthquake, common to the region, could have flattened the palaces and made the land inhospitable, while at the same time triggering the Santorini eruption—a common occurrence."

THE SETTLEMENTS ON SANTORINI

U NTIL HEINRICH SCHLIEMANN'S excavations on the Greek mainland in 1876, hardly anything was known about the Aegean Bronze Age. In fact, it was generally assumed that Greek culture commenced somewhere around 776 B.C., the year of the first Olympiad. Prior to that date, Greek prehistory consisted of the epic poems of Homer: the *Iliad* and the *Odyssey,* the heroic tales of the confrontation between Achilles and Hector, and the Trojan War. The storied culture of the ancient Greeks was thought to consist of romantic fables with no basis in historical fact.

Because Schliemann was committed to finding the legendary city of Troy, he believed he had found it when he uncovered royal shaft graves at Mycenae, and that the artifacts in the tombs had belonged to the heroes of the Trojan War. Also in the 1860s, during excavations in the volcanic debris on the island of Thera, Bronze Age settlements were unearthed that corresponded with the Mycenaean shaft graves. Although some evidence of prehistoric settlements was uncovered, Santorini would remain undisturbed by inquisitive archaeologists until 1967, when Spyridon Marinatos began to dig at Akrotiri.

In 1965, Marinatos made his first reconnaissance of the island of Santorini. He reasoned that the little village of Akrotiri, located on the southern hook of the island, offered a safe harbor from northwesterly storms and might have been the site of an early settlement. His instincts were rewarded when he was

PROFESSOR SPYRIDON MARINATOS (right) supervising the dig at Akrotiri

told about certain places where the soil had subsided in such a way as to indicate that it might be layered atop ruined buildings. He also found donkeys drinking out of stone troughs that he recognized as massive prehistoric mortars. He decided to dig in the shallow ravine that ran from Akrotiri to the sea, and within hours, he realized that he had found the remains of a prehistoric city.

In 1968, during the second season of excavations at Thera, Marinatos found fragments of a wall painting that contained the head of a man, several birds in flight, and the head of a monkey. Then they found another monkey fresco, this one showing a band of blue monkeys scrambling over a rocky landscape. Indeed, Akrotiri's most significant contribution to the opening of the long-closed book on Aegean prehistory is its graphic arts, particularly the wall paintings. The colors available to the artists of Akrotiri were red, black, yellow, blue, and cream, with the lighter colors often serving as background. They painted on small areas, such as the space between two windows, and on full expanses of blank walls. Although the paintings were begun on wet plaster, the artists evidently did not try to maintain the wet condition, and often completed the paintings when the plaster was completely dry. For this reason, the term "fresco" (from the Italian for "fresh") is not strictly accurate. Paintings on dry plaster tend to flake, while those painted when the plaster was wet are much better preserved. They painted wild animals, such as antelopes and monkeys, semidomesticated animals like cats and goats, various mythological creatures, and the subjects that give us our best view of life in prehistoric Greece: people.

Most of the frescoes discovered at Akrotiri were fragments, sometimes found in the dust, sometimes barely clinging to the crumbling walls. For those that had fallen, the pieces had to be painstakingly reassembled, and often, large portions of a mural were lost and had to be reconstructed. As Marinatos and his crew (which included his daughter Nanno, the British scholar Colin Renfrew, and Christos Doumas, the second-in-command, who would go on to become the project's director) slowly removed the piled-up volcanic ash, they saw what Renfrew described as "one of the most perfect works of art to have been preserved for us from prehistoric times." It was a wall painting, completely intact, of a rocky landscape with lilies growing on the rocks, and swallows swooping overhead.* This spectacular painting is now known as the "Spring Fresco" or the "Fresco of the Lilies." The lilies and the swallows are realistic, but the contours of the red and gray rocks—obviously of volcanic origin—are highly exaggerated, prompting Nanno Marinatos to write that she was "not at all convinced by the suggestion that they depict a typical pre-eruption Thera setting. Rather they represent the idea of rocky ground using the conventions of Minoan art."

In his first excavations, Marinatos found rooms that contained cups and lamps, but reasoned (correctly) that he had discovered the upper story of a multistory building, and took pains to protect it from the elements. He covered the site with corrugated sheet metal, which protected the fragile buildings from the rain, and fiberglass to let in the sunlight as they continued their work. Ten complete buildings were uncovered, which Marinatos identified with a complex system of names, including alpha, beta, gamma, and delta for the first four, then Xesté (the Greek term for the dressed stone blocks known as ashlars), with Arabic numerals employed to identify particular buildings (e.g., Xesté 3), and, finally, names that referred to particular features or loca-

* In the 1975 John Huston film *The Man Who Would Be King*, based on the story by Rudyard Kipling and starring Michael Caine, Sean Connery, and Christopher Plummer, two soldiers, mustered out of the British army in India, decide to cross the Himalayas to "Rajistan," where they intend to proclaim themselves kings and loot the country's fabled riches. In the film, the "treasury" contains the sumptuous booty of Alexander the Great, evidently stored there since he invaded northern India some two thousand years earlier. The walls of the Himalayan palace are decorated with exact replicas of the paintings of the lilies and swallows of the "Spring Fresco" in room Delta 2 at Akrotiri.

THE "FRESCO OF THE LILIES," or "Spring Fresco," in building Delta 3 at Akrotiri, with swallows flying over the flowers. This design was copied for the "treasure room" in the 1975 film *The Man Who Would Be King*, which has nothing whatever to do with the Aegean.

tions, such as the House of the Ladies, where, on facing walls (the east and the west), are two incomplete murals showing mature women, identifiable by their long hair and full breasts. In the next alcove to the north are frescoes showing tall papyrus plants. (This and the "Spring Fresco" are the only rooms that show solely plants.) Papyrus did not grow in Thera, and probably not even in Crete. When he found what was obviously a street that ran north-south between several buildings—one of which yielded some artisans' tools—Marinatos named it Telchines Street, after a primitive tribe that was sometimes represented in mythology as the inventors of the useful arts. As of 1992, an area of about 10,000 square meters (32,800 square feet) of Akrotiri had been excavated, and it is estimated that this may be half or less than the total.

Spyridon Marinatos died of a stroke on October 1, 1974, while supervising the installation of a new device for removing ash from the dig at his beloved Akrotiri. According to his daughter, he had been working "intensively and without interruption" since 1967. He concluded his 1972 *National Geographic* article with these words: "Eventually [visitors] will be able to stroll through the streets and glance through the doors and windows of a once-flourishing Minoan city, a city that died by violence, a city that in the pathos of its ruin—its pulse of life stopped virtually in mid-beat—stands as an epitaph for the brilliant, seagirt world of Minos." Pursuant to his instructions, Marinatos was buried in room 16 of the Delta Building. Christos Doumas, Marinatos's deputy, assumed command of the project, and in addition to his prodigious output of papers and articles, and his chairmanship of numerous symposia dedicated to Theran studies, he is the author of *The Wall Paintings of Thera,* the definitive study of these monuments in the history of art. Nanno Marinatos, educated in the United States (she has a Ph.D. from the University of Colorado at Boulder), maintained the family tradition of passionate interest in Thera. She became an authority on the interpretation of Theran frescoes and, in 1985, published *Art and Religion in Thera: Reconstructing a Bronze Age Society.*

The building known as "Building Beta" ("B1") was so badly damaged by a later flood that it has not been possible to locate the entrance. Nevertheless,

THE ANTELOPES and "boxing boys" from Beta 1 at Akrotiri. Like everything else about the wall paintings of Thera, the reason for the juxtaposition of these disparate images is unknown.

excavators have uncovered enough pottery vessels to infer that this was a private residence, its upper stories decorated with intriguing wall paintings, including a realistically drawn pair of antelopes. Spyridon Marinatos had originally identified them as oryxes (*Oryx beisa*), but his daughter says "they are a hybrid of the Thomson and Grant's Gazelle and also *Oryx beisa*.* It is thus probable that the iconographical form is derived from other pictures and that the painter had never seen the real animals. . . . The animals are rendered with surprising liveliness in simple, outline form." Because antelopes are not known in the Aegean islands, this iconography is probably borrowed from Egypt, but as Vanschoonwinkel notes in his 1990 study of animal representations in Theran and other Aegean arts, "The steps in the transmission of this motif are missing at this time."

The "Blue Monkey Fresco" in Beta 6 again shows an animal not native to the island as the subject of a major painting. But unlike the single, supplicant monkey in Xesté 3, the simians in Beta 6 cavort in great numbers all over one wall. These monkeys are identifiable as to type and, therefore, as to origin. They are guenons, long-tailed ground dwellers from Africa, and even though color is not a good determinant (the Minoan wall painters had a very limited palette), the monkeys in the paintings closely resemble the species coincidentally known as "blue monkeys," *Cercopithecus mitis.* Found from central to south Africa, blue monkeys are characterized by their solid, slate-gray to bluish coloration, with a distinct white band across the forehead, clearly visible in the Akrotiri paintings.

Aris Poulianos (1972) describes a petrified skull, referable to the genus *Cercopithecus,* that was found in the ruins of Thera, which suggests to him that the monkeys were drawn from real animals, perhaps kept as pets as they were in Egypt.† The skull was found "among the sea pebbles and rocks on the east side of Thera on the Monolithos coast in the summer of 1966" by Edward Loring, who is described by Poulianos as "a foreign scientist looking for evidence of the

* Gazelles are small, delicate creatures, and the only aspect of the Akrotiri paintings that is at all gazelle-like is the curving horns. Oryxes, on the other hand, are heavyset antelopes (classified with the group commonly known as "horse antelopes") with straight or slightly curved horns. Everything about the Akrotiri antelopes calls to mind an oryx—including the striking body and face pattern—but the horns say "gazelle," which suggests that Nanno may be correct in her "hybrid" theory; not that the antelopes were actually hybrids, but that the artist combined the characteristics of animals he had never seen.

† In his 1969 *Atlantis: The Truth Behind the Legend,* Galanopoulos identifies a "fossilized monkey's head found on Santorin in 1966" as "a gibbon, probably of the species *Colobinae,* mostly found in Ethiopia." Gibbons are not monkeys (they are apes); they are not found anywhere near Ethiopia (they are Asiatic); and they are not members of the subfamily Colobinae, which actually includes such diverse monkeys as the guerezas of Africa, the sacred langurs of India, and the proboscis monkeys of Borneo.

THE SO-CALLED monkey's-head fossil, found at Santorini in 1966. Used to demonstrate that there were monkeys killed in the volcanic eruption, the "fossil" is actually a lava bomb.

lost continent . . . [who] actually spent many summers actually combing the island for evidence." Whatever Loring was looking for, he seems to have found the only "evidence" of a living creature that perished in the eruption of Thera around 1500 B.C. In his discussion ("The Discovery of the First Known Victim of Thera's Bronze Age Eruption"), Poulianos wrote, "Perhaps his masters were less fortunate than he and were burned off behind, and this monkey was assigned by fate to give us sole testimony of this biblical destruction." In later years, Loring's "monkey skull" was dismissed as spurious; if not an outright fake, it was certainly not what Loring (or Poulianos) said it was. Also, as Dorothy Vitaliano points out, "neither Mavor, nor Galanopoulos and Bacon offer any explanation of what would constitute an unprecedented case of fossilization—replacement by lava—in terms that would satisfy any paleontologist." The monkeys of the frescoes, however, are included in this discussion because, as we shall see, their presence in ancient Greece might have contributed to the Plague of Athens, a catastrophe that may have been peripherally included in Plato's discussion of the downfall of Atlantis.

In addition to those of Beta 6, monkeys appear in three other Theran wall paintings: in Xesté 3, a young woman sits on a platform flanked by a griffin and a monkey; in Room 2 of the West House, there is a fragmentary frieze showing monkeys holding swords or playing a lyre; and Sector A shows part of a monkey with its forepaws raised in front of an altar.

No palace has been found at Akrotiri—nor is one expected—but in addition to the ordinary houses, there are "mansions," which include ceremonial rooms and smaller rooms that appear to have been service areas used for the storage and preparation of food. Xesté 3, for example, can be divided into two distinct sections, identified as eastern and western. The small rooms of the western section contained storage jars and pottery and were therefore probably used for food preparation; the eastern section has two large rooms and two stairways, and when the doors between the rooms were opened, a large space was formed, which Nanno Marinatos believed was "suitable for public gatherings." This building also contains a small, square room similar to those that Arthur Evans had found at Knossos, and that he had decided were "lustral basins," employed in ritual purification ceremonies. Others saw them as baths, but since there are no drains attached to these rooms, they have now been interpreted as holy areas known as *adyta* (singular: *adyton*), into which priests would descend to make offerings. The second story may have been used for sleeping quarters, but most of the upper level collapsed into the lower, and is less easy to read. This building also contains the "Goddess Fresco," and, with the *adyton,* indicates that Xesté 3 was a building with a primarily religious function—as Nanno Marinatos describes it, "suitable for cult activities of a mystical character." It is obvious that the wall paintings in Xesté 3 were more than mere decorations; they depicted specific events or symbolic iconography that had substantial importance to the inhabitants of Akrotiri.

The "fishermen" paintings, one of which is much better preserved than the other, show two naked youths with their heads shaven (indicated by the bluish color), with only topknots of hair remaining. The fisherman on the west wall holds one bunch of three mackerel; on the north wall, the boy holds seven dolphinfish (also known as dorado or mahimahi) in his right hand, and five more in his left. Both these species of fishes are fast swimmers and would not be—even today, with sophisticated spearguns—catchable by divers. Why, then, are these two naked boys shown with strings of these particular fish? Nanno Marinatos writes that "their blue heads, which denote partial shaving, and their nudity" indicate that they are "performing a special function as youthful adorants," and suggests that they are making an offering to their deity.

The "priestess" (on the southeast doorjamb of Room 4 where it connects to Room 5) is dressed in a floor-length chiton of a terra-cotta color, with blue and white trim. She wears heavy gold earrings, a necklace, bracelets, and a snakelike device in her blue hair. (Nanno Marinatos sees her coiffure somewhat differently: "If the blue color of her hair denotes partial shaving, then the lock on top of the head is dressed in such a way as to resemble a snake.") Her lips and left ear (she is shown in left profile) are painted red, and in her hands she holds a glowing brazier. "Perhaps," wrote Nanno Marinatos, "she passed

THE YOUNG "fisherman" painted on the wall of West House carries seven dolphinfish (dorado or mahimahi) in his right hand, and five more in his left. Did he catch them, or is there another explanation?

from room to room censing it or perfuming the air of the house. This is why she is depicted on a door jamb."

According to Christina Televantou's 1990 reconstruction, the "Miniature Frieze" ran around all four walls of Room 5, even though there are no fragments to indicate that there was a painting on the west wall. The piece entitled "Frieze with the Fleet" shows ships heading from one end of the wall to the other, crossing open water from one settlement to another, powered by ranks of oarsmen. It has been suggested (Doumas 1992) that "the painter of the Miniature Frieze sought to tell the story of a major overseas voyage, in the course of which the fleet visited several harbours and cities, five in all, which the artist has successfully depicted on the four walls of Room 5." An alternative interpretation, proposed by Nanno Marinatos, is that the friezes show a religious festival, exemplified by the festive ornamentation of the ships; the existence of a woman of high rank seated near the symbolic horns of consecration; the fact that the ships are being paddled, rather than rowed, which suggests a ceremonial function; and the presence of a group of youths leading an animal to a religious sacrifice. Further, she sees the festival as celebrating war or aggression, shown by the boat crews' shields and spears, the grappling iron, and the floating bodies, which suggest a battle, not a shipwreck.

As shown in the frescoes, the island settlements contain buildings in the

Minoan style; multistoried structures of different heights, built of trimmed blocks. Town II is seen as a coastal community, with pastoral activities depicted in the upper portions of the painting, including herdsmen with sheep, goats, and cattle; a troop of helmeted warriors with shields and spears; and, below them, the wrecks of ships with drowned victims floating in the water. On the east wall is a frieze that shows a river, and thus interrupts the "voyage" of the ships. We see the river from above, and among the palm trees and bushes are various animals, including a wildcat and a jackal in pursuit of ducks. This scene also contains a drawing of a griffin, with the wings and head of an eagle and the body of a lion. The river continues into the next segment of the frieze, and may in fact be a continuation. The landscape at the left, from which the ships are departing, shows not only a town (Town IV) but the mountainous

landscape in which the town is set, complete with rocks, trees, streams, and heavy-antlered deer being pursued by a lion. It is not evident that the painter of the frieze intended it to portray a particular location, but, writes Nanno Marinatos, "even if the artist wanted to draw imaginary places, he would incorporate elements with which he was familiar." Thus we see a depiction of the naval and terrestrial architecture of Thera, from approximately 1600 B.C. In this scene, which is believed to show some sort of ritual "nautical festival," the largest ship, dubbed "the Admiral's," is festooned with crocus pendants strung over the covered pavilion, in which the passengers are seated comfortably. Dolphins frolic around the vessels, and the "the Admiral's" ship is decorated with paintings of

ALTHOUGH WE DO NOT know the true identity of the woman depicted in this Akrotiri wall painting, she is commonly referred to as the "priestess."

lions and dolphins. Each of the large vessels has a figurehead at the stern, usually in the form of a lion, and a long, graceful bowsprit. A single mast is stepped
amidships, and while most of the ships are being rowed by oarsmen, one of the
smaller ships has a single square sail raised, and the details of the rigging are
clearly shown. They are headed for Town V, a series of stacked buildings with
people looking out over the sea at the arriving flotilla from the flat rooftops,
and from open windows. Doumas (1992) writes that "the topographic features
of the landscape, the configuration of the harbour and the beached boats, the
multi-storied buildings with Aegean architectural traits, and the appearance of
the inhabitants argue for the identification of Town V as Akrotiri."

In her 1990 discussion of the friezes ("New Light on the West House Wall-
Paintings"), Christina Televantou summarized her interpretations:

> We are of the opinion that the pictorial programme of the West House was
> organized so as to project a highly complex central idea, the age-old relation-
> ship between man, in this case the Theran, and the sea. . . . Firstly through the
> projection of the activities of the Aegean fleet in the Eastern Mediterranean,
> which we believe is the setting in which some of the events depicted on the
> Miniature Frieze are enacted, though with special emphasis on the participa-
> tion of the Theran fleet. Secondly by projecting martial alertness of this fleet,
> and, by extension, the economic and political role of the Therans in the
> Aegean and perhaps the Aegean peoples in the Eastern Mediterranean. . . .
> Finally, the significant role of sea-faring activities in the upbringing of Theran
> youth is also projected.[*]

Except for domesticated animals, beasts of burden, birds of the air, and
fishes and dolphins of the sea, the Greek islands are largely devoid of exotic
wildlife. There are no native monkeys, antelopes, deer, or lions.[†] There are certainly no griffins. However they got there, lions appear prominently in the

---

[*] It is worth noting here that Plato described the harbors in the metropolis of Atlantis as consisting of
"two rings of land, and three of sea, like cartwheels, with the island at their center and equivalent from
each other, making the place inaccessible to man (for there were still no ships or sailing in those days)."

[†] The closest lions at that time were probably in North Africa, six hundred miles across the Mediterranean. Of course, Egypt was also in North Africa, and lions were probably hunted by royalty, although
they do not appear in Old Kingdom reliefs. The famous Lion Gate at Mycenae, made around 1250 B.C.,
shows two lions heraldically positioned around an architectural column with their forefeet resting on
an altar in the Cretan style. Around 650 B.C., long after the Minoan and Mycenaean civilizations had
fallen, the great cats would appear in the spectacular Assyrian reliefs of Assurbanipal's lion hunts, which
were unearthed in 1849 by Austen Henry Layard at Kuyunjik, on the banks of the Tigris in what is now
Iraq. Of these remarkable works, art historian Kenneth Clark wrote, "On these Assyrian reliefs, exe-
cuted over a period of more than two hundred years, the depiction of lion-hunts produced a series of
masterpieces unsurpassed in the ancient world."

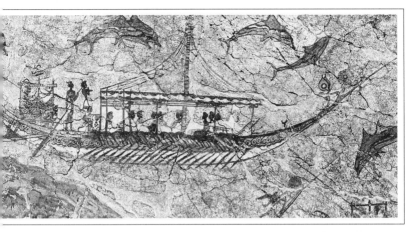

THE "ADMIRAL'S SHIP" in the long frieze in the West House at Akrotiri, showing a high-ranking official being transported. Other than that, we know nothing about this sophisticated painting.

wall paintings of Akrotiri, in landscapes, as the painted decorations and figure-heads on ships, and even on libation cups—but there are hardly any lions on the Minoan artifacts from Crete.

According to Fouqué (1869), "The men of Santorini were laborers or fisher-men; they cultivated cereals, made flour, extracted oil from olives, raised flocks of goats and sheep, fished with nets; they produced decorated vases and were acquainted with gold and probably copper." It is clear that Minoan Akrotiri had been a town of some consequence. For its time, it was also immense, covering some thirty-one acres. There were two- and three-story buildings, separated by narrow, winding streets; houses with substantial doors and stone staircases, with large windows to let in the sunlight for which the Cyclades are still renowned. Some of the bigger buildings, such as the West House and the House of the Ladies, were freestanding, while many of the others seem to have had common walls and were bunched together. These "apartment blocks," such as the Beta, Gamma, and Delta buildings, comprise many rooms, some of which have been identified as dwellings, but not as many kitchens as might have been expected have been found, suggesting that more than one family may have used the cooking facilities. The buildings identified as the "North Magazine" appear to have been used for storage and food preparation (many storage jars and a hearth have been found there), and the presence of large windows facing the street at ground level has prompted the suggestion that they might have served for the distribution of goods to the townspeople. A lion's-head rhyton found in the magazine may indicate that cult activities were also carried out there. In the upper level of the mill building, a rhyton in the form of a cropped-horn bull covered by a net was found, of which Nanno Marinatos wrote, "It seems that this bull is a representation of a sacrificial animal because the net and the cutting of the horns suggest a ritual preparation. It is very probable that the sacrificial ritual was connected with the harvest of grain or with its grinding into flour in Crete."

The houses were built of local materials, including small stones, held together with a mortar of mud and straw. As at Knossos, the walls were strengthened with wooden beams, which were often exposed indoors and out.

Trimmed ashlar blocks were used to face the larger buildings, many of which included multiple rooms to serve different functions. There were bathrooms with terra-cotta tubs, and on the second floor, to take advantage of the gravity flow, stone toilets (that may once have had wooden seats), connected by a series of clay pipes to a drainage system that ran beneath the streets. Theran potters appear to have turned out great quantities of ceramic vessels, including cookware, incense burners, ewers, jugs, drinking cups, and storage jars, all ornamented with brilliantly colored images of flowers, ears of barley, birds, fishes, dolphins, and abstract designs.

There is little question that the settlement at Akrotiri was Minoan. Sinclair Hood (1990) has analyzed the architecture

A LARGE ROOF has been constructed over the entire dig at Akrotiri to ensure that the excavated ruins are not affected by the weather.

and found that it "suggests a basically similar way of life at Akrotiri and in major Cretan centers." J.-C. Poursat's observations on the commercial interactions between Crete and Thera (also published in the 1990 *Thera and the Aegean World III*) address the importance of Thera as a port and indicate that it might have been the most significant international harbor of its time. Indeed, the dominance of the Cretans (what M. H. Wiener calls the "Minoan Thalassocracy") influenced the Cyclades, the Dodecanese, and even the coasts of Asia Minor.

Frescoes in Thera have a white background, while those of Knossos are polychromed, but the subject matter and style are largely similar.

During the 1890s, von Gaertringen excavated the ancient city of Thera. (The *island* is also known as Thera, and the capital city, overlooking the caldera, is Phira, sometimes spelled Fíra.) "Ancient Thera" (as the guidebooks call it) is a settlement high on the hill called Mesa Vuono, originally settled by the Greeks of the ninth century B.C., some six hundred years after the devastating volcano eruption. Because it sits on a ridge 1,000 feet above sea level, the town commands the most dramatic position on the island, probably chosen for reasons of defense. Following the configuration of the ridge, ancient Thera runs on a northeast-southwest axis, and is a long, narrow settlement, with the Gymnasium of the Ephebes at one end, the Gymnasium of the Guard at the other, and various Hellenic buildings, such as the Temple of Dionysus, the Temple of Apollo Karneios, and various public and private buildings in between.

In Akrotiri, pottery pieces and many complete examples are the dominant artifactual evidence of the settlement. More than fifty different shapes have been distinguished, many of them locally produced and others imported, probably from Crete. They range in size from the *pithoi,* which are large storage jars, often taller than a man, to vases and drinking cups. Their shape and decoration define and date them, and their provenance helps to date the settlement itself. The pottery of Akrotiri was decorated with a variety of themes, including abstract designs and representations of the plant and animal kingdoms. Small oblong vessels, known as *kymbai* and resembling miniature bathtubs, and decorated with dolphins, swallows, or chamois, have been found only at Akrotiri.

Rhytons are libation cups, usually in exotic shapes, but sometimes they are just elongated cones. At Akrotiri, there have been found rhytons in the shape of a polled bull, a boar's head, the head of a lioness, and, probably most dramatic of all, given the importance of the bull in Minoan culture, the bull's head. A spectacular rhyton, made of black steatite in the shape of a bull's head, was found in the palace complex at Knossos, and another of the same shape was found in the "Hall of Ceremonies" at Zakros. Each one was badly shattered, but they were reconstructed to show a hole at the nape of the neck, and another at the tip of the muzzle, respectively for filling the vessel and for pouring the libations. The Knossos rhyton, half of which was intact, had eyes made of rock crystal, jasper, and clamshell. The shape of the horns, missing in both cases, has been reconstructed on the basis of a silver rhyton, found at Mycenae—undoubtedly imported from Crete—in which the gracefully curved horns were made of gilded wood. Two more rhytons, both made of faience in the shape of a hornless bull (or perhaps a cow), were found at Zakros. (Also at Zakros, a foot-high, cone-shaped rhyton was found that was decorated with raised images of goats and numerous representations of the altars crowned with ceremonial horns.)

THE BULL'S-HEAD RHYTON from the Little Palace at Knossos. Found without the horns, the eight-inch-high head is made of black steatite, and the eyes are rock crystal.

In Ninkovich and Heezen's synopsis, "The greater part of the settlement . . . together with the central part of the island, fell into the magma chamber during the big eruption." It has been too easy to attribute the fall of Knossos to a destructive volcano, but a careful examination of the archaeological and geological evidence does not support this simplistic resolution of one of the great mysteries of prehistory. Knossos was in decline—indeed, it may have been conquered and burned—before the volcano erupted in 1450 B.C. (Marinatos discovered that objects found beneath the lower tephra in Santorini cannot be dated later than 1520 B.C., suggesting that the big eruption occurred after the Minoan settlement had been destroyed.) The central settlement at Knossos, which Arthur Evans believed was ruled by King Minos, was rebuilt and struggled on for years before collapsing altogether. R. W. Hutchinson (1962) accepted Marinatos's theory of the volcanic destruction of LM-I palaces, but believed that the decline of Minoan Crete was the result of an invasion by the Mycenaeans (Achaeans). The palaces at Knossos survived the pillaging Mycenaeans, but the eruption of Thera closed the book on one of the greatest unsolved mysteries in the history of civilization. Only through the concerted efforts of archaeologists, historians, and geologists are we beginning to get an idea of the glory that was Crete.*

The discovery of Minoan pottery, frescoed walls, and storerooms with amphorae still in place paled beside the discovery that under the fallen stone walls there was no trace of the pumice that covered everything else. Based on that evidence, Marinatos concluded that "a strong earthquake had destroyed the building; thereafter a shower of tephra from an exploding volcano buried it." Marinatos decided that the eruption of Thera had ended Minoan culture.

Revelations about the Minoan civilization, combined with information about the eruption of the volcano, have produced any number of studies, culminating in the establishment in 1989 of the Thera Foundation, dedicated to the study and dissemination of information on every aspect of the history of Thera. The foundation has sponsored (so far) four symposia and issued no fewer than six massive volumes of learned papers on every aspect of Theran studies. In his concluding remarks to the Third Congress, Dr. Vassos Karageorghis coined a new category for the archaeological lexicon: "Therology." While Pliny gave his name to a type of eruption, and Stromboli and Pelée have types of volcanic eruptions named for them, Thera is the only volcano immortalized by a whole field of study. One effect of this concentrated study is that it supersedes previous work, mostly by utilizing that previous work as a substructure for the more recent studies. Thus, the eruption, the archaeology, and the history of Santorini (as well as the influences of mainland Greece, Crete, and other Aegean islands) are probably best interpreted through the most recent publications—most often, those of the Thera Foundation. In the capital city of Thera, the foundation has reconfigured an earthquake-damaged building into a thoroughly modern conference center, which was the site of the 1996 symposium on the wall paintings of Thera. And just in time, since at the site, Professor Doumas and his dedicated corps of students and volunteers

---

* In *Four Thousand Years Ago: A World Panorama of Life in the Second Millennium B.C.*, Geoffrey Bibby re-creates the daily life of Minoan nobles at Knossos, including the bull games (where an occasional amateur "sprang into the ring in the pauses between the teams, to make a pass or two at one of the bulls and to retire to polite applause after a single somersault"), trade with Egypt, and, finally, the invasion of the Achaeans, who burned the palace and enslaved the Minoans. Those who escaped, he says, settled in Lebanon, Egypt, and Cyprus.

are uncovering and reassembling even more fascinating examples of this site-specific art form.

Santorini is one of the most popular tourist destinations in the Aegean, for all the wrong reasons. It is probably the most spectacular of the Cyclades—in fact, it is one of the most spectacular islands in the world. (In the 1994 guidebook *The Cyclades,* it is referred to as "most people's favourite Greek island . . . with the awesome mixture of towering, sinister, multi-coloured volcanic cliffs, dappled with the 'chic'-est, most brilliant-white, trendiest bars and restaurants in the country. . . .") It looks not unlike an atoll: a hollowed-out circle, with high, striated cliffs surrounding a deep blue crater. In the middle of this volcanic caldera—for that is what Santorini is—two black lava islands rise, a silent testimony to its unbelievably violent history.

CHRISTOS DOUMAS, archaeologist in charge of the recent excavations of the Minoan settlement of Akrotiri, on the island of Santorini

The tourists arrive by plane, by ferry, and by cruise ship. Usually less than a day is allocated to the exploration of Santorini, with a pronounced emphasis on shopping. Shops sell everything from ice cream and doughnuts to museum replicas of Greek antiquities and expensive gold jewelry. In the summer, the main city of Thera (also called Phira) attracts nomadic students in hordes. During the day, they cruise the narrow roads of Santorini on buzzing mopeds, motorbikes, and motorcycles, going to the beaches, and in the evening—and all through the night—they hang out, drinks in hand, making contact with their fellow travelers from every possible location in Europe and America.

But behind the "happy-tourist-in-the-Greek-Islands" façade there lurks a story of a stupendous volcanic eruption that blew up most of an island; an entire civilization that abruptly vanished from the face of the earth; and—not surprisingly—intimations of the Lost City of Atlantis.

The archaeological dig at Akrotiri belongs on the itinerary of visitors to Santorini. Because of the fragile nature of the dig, only forty people at a time are allowed to walk through, on specified paths and under the watchful eye of a guide. As the tourists gawk, archaeological students and volunteers under the direction of Christos Doumas are carefully removing fragmented evidence of the Minoan occupation of the site, some thirty-five hundred years ago.

Spyridon Marinatos's dream of a "walk-through" Minoan civilization will not be realized in our lifetime. (The closest we will come to such a concept is Evans's "reconstructions" at Knossos.) Excavations of this sort go painfully slowly, as each wall, stairway, and fragment of wall painting has to be gently uncovered, often with a tiny brush, and then photographed, mapped, and carefully removed. As it is cleared away, the ash is placed in leather buckets, and then transported by wheelbarrow to a dump site outside the dig. (Archaeology may have made some technological advances, but the method of removing unwanted ash or dirt is the same now as it was in Schliemann's time, the difference being that researchers today are much more careful than Schliemann was.) In the case of pottery or frescoes, that is only the beginning, since the restorers then have to try to reassemble the pieces, often without a clue as to the appearance of the final artifact. Professor Doumas has dozens of assistants, volunteer and otherwise, meticulously reassembling wall paintings and pottery. They are nowhere near up to speed, however, since there are batteries of filing cabinets and boxes containing thousands of fragments that will not see the light of day for many years. Even if he had the money—which he does not—to pay more restorers, the sheer weight of the archaeological evidence would occupy hundreds of people for decades.

With its sophisticated art and architecture and its wealth of archaeological mysteries, not to mention the mysterious disappearance of its people, it is tempting to align the Minoan civilization with Atlantis. Indeed, many people have done just that. Just as Atlantis represents one of the greatest mysteries of ancient literature, so then do the palaces at Knossos and Phaistos, and the settlement at Akrotiri, exemplify one of the greatest puzzles in all of archaeology.

WALLS OF WATER

Here from the ground a roar like Zeus's thunderclap
came sounding heavy round us, terrible to hear.
The horses raised their heads and pricked their ears
right up into the air, and on us fell as lively fear,
wondering what the sound could be.
And when we looked along the foaming shores,
we saw a monstrous wave towering up into the sky,
so big it took away the view of Sciron's promontory
from my eyes. It hid the Isthmus and Asclepius' rock.
Next, swelling up and surging onward, with, all around,
a mass of foam, and with the roaring of the sea,
it neared the shore where stood the four-horse chariot.
And in the very surge and breaking of the flood,
the wave threw up a bull, a fierce and monstrous thing,
and with his bellowing the land was wholly filled,
and fearfully re-echoed.

—EURIPIDES
Hippolytus

NCORRECTLY REFERRED TO as "tidal waves"—they have nothing to do with tides—tsunamis are among the most destructive forces in nature.* In his introduction to Douglas Myles's book *The Great Waves,* George Pararas-Carayannis wrote, "The impact of tsunami [he chooses the Japanese plural, although most authors prefer "tsunamis"] on human societies can be traced back in written history to 1480 B.C. in the Eastern Mediterranean when the Minoan civilization was wiped out by such great tsunami waves generated by the volcanic explosion of the island of Santorin." (Pararas-Carayannis's opinions are to be taken seriously; the Greek-born seismologist is the director of the International Tsunami Information Center in Honolulu.) In Japanese, the word *tsunami* means "large waves in harbors," which is another unfortunate misnomer, since most of these waves are generated deep under the open ocean, and then run up on shore. Among the currently accepted terms are "seismic sea wave," "seismic wave disturbance," and "oceanic shock wave," all of which acknowledge the earthquake as the progenitor of these phenomena.

---

* There are indeed "tidal waves," also known as "bores," which are the sudden surges with which incoming tides arrive in some parts of the world. Among the most famous of these are the bore of Britain's Severn River; and on the Seine, the Mascaret, which has been known to arrive at Paris as a 24-foot-high wall of water. Between New Brunswick and Nova Scotia in eastern Canada, the Bay of Fundy has the highest tides in the world, which can produce rises of 50 feet.

When the image of giant waves comes to mind, we usually envision great curling combers, like the 30-footers that daredevil surfers ride at places like Waimea Bay on the north shore of the Hawaiian island of Oahu. In fact, tsunamis do not look like that at all, but the popular perception is that they are gigantic, cresting, breaking waves.* Ocean waves, including the big surf of Hawaii, are generated by eastwardly moving low-pressure storms—called "extratropical cyclones" by meteorologists—that are born off the western sides of the great oceans and mature as they travel across them. The warm, light air of the low-pressure systems passes near the cool, relatively heavy air of a high, and as the air from the high rushes toward the low to equalize atmospheric pressure, wind is created, and wind creates waves. The distance over which the wind blows (known as the "fetch"), the wind velocity, and the duration of the wind directly affect the height and length of the waves. Winter storms are the largest, and thus create the largest waves. Many other factors, such as the depth of the water over which the waves form, the shape of the bottom, the slope of the shoreline, and the wind direction, affect the formation of waves. The most powerful of wind-driven waves travel at a speed of perhaps 60 miles per hour. Before they are slowed down by contact with the shelving bottom and eventually the shore, tsunamis can achieve speeds of more than 500 miles per hour—about the cruising speed of a jetliner.

The tsunami following the June 26, 1896, earthquake at Sanriku, Japan, was recorded on tide gauges in San Francisco, some five thousand miles away, ten and a half hours later, giving it an average speed of 480 miles per hour. A violent seaquake 120 miles from Japan occurred 32,000 feet down, in the Tuscarora Deep, a notorious source of seismic activity. "Such a trench," wrote Rachel Carson, "is by its very nature a breeder of earthquakes, being a place of disturbed and uneasy equilibrium, of buckling and warping downward of the sea floor to form the deepest pits of all the earth's surface." At Sanriku, on the northern coast of Honshu, the seas began to recede, and in the ominous silence that followed, heads turned to watch the ocean where an impossible wall of water, 110 feet high, was bearing down. "It came at first as a far-off whis-

---

* Unfortunately, the dust jacket of Myles's book, which is primarily about tsunamis, is decorated with a photograph of a curling shorebreak wave, which contradicts this important distinction. A painting by Darrel Millsap, first used on the cover of the November 1971 issue of *Oceans* magazine and reproduced frequently thereafter, shows a wave towering over the Scotch Cap lighthouse in the Aleutians—a gigantic comber about to break. Probably the most familiar single wave in all of art, Katsushika Hokusai's *Great Wave near Kanagawa* (from his *Thirty-six Views of Mount Fuji*) is a very large wave indeed—it dwarfs the boats in the picture—but it is not a tsunami.

per," wrote Michael Mooney, "similar to the sound of falling rain on water. The whisper became a hiss, then a steady rush, growing louder by the second until it reached a watery crescendo of stupefying proportions." Millions of tons of seething, frothing water and sand engulfed the coast for hundreds of miles. More than ten thousand houses were destroyed, and as many as twenty-seven thousand people were killed.

On April 1, 1946, when residents of the town of Laupahoehoe on the eastern shore of the Big Island of Hawaii noticed that the ocean was receding, they were completely unaware of the possible consequences. After the Pacific rolled back in and then out again, many of them ventured onto the exposed wet sea floor to pick up the dead and dying fish. But a monstrous wall of water came roaring in, smashing buildings and drowning people. It receded again, but returned with even greater force, destroying almost everything in its path. It was—and still is—the largest tsunami of this century.

Often the receding of the ocean from the shore is the first sign of an approaching tsunami. In a "seaquake," there is an abrupt collapse of a part of the ocean bed, and the sea above it drops, leaving a depression on the surface, which is filled by the surrounding waters. This leads to a wild oceanic turmoil, where the sea flows back and forth, each time higher and faster than before. The first return wave generally appears within fifteen minutes, but it might take much longer. In *Waves and Beaches,* oceanographer Willard Bascom described the process:

> The first jolt [of three generating forces] is a simple fault in which tension in the submarine crustal rock is relieved by the abrupt rupturing of the rock along an inclined plane. When such a fault occurs, a large mass of rock drops rapidly and the support is removed from a column of water that extends to the surface. The water surface oscillates up and down as it seeks to return to mean sea level, and a series of waves is sent out. If the rock falls in compression, the mass of rock on one side rides up over that on the other, and a column of water is lifted, but the result is the same: a tsunami.

Not all deep-ocean seismic activity produces receding waters. When an island is born as a result of an underwater volcano, as with Surtsey, for example, the eruption causes land to emerge from the sea, displacing large volumes of water and generating concentric waves away from the source. Another instance in which there would be no receding is when a terrestrial event such as a landslide dumps large amounts of material into the ocean. The largest wave ever accurately measured climbed up the wooded slopes of Lituya

Bay, Alaska, in 1958, when an earthquake-triggered landslide consisting of 40 million cubic yards of rock weighing some 90 million tons fell from a maximum height of 3,000 feet and crashed into the bay, sending a wall of water over a 1,740-foot-high promontory. (This is not a typographical error; the figure is *one thousand seven hundred and forty* feet.) That the water reached this un-believable height was determined from the examination of trees on the slope which had been knocked down by the water. It was estimated that this monster wave—technically known as a "swash"; only when it leaves the enclosed bay and enters the sea does it begin to qualify as a tsunami—was by far the largest in recorded history. (For comparison, the Washington Monument is 555 feet high, and the Sears Tower in Chicago tops out at 1,454 feet.)

Against giant waves, there are absolutely no protective measures that can be taken, except to vacate the area. As Frank Lane has written (in *The Elements Rage*), "The sea defense does not exist which can repel a great tsunami; a vast wall of water, 50, 100, even 200 feet high, weighing untold millions of tons, crashing inland at 100 or even 150 mph." Although the unfortunate victims of the Laupahoehoe tsunami were killed by the waves—there were four in all—the real killer, according to Gerard Fryer, was ignorance. Had they known what was happening, they could have evacuated the area, instead of foolishly waiting for the "tidal wave." Tsunamis do not crest like ordinary waves, but approach the shore the way a bore does, as a wall of water with higher water behind it. True, tsunamis grow as they approach the shore—they are slowed and raised by the shoaling bottom—but even as the leading edge of the wave slows down, the vast amount of water behind it is still barreling along at speeds that can approach 500 miles per hour. This power can drive the water across half a mile of low-lying shoreline, as it did in Hawaii in 1946. Four and a half hours after the Unimak quake, the tsunami was recorded on the Honolulu tide gauges, having traveled 2,240 miles at 490 miles per hour. The water first rose eight inches in six minutes, then fell two feet in seven and a half minutes.*

Because of the unpredictable nature of tsunamis, it is rare that eyewit-

---

* Rarely do terrestrial landslides create tsunamis, but underwater landslides are a story of a different magnitude. In a 1995 article on tsunamis, University of Hawaii geophysicist Gerard Fryer suggests that the tsunami that overwhelmed Hilo, Hawaii, in 1946, killing 159 people and setting off the giant wave that crushed the Scotch Cap lighthouse on Unimak Island in the Aleutians, "was caused by a massive slope failure of the sedimentary wedge: a submarine landslide. . . . Several investigators have suggested that a similar sequence caused the Sanriku, Japan, tsunami of 1896, which killed between 22,000 and 27,000 people in Japan and wreaked massive damage in Hawaii, California and Chile."

nesses publish detailed descriptions of these phenomena, and rarer still that an eyewitness would be an authority on the formation and character of the sea floor. In April 1946, marine geologist Francis Shepard, the author of many scientific papers, *The Earth Beneath the Sea,* and *Submarine Canyons,* was living near the beach on the north shore of Oahu when he was awakened by "a loud hissing sound, which sounded for all the world as if dozens of locomotives were blowing off steam directly outside our house." Looking out the window, Shepard reported that "where there had been a beach previously, we saw nothing but boiling water, which was sweeping over the ten-foot top of the beach ridge and coming directly at the house." The wall of water rolled into the house, smashed the windows, and carried the refrigerator out into a cane field. As Shepard and his wife ran for the highest ground they could see, a third wave rolled in, and then a fourth, fifth, and sixth, destroying fields, uprooting trees, and demolishing houses. As soon as possible after his harrowing ordeal, Shepard checked the literature to see if he could find anything to suggest that the waves continue to increase in size, but he found nothing. Throughout the Hawaiian Islands, but mostly on the north shore of the Big Island, 159 people were killed by this series of waves.

The source of this killer tsunami was thousands of miles from Hawaii, in the eastern Aleutian Islands. An earthquake occurred at about 2:00 a.m. on April 1, 1946, some eighty miles southeast of Unimak Island (the actual location is 53°5′ north, 163° west), where the ocean is 12,000 feet deep on the steep slope of the Aleutian Trench. At the Coast Guard station on Unimak Island, the five guardsmen in the Scotch Cap lighthouse felt a sudden, severe shudder that lasted almost a minute. Forty-seven minutes later, a series of monstrous waves thundered in and engulfed the lighthouse, shearing it off at its base and killing everyone inside. One of the waves generated by the earthquake rolled over Laupahoehoe, and hours later, another one damaged buildings, piers, and boats along the California coast. Japan, Samoa, Chile, and New Zealand all reported damage from the run-up of waves. "The entire Pacific," wrote Fryer, "more than a third of the earth's surface, was quivering."

It was long assumed that the epicenter of the earthquake responsible for the Hawaiian tsunamis occurred because the Pacific Plate, subducting beneath the North Pacific Plate at the Aleutians, dragged the edge of the upper plate down, flexing it like a spring; then it snapped back, causing what is known as a "shallow-thrust earthquake." But contemporaneous measurements of the Unimak earthquake showed that it registered 7.3 on the Richter scale, powerful enough to destroy a large city, but not great enough to have touched off such a huge tsunami. The Richter scale* measures ground motion within twenty seconds but understates the magnitude of larger earthquakes, which release most of their energy in the form of waves with longer periods (a period is the length of time required for two successive crests to pass a given point). Recent analysis has shown that the Unimak quake had a moment-magnitude reading of 8.0, making it twenty-five times more powerful than its Richter reading indicated, and therefore quite capable of generating the force necessary to launch the tsunamis. Also, the interaction of the plates might have caused a massive landslide powerful enough to initiate the deep movement of the waters that wreaked havoc on the surface. In other words, the changes in the sea floor may be more important in the development of tsunamis than the amount of seismic energy released.

One might think that a tsunami that killed 159 people in Hawaii would serve as an object lesson, and that people might have learned what to do and what not to do in the event of a receding ocean. Yet at Hilo, in May 1960, when residents were warned that a tsunami was en route across the South Pacific (as a result of a massive earthquake in Concepción, Chile, five thousand miles away), sightseers flocked to the water's edge to watch the spectacle. They should have headed for the hills. According to one eyewitness, "The roar of the massive wall of water blended with the crashing of dozens of stores and apartments and theaters and restaurants—and with the screams of dozens of persons for whom the final noisy warning came in the same moment with death" (Lane 1965). The business district of Hilo was smashed; 282 people were injured and 61 were killed.

The 1960 Chilean earthquake, at a magnitude of 9.5 the most powerful ever recorded, is believed to have resulted from a 600-mile-long rupture of the Chilean subduction zone, which probably slipped all at once. Along 140 miles of coastline, from Puerto Saavedra to Osorno, the shoreline subsided 6 to 12 feet, leaving it open to invasion by the sea. Turbulent waves estimated at 12 to 15 feet high flooded the towns, destroyed boats and buildings, and then hissed out again, returning in a 26-foot-high wall of green water at 125 miles an hour. By the time the third and fourth waves rolled in, there was hardly anyone left,

---

* The Richter scale, developed by physicist Charles Richter in 1935, is used to indicate the magnitude of earthquakes, by using a seismograph to measure the amount of energy released underground. In recent years, seismographers have switched to the "moment-magnitude scale," which (in part) multiplies the area of the fault's rupture surface by the distance the earth moves along the fault. The 1906 San Francisco earthquake has been estimated at 8.3 on the Richter scale and calculated at 7.7 on the M-M scale. Loma Prieta has been adjusted from 7.1 (Richter) to 7.0 (M-M), and Northridge, which was given a reading of 6.4 on the Richter, is now calibrated at 6.7 on the M-M scale.

and virtually every building near the beach had been demolished. The total number of Chileans drowned will never be known, but it has been estimated at more than one thousand.

Concentric circles of waves radiated through the Pacific, flattened much of Hilo, unleashed destruction over an area of 90,000 square miles, destroyed some fifty thousand buildings, and killed six thousand people. Twenty-two hours after its inception, the quake drove a 20-foot-high wave ashore in the harbors of the Japanese islands of Honshu and Hokkaido, ten thousand miles from Chile, flinging fishing boats into dockside buildings like battering rams, killing 180 people and causing an estimated $350 million worth of damage.

We will never know what actually happened when the Aegean volcano erupted around 1500 B.C., but recent analysis of tsunamis generated by earthquake-derived movement on the sea floor suggests that it is possible to imagine a huge wall of water rolling over Crete when the island of Santorini exploded. Even without an underwater landslide, the cataclysmic explosion of a volcano can produce immense seismic waves, like the one that resulted from the eruption of Krakatau (where thirty-six thousand people were drowned by walls of water up to 135 feet high), and the eruption of the volcano in Santorini is believed to have exploded with as much as or more force than the Indonesian one. (In his 1975 article on tsunamis, Michael Mooney calls the eruption of Thera "the greatest known cataclysm in recorded history. . . . [E]xperts have calculated its force as four times that of Krakatoa.")

A F T E R T H E Y H A V E escaped the storm that sinks their ship, Dr. Pangloss and Candide make their way to Lisbon. The year, unfortunately for them, was 1755. In his 1759 novel, named for that innocent disciple of Pangloss, Voltaire wrote that "they had scarcely set foot in the town when they felt the earth tremble underneath their feet; the sea rose in foaming masses in the port and smashed the ships which rode at anchor. Whirlwinds of flame and ashes covered the streets and squares; the houses collapsed, the roofs were thrown upon the foundations, and the foundations were scattered; thirty thousand inhabitants of every age and both sexes were crushed under the ruins." Voltaire's description is accurate; only the number of people killed is understated.

Harry Fielding Reid wrote in 1914 of the Lisbon earthquake: "The region in which the earthquake occurred, its severity, the damage and the loss of life due to it, the distance to which it was felt, the great sea waves to which it gave rise, the agitation of the waters of distant lakes and ponds which it caused, have all

DURING THE GREAT Lisbon earthquake of 1755, buildings collapsed, fires broke out, and walls of seawater inundated the city, killing an estimated sixty thousand people, but the events did not all occur simultaneously, as shown in this nineteenth-century engraving.

united to make it the most notable earthquake of history."* Initiated by a violent rupture of the tectonic plates that meet at the Mid-Atlantic Ridge, the Lisbon quake first shook the city—population estimated at 250,000—at 9:40 in the morning of November 1, 1755, causing churches and other tall buildings to topple, crushing hundreds in the cascading rubble. Candles that had been lit in celebration of the Mass of All Saints' Day started fires in the churches that quickly spread to the neighboring buildings. The royal palace and other buildings were shaken from their foundations and fell on their inhabitants, but

* In terms of fatalities, the worst quake in history occurred in 1556 in Shenshu, China, where more than 830,000 people died; and again in China, the 1920 Kansu earthquake took almost 200,000 lives. In 1737, the Calcutta earthquake claimed 300,000 fatalities, and in 1923, most of Tokyo was destroyed by the great Kanto earthquake, in which 140,000 people died. The Chinese city of Tangshan was completely demolished on July 28, 1976, by two quakes, several hours apart, each of which was equivalent to the San Francisco quake of 1906. Collapsing mine tunnels under the city contributed to the disaster, in which 240,000 people died. What remained of the city was compared to the aftermath of the destruction of Hiroshima. Concerned for the safety of Beijing's 6 million inhabitants, only eighty-five miles away, Chinese officials ordered all residents out of their houses, where they remained for two weeks.

King José was spared because he was out of town. When the first tremors sub-sided, people ran toward the sea to escape the blistering heat of the burning city. Those who could boarded any available ship and headed away from the conflagration; others massed on the marble quay, no doubt taking solace from its massive strength. As thousands of hapless citizens watched, the sea receded in Oeiras Bay (an estuary of the Tagus River), leaving ships heeled over and fish flapping on the exposed bottom. A 50-foot wall of churning black water came roaring in, drowning the poor souls who had sought refuge away from the fires and crumbling the quay to rubble. A realistic estimate of the number of casualties is sixty thousand.

Because it occurred long before the introduction of the Richter scale, the magnitude of the Lisbon earthquake could not be measured, but based on its effects, it has been retroactively estimated at 8.75 to 9.0—the most violent earthquake in history until 1960, when hundreds of miles of the coast of Chile rippled. The shock waves generated by the Portuguese quake, whose epicenter is believed to have been almost directly beneath Lisbon, traveled north to En-gland, south to Africa, and across the Atlantic to North America and the Caribbean. The Moroccan cities of Fez and Mequinez were heavily damaged, leading to speculation that there might have been another focus in North Africa, part of the same fault system. Madeira and the Canaries, islands off the northwest coast of Africa, were inundated by giant waves, and although unsubstantiated, there are stories that a 50-foot wave swamped the Andalusian port city of Cádiz.

As early as 1939, Spyridon Marinatos was suggesting that the palaces on Crete were destroyed by an earthquake that generated a giant sea wave. In "The Volcanic Destruction of Minoan Crete" (published in *Antiquity*), he wrote:

> No historical account survives of this great earthquake, but fortunately we have an excellent means of reconstructing all the phenomena which accom-panied this disaster, in the eruption of Krakatau in the Dutch East Indies on 26–27 August 1883. Geologically speaking, both volcanoes belong to the same family, and the phenomena of their eruptions are therefore analogous. The island of Krakatau is much smaller than Thera and the part of it which was submerged was about a quarter of the other (22.8 sq. km. against 83 in Thera). . . . Vast quantities of pumice covered both the island and a great part of the sea round about. . . . A tremendous roar accompanied the explosion and was heard over 2000 miles away—just one-twelfth of the earth's circumfer-ence. . . . But worst of all was a series of terrific waves which rose after the explosion. They were as much as 90 feet high, and broke with devastating force

and speed against the coasts of Java and Sumatra. Where they struck a plain, they swept inland, and as far as 1000 yards inland they were still 15 yards high. Whole towns, villages and woods were destroyed, and great masses of stones from the sea were hurled far inland.... This amazing catastrophe cost over 36,000 lives.

The magnitude of the Santorini eruption is a matter of conjecture, but the largest explosion ever recorded—volcanic or otherwise—was the 1815 eruption of the volcano Tambora on the Indonesian island of Sumbawa, which is believed to have exploded with a force of 25,000 megatons, compared with the 500 megatons calculated for Krakatau. Sometime in late 1814, the mountain began to emit small showers of ash, and on the night of April 5, 1815, a strong earthquake was felt. Sir Thomas Stamford Raffles, the lieutenant governor of Java, dispatched two boats to investigate what he thought was cannon fire; and some nine hundred miles away, at Macassar on the island of Celebes, the captain of the East India Company's *Benares* heard what sounded like an artillery barrage, and sailed into the Flores Sea looking for pirates. Had they correctly identified the origin of the noise, they probably would not have lived to tell about it, since it was the most powerful explosion in history. Tambora, which had been a 13,000-foot-high mountain, had blown almost a mile off its crown, covering the island with a two-foot-thick coating of ash and mud. The eruption itself killed ten thousand people. On the island of Sumbawa, boats were driven ashore as the sea rose 2 to 12 feet, then subsided. On April 10, five days after the initial explosion, a 14-foot-high wave rushed in and caused great havoc, then receded three minutes later. Subsequently, another eighty thousand people would die of famine and disease, and the ash cloud, carried around the world, cooled cities such as Geneva and New Haven to such an extent that 1816 was referred to as "the year without a summer." It snowed in June throughout New England, and a killing frost on August 21 destroyed crops and gardens from Maine to Connecticut. In his 1994 study of earthquakes and volcanoes, Jon Erickson wrote that Tambora exploded with the equivalent of 20,000 megatons of TNT (one megaton equals 1 million tons); Krakatau exploded with 1,500 megatons; and the atomic bomb dropped on Hiroshima, with 0.02 megaton. (The eruption of the volcano in Thera in 1500 B.C. is estimated to be the second-largest explosion in history, at some 7,500 megatons.) The explosion at Tambora ejected a greater volume of matter than any other volcano, spewing some 36 cubic miles, or 1.7 million tons, of debris into the atmosphere.

BEFORE THE 1883 eruption, the Indonesian island of Krakatau looked like this.

The volcano known as Krakatau* began to signal its intentions with violent earthquakes in May 1883. The island was located in the Sunda Straits, between the large islands of Sumatra and Java, and was composed of three peaks: Rakata, at 2,600 feet; Danan at 1,400; and 300-foot-high Perboewatan. (The past tense is employed when describing the island, because most of the original landmass is gone.) After three months of rumbling earth tremors, on the morning of August 27 the island blew up with a succession of blasts that could be heard three thousand miles away. (If Pikes Peak in Colorado had exploded with the same force, every person in North America would have heard it.) There were four detonations over the course of five hours; the last, occurring at 10:52 a.m., was one of the biggest explosions in history.

A hail of hot pumice fell on ships, whose officers reported a period of threatening quiet followed by a series of titanic explosions that culminated in a cloud estimated at 20 miles high. From his vantage point aboard the *Sir Robert Sale,* Captain W. T. Wooldridge noted that "the sky presented a most terrible appearance, a dense mass of clouds being covered with a murky tinge, with fierce flashes of lightning." The cloud above the volcano appeared to him as "an immense pine tree, with the stem and branches formed of volcanic lightning." An hour after the explosions, a towering cloud rose from what was left

* A Hollywood movie entitled *Krakatoa, East of Java* was made in 1968, a muddled story of treasure hunters foiled by the eruption of a volcano and a "tidal wave." Unfortunately for those who named the movie, Krakatau is *west* of Java. When the movie was made, the volcano was popularly known as "Krakatoa," but the spelling has now been revised to conform to the Indonesian pronunciation.

DRAWN FROM a photograph, this is the only contemporaneous illustration of the 1883 eruption of Krakatau, one of the largest and deadliest events in volcanic history.

of the island, and as lightning stroboscopically lit up the blackening skies, a thick, muddy rain fell on Batavia (now Djakarta). Red-hot debris from the blast, some chunks eight feet around, fell over an area larger than France. The great discharge from the explosion created a hole in the ocean floor, and what remained of the mountain collapsed into this abyss, causing the sea to rush in. As the cold waters contacted the red-hot magma—what Frank Lane called "the titanic battle between Vulcan's fires and Neptune's waters"—the steam exploded with catastrophic violence, and 4 cubic miles of rock and ash were hurled into the stratosphere, some of it shooting 40 or 50 miles high. Since the island was uninhabited, nobody on Krakatau was killed, but giant tsunamis, some reaching a height of 135 feet, rolled out in all directions, flooding the coasts of Java and Sumatra, submerging more than three hundred towns and villages, and drowning more than thirty-six thousand people.

Unlike the waves that devastated Hilo, the shorelines of the Indonesian islands and bays were relatively close to the causative eruption. Hilo is more than two thousand miles from Unimak Island; some of the islands and villages affected by the sea waves when Krakatau exploded are only a couple of miles away. Calymer, the island immediately to the west of Krakatau, was completely demolished. An 87-foot-high wave engulfed and totally destroyed the town of Teluk Batung, at the head of Sumatra's Lampong Bay, killing five thousand people. (It was here that the Dutch warship *Berouw* was carried over the drowned village, to come to rest more than a mile inland.) Shortly thereafter, a huge wave roared into Semanka Bay (the next embayment to the west) and overran all the villages and towns on either shore. Twenty-five hundred drowned at Beneawany, and hundreds more at Beteong, Tandjoengan, and Tanot Bringin. The water cascaded into the town of Tangerang, and when it swept out again, it carried away people, animals, houses, and trees. The death toll at Tangerang was reckoned at 1,974. To the accompaniment of thunderous explosions, the wave swept around St. Nicholas Point in Java and headed for Batavia, ninety-four miles from the epicenter. At 11:30 a.m., two hours after the initial explosion, the sea roared into the capital city. It receded, and then came back. An estimated six thousand ships, ranging in size from steamships to small proas, were destroyed in Batavia's harbor. A reporter (quoted in Rupert Furneaux's *Krakatoa*) described the scene:

> To give some idea of the tidal waves which agitated the sea and rivers, we need only say that at Tanjang Priok, the water rose 10 feet within a few minutes, that it not only overflowed a portion of Lower Batavia quite suddenly, but also bore fully laden proas like straws. This phenomenon was repeated at 2 p.m. but not so violently. However great was the force exerted by this heavy flow, there came a moment, after it had raged its utmost, when the water in masses of immense height suddenly ebbing away vanished, and left the river beds and sea bottom dry.

No one knew that the waves would come back after they had receded. It is likely that many people believed the worst was over and returned to their shoreside villages, only to experience another, more catastrophic inundation. The town of Merak, which had suffered little damage from the first series of waves, was destroyed by the second and third. A 50-foot wave, traveling at hundreds of miles per hour, entered the narrow bay, and as the shoaling beach slowed down the leading edge of the wave, millions of gallons of water began piling up behind, until the wave reached the astonishing and totally terrifying height of 135 feet. This mountain of seething water rolled over poor little Merak, obliterating everyone and everything in its path. Anjer Lor was drowned by a 33-foot wave, and Tyringin, twenty-four miles from the volcano, was smashed to smithereens by a 70-foot-high locomotive of roiling water.

It was these waves, a by-product of the eruption, that caused the death and destruction. As Douglas Myles wrote, "When all the talk of Krakatoa is done

ANAK KRAKATAU (the "Child of Krakatau") sends smoke and steam into the air in 1983, one hundred years after the devastating explosion of its parent, which killed more than thirty-six thousand people.

and all the statistics evaluated, one salient fact remains. Despite the frightful power of the eruption itself, the emission of noxious gases, flame, smoke, volcanic bombs, and other ejecta, it was not the mountain's fury which destroyed those unfortunate thousands, except indirectly. It was the terrible power of water. In the vast majority of instances death came at the hands of seismic sea waves." Nine hours after the eruption, three thousand riverboats were swamped and sunk in Calcutta, two thousand miles away, and ships strained at their anchors five thousand miles distant, at Port Elizabeth, South Africa.

Where once there had been a pretty little tropical island, there was now a hole in the ocean floor that was 1,000 feet deep and 6½ miles across. Like that of Tambora, Krakatau's explosion generated a climate-altering ash cloud that produced lurid red, blue, green, and copper-colored sunsets and lowered temperatures around the world. What was left of Krakatau remained dormant until January 25, 1928, when a cone of basaltic rock and pumice rose out of the sea: Anak Krakatau, the "Child of Krakatau," was born.

On December 12, 1992, as a result of a 7.5 earthquake just north of the Indonesian island of Flores, two thousand people were killed, and another two thousand injured; approximately half of these figures are attributed to tsunamis. The little village of Riangkroko was completely washed away, and every one of the 137 inhabitants was killed by a wave that was later estimated to have been 65 feet high. Two villages on the island of Babi, some three miles from the epicenter, were completely destroyed, and some of the 263 people who died were found suspended in the branches of trees. Harry Yeh et al. (1993), who visited the site seventeen days after the earthquake, opined that massive land slumps and soil liquefaction were caused by the earthquake, which produced this unexpectedly high tsunami. Less than two years later, on June 3, 1994, another earthquake occurred in the Java Trench, generating a powerful tsunami that violently struck southeast Java and extended to southwest Bali. Some two hundred people were killed, another four hundred injured, and one thousand houses destroyed. The "run-up heights" were 16 feet on Java, and 46 feet on Bali. The earthquake occurred in the ocean about 150 miles from the hardest-hit area, and there was no ground-shaking to warn the inhabitants of the impending catastrophe (Synolakis et al. 1995).

Outside the caldera of Santorini, there is a submarine promontory known as Coloumbos that erupted on September 14, 1650, and produced a steaming volcanic cone that appeared above the surface of the sea. On September 29, a violent earthquake occurred, and a huge tsunami swept over the east coast of Santorini, leaving the valleys filled with pebbles and dead fish. On the island of

Ios, twenty miles away, there were waves recorded at 50 feet, and on Crete, ships were torn from their moorings and sunk in the harbor of Herakleion. When the waters receded on Santorini, remains of the ancient towns of Kamari and Perissa were revealed. The Coloumbos eruption lasted for three months, and poisonous gases killed forty people. The "island" of Coloumbos has receded beneath the surface, and the top of the cone is now 60 feet below the surface.

WHEN JULES VERNE WROTE *Journey to the Center of the Earth,* published in 1864, he omitted Atlantis altogether—perhaps because he was planning to use it in *Twenty Thousand Leagues Under the Sea.* But in 1959, filmmakers realized that they could make up for Verne's unfortunate oversight. After a series of underground adventures that bear only the vaguest resemblance to those in the book, Professor Lindenbrook (played by James Mason), Mrs. Goteborg (Arlene Dahl), Alec McKeown (Pat Boone), and a Viking named Hans cross the "Central Sea" (in this book, the center of the earth is *water*) and fetch up in Atlantis. Rummaging around in the remains of the crumbled city, they find a haversack filled with gunpowder. They are also trapped far below the surface of the earth, and threatened by a huge red lizard that seems to attack people with its tongue. Lindenbrook says, "We can use the gunpowder to open the clogged vent of the volcano, which will then shoot us right out of here." So they climb into a sort of Atlantean saucer that resembles a cheap amusement-park ride, and as McKeown lights the fuse, the entire cast is propelled to the surface on a rising pillar of molten lava that eventually erupts them right out of the mouth of the volcano Stromboli and into the Mediterranean, where they are rescued by Italian fishermen. The giant red lizard, Atlantis, and the volcano ride are more fantastic than anything Jules Verne could possibly have invented.

When Atlantis appears in literature—as opposed to the fantasies of Igna-

JULES VERNE, "the father of science fiction," was
born in 1828 in Nantes, France. *Twenty Thousand Leagues
Under the Sea,* published in 1870, contains an imaginative
visit to Atlantis.

tius Donnelly or Otto Muck—it often takes the form of a Greek city that sank
because of some catastrophe, and is discovered millennia later by underwater
explorers, such as Captain Nemo or Professor Arronax.* In *Twenty Thousand
Leagues Under the Sea,* after locating a massive hoard of gold and silver "off the
southwestern point of the Spanish peninsula," Captain Nemo brings the submarine *Nautilus* about, and heads south-southwest into the open Atlantic. At
a spot carefully identified as "16° 17′ longitude and 33° 22′ latitude" (a location
that actually puts them quite close to the island of Madeira), Nemo asks Arro-

* Atlantis also appears in science fiction. As L. Sprague de Camp wrote, "To the novelists, Atlantis has
been a gift of the gods, and recently, the lost continent has become, like the other planets and the
remote future, a standing setting for stories of the science-fiction *genre.*" A respected practitioner of the
genre himself, de Camp has conducted a detailed study of the appearance of Atlantis in science fiction, up
to the publication of his book in 1954, which leaves another fifty years unaccounted for. The 1995 *Encyclopedia of Science Fiction* picks up where de Camp left off, and lists some of the more important recent
authors of "Atlantis" fiction, such as Marion Zimmer Bradley, David Gemmell, and Ursula K. Le Guin.

nax if he would like to join him on a nocturnal underwater excursion. At 150 fathoms, clad in their diving costumes and without underwater lights, the two men march toward a "large light shining brilliantly, about two miles from the *Nautilus.*" The intrepid submarine hikers push on, until Arronax realizes that they are walking along huge, regular furrows, defined by a border of large stones. The light that they'd seen from so far away was "simply a reflection, developed by the clearness of the waters. The source of this inexplicable light was a fire on the opposite side of the mountain."

They climb the 800-foot-high mountain, pass through a copse of dead trees (with fish flitting through the branches), and come upon a field of broken rocks, with dark crevices inhabited by "giant lobsters . . . titanic crabs . . . and

ILLUMINATED BY a splendid display of pyrotechnics from an underwater volcano, Captain Nemo and Professor Arronax gaze at the ruins of Atlantis in *Twenty Thousand Leagues Under the Sea.*

frightful-looking poulpes [squid or octopuses] interweaving their tentacles like a living nest of serpents." Unfazed by the *articulata* ("Nemo, well acquainted with these terrible creatures, was ignoring them"), the hikers continue upward until they reach the top, where Arronax sees that the mountain is a live volcano, "vomiting forth torrents of lava which fell in a cascade of fire into the bosom of the liquid mass."*

Lit by the incandescence of the erupting volcano, Arronax observes a town,

its roofs open to the sky, its temples demolished, its arches in pieces, its columns on the ground, but its proportions were clearly outlined, reminding me of the stately architecture of Tuscany. Farther on were the remains of a gigantic aqueduct; here were the encrusted remains of an Acropolis, with the floating forms of a Parthenon; the remains of a quay, also, vestiges of an ancient port on the shore of a vanished sea, which had given shelter to merchant ships and craft of war; farther still, the outlines of crumpled walls and long lines of wide, deserted streets, an ancient Pompeii buried beneath the sea.

"Where was I?" Arronax wants to know, and Nemo picks up a piece of chalky rock and uses it to inscribe a single word on black basalt: ATLANTIS. "What a light shot through my mind," says Arronax, and expounds the full range of his (rather Francophilic) knowledge of the Lost Continent:

Atlantis the ancient Meropis of Theopompus,[†] the Atlantis of Plato, that continent denied by Origen, [Porphyry,] Jamblichus, D'Anville, Malte-Brun, and Humboldt, who placed its disappearance amongst the legendary tales admitted by Posidonius, Pliny, Ammianus, Marcellinus, Tertullian, Engel, [Sherer, Tournefort,] Buffon, and D'Avezac. I had it there before my eyes, bearing upon it the unexceptionable testimony of its catastrophe. The region thus engulfed

---

* Although none had been discovered in Verne's time (1828–1905), there are indeed underwater volcanoes that spew forth molten lava. Of course, contact with the seawater quenches the fire, so it is only for a moment that the fiery nature of the melted rock can be observed. Verne writes that there were no flames, because "flames require oxygen of the air to feed on, and cannot be developed under water, but streams of lava, having in themselves the principles of their incandescence, can attain a white heat. . . ."

[†] According to Lewis Spence, "Theopompus of Chios [was a] Greek historian of the fourth century B.C., none of whose works has survived, save in the *Varia Historia* of Aelian, a compiler of the third century A.D., [who] alludes to an account of the Atlantic area given by the Satyr Silenus, the attendant of Dionysus, to Midas, King of Phyrigia, who seized him when intoxicated, and recovered much ancient wisdom from his lips. 'Silenus,' (says Theopompus) 'told Midas of certain islands named Europa, Asia, and Libya, which the ocean surrounds and encompasses. Outwith this world there is a continent or mass of dry land, which in greatness was infinite and immeasurable, and it nourishes and maintains by virtue of its green meadows and pastures many great and mighty beasts. The men who inhabit this clime are more than twice the height of human stature, yet the duration of their lives is not equal to ours.' "

was beyond Europe, Asia, and Libya, beyond the Columns of Hercules, where those powerful people, the Atlantides, lived, against whom the first wars of ancient Greece were waged.

After a brief history of Plato's Atlantis, Verne/Arronax identifies the Madeiras, Azores, Canaries, and Cape Verde Islands as the highest peaks of the drowned continent which still stand above the sea. "Some day," he writes, "some new volcanic eruption would return these ruins to the surface! Many a ship's crew has reported tremors as they sailed over these tormented depths. Some have heard rumblings indicating some dispute between the elements, others have caught volcanic fragments thrown out of the sea."*

In 1929, Arthur Conan Doyle (1859–1930) published a novel called *The Maracot Deep,* in which three adventurers—Professor Maracot, Cyrus P. Headley of the Zoological Institute of Cambridge, Massachusetts, and an American mechanic named Bill Scanlan—descend into the Atlantic Ocean in an airtight contraption designed by the professor and land almost on top of the fabled Lost City. It would appear that Conan Doyle was familiar with the work of Jules Verne, published some sixty years before his version, and also with certain works referring to deep-sea biology and oceanography as it was known in the 1920s. Conan Doyle was born in 1859, trained as a doctor, and practiced medicine until 1891, at which point he devoted himself to the writing of stories, most of which, of course, concerned the exploits of a certain detective. He was also a Spiritualist, and "channeled" information from his guide, Phineas. Apparently he was particularly interested in Atlantis, for he participated in a séance in 1928 during which he asked Eileen Garrett, a celebrated British medium, if her contact, a twelfth-century Persian named Abdul Latif, "could give any approximate date for the sinking of Atlantis." As reported in Alan Vaughan's 1996 article, Latif responded, "Many people will tell you that Atlantis disappeared so quickly. That is not true. There was a series of three cataclysmic eruptions that caused the gradual disappearance of the land. There are great monuments, tombs to be opened, there will also be cataclysms that will bring up to you that which I swear in the name of almighty God to be true."

The Maracot Deep takes place far offshore, some two hundred miles south-

* The area in which Verne placed the drowned continent is, of course, along the Mid-Atlantic Ridge, where tremors and eruptions—if not flying volcanic fragments—are the rule rather than the exception. The island groups are the highest peaks of the Ridge, proving, unfortunately for Verne, exactly the opposite of what he suggests. The Mid-Atlantic Ridge is the volcanic origin of the sea floor, moving the continents apart—thus unlikely to appear at the surface with ruined temples and fallen arches.

west of the Canary Islands. On board the ship *Stratford* out of London, Headley (the story's principal narrator) is shown some strange equipment belowdecks, which he describes as "four flat sheets of steel with elaborate bolts and rivets along the edges. Each sheet was about ten foot square and an inch and a half thick, with a circular gap of eighteen inches in the middle." The circular gaps are for "crystal windows," and the plates are to be assembled into a "pressure-proof lookout station" equipped with electric searchlights all around, and with an arched top to which is affixed "a great ring for a chain or a rope." Professor Maracot, it seems, is planning to lower himself a third of a mile down, "to make such observations as we can." (Maracot believes that "the current doctrine as to the extreme pressure of the ocean at great depths is extremely misleading," and that "other factors exist which neutralize the effect, though I am not prepared to say what these factors might be.")

As they descend in this squared-off ancestor of the research submersible, Maracot and his colleagues see the color of the sea change from light green to olive, then to "a wonderful blue," a dusky purple, and at 600 feet, they encounter utter darkness. The searchlights reveal "the wonderful world of water as it really was," and all sorts of real ("the black ceratia, all spikes and mouth") and imaginary creatures ("one terrifying creature had luminous teeth"). When they reach the end of their tether, Maracot tells his fellow aquanauts that it "confirms my previous view that this ridge is part of a volcanic formation."* Poised on the volcanic ridge at the edge of a vast abyss, they see a "great creature" climbing toward them: "A beast unknown to Science . . . too long for a huge crab and too short for a giant lobster, it was moulded more upon the lines of the crayfish, with two monstrous nippers outstretched on either side, and a pair of sixteen-foot-long antennae which quivered in front of its black dull sullen eyes. The carapace, light yellow in colour, may have been ten feet across, and its total length, apart from the antennae, must have been not less than thirty."

Always the scientist, Maracot gives it a name ("Crustaceus maracoti"), but unmindful of this new honor, the giant crayfish snips the hawser that connects them to the *Stratford* at the surface, and they tumble into the abyss. They land in "the thick, soft elastic ooze of the bottom," 26,700 feet deep. To everyone's surprise, it is not dark down there, but "there was a dim, misty light which streamed through our porthole, like the cold radiance of a winter

---

* In the story, they were dropped somewhere west of the Canary Islands, and while Conan Doyle could not have known it in 1925, his description of "a volcanic formation" would prove to be correct thirty years later, when the Mid-Atlantic Ridge was discovered.

morning." Maracot asks: "What is this pteropod or globigerina ooze? Is it not the product of decay, the mouldering bodies of a billion billion organic creatures? And is decay not associated with phosphorescent luminosity?" Light or no light, they cannot raise their steel cube, and they cannot venture out into the darkness, so as the air becomes "stagnant and dreadful," the explorers prepare to die. Just as they are about to drift into unconsciousness, they see a human face through the porthole.

It is, of course, a citizen of Atlantis, a fact they discover when they are taken to the underwater city that sank into the Atlantic some eight thousand years earlier, "before the Egyptian written records begin." The Atlanteans communicate in a language that not one of the terrestrials—not even the polyglot Maracot, who speaks classical Greek—can understand, but this doesn't matter, because the Atlanteans can project their thoughts onto a screen, and thus show what amounts to movies of subjects they wish to describe. (They teach Maracot, Headley, and Scanlan how to do this, too, so the conversations are not totally one-sided.) Using this "thought-cinema," the Atlanteans are able to visualize their original settlement, which pretty much corresponds to Plato's description. They see

> a glorious rolling country, enormous in extent, well-watered and cleverly irrigated, with great fields of grain, waving orchards, lovely streams and woody hills, still lakes, and occasional picturesque mountains. It was studded with villages and covered with farmhouses and beautiful private residences. Then our attention was carried to the capital, a wonderful and gorgeous city upon the seashore, the harbor crammed with galleys, her quays piled with merchandise, and her safety assured by high walls with towering battlements and circular moats, all on the most gigantic scale.

All is not so tranquil, however, since this beautiful civilization is much given to excesses of the flesh, and is warned by a prophet in a trance that unless they mend their ways, they will be in a lot of trouble. He gets them to build an ark, but it does them no good, for despite the efforts of the faithful, doom arrives in the form of "a huge sleek mountain of water" that rises "to an incredible height out of a calm ocean" and covers the entire city until nothing remains but "dead men and animals, chairs, tables, articles of clothing, floating hats [*hats?*] and bales of goods, all bobbing and heaving in one huge liquid fermentation." The leader instructs fifty or sixty of his followers to save themselves by digging into the bowels of the earth, and teaches them essential survival skills, such as how to rearrange the chemistry of various compounds in order to change them—after all, says Maracot, "The molecules of the elements are like bricks, and these bricks lie all around us. We have only to learn how to pull out certain bricks—sometimes just a single brick—in order to make a fresh substance. Sugar becomes starch, or ether becomes alcohol, just by a shifting of the bricks."

The citizens of drowned Atlantis can function underwater by wearing transparent glass bubbles equipped with sketchily detailed breathing devices that produce fresh air and somehow remove carbon dioxide. But they need these only when they are out of the city, because the Atlanteans can live comfortably in their city by pumping out the water, supplying a "fresh current of air which came through small holes in the wall," and even providing central heating, although "no stove was visible." All this engineering was accomplished long before the land sank beneath the waves, since "such precautions could not have been taken after the event." They eat food (milk, bread, honey) that seems to have been created by the rearrangement of molecules, and various fish products. They occasionally venture out of their sanctuary to hunt, and the visitors experience—much like those underwater hikers in *Twenty Thousand Leagues*—the marvels of the deep, including fields of shark's teeth and whale earbones, working coal mines, and the glowing bathybius of the sea floor. They also see the remains of the fallen city, described as not unlike the temple of Karnak at Luxor, with huge, towering statues; and a pier with a lighthouse at the end, showing that the city had been a seaport. Of course, they also see some of the dangers of the deep, including "a loathsome black squid, its foul body rising and falling in a slow, steady rhythm so that it seemed like some evil heart which still beat in the center of this wicked place," and black-and-white "tiger crabs, each about the size of a Newfoundland dog." They are also vouchsafed a view of the fabulous "blanket fish, well known to ichthyologists" (which smothers its victims by draping itself over them); and, mirabile dictu, a "real sea-serpent, a creature which has never appeared before the human eye . . . some ten feet in height and two hundred in length, black above, silver-white below, with a high fringe upon the back, and small eyes no larger than those of an ox."

The travelers are happy in Atlantis—Headley has fallen in love with the beautiful Mona, daughter of Manda—and Scanlan has managed to build a radio receiver, but not a transmitter. ("It seemed funny to me," he said, "with all this electricity to hand, and with their glasswork ahead of ours, we couldn't vamp up something that would catch an ether wave, and a wave would surely travel through water just as easy as through air.") The sounds of Old England make them homesick, and they decide to escape by stringing together several of the buoyant "vitrine bells" that they wear for sea-floor strolling, and shoot to the surface, where they will be picked up by a ship that they have already signaled by sending a message to the surface in a bottle.

Among the videos they watch are those that show Headley as an Atlantean dying in the destruction, along with his beloved Mona. Watching yourself die and then writing about it produces some rather peculiar constructions ("An ax gleamed in the air and crashed down upon my head. I fell forward dead upon the lady, bathing her white robe in my blood"), but it also enables Headley to acknowledge the reincarnation that explains why Atlantis and its inhabitants are so familiar to him. "Now I understood that deep soul thrill," he says, "which I encountered when my eyes met those of Mona. It came from the depths of my own subconscious self where the memories of twelve thousand years still lingered."

The travelers do indeed escape from Atlantis (Mona joins them), but before they leave, they make an unauthorized visit to "the Palace of Black Marble," a building that the Atlanteans had expressly forbidden them to investigate. Professor Maracot acknowledges that we have learned about Atlantis from Plato ("Our knowledge of the conditions there came to us chiefly by way of Egypt," he says. "[I]t is what the Priests of the Temple at Sais told Solon"), but then, as an added twist, he says that the party responsible for the destruction of the Atlantean civilization was none other than "the Lord of the Dark Face," that is, the Devil. And guess who they find waiting for them in the palace?

> Against one of the pillars of the hall a man was leaning, his arms folded upon his chest and his malevolent eyes fixed with a threatening glare upon ourselves. . . . Outwardly he was a magnificent creature, not less than seven feet in height, and built upon the lines of a perfect athlete, which was the more noticeable as he wore a costume which fitted tightly upon his figure, and seemed to consist of glazed black leather. His face was that of a bronze statue—a statue wrought by some master craftsman in order to depict all the power and also the evil which the human features could portray.

The Devil, who speaks perfect English and can read their thoughts, tells them that it was he who brought Atlantis to its height and encouraged its "orgy of wickedness," only to have some of the inhabitants escape. But now he is prepared to rectify that unfortunate incident, and plans to destroy the underwater city. The visitors try to figure out how to save Atlantis (and themselves, of course), and Bill Scanlan produces a six-shooter and says, "Maybe if I made as many holes in the big stiff it would let out some of his magic," but "Baal-Seepa," the Dark Lord, invisibly wrests the revolver from his hand and sends it clattering to the floor. "If any human brain could solve our problem," muses Headley, "it would be Maracot's." And Maracot's brain does solve the problem: he confronts the Lord of the Dark Face at a sort of a mass meeting where the Devil is telling the Atlanteans that they are doomed, and says, "Your time has come. You have overstayed it. Go down! Go down into the Hell that has been waiting for you for so long. You are a prince of darkness. Go where the darkness is." Maracot has managed to summon up the spirit of Warda, the benevolent force that saved the Atlanteans in the first place, and realizing this, the Devil says, "Oh, curse you, Warda. Curse you! Curse you!" and melts into a "semi-liquid heap of black and horrible putrescence which stained the dais and poisoned the air." "We have won," mutters Maracot, just before he collapses on the floor. And when he recovers, they shoot to the surface, leaving the Atlanteans to live happily ever after. The story ends:

> Dr. Maracot actually talks about going back. There is some point of ichthyol-
> ogy upon which he wants more precise information. But Scanlan has, I hear,
> married his wren in Philadelphia, and has been promoted as works manager of
> Merribank's, so he seeks no further adventure, while I—well, the deep sea has
> given me a precious pearl, and I ask for no more.

JULES VERNE NEVER SAW anything like his *Nautilus* take to the sea; when he died in 1905, the submarine had been developed, but the submers-ible—an underwater vessel with windows—was still far in the future. In 1930, the year of Arthur Conan Doyle's death, William Beebe would descend to a depth of half a mile in a bathysphere, and while he found no Atlantis, he found the underwater world to be even more fascinating than the fantasies of the writers of science fiction.

Because of the melodramatic nature of the subject, with its lost cities, vast riches, and historical orientation, it is not surprising to find Indiana Jones involved in the search for Atlantis. In a four-part comic-book series, published in 1992, the swashbuckling archaeologist, who made his first appearance in the 1981 movie *Raiders of the Lost Ark,* joins such luminaries as Ignatius Donnelly, Angelos Galanopoulos, and Otto Muck in the search for the Lost City. Of course, "Indy" goes about it a little differently, since few practicing archaeolo-gists go into the field brandishing a bullwhip or punch their rivals in the nose in an attempt to establish ownership of artifacts. But movie and comic-book archaeologists are rarely inhibited by the exigencies of scholarship, so when a German brings Jones a strange-looking key, it serves to launch a series of frantic adventures that take Jones all over the globe, first to Germany (the story takes place in 1939) and then, in rapid succession, to Iceland, the Azores, the Yucatán, Leningrad, Morocco, and, finally, Crete, where they discover that the mysterious key opens a heretofore hidden door to the Labyrinth of the Minotaur, which has in it a scale model of Plato's Atlantis, circular canals and all.

It is obvious that the writers did their homework about Atlantis, since Indiana Jones gets to go to all sorts of places that have been implicated in various Atlantis narratives, and when they are not dodging fists or bullets, they are quoting Plato. Indeed, they arrive at Knossos, as evidenced by a panel showing the bull-leaper fresco, and another that depicts the "horns of consecration." The key to the mystery is Plato's mysterious "orichalcum," which the Nazis want because it has magical properties that they can use to build a superbomb. Indiana Jones outwits the Nazis, but in the process, Atlantis blows up (too much orichalcum in the machine), and Professor Jones and archaeologist Sophia Hapgood return to Barnett College just in time to watch the homecoming football game.

The Atlantis legend, with its sinking cities and catastrophic volcanic explosions, also seems a natural for cinematic interpretation, so it is somewhat surprising that the first Atlantis movie takes place in the desert. Made in France in 1921, *L'Atlantide* was a silent film based on the Pierre Benoît novel in which French adventurers discover Atlantis in the sands of Algeria. In his *Film Guide,* Leslie Halliwell wrote, "Two explorers find the lost continent of Atlantis and fall in love with its queen. Highly commercial adventure fantasy of its day; it cost two million francs and ran in Paris for a year. Some scenes still sustain, and the desert scenes are impressive." G. W. Pabst made a German version of the same novel in 1932 (with Brigitte Helm as the queen), and in 1948, *L'Atlantide* arrived in Hollywood.

In *Lost Continents,* L. Sprague de Camp reviewed the United Artists version, which was rechristened *Siren of Atlantis:*

> The late Maria Montez was cast as Antinéa with a series of eye-filling gowns and a Spanish accent, while Jean-Pierre Aumont, her real-life husband, gave a glassy-eyed performance as the hapless French officer beguiled by Antinéa into murdering his best friend, a brother officer who has antagonized the temptress by resisting her lure. Although the story has considerable cinematic possibili-

ties, the production in this case was so hammy that the final result was unintentionally funny. The picture was such a financial disaster that the following year Señorita Montez sued the producer (a man with the Atlantean-sounding name of Nebenzal) for the unpaid balance of her salary, and got a $38,000 judgment against him.

In the 1930s, kids used to go to the movies on Saturday afternoons to see the serials, weekly installments of a "cliff-hanger" that starred an action hero (or heroine) in impossible predicaments. What could be more impossible than Crash Corrigan descending in a "rocket submarine" to the undersea world of Atlantis? In the 1936 serial *Undersea Kingdom,* a series of earthquakes have been disturbing American cities, so Professor Norton, his son Billy, ace reporter Diana, and naval lieutenant Ray "Crash" Corrigan, descend in a rocket submarine to investigate. As they reach 7,000 feet, a mysterious force grips their ship and drags it another 3,000 feet down, until they surface in "an inland sea" in Atlantis, 10,000 feet below sea level in "another world." (Ingress and egress to Atlantis are dealt with in a rather perfunctory manner; it is never made clear how the adventurers get in or out.) They leave the submarine, only to be captured by the "black robes" of Unga Khan, the evil warlord of Atlantis.

In this twelve-part serial, the plot revolves around the rivalry between Unga Khan (who looks not unlike Genghis Khan) and Sharad (William Farnum), the high priest of Atlantis, who puts his faith in Poseidon and wears a sort of silk popover on his head. Crash and his cronies, finding themselves in Atlantis, join forces with Sharad against the sneering Unga Khan, who wants to take over the Upper World or destroy it. In chapter 2, we are warned that a shot fired from a cannon will break the orichalcum roof and bring the ocean crashing into Atlantis, but this advice is ignored in the remaining chapters, since every kind of weapon, from a pistol to a missile to a disintegrator ray, is fired in every direction. Indeed, after the submarine adventure, there is no reason to believe that the story is taking place anywhere but on dry land—dry land that looks suspiciously like the American West. Under clear skies, and with a background of mesas, canyons, and buttes, everybody waves their swords and gallops around madly. The preferred mode of travel in Atlantis is horseback, but there are also many chariots to be seen, and sometimes the "Juggernaut" appears, an armored vehicle that whines into view and disgorges the "Vulkites," men in soup-can armor who shoot atom-ray guns.

Unga Khan and his henchmen can see what is going on anywhere—even in the Upper World—simply by flicking on the "refracto," a sort of primitive

CRASH CORRIGAN REMOVING the "Vulkite" armor that enabled him to fool
Unga Khan, the evil warlord of Atlantis. Nice sandals, Crash.

television system that doesn't seem to require cameras. The warlord wants
Professor Norton to build "rocket motors" that will propel his tower up and
into the Upper World, where he plans to wreak havoc and take over. Crash
cannot stop the launching, and we see the tower heading up through the
water (somehow it has passed through the orichalcum roof) until it bobs to
the surface. From the submarine (which they have reboarded), Crash sends a
message to the U.S. Navy that "this power is equipped with machinery capable
of destroying our entire continent. I recommend that you dispatch battle fleet
immediately while I try and stop him from using his disintegrator." The battle
fleet is dispatched, the tower surfaces, and the Navy shoots it. This suffices as
the end of Atlantis—it is blown out of the water by heavy artillery. Unga Khan
gets his just deserts, and Crash and Diana head for City Hall to get a marriage
license.

Undersea Kingdom (also titled *Sharad of Atlantis*) is a terrible movie, with wooden
acting, cheesy sets, and no discernible plot. Regardless, it probably thrilled a
generation of young Saturday-matineegoers, who must have thought that
Crash Corrigan's heroics were pretty nifty. But if they thought that the real

story of Atlantis had lines in it like, "Before this day is over, I shall make myself supreme ruler of the Upper World" or "Drop your swords," they missed a much better tale than the one they saw on successive Saturdays.

G E O R G E   P A L $(1 9 0 8 - 1 9 8 0)$, a Hungarian filmmaker who specialized in movies for children with elaborate animation and special effects, made *Atlantis, the Lost Continent* in 1961.* Leonard Maltin's capsule review reads as follows: "Famed sci-fi producer George Pal's worst film is set on the island of Atlantis, in the time of ancient Greece. Heroic young fisherman becomes involved in tedious intrigue before, finally, the palace sinks. Lots of stock footage, poor effects. Occasionally funny—too bad it's not on purpose."

The film opens with a map of the Atlantic Ocean, on which a new continent appears as the narrator solemnly intones, "There once was another continent: Atlantis." Long shot of a boat, containing the poor (but 1960s-handsome, which means big hair in a teased pompadour) fisherman Demetrius and his father. They spot a raft in the distance, and Demetrius immediately leaps into the water to investigate. He climbs aboard the raft to find a sleeping beauty, whom he revives with a nip from his flask. They take her to their humble fishermen's cottage, which offends her because she is used to only the finer things, since she is a princess from "beyond the Pillars of Hercules." She is not so offended that she doesn't pat a little flour on her face, redden her lips with a juicy cherry, and go in search of Demetrius, who is drying the nets. The princess Antillea tells him where she comes from (but not how she came to be floating around on a raft), and of course he does not believe her, because he knows that there is nothing beyond the Pillars of Hercules. She pleads with Demetrius to take her home, telling him that if he does, her father will shower riches upon him, but he says he has everything he needs, "save for one thing," and makes a grab for Antillea. She runs from him crying, "And that is one thing you shall never have, fisherman," and dashes off. Anxious to return to her homeland, she steals a boat and sails away, presumably toward Atlantis in the west. Brave Demetrius follows, and before long, they encounter Poseidon, a big green man with a yellow beard and a triton, and then a submarine with fins, which contains various Atlantean officials who have been searching for

---

* Not to be confused with a 1968 film named simply *The Lost Continent.* In this British entry, a tramp steamer wanders into uncharted, swampy seas and encounters assorted monsters, as well as remnants of the Spanish Inquisition, outfitted in conquistador armor and Ku Klux Klan robes. Leslie Halliwell calls this film "hilariously imaginative hokum."

the missing princess. They bring her home, and as the submarine surfaces, we can see the reason that George Pal made this movie in the first place: a great city sits on the shore, its temples and palaces perched in the shadow of a towering, conical volcano that is just waiting to explode and dump Atlantis into the sea.

Unbeknownst to Antillea, Demetrius has been made a slave, whose job seems to consist of breaking up large diamonds that are found lying on the ground. (It is at this time that Demetrius sees the minotaurs: men in bull's-head masks, who have been transformed by the sorcerer. The author of the screenplay probably remembered something about Theseus and the Minotaur being related to Knossos—which was somehow related to Atlantis.) Before the sorcerer can turn him into a bull, however, Demetrius has to undergo the torture of "fire and water," in which he fights an ogre in a fiery pit that then turns into a swimming pool. He wins, of course (and wins his freedom), to the dismay of Zaron, the prime minister with the evil grin, bad blond-dye job, and curly-toed shoes. All of this huffing and puffing is just preamble, of course, to the big denouement, which comes after the villains have decided to conquer the rest of the world with their giant crystal ray gun. "We must conquer or be conquered," declares Zaron. "Are we not the master race?" The birds and the bees desert Atlantis "because they sense something evil," and the clouds turn red, which means that the end is nigh. The holy man Azar warns that evil will destroy Atlantis, even before the nasty Zaron can begin his conquest of the rest of the world, so Demetrius leads the slaves in revolt for reasons that are not clear, since the place is obviously going to blow up anyway. They all run toward the harbor so they can board the ships before the mountain erupts, and sail back into the "Hidden Sea" (the Mediterranean).

The mountain in the background begins to smoke, flames shoot from the ground, molten lava oozes through the countryside, people leap into the sea, and the white-columned city stands precariously silhouetted against billowing black smoke. The minotaurs attack the sorcerer who turned their heads into Halloween masks, and to a background cacophony of people yelling and buildings exploding, the city of Atlantis begins to crumble into the sea. Zaron's remedy for the destruction of his beloved Atlantis (which is now burning like Atlanta in *Gone With the Wind*) is to shoot his crystal ray gun at anything that moves, including Demetrius and the princess Antillea. But just before he can zero in on the lovebirds, Azar the Good tackles him and they roll down the stairs, leaving the ray gun zapping away aimlessly. It vaporizes Zaron at the foot of the stairs, and the great city collapses into the sea as Demetrius and

FROM THE BEGINNING of George Pal's *Atlantis, the Lost Continent,* it was clear that the volcano was going to blow and the city was destined to tumble into the sea. (We might even have deduced that from the title.)

Antillea watch from their boat.* The clouds disperse, the sun comes out, and as the film ends, a somber voice tells us that "Atlantis is gone, but three men, wise men, carried the culture from the mother empire to the four corners of the earth." From the antics of the Atlantean warlords, it would seem that the only aspects of culture they could spread were diamond-breaking, ray-gun construction, and the superiority of the master race, but never mind. The idea that the "Lost City" would be discovered later by underwater adventurers is also rendered difficult, since every building crumbled into tiny pieces before splashing into the sea. Maybe they will find the Hollywood model shop where the miniature "Atlantis" was built, or the tank into which it crumbled.

The 1978 *Warlords of Atlantis* is a surprisingly ingenious recombination of some of the assorted Atlantis legends, suggesting that the writers had done research before they wrote the script. (However, Leslie Halliwell writes that it is "a predictable compote of monsters and unwearable costumes, without a trace of wit in the script. For infants only.") In addition to the obvious ingre-

---

* In *Atlantis: Lost Lands, Ancient Wisdom,* Geoffrey Ashe wrote that this film was based "partly on the Theosophists' accounts of Atlantean magicians in conflict, partly on C. J. Cutcliffe Hyne's novel, *The Lost Continent,* [which was] written in the wave of enthusiasm launched by Donnelly, Madame Blavatsky, and Scott-Elliot."

dients, such as erupting volcanoes, cities crumbling into the sea, and the inevitable escape of the hero and heroine, *Atlantis* and *Warlords* share an emphasis on a "master race" and slavery, which suggests either that the later film was dependent upon the earlier; that the writers were familiar with the works of Lewis Spence, whose Atlanteans were superior beings; or (least likely) that they had actually read Plato's *Timaeus,* in which he talks about the Atlanteans' plan to "enslave . . . your country and ours, and all the territory within the strait." They may even have known of Karl Georg Zschaetzsch, who in 1922 wrote about a race of superior, blond, blue-eyed Aryans that originally inhabited Atlantis. Of course, there are also the requisite underwater monsters, including a sort of marine dinosaur identified as "a living placoderm" (a name that actually denotes a class of long-extinct armored fishes), some assorted terrestrial reptiles, and, at the finale, the ultimate giant octopus. Shot in Malta and Pinewood Studios, England, this film is about a band of Victorian explorers, led by Professor Aitken, who descend in a bathysphere to the ocean floor, where they find a golden statue that guards the lair of a giant octopus. The adventurers snatch the statue, an act that will eventually have serious cephalopod repercussions. In this unique bathysphere, which is open-bottomed and whose source of power remains unidentified, the explorers maneuver around underwater until they bob up off a beach where the members of the crew, previously seen to have been captured and dragged into the octopus's cave, are now seen languishing. There they are found by the Atlanteans, represented at first by Atmir, a handsome chap in a silvery, fish-scale tunic and a Prince Valiant haircut. He throws the seamen and the "engineer" (Doug McClure) into the dungeons, but takes Charles Aitken (the son of the professor, who has remained aboard the ship) to meet the Atlantean royalty. In the role of Atsil, queen of the Atlanteans, is Cyd Charisse, and she and Atraxon the Royal Inquisitor have selected young Aitken because he is a "superior person," and they outfit him with a crystal helmet that enables him to see the future. The warlike Atlanteans reveal themselves as a "master race" that arrived from Mars, and show Aitkin the future. By means of the magical hat, Aitken sees an image of the future that shows they will evolve into jackbooted Nazis and take over the world. Why? So they can create "neutron energy" to return to their world, of course. A weak but ambitious man, Charles Aitken is all set to sign on and abandon his friends when the rest of the crew, having escaped from prison, find him and smash the helmet to bits. At that moment, the city is attacked by a horde of wall-climbing, armored dinosaurs, and in the confusion, the prisoners escape. They outrun Atmir and the "guards" (half-fish, half-man mutants armed with repeating rifles) and leap off a cliff to the conveniently waiting bathysphere. Collinson drives them through various caves and grottoes away from Atlantis, and they return to the ship, which still has the golden idol aboard.

Although we are never told why, the giant octopus is highly proprietary about this statue, and as soon as the crew reassembles on board, the monster returns. As cinematic model octopuses go, this is a pretty good specimen. The first time we see it, it is swimming past the bathysphere, with its writhing arms spread wide like a tentacled parachute, but when it surfaces, it looks surprisingly real. The octopus attack, with tentacles squirming down the stairwells and in through the portholes to grab sailors, is a bad version of a similar scene in the Disney *Twenty Thousand Leagues Under the Sea,* since the wires employed to move the arms are often clearly visible. The octopus now appears to be *really* angry, for it not only grabs the crew members again but this time also wields the statue like a club to smash up the ship. With its grasping tentacles everywhere—down the hatches, up the masts, in the portholes—the octopus succeeds in sinking the ship, but the heroes escape in a convenient lifeboat that was knocked overboard in the melee. Like Professor Maracot, Charles Aitken talks about going back to Atlantis, but Engineer Collinson cleverly says, "I think maybe we went a little bit below our depth."

"The Man from Atlantis" was a popular television series in the late 1970s, but the amphibious human (played by Patrick Duffy, who later went on to greater things as J. R. Ewing's younger brother Bobby on "Dallas") made his debut in a 1977 film about an Atlantean who washes ashore and is taken into custody by the U.S. Navy. Because the Navy has lost a research submarine 36,000 feet down in the Mariana Trench, they requisition the aquanaut—who has, for convenience' sake, been named "Mark Harris"—and send him down to locate the missing vessel. Eschewing any equipment (he can breathe underwater), Mark Harris dives straight down for seven miles, and when he reaches the bottom, he finds a complex underwater habitat that has been built by a mad scientist named Schubert, who intends to turn all the missiles of the world against one another and start the world over with a less warlike—by which he means water-breathing—people. The man from Atlantis foils this dastardly plan and returns to the surface, where he bids farewell to the admiral who put him to work, and also to the lovely Dr. Elizabeth, who saved him. As he descends to his homeland beneath the sea (off San Diego?), "Mark Harris" reviews the events of the recent past, and decides to forsake his ancestral home (are there any more at home like him?) and return to dry land, where the beautiful Dr. Elizabeth awaits.

Atlantis lives on, not only in mythology and science fiction but on Paradise Island in the Bahamas. Advertising "man-eating creatures, ancient ruins, and sun worshippers," as well as a 3.2-million-gallon saltwater tank that contains "35,000 pounds of tropical fish guests," the resort Atlantis opened in 1994. (Quotations are from a 1996 article that appeared in *Carnival Air,* the in-flight magazine of Carnival Airlines.) "The $125 million construction and development project includes a 14-acre waterscape that not only features every kind of water recreation imaginable, but preserves, showcases, and celebrates the wonder of ocean life in all its variety, brilliance, and beauty." If possible, the new Atlantis is even more luxurious than the original. There are 1,147 guest rooms, 12 restaurants, an 18-hole golf course, a Las Vegas–style review, and a Sports Bar.

Atlantis also flourishes in cyberspace, and a Net search produces hundreds of entries that incorporate the name of the Lost City. For example, the new oceangoing research vessel out of the Woods Hole Oceanographic Institution is christened *Atlantis;* there are *Atlantis* tourist submarines in the Cayman Islands and Hawaii. The spacecraft that rendezvoused in February 1996 with the Russian *Mir* was named *Atlantis.* You can learn the rates for the Atlantis Hotel at Knossos in Crete; or discover what happened to the original Atlantis Beach Club in Nags Head, North Carolina. (You can also check into the Atlantis Resort's home page and read for yourself about their "35,000 pounds of tropical fish guests.") You can drink the "Ancient Whale Ale" brewed by the Atlantis Brewing Company in Denver; take Atlantis vitamins and supplements; or bedeck yourself with Atlantis crystal necklaces. You can avail yourself of the annual report of the Atlantis Plastics Corporation, or stay at the Atlantis Motor Inn in Cape Ann, Massachusetts. There is a CD-ROM of the Indiana Jones story, and Peter James's *Sunken Kingdom* (see pp. 94–5) is for sale on the Net. There are dozens of links to computer games, and if you have the right equipment, you can listen to the "eminently danceable rootsy neo-raggle-taggle pop-skiffle" songs of a British band called "the Lost T-shirts of Atlantis."

CONCLUSION

W AS THERE EVER a continent—or an island, or a city—known as Atlantis? A legend that can trace its roots back ten thousand years probably has some basis in fact, no matter how distorted the story has become over time. Whether Plato fabricated his account out of whole cloth or incorporated some vaguely remembered tales out of the collective Greek past, we will never know for certain. Plato told us precisely where Atlantis was located, and approximately how big it was ("opposite . . . the Pillars of Heracles, an island larger than Libya and Asia combined"), but because they are unable to reconcile these data with their own presumptions, Atlantologists have repeatedly rearranged its size and location.

Without identifying his sources, Arthur C. Clarke says that "there is some evidence that to the early Greeks the Pillars of Hercules did not mean the Straits of Gibraltar at all." He then suggests that the Straits of Messina, between the toe of Italy and the island of Sicily ("one of the most dangerous passages in the world because of its furious tide races"), may be the place originally identified as the Pillars of Hercules. If this is so, it would locate Atlantis in the western basin of the Mediterranean, between Italy and Sardinia. "Now this makes a great deal of sense," writes Clarke. "The Mediterranean is a new sea, not an ancient ocean like the Atlantic or the Pacific, which have both existed for millions of years. Men were alive when the bed of the Mediterranean was a fertile valley, and Spain met Africa to form a barrier against the

Atlantic. Many geologists believe that this barrier went down some twelve thousand years ago, which agrees very well with the date given by Plato for the fall of Atlantis."

It appears that most authors, unless they have another solution to the problem of Atlantis in mind, are prepared to accept the idea that Plato made it up. (Of course, if they had not had a solution in mind, they would not have written a book defending their theory.) There are so many such authors that it would be an exercise in redundancy to repeat too many of them, but let me choose a few, from various disciplines.

L. Sprague de Camp (science fiction and science writer): "Plato's story is based on many things that Plato had heard or read about, woven into a charming fiction to set forth his ideas of a perfect state. The glittering city of Atlantis is probably based on the rich trading and mining city of Tartessos, in south-eastern Spain near modern Cádiz. The earthquake that submerged Atlantis is derived from the earthquake wave that overwhelmed the little Greek island of Atalanté, the year before Plato was born. Plato also employed the legend of the demi-god Atlas, who in more orthodox myth was turned into the Atlas Mountains when he wearied of holding up the heavens and the gods took pity on him. Plato's Atlantean elephants are probably based upon the elephants that roamed the valleys of the Atlas range."

Edwin S. Ramage (professor of classical studies): "By now it is perhaps unnecessary to point out that the driving desire to explain Atlantis at all costs has also been responsible for a great deal of out-and-out rationalizing and wild theorizing without any evidence at all. As we have seen, Spence created a whole new island, Antilla, to get his Atlanteans to the New World at the proper time after the destruction of their island. Folk memory, movements of peoples in Central Asia, comets, Atlantis the source of all civilization, land bridges, and whole continents in the North Atlantic are just a few of the many devices that have been invented to explain different aspects of different theories."

Encyclopaedia Britannica: "legendary island in the Atlantic, just beyond the Pillars of Hercules, finally overwhelmed by the sea. It was described by Plato in two dialogues, the *Timaeus* and the *Critias*. The legend of its existence persisted throughout the Middle Ages, and, since the Renaissance, it has been variously identified with the Americas, Scandinavia, the Canary Islands, and Palestine."

Arthur C. Clarke: "On this slender basis [Plato's account in the dialogues], hundreds of books have been written, and men have devoted their entire lives to unraveling the truth about Atlantis. Unfortunately, most of the literature on the subject is not merely worthless—it is misleading nonsense produced by cranks. This is a great pity, for the legend of Atlantis may well be based on truth, and serious students have been scared away from it by the crackpots. . . . And since there have been so many towns and even whole islands swallowed by the sea, Plato's account is completely plausible, even though he certainly exaggerated for the sake of effect when he described the great city of Atlantis with its buildings ornamented with gold, silver, and brass."

L. Don Leet (seismologist): "The all-time favorite among tall tales involving earthquakes, volcanoes, tidal waves, and hurricanes, is the story of Atlantis by the Greek philosopher Plato. The story is pure political philosophy. It points up the prosperity that results when pious, law-abiding, industrious pioneers develop a civilization that prospers in peace and the fate which awaits that civilization when it falls apart in the midst of avarice, aggression, bickering, and sloth. Plato would have been chagrined and disheartened indeed had he known that over 2,000 years after he spun his yarn with a moral, citizens of an age fantastic beyond belief would be tearing at each other's throats exactly according to the pattern of his prophecies, in tiresome repetition of the actions of previous civilizations on whose bones they trod, when they remembered his story only for the legendary destruction of Atlantis by earthquakes and its disappearance beneath the sea. . . . There is no evidence at present known to support the belief that any such land mass foundered in the Atlantic within the past 11,000 years. Attempts to relate this supposed event in some way to the topographic feature traversing the bottom of the Atlantic Ocean as the Mid-Atlantic Ridge are too farfetched to warrant serious discussion. The ridge lies roughly under 10,000 feet of water as compared with an average of nearer 15,000 feet for the ocean elsewhere. There seems to be no doubt that Plato's account is strictly imaginative in its geological features. His explanation that oceanic islands are erosional remnants of continents, is, of course, erroneous as well."

J. Rufus Fears (classical historian): "For us it is enough to point out how ill-founded are any attempts to establish a case for the historical existence of

Atlantis upon the ephemeral foundations of a pre-Hellenic Cretan empire. Neither archaeology nor Greek mythology offers any support for the view that the tale of Atlantis reflects the imperial power and sudden disappearance of Minoan Crete. When this is combined with the clear evidence that Plato's tale of Atlantis is his own invention and not the reflection of a valid historical tradition, it becomes clear how futile must be any search for historical elements in the myth of Atlantis. Atlantis is not a remembrance of things past, but rather a complete poetic fantasy."

Sir Desmond Lee (translator of Plato's dialogues the *Timaeus* and the *Critias*): "I have suggested that the *Critias* is the first essay in science fiction. For science fiction there seem to be two motives. First, the attempt to peer into the future and guess what man's growing control over nature may enable him to do. This motive, you will say, can hardly have operated with Plato. Yet if Atlantis is situated in the past, it is nonetheless a society with an advanced material civilization, a construction by the imagination of what man's ingenuity could achieve. . . . Some science fiction adds sentiment to speculation, as in the story in which the hero first sees the heroine in a bubble-bath aboard a space ship. Plato was not given to that sort of escapism. But in the story of Athens and Atlantis he has yielded to escapism of another kind. For surely if you cannot see how your Utopia can ever work in the real world, it is mere escapism to project it either into the distant past or into the distant future."

S. Casey Fredericks (mythologist): "It is time for the modern imagination to recognize that Atlantis never existed, either in time or space, and to realize that the actual location of Atlantis all along has been the world of the mind and its most fascinating imaginative product, myth. The universe of the imagination remains the only landscape where exploration, perhaps even further discovery, awaits Atlantists of the future."

Christos Doumas (archaeologist of Akrotiri): "The destruction of a civilization (the Minoan) was attributed to the sinking of an island where this civilization flourished (Crete), while in reality it was Thera that sank, and that not completely. However, it is not improbable that Plato used these real events as the nucleus of his myth of an ideally organized state which flowered and prospered for as long as men respected and enforced the laws and worshipped the gods who had given them the legislation. When, however, the men became arrogant and ceased to obey the laws of their state, the wrath of the gods was such that they were condemned to annihilation."

Quoting only those who agree with you is a poor way to prove a point, but I have given those who would argue that Plato did not make up the story of Atlantis latitude to present their cases. One may close this book believing that Atlantis was in the Sahara Desert, underwater in the Bahamas, or reposing on the bottom of the Atlantic Ocean, but for the record, I think it was entirely Plato's creation.

Was Knossos—or some other palace in Crete—the fabled Atlantis? Forgoing for the moment the problems of timing, let us compare what we know of Knossos with Plato's description of Atlantis. After locating it at the center of concentric rings of land and water, joined by tunnels and bridges, Plato describes the palace:

> The construction of the palace within the acropolis was as follows. In the center of the shrine sacred to Poseidon and Cleito, surrounded by a golden wall through which entry was forbidden, as it was the palace where the family of the ten kings was conceived and begotten. . . . There was a temple of Poseidon himself, a stade in length, three hundred feet wide, and proportionate in height, though somewhat outlandish in appearance. The outside of it was covered all over with silver, except for the figures on the pediment, which were covered with gold. Inside, the roof was ivory picked out with gold, silver and orichalch, and the walls, pillars and floor were covered with orichalch. It contained gold statues of the god standing in a chariot drawn by six winged horses, so tall that his head touched the roof, and round him, riding on dolphins, a hundred Nereids (that being the accepted number of them at the time), as well as many other statues dedicated by private persons.

This is no closer to a depiction of the palace of Knossos than it is to a description of the Empire State Building. Knossos was constructed of dressed limestone blocks, which were not covered in gold—or anything else, for that matter. There were no freestanding statues, and no horses, winged or otherwise, in Minoan Crete. But Plato did not have to look into the obscure historical past, for there was a gigantic temple, in existence during his lifetime, that came remarkably close to his description of the palace of Atlantis. The Temple of Artemis at Ephesus, one of the seven wonders of the ancient world, was built around 550 B.C., by King Croesus of Lydia. It was in that part of Greece then known as Anatolia, now part of Turkey. (The ancient city of Ephesus was near the modern town of Selçuk, about fifty kilometers [31 miles] south of Izmir.)

According to Pliny (who was writing in the first century A.D.):

The temple was completed in 120 years with contributions from all over Asia. Standing on a marble base, it was 425 feet long, 225 feet wide, and had 127 columns each 60 feet in height, and each built by a different king. Thirty-six of these were decorated with high reliefs, and at least one is known to be the work of Scopas, a well-known sculptor of the time. The architects were Chersiphron and his son Metagenes. In this magnificent temple stood a statue of Artemis, made of either cedar or ebony. . . . Ancient writers who had seen the temple could not help being impressed by its splendor and by the great numbers of fine pieces of art that had been assembled there. The ceiling was made of cedar, the doors of cypress, and each step of the stairs leading to the roof was made of the solid stock of the grape-vine.

Even before Schliemann began excavating at Troy in 1870, John Turtle Wood was digging in the floodplain of the Kaystros River in Ephesus. In the mud, he found the remains of the foundation of the temple—also known as the Artemesium—which confirmed Pliny's description of its great size, and he also unearthed one of the "high-relief" sculpted column bases. The 127 columns reported by Pliny have not been found, but the ground plan reveals a veritable forest of columns, set on a stepped marble platform. "We have no proof that the cult statue of Artemis Ephesia dominated the sacred room," wrote B. L. Trell in her 1988 discussion of the temple, "as did the statues of Athena at Athens or that of Zeus in the sanctuary at Olympia," but the depiction of this goddess was a particularly dramatic one. As the symbol of fertility, she was represented as a many-breasted mother goddess (thus her name "Artemis Polimastros") standing rigidly upright, with her lower portion resembling an Egyptian mummy case, elaborately decorated with lions, sphinxes, and stags. Around her neck there is an elaborate necklace, and on her head, a crown composed of miniature versions of the temples in which she was venerated.*

Even allowing for some exaggeration on Pliny's part, this temple is much closer to Plato's description of the palace at Atlantis than any possible manipulation of a rendering of Knossos. As described in the *Critias,* the temple at Atlantis was "a stade [an eighth of a mile, or 660 feet] in length, three hundred feet wide, and proportionate in height." (Knossos was roughly square, about 500 feet on a side, with an open-air central court.) Plato's temple of Atlantis was

---

* Two marble statues of Artemis Ephesia were found by Austrian archaeologists excavating in 1956, one life-size and the other twice that (Miltner 1958). They are Roman reproductions, probably made during the time of Hadrian (117–138 A.D.). Coins minted at Ephesus at the same time show the goddess in conjunction with the temple, and also the sculpted drums at the bases of the Ionic columns.

twice as large as Artemis at Ephesus, not at all an unreasonable exaggeration for one who wishes to make his fictional edifice larger and grander than anything known.

Did Plato know of this temple? He is not believed to have visited Anatolia, but some of his contemporaries certainly did, and they must have told him of this fabulous building. On the night of July 21, 356 B.C., Herostratus burned the temple to the ground in an attempt to immortalize his name, but he was overshadowed, since that was also the date of the birth of Alexander the Great. (Herostratus burned the temple while Plato was alive, so it is also possible that the philosopher could have incorporated the destruction of this magnificent edifice into his Atlantis story.) Over the next two decades, the temple was rebuilt, and it lasted until 262 A.D., when it was devastated by the Goths.

There is also the possibility that Plato simply embellished his portrayal of a famous temple that he would have known from firsthand observations. The Parthenon, commissioned by Pericles and designed by Ictinus and Callicrates, overlooked Athens while Plato was growing up, and he could see it on his daily walks.

Plutarch wrote that Pericles told the Athenians that after they had provided the city "with all things necessary for war, they should convert the surplus of its wealth to such undertakings as would, hereafter, when completed, give them eternal honor. . . . [T]o that end he thought fit to bring in among them, with the approbation of the people, these vast projects of buildings and designs to work, that would be of some continuance before they were finished, and would give employment to numerous arts, so that the part of the people that stayed at home might, no less than those that were at sea or in garrisons or on expeditions, have a fair and just occasion of receiving the benefit and having their share of public moneys." Plutarch continues:

> The materials were stone, brass, ivory, gold, ebony, cypresswood, and the arts or trades that wrought and fashioned them were smiths and carpenters, molders, founders and braziers, stone cutters, dyers, goldsmiths, ivory workers, painters, embroiderers, turners. . . . As the works went up, proud in their grandeur and exquisite in form, the workmen striving to surpass the material and design with the beauty of their workmanship, yet the most wonderful thing was the speed of their execution.

Situated dramatically on the craggy hill in Athens known as the Acropolis, the Parthenon is probably the world's most famous building. It was begun in 447, and it was consecrated in 438 B.C., approximately ten years after Plato was born. Officially the Temple of Athena Parthenos (the "Virgin's Chamber"), it is a perfect example of Doric architecture. Built entirely of Pentelic marble, it is 228 feet long, 100 feet wide, and 65 feet high. It has eight fluted, baseless columns at the ends, and seventeen on each side, each column a little over 34 feet in height and composed of twelve drums. As they gazed at the temple, only a few of the Athenians would have known of the imperceptible convexity of the columns as they diminish in diameter toward the top (entasis), or the subtle thickening of the four corner columns to counteract the thinning effect of being seen silhouetted at certain angles against the sky. Inside was a walled interior chamber, originally divided into three aisles by two smaller colon-nades. One entered through the east portico (the *pronaos*), and then passed into the great east room, or *cella,* which was known as the *hekatompedos neos,* or "hun-dred-foot temple." In this room was Phideas's celebrated chryselephantine (gold and ivory) cult statue of Athena. Finally, there was the west portico, des-ignated the *opisthodomus,* or rear chamber.

The Parthenon is admirable not merely for its impressive and perfect pro-portions and its architectural beauty and finish, but also for the wealth of its sculptural ornamentation, originally lavishly adorned with colors and gilding. The tympana of the pediments were filled with groups of colossal statues, those on the eastern pediment representing the birth of Athena; on the west-ern pediment, Plato could see the contest between Athena and Poseidon for the land of Attica. In the frieze of the entablature, the triglyphs (vertically grooved blocks) alternated with the metopes, which were filled with ninety-two high-relief sculptures representing scenes from Attic mythology: on the south, the battles between Greeks and centaurs, and on the west, Greeks and Amazons. Running completely around the building was the Ionic frieze, some 524 feet in length and 3¼ feet high, which soared 40 feet above the floor of the outer corridor. Carved in low relief, this frieze represents the Panathenaic pro-cession, which occurred every four years on the occasion of the great festival. It does not require a great leap of the imagination to picture Plato taking this familiar building, the most magnificent temple in Athens, and, by modifying and enlarging it, locating it in the imaginary urban landscape of Atlantis.*

---

* Among Pericles' other contributions to Athenian architecture were the four-mile-long "Long Walls" that connected Athens to the harbors at Piraeus. (Pericles had the walls built, but it was Themistocles' idea.) This construction bears a superficial resemblance to the "rings and bridges" of Atlantis that Plato described as "enclosed by a stone wall all round, with towers and gates guarding the bridges on either side where they crossed the water." The Spartans destroyed the Long Walls during the Peloponnesian War, but they were rebuilt in 394 B.C.

I N I 9 6 9 , three books about Atlantis were concerned with the possibility that the answer to the puzzle could be found in Minoan Crete. Galanopoulos's *Atlantis: The Truth Behind the Legend,* Luce's *Lost Atlantis,* and Mavor's *Voyage to Atlantis* were all published in that year, and in the *Journal of the Folklore Institute,* Dorothy Vitaliano reviewed all three. She acknowledged that the idea originated with K. T. Frost* in 1913, in his anonymous essay, "The *Critias* and Minoan Crete," but since he had no idea about the volcanic destruction of Thera, he could not imagine what force could have caused the destruction of the Cretan palaces. (He wrote, "Knossos and its allied cities were swept away just when they seemed strongest and safest. It was as if the whole kingdom had sunk into the sea, as if the tale of Atlantis were true.") In the *Geographical Review* in 1917, Edwin S. Balch published an article called "Atlantis or Minoan Crete," in which he suggested that Plato's Atlantis was a poetic memory of the Minoan civilization in Crete. It was not until 1939 that Spyridon Marinatos recognized that the volcano that had wreaked such havoc on Crete was only sixty miles away; and, of course, Marinatos had begun working on Santorini when Mavor arrived in 1967. The possibility of contemporaneous earthquakes was dismissed by Marinatos, who wrote, "When, however, we attempt to explain the various catastrophes throughout the island by common earthquakes, the problem begins to present difficulties. The other parts of Crete are less susceptible; many districts, indeed, are almost wholly immune. Moreover, earthquakes are usually confined to a very small area." So if earthquakes did not destroy the palaces and civilization of Crete, what did? The discovery by Ninkovich and Heezen that the tephra from the erupting volcano had blanketed a vast area of the Aegean—including much of Crete—provided a partial answer to the question.

Spyridon Marinatos has probably made the most substantial contributions to the traditional and current mythology of Atlantis. In 1939, he published "The Volcanic Destruction of Minoan Crete," which led to the various associations of the Cretans with the Atlanteans. After a distinguished thirty-year career as an archaeologist, Marinatos began digging at Akrotiri, and eventually unearthed the remains of the Minoan settlement on Thera. In 1967, he

---

* It is bad enough that James Mavor refers to K. T. Frost as "J. K. Frost," but in an egregious display of careless writing and scholarship, he writes, "Thirty years later [after 1909], the British archaeologist J. K. Frost gave his endorsement to the theory that the Minoan culture of Crete and Atlantis were one and the same, and admitted that he had been the author of the anonymous article in 1909." By 1939, Frost had been dead for twenty-three years.

joined—more or less reluctantly, as we have seen—in the ill-fated "expedition" of James Mavor to Santorini, and even after he died, he was dragooned into participating in Charles Pellegrino's exposition of Atlantis. Because his contributions were so important to the story of Thera, Marinatos has been quoted in support of just about every theory about Atlantis. Do we know what he really thought about the subject?

We do. In his 1950 essay "On the Legend of Atlantis" (reprinted in 1969 by the Athens Museum, with a new introduction by the author), he said, "Plato's imagination could not possibly have conjured up an account so unique and so unusual to classical literature. . . . For this reason, the account is usually called a 'tradition' by Plato. I should also like to add that if in some parts the account chances to bear the stamp of the fable, this must be attributed to the Egyptians and not to Plato."* Marinatos then recounts a story from the Middle Kingdom of Egypt about a shipwrecked traveler who was cast ashore on an island where a dragon took the sailor to another island that had once been burned to a cinder by a falling star, and on which the dragon's seventy-five children lived. "This tale of a supremely happy island," wrote Marinatos, "which later became submerged and vanished was, therefore, clearly familiar to the Egyptians. This is the tale the Saïte priests confused with other traditional accounts concerning Atlantis because they contained similarities." This seems to be an unusually weak argument, and although Marinatos then presents a lengthy explication of how historical legends are handed down to the people ("Names become changed or corrupt. Events actually having occurred are intermixed with imaginary accounts. The districts where the events took place are changed to others, and moreover, time is projected indefinitely back into the past . . ." and so on), he has to work very hard to bring this explanation anywhere within range of Plato's story. "Therefore," he says, "we can only accept the historical core of the traditions on Atlantis as a fact, but time and place we cannot accept."

To rearrange the time and place, Marinatos writes that the Egyptians

---

* In *Lost Continents*, L. Sprague de Camp wrote, "If all Atlantists would read the rest of Plato's writings as well as his Atlantis story, and realize what a fertile myth-maker he was, they might be less cocksure about his reliability as a historian." He lists examples in the philosopher's collected works where Plato demonstrated his ability to create fictional settings and "pseudo-myths": "In the tenth book of *The Republic* he had Socrates tell a story of Er, the son of Armenios, a Pamphylian whose soul went to the other world but returned to its body just in time to save the latter from being burned. . . . In *Phaidon* he speaks of 'hollows of various forms and sizes . . . in all parts of the earth . . . into which the water and the mist and the air collect, and of islands floating in the sky . . .' in *Gorgias* he mentions the Island of the Blest. The *Politikos* describes the Golden Age of King Kronos, which lasted until Zeus released his grip on the management of the universe, which . . . went to ruin because of the growth of materialism. . . ."

invented the myth of Atlantis based on their erroneous interpretation of the story of the explosion at Thera:

> A large powerful island lost within the region of Egyptian awareness other than Crete did not exist. But that they should have invented a myth about its being submerged, even though they had their own story of the Shipwrecked Traveler, seems difficult. We then have the army of the Athenians which the "earth engulfed" to a man after frightful earthquakes and deluges within a single day and night together with Atlantis. The Egyptians must have learnt of an island becoming submerged and this was Thera, but being so small and insignificant, they did not know of it. They transferred the event to Crete, the island so grievously struck and with which all contact they suddenly lost. The myth of an army being engulfed stemmed from the news of the loss of thousands of souls. With the lack of cohesion and logic that characterizes myths— as well as all other products of the peoples' imagination—not even Plato sensed the inconsistency of Atlantis in the Atlantic Ocean and the entire armed forces of the Athenians, in Athens of course, being submerged at one and the same time!

Marinatos weaves a convoluted story, based on his idea that historical events are often so distorted that they become virtually unrecognizable over time. When the Egyptians lost contact with the Cretans after the volcano erupted, earthquakes toppled the buildings, Crete was swamped with tsunamis, and ash blanketed the island. "The transference of the island to the Atlantic Ocean is explained by the circumnavigation of Africa by the Phoenician sailors, and the invasions by central Mediterranean peoples were added to the myth as invaders from Atlantis. . . . The core of these events, embodied in a single historical myth, is the eruption of Thera, and the year is about 1500 B.C."

Acknowledging Marinatos's contributions, Rhys Carpenter advances the idea that "the natural catastrophe which overwhelmed the Aegean island of Santorin, in antiquity known as Thera, was of such magnitude as to have altered the entire course of human history in the lands surrounding the Aegean." In *Discontinuity in Greek Civilization,* Carpenter says that the severe eruption of Santorini "must have been sufficiently intense and prolonged to have heaped up an enormous layer of volcanic ash and pumice that still covers the island and has in places a depth of 100 feet. . . . Crete . . . must have been wrapped in darkness of falling ash amid terrifying storms of wind and rain." He continues:

> Who is not reminded of the vivid description of the destruction of the island of Atlantis as recounted to Solon by the Egyptian priest in Plato's *Timaeus,* how

there were tremendous earthquakes and inundations and in a single ensuing terrible day and night the island sank into the sea and disappeared? Since the priest, according to Critias' account, asserted that "whenever anything great or glorious or otherwise noteworthy occurs, it is written down and preserved in our temples" and since Egypt, less than 500 miles distant from Santorin in direct air line and regularly visited by Minoan and Mycenaean traders and emissaries, could not conceivably have failed to have knowledge of the great disaster in the Aegean, is it not entirely reasonable to interpret Santorin as the ultimate origin of the legend of Atlantis?

Carpenter comes down in full support of Marinatos, and writes, "I am accordingly prepared to maintain that in Solon's day there was preserved in Egyptian temple chronicles the mention of an island that had sunk beneath the sea during a tremendous marine upheaval, and that this island—for which Plato invented the name Atlantis—was no other than Santorin." (Carpenter presented these ideas in a series of lectures in 1965, shortly before Marinatos began to dig at Akrotiri. At that time, a settlement on the island of Keos had been excavated and showed evidence of having been destroyed by an earthquake around 1500 B.C.)

Is Marinatos's interpretation any better or worse than that of Galanopoulos? It is considerably better, because Marinatos has only rearranged legends and myths, and not tampered with reputable geological data. Galanopoulos demonstrates that a map of Atlantis—derived from Plato's descriptions, but with the dates reduced by an order of magnitude—can be overlaid on the caldera at Thera to show the concentric rings of the harbor, but this is a stretch, and he admits that "it could perhaps be admitted that the traces of the harbors on the caldera floor might be a coincidence resulting from its morphological features." Even if Santorini *was* the metropolis of Atlantis, subsequent eruptions would have long since covered any evidence of the "harbors" in the caldera, where the Kameni Islands now stand. Galanopoulos, of course, believed that Atlantis actually *was* Thera, and explained that while Thera blew up, the "Royal City" was in Crete. (He places the "Metropolis" square in the center of the caldera of Thera, and says that the "uniformly flat plain" that Plato locates on "the rest of the island" was actually in Crete, another island some seventy miles from Thera.)

Angelos Galanopoulos was not the only author who tried to force Plato's Atlantis story into a Theran framework; this interpretation is so filled with discrepancies that the only people able to accept it are those who are predisposed to do so. In the dialogues, Plato never connects Atlantis with Crete (an island he certainly knew about), nor is there any mention of a volcano as the causative agent. And those concentric circles bear no resemblance whatever to Knossos—or to any other known site, for that matter. In his incisive discussion of the mythological perspective of Atlantis, S. Casey Fredericks wrote:

> The works of the archaeologically oriented who write about Atlantis are as a rule crammed with charts, site maps, brilliant photographs of landscapes and archaeological finds, and chronological tables—but none of this has anything to do with Plato's story. The alleged connections between Thera and Plato's two dialogues is both artificial and unnecessary. What happens again is that the ancient literary text is dissected into fact and fiction, the former category being applied in a Procrustean fashion to whatever in the archaeological evidence looks as if it might fit the preconceived theory.

Fredericks also points out that Plato's story is not a Greek legend at all. Because Solon is said to have heard the tale from the Saïte priests, the story had to have originated in Egypt—just as Marinatos said it did. Greek, Egyptian, and Near Eastern mythologies all contain references to a catastrophic deluge, evidently derived from an ancient Mesopotamian tale.

A common motif in Greek and Near Eastern mythology is the gods' decision to destroy a society gone corrupt, often with a flood. Plato tells us that the Atlanteans "ceased to be able to carry their prosperity with moderation. To the perceptive eye the depth of their degeneration was clear enough, but to those whose judgment is defective, they seemed, in their pursuit of unbridled ambition and power, to be at the height of their fame and fortune. And the god of the gods, Zeus, who reigns by law, and whose eye can see such things, when he perceived the wretched state of this admirable stock, decided to punish them and reduce them to order by discipline." Zeus summons all the gods to his most glorious abode in order to explain his punishments, but there the dialogue (the *Critias*) abruptly ends. How different is this from the Bible's Genesis, where

> God saw that the wickedness of man was great in the earth, and that every imagination of the thoughts of his heart was only evil continually. And it repented the Lord that he had made man on the earth, and it grieved him at his heart. And the Lord said I will destroy man whom I have created from the face of the earth; both man, and beast, and the creeping thing, and the fowls of the air; for it repenteth me that I have made them. . . . In the six hundredth year of Noah's life, in the second month, the seventeenth day of the month, the same day were all the fountains of the great deep broken up, and the windows of heaven were opened. And the rain was upon the earth forty days and forty nights.

Fredericks concludes his discussion with these words:

> Atlantis is a distant echo of the old flood myth which manifests a rather com-
> plex history. First, Plato had recategorized the flood legend along with all
> other stories of the destruction of civilization and formed a new class, that of
> "catastrophes." Second, Plato conceived of all these catastrophes as illustra-
> tions of a universal pattern of cyclical time, and third, he thought that con-
> temporary rational sciences could explain their real nature. Fourth, Plato's
> account of Atlantis cannot be separated from his quasi-Euhemeristic theory of
> myth which it documents, and finally, Plato's self-conscious orientation
> toward the Golden Age reinforces the conclusion that the Atlantis myth is
> based upon earlier Greek myths. In the face of these determining factors, all
> modern Atlantis scholarship which believes Plato is describing a real prehis-
> toric event has fallen into the logical fallacy of recapitulating a false ancient
> theory of myth.

Since the publication of Galanopoulos's and Mavor's claims that they had
actually found the Lost Continent, there has been a tendency to accept their
identification of Minoan Crete as the civilization that sank into the sea. But
Crete, the site of the great palaces, did not disappear. It remains where it always
was, above water in the eastern Mediterranean, far from the Pillars of Hercules.
(It is not even near the "other" Pillars of Hercules.)

Could Atlantis have been Santorini? Not easily. Like Crete, Santorini is
in the Aegean, but unlike Crete, it had no sumptuous palaces. It did have
Akrotiri, with its fabulous frescoes and evidence of the astonishing creative
artistry of the Minoans, but the island was only ten miles across, not "larger
than Libya and Asia combined," as Plato described it in the *Timaeus*. I believe
that Plato fabricated the story to make some specific points about the society in
which he lived.

If it was not the Minoan collapse that inspired him to write about a city
that sank beneath the sea, could there have been other incidents that provided
him with inspiration? Indeed there were. There was an event much closer to
fifth-century Greece than the explosion of Thera and the disappearance of
Minoan Crete. In fact, such an incident occurred in Greece, and during Plato's
lifetime.

In her discussion of tsunamis in *The Sea Around Us,* Rachel Carson says, "One
of the earliest of record rose along the eastern shores of the Mediterranean in
A.D. 358, passing completely over islands and low-lying shores, leaving boats on
the housetops of Alexandria, and drowning thousands of people." (There is no
mention of this date or event in Stothers and Rampino's discussion of some

thirty-five Mediterranean eruptions; one wishes Carson had provided some sort of documentation for this statement.) Although they are not as common as they are in, say, Indonesia, Hawaii, or Japan, tsunamis are not unknown in the Mediterranean. Stothers and Rampino combed the classical literature to assemble a list, but their only reference to a "great wave" accompanies the description of the A.D. 46 eruption of Thera, when "a new island, Thia, arose between Thera and Therasia . . . [and] an earthquake and tsunami struck Crete."

In 1960, while spending a year at the Institute for Advanced Study in Princeton, Spyridon Marinatos wrote an article for *Archaeology* entitled "Helice: A Submerged Town in Classical Greece." It begins: "In the year 373/2 B.C., during a disastrous winter night, a strange thing happened in central Greece. Helice, a great and prosperous town on the north coast of the Peloponnesus, was engulfed by the waves after being leveled by a great earthquake. Not a single soul survived. No natural devastation of such an extent had occurred on Greek soil since more than a thousand years earlier, when the terrific explosion of the volcano on Thera destroyed this area and the surrounding area." The next day, when men arrived to bury the dead, they found that every single inhabitant of Helice had been carried to the bottom of the Gulf of Corinth, along with the entire town. As Marinatos described it, "Helice was a very old town, with traditions harking back to the heroic Mycenaean Age. It had a famous sanctuary, great religious prestige, and an important position as a political center. . . ."

"The first systematic and nonmystical treatment of earthquakes," wrote Bruce Bolt in *Earthquakes,* "occurred in Greece, where its people experienced Aegean volcanoes and earthquakes along the Mediterranean Sea, sometimes accompanied by 'tidal' waves (tsunamis). A number of Greek philosophers offered mechanical explanations for these natural events. Strabo, for example, noted that earthquakes occurred more frequently along the coast than inland. He, like Aristotle, suggested that earthquakes were caused by rushing subterranean winds, igniting combustible materials underground." In 1939, Marinatos wrote, "We know, too, that at the time of the great disaster at Helice, where the population was drowned to a man as a result of a great earthquake, the neighboring Voura sustained serious damage but no more distant Aigion (40 stades) did not suffer at all." Helice—also spelled "Helike"—which was located on the south coast of the Gulf of Corinth (therefore the north coast of the Peloponnese), slid into the sea in 373 B.C., after a landslide initiated by an earthquake, accompanied by a tsunami. In his 1928 *A Commentary on Plato's*

Timaeus, A. E. Taylor wrote that there is "no reason to suppose that the whole narrative is more than a fiction of Plato's own," but Taylor believed that some of the inspiration came from the disastrous earthquake and tidal wave which devastated the Achean coast in 373 B.C. (In a 1983 article entitled "Volcanic Eruptions in the Mediterranean Before A.D. 630," Stothers and Rampino also mention Helice, but give the date as 375 B.C., when a "great inundation of the sea overwhelmed Helice.")

The Greek traveler and geographer Pausanias, who wrote his *Description of Greece* sometime in the second century B.C., discusses the destruction of Helice in book 2, which is devoted to the northern Peloponnesian regions of Elis and Achaea. The text of Pausanias's description of the earthquake (and the responsible agent) reads as follows:

> But at a later time, when the Achaians of this place pulled ritual supplicants out of the sanctuary and murdered them, the vengeance of Poseidon was unhesitating. There was an earthquake in the country that effected the demolition of every constructed thing, until the very foundations of the city were lost beyond the inquisition of future ages. The god gave the same warnings he generally does give of the most enormous and far-reaching earthquakes: for a long time before an earthquake there are continuous rainstorms or droughts; the weather becomes unseasonably sultry in winter, and in summer the orb of the sun hazes over in an unusual reddish glare of an almost dusky tinge; the water dries up in the springs; and sometimes violent storms of wind rush across the countryside uprooting trees, or electrical storms break out in mid-heaven with a lot of lightning; there are new configurations of stars that terrify the observers, and even a powerful rumbling from the air-currents underground; the god gives these signs and many others before every forceful earthquake. There is more than one kind of tremor, and the original scholars of this subject and their pupils have been able to distinguish different kinds of earthquakes in the following way. The gentlest kind, if it is permissible to conceive anything good about so terrible an evil, is when, after the first tremor and toppling over of buildings, a reverse tremor throws back what has already toppled. In this kind of shock you can see columns settling upright when they were all but completely down, and the walls that had gaped apart coming back into place, beams that the tremor had slid out of position came back to true, and artificial channels and every kind of conduit having their cracks jammed tighter than a craftsman could close them by any mechanical means. The second kind of shock demolishes everything shakable, and whatever it attacks it slams down at once like a battering ram. But the deadliest kind . . . is the way an earthquake penetrates below buildings and upheaves the foundations just like mole-hills being thrown up from underground. This is the only

kind of tremor that leaves no trace of inhabitation in the ground. They say now that an earthquake of this kind uprooted Helike from the foundations and the same winter brought a further punishment: the sea flooded in far over the land and overwhelmed the entire circuit of Helike, and the swell of the sea so covered the sacred grove of Poseidon that nothing could be seen but the tops of the trees. There was a sudden shock from the god, and with the earthquake the sea ran back, dragging down Helike in its backwash with every living man.

In his translation and commentary, the classicist J. G. Frazer (author of *The Golden Bough*) wrote:

> According to the testimony of a contemporary, the historian Heraclides Ponticus, the destruction of Helice by an earthquake took place on a winter night in the year 373 B.C., two years before the battle of Leuctra. The city was situated a mile and a half from the sea, and all this intermediate space, along with the city itself, vanished under the waves. Two thousand Achaeans were sent to bury the dead, but they could find none. Eratosthenes, who visited the site many years afterwards, was told by sailors that a bronze statue of Poseidon was standing under water and formed a dangerous shoal. See Strabo, viii. p. 384 *sq.*

The "Strabo" reference cited by Frazer is in volume I of the *Geography,* and is similar to Pausanias's account (Pausanias preceded Strabo, who was born around 63 B.C. and died around 24 A.D.), but Strabo adds a discussion of a bull sacrifice:

> For the sea was raised by an earthquake and it submerged Helice, and also the temple of the Heliconian Poseidon, whom the Ionians worship even to this day, offering there Pan-Ionian sacrifices. And some suppose Homer recalls this sacrifice when he says, "but he breathed out his spirit and bellowed, as when a dragged bull bellows round the altar of the Heliconian lord." And they infer that the poet lived after the Ionian colonization, since he mentions the Pan-Ionian sacrifice, which the Ionians perform in honor of the Heliconian Poseidon in the country of the Prienians; for the Prienians themselves are said to be from Helice; and indeed as king for this sacrifice they appoint a Prienian young man to superintend the sacred rites. But still more they base the supposition in question on what the poet says about the bull, for the Ionians believe that they obtain omens in connection with this sacrifice only when the bull bellows while being sacrificed.

In that part of his description of Atlantis that is in the *Critias,* Plato also describes bull sacrifices, as follows:

In the sacred precincts of Poseidon there were bulls at large; and the ten kings, after praying to the god that they might secure a sacrifice that would please him, entered alone and started a hunt for a bull, using clubs and nooses but no metal weapon; and when they caught him they cut his throat over the top of a pillar so that the blood flowed over the inscription. And on the pillar there was engraved, in addition to the laws, an oath invoking awful curses on those who disobeyed it. When they had finished the ritual of sacrifice, and were consecrating the limbs of the bull, they mixed a bowl of wine and dropped a clot of blood for each of them, before cleansing the pillar and burning the rest of the blood.

The sacrifice of the bull and the mention of Poseidon are surprisingly similar, suggesting again that Plato artfully employed the story of Helice in his re-creation of Atlantis.*

In his *On the Characteristics of Animals,* Aelian also included an account of the event, written some five hundred years after the fact:

When a house is on the verge of ruin, the mice in it, and the martens also, fore-stall its collapse and emigrate. This, you know, is what they say happened at Helice, for when the people of Helice treated so impiously the Ionians who had come to them, and murdered them at their altar, then it was that "the gods showed forth wonders among them." For five days before Helice disappeared, all the mice and martens and snakes and centipedes and beetles and every other creature of that kind in the town left in a body by the road that leads to Cerynea. And the people of Helice seeing this happening were filled with amazement, but were unable to guess the reason. But after the aforesaid creatures had departed, an earthquake occurred in the night; the town collapsed; an immense wave poured over it, and Helice disappeared, while ten Lacedaemonian vessels which happened to be at anchor close by were destroyed together with the city I speak of.

The first modern scientist to speculate on this ancient disaster was Julius Schmidt, a German astronomer who was director of the observatory at

* Although serendipitously found by sponge divers and not by the methodical searching of archaeologists, a bronze statue of Poseidon was recovered from the sea in 1907 off the island of Symi in the Dodecanese, just north of Rhodes. Part of a shrine that had toppled into the water, the statue remained submerged for two thousand years until it was hauled up by divers. The famous statue known as *Thundering Zeus,* a cast of which stands in the UN headquarters in New York, was recovered from 60 feet of water off Cape Artemesium on the northern coast of Euboea in 1928. The 7-foot-tall statue, dating from around 450 B.C., is now believed to represent Poseidon, but the thunderbolt or trident that would make for positive identification still lies on the bottom of the sea.

Athens. In 1861, another earthquake struck Helice, and when an eight-mile-long crack appeared along the foot of the mountain, the coastal plain slid slowly into the sea. The trees and reeds on the plain were buried until only their tops showed above the mud—just as Pausanias had described the circumstances at Helice some 2,234 years earlier. The disaster of 373 B.C. was estimated to have been ten times greater than the 1861 earthquake, but the chronology of the events at Helice is somewhat muddled. There were no survivors (and therefore, no eyewitnesses), so we must trust later historians, who had to rely upon hearsay. Pausanias wrote that first an earthquake uprooted Helice from its foundations; the sea flooded and overwhelmed the city, and then the sea ran back, dragging Helice into the sea in its backwash. Aelian, writing even later (and evidently not restricted by adherence to the truth), said that first came the earthquake, then the town collapsed, and then an immense wave poured over it. In his summary, Marinatos reconstructs the 373 scenario:

> 1) The earthquake destroyed the town and at the same time the ground began to slip *slowly.* 2) The sinking continued slowly until the highest tree tops disappeared, but it stopped when the remains of Helice were still in shallow waters, so that they were visible for five centuries or more. 3) The ground showed numerous cracks similar to those observed by Schmidt in 1861, but much larger and deeper.

There has been little success in finding the lost city of Helice. Spyridon Marinatos first mentioned it in 1939, and then discussed it in more detail in his 1960 *Archaeology* article. He wrote:

> For more than twenty years I have been working on submarine research in Hellenic waters. . . . The first attempt (in 1938–39) was to attract the interest of the staff of the American excavations of the Athenian Agora. Mr. Adossides, then their legal counselor, became an ardent supporter of the idea. Unfortunately, neither he nor Dr. Shear, director of the excavations, survived the Second World War. At the same time I spoke to Stanley Casson, who promised to promote the idea. He too perished. . . . After the war my efforts began with the late Professor Demangel, Director of the French Archaeological School at Athens, who discussed the idea of some French amateur divers diving at Artemision. . . .

In 1950, a French diving team under the direction of Dr. Henri Chévenée was invited to search for the lost city, which had been referred to (by Professor

Demangel) as "an underwater Pompeii." Demangel told Chévenée that "the town lies on the northern coast of the Peloponnese, entire if not intact, under between 50 and 130 feet of water at a distance of between 550 and 1,600 yards from the present-day shore." (This account comes from *Man and the Underwater World* by Pierre de Latil and Jean Rivoire.) In the heavily silted waters, the divers found no remains of Helice, but they did manage to locate the hulk of a German vessel that was sunk in 1941. It was so deep in the mud—only the superstructure showed—that they gave up the search, because "if a vessel sunk less than a decade ago was buried that deep in the silt, what must have happened to a town engulfed twenty-three centuries before?" Rather than lying on the bottom just offshore, the lost city of Helice may now be under solid ground. Over the past twenty-four hundred years, alluvial deposits may have increased the shoreline by well over a mile, so instead of sending divers to look for the crumbled buildings, the best course might be to search under the land—a more difficult proposition.

In the early 1960s, Marinatos began a correspondence with Harold Edgerton, who had developed a "mud-pinger," a device that used echo-sounding to locate objects buried under thick layers of sediment. Together they petitioned the National Geographic Society and the Greek Archaeological Office for financial assistance in 1966, claiming that "a city which sank almost instantly and which belonged to the golden age of Greece might be expected to provoke great interest. . . ."

The National Geographic Society gave Marinatos and Edgerton a small grant, and in Edgerton's report to the society, he stated, "Our studies covered not only the area between the Selinous and Cerynites Rivers, but also the area to the northwest, as suggested by Professor Marinatos, who was working in the field with us. A series of seismic profiles, together with navigational data, were obtained between November 10 and 18, 1966, and turned over to Marinatos for his use." The records showed interesting "holes" and "bumps," but no signs of a buried city. Commander Jacques Cousteau, a friend of Edgerton's, offered to join them, but the 1967 Six-Day War prevented Cousteau's ship *Calypso* from passing through the Suez Canal, and the rendezvous at Helice never took place.

Then underwater archaeologist Peter Throckmorton (who had suggested to Edgerton that the 1966 expedition might prove fruitful) wrote that he and Edgerton went looking for Helice in 1971: "We found a likely-looking mound in deep water bearing shells from A.D. 640, plus or minus 110 years, but no trace of buildings. Our conclusion was that Helice may no longer be under the sea at all. The site of the ancient city may lie beneath the alluvial plain that is constantly being built up by mud washed down from the mountains. The rate of sedimentation is such that, even if Helice was one hundred feet under water two thousand years ago, by now the site may well have been filled in by land."*

We have only the words of Strabo and Pausanias to go on, but there appears to be no question that this city was destroyed by an earthquake in 373 B.C. and slid into the Gulf of Corinth. Plato was born in Athens around 428 B.C., and died in 347, which means that he was fifty-five when Helice disappeared. The dialogues the *Timaeus* and the *Critias* were written after the disaster at Helice. It is therefore possible that Plato combined his contemporaneous knowledge of Helice with a vague story of a Carthaginian island outside the Pillars of Hercules, and perhaps even with some tales he had heard about the disappearance of a "civilization" some nine hundred years earlier, using them as the geographical and historical matrices into which he wove the tale of Atlantis.

Plato undoubtedly knew of another disaster that had befallen Athens shortly before 428 B.C. Nowhere in the *Timaeus* or the *Critias* does he mention a plague, but from approximately 430 to 425, the city was struck by a horrific epidemic that felled one in four of its citizens. The disease was first encountered in Piraeus (the port of Athens), but soon spread to the upper city, where the citizens experienced "violent heats in the head, and redness and inflammation in the eyes, the inward parts, such as the throat or tongue, becoming bloody and emitting an unnatural and fetid breath." Thucydides—who described the plague in his *History of the Peloponnesian War*—had no idea of its nature or cause, so he "simply set down its nature, and explain[ed] the symptoms by which perhaps it might be recognized by the student, if it should ever break out again." Further symptoms included sneezing and hoarseness, chest pains, discharges of bile, retching, violent spasms, and skin that broke out in small pustules and ulcers. In the final stages, there was bleeding diarrhea, loss of fingers and toes, and blindness.

Among the suggestions that have been made to account for this massive disaster have been smallpox, bubonic plague, scarlet fever, measles, typhus, typhoid fever, or some unprecedented combination. Alexander Langmuir of Johns Hopkins, the epidemiologist who (with his colleagues) proposed the name "Thucydides syndrome," suggested influenza complicated by toxic shock as the cause of the Athenian plague, even though, they wrote, "the extremely

---

* As far as I can tell, no one involved in the Helice expeditions—not Marinatos, Edgerton, or Throckmorton—ever suggested that they were looking for Atlantis.

high mortality in Athens is out of proportion to that of all known influenza epidemics. Mortality rates of 3 to 5 per cent were the highest recorded in other than primitive, remote, isolated areas in 1918." To this deadly constellation of pathogens, Langmuir et al. added staphylococcal enterotoxic food poisoning, and wrote, "The well-known capacity of both the influenza virus and the staphylococcus to mutate, transfer, adapt, survive and 'plague' the human race raises the possibility that the Thucydides syndrome may reappear as a minor or even major manifestation of some future epidemic or pandemic of influenza."

In a 1994 article in the *American Journal of Epidemiology,* David Morens and Robert Littman carefully examined the extensive literature on the subject, and ruled out influenza and toxic shock syndrome, but did not eliminate typhus, plague, anthrax, smallpox, or an arboviral disease (transmitted by houseflies or ticks). The epidemiology of the Plague of Athens has long confounded medical and other historians. Thucydides (who contracted the disease but survived) never says how many Athenians died in the epidemic, but he does tell us that during an expedition to Potidaea that embarked two months after the epidemic struck, 1,050 of the 4,000-man force (26 percent) caught the disease and died. At that time, the population of Athens was between 250,000 and 300,000, so extrapolating from the number that died in Potidaea, Morens and Littman suggest that between 65,000 and 78,000 Athenians died in the four-year duration of the plague.* In a city of the population density of ancient Athens, this figure is too low for influenza; they wrote, "Even the bare minimum estimated degree of crowding (20,000–25,000 persons per square mile) could not possibly have sustained influenza in a completely enclosed city for 2–5 continuous years." (In the same journal, Langmuir responded to the Morens and Littman paper by commenting that he was "greatly amused and somewhat disheartened to realize that competent and respected scientists and classicists can examine the same evidence and draw diametrically opposite conclusions with such emotion.")

Since the Greeks cremated their dead, there is no way of testing any of the hypotheses, but in the medical journal *Emerging Infectious Diseases* of April–June 1996, Olsen et al. recognized many of these symptoms as those of the Ebola virus, and wrote, "The profile of the ancient disease is remarkably

---

* Among those who died was Pericles, Athens' greatest statesman and the leader of the Athenians against the invading Spartans in the Peloponnesian War. As Plutarch wrote, "The plague seized Pericles, not with sharp and violent fits, as it did others that had it, but with a dull and lingering distemper, attended with various changes and alterations, leisurely, little by little, wasting the strength of his body and undermining the noble faculties of his soul."

similar to that of the recent outbreaks in Sudan and Zaire, and offers another
solution to Thucydides' ancient puzzle. A Nilotic source for a pathogen in
Piraeus, the busy maritime hub of the Delian League . . . is clearly plausible."
One of the suspected vectors of the Ebola virus is the vervet or blue monkey (*Cercopithecus aethiops*). These monkeys—or their close relatives—are
known to have been on the Aegean island of Santorini, since they appear in
the Minoan frescoes at Akrotiri (see pp. 171–76). The presence of blue monkeys in ancient Greece—even a thousand years before the Plague of Athens—
suggests that these monkeys might very well have been responsible for the
spread of this virulent epidemic. Since the inhabitants of Atlantis all disappeared (along with their city) in a single day, the plague probably has nothing
to do with Plato's tale, but it is certainly possible that he might have been
thinking of the sudden death of tens of thousands of Athenians when he
wrote his story.

In Plutarch's life of Pericles, we read that the Plague of Athens had some
consequences that would seem to tie it even more closely to the dramatic
demise of Atlantis. Pericles believed that the "small tenements and over-
crowded hovels" of the city were the cause of the plague, so he arranged for 150
galleys to leave Athens, partly to relieve the crowded conditions, but also to
demonstrate to the Spartans that the Athenians could still muster a powerful
fighting force:

> And now the vessels having their complement of men, and Pericles being gone
> aboard his own galley, it happened that the sun was eclipsed, and it suddenly
> grew dark, to the affright of all, for this was looked on as extremely ominous.
> Pericles, therefore, perceiving the steersman seized with fear and at a loss for
> what to do, took his cloak and held it up to the man's face, and screening him
> with that so he could not see, asked him whether he imagined there was any
> great hurt, or the sign of any great hurt in this, and he answering No, "Why,"
> said he, "and what does that differ from this, only that what has caused that
> darkness there is something greater than a cloak?"

P A S S E D   D O W N through the centuries, Plato's story seems to be composed
of several disparate parts, combined in the two dialogues. Of these pieces,
probably the least useful (although certainly the most dramatic) is the history
of the destruction of Minoan Crete. Unfortunately for those who would tie
Crete to Atlantis, there are hardly any elements that can be made to fit. Only
the large buildings, the seafaring nature of the occupants, and the disappear-

ance of a large number of people coincide with Plato's description, and this seems a meager congruence indeed. It is also unlikely that Plato—or any fifth-century B.C. Athenian—knew anything about the volcanic destruction of an island almost a thousand years earlier. As Critias comments, the Egyptians thought that the Greeks were "all children," by which he meant that they had no recollection of their own ancient history. ("Our traditions are the oldest preserved," says the Egyptian priest. "We have preserved from earliest times a written record of any great or splendid achievement or notable event . . . whether it occurred in your part of the world or here or anywhere else.") The Egyptian seems to be referring specifically to floods, for he says, "You may remember only one deluge, though there have been many, and you do not know that the finest and best race of men that ever existed lived in your country. . . ."

Marinatos and others were probably correct in attributing the origins of the story to some Egyptian tales, especially since Critias tells Socrates that the tale is actually Egyptian. Plato himself tells us that he has taken the story told by the Egyptians and adapted it to the Greek environment; in the *Timaeus,* he has Critias say: "I am ready to tell the story, Socrates, not only in outline but in detail, as I heard it. We will transfer the imaginary citizens and city which you described yesterday to the real world, and say that your city is the city of my story and your citizens those historical ancestors of ours whom the priest described. They will fit exactly, and there will be no disharmony if we speak as if they really were the men who lived at that time." To this Plato might have added a variation on the story of Helice, which he surely had known about; stirred in a bit of the splendor of the Temple of Artemis at Ephesus; and incorporated a portion of Greek mythology, in which Poseidon and Cleito produced five pairs of twins who divided the island of Atlantis between them. Because thousands of Athenians died suddenly, it is difficult to ignore the Plague—and fall—of Athens as possible components of Plato's story.

Pericles, who was born around 495 B.C. and died in 429, was the general and statesman whose intentions were to make Athens the political and cultural center of Greece. During the "Periclean Age" (sometimes called the "Golden Age of Pericles" or the "Golden Age of Athens"), the philosophers Anaxagoras, Protagoras, Empedocles, and Socrates held forth; Hippocrates roamed through Greece teaching and practicing medicine; Sophocles wrote *Antigone;* Euripides wrote *Medea;* and on the hill of the Acropolis, the Propylaea, the Erechtheum, and the Temple of Athena Nike were built, along with the Parthenon. But this powerful and successful city-state was not destined to perdure; the plague ravaged the proud city of Athens, and the Peloponnesian War, which began in 431 and lasted until the defeat of the Athenian navy in 405, resulted in conquest by the Spartans.

As reported by Thucydides, Pericles delivered the famous funeral oration over the bodies of the Athenians who died in battle and from sickness. He said (in part):

> You, in your private afflictions, are angry with me that I persuaded you to declare war. Therefore you are also angry with yourselves that you voted for me. You took me to be what I think I am, superior to most in foresight, in oratorical ability—for if a man cannot explain himself clearly, he might as well have no foresight—in patriotism, and in personal honesty. But if you voted with me because you took me to be like this, you cannot fairly charge me with doing you an injury. I have not changed; it is you who have changed. A calamity has befallen you, and you cannot persevere in the policy you chose when all was well; it is the weakness of your resolution that makes my advice seem to have been wrong. It is the unexpected that most breaks a man's spirit.

"By this speech," wrote Thucydides, "Pericles tried to divert the Athenians' wrath from himself and their thoughts from their present distress." Only a few months after delivering this speech, Pericles died of the plague.

After the death of Pericles in 429, Cleon (according to Thucydides, "the most persuasive speaker in the Assembly") became the leader of the Athenians, in politics as well as on the battlefield. His army was defeated and he was killed at Amphipolis, and Nicias, a former supporter of Pericles, took over. The war appeared to have ended in 421, when Nicias persuaded the Athenian assembly to accept Sparta's overtures for peace, but by 415, fighting had broken out again. The terms of the "Peace of Nicias" were never implemented, and in an attempt to end the war in one powerful maneuver, the Athenians decided to send a great armada to invade Sicily. The expeditionary force was led by three generals—Alcibiades, Lamachus, and Nicias—but the invasion ended in a complete disaster, when Lamachus was killed, Nicias fell ill, and Alcibiades, who had been recalled for sacrilege, escaped and transferred his allegiance to Sparta. It was Alcibiades who led the Spartans in the final naval victories of the war. The Spartans had allied themselves with the Persians, and at the battle of Aegospotami (on the European side of the Hellespont), the Persians under Cyrus completely destroyed the remnants of the Athenian navy. In 404, the troops of the Spartan admiral Lysander demolished the great walls of Piraeus, and Athens was stripped of her empire, fleet, and fortifications. The Spartans

portentous advice by saying, "You are my father's brother, and that alone saves you from paying the price your empty and ridiculous speech deserves!")

On land, the Greeks occupied the narrow pass of Thermopylae, and under the leadership of Leonidas defended it bravely against the Persian infantry. They fought to the death, but Thermopylae fell to the Persians. Xerxes advanced to Athens and sacked the city, but the Greeks retreated by sea, trapping the Persian fleet in the narrow waters of the Straits of Salamis, where they won the decisive battle under the inspired leadership of Themistocles. That winter, Greek ground forces defeated the Persians at Plataea and Mycale, resulting in the complete rout and defeat of the invaders. A treaty of peace was signed in 448, and the Persian king Ataxerxes I recognized the liberty of the Greek states.

It requires very little imagination to equate Plato's tale of the rise and fall of Atlantis with Herodotus's account of the Greco-Persian Wars and, to a lesser extent, with Thucydides' description of the Peloponnesian War. In both cases, Athens is at war: in the first, she is triumphant; in the second, she is defeated. It is not at all difficult to imagine that Plato was describing the invading Persians when he wrote, "Our records tell how your city checked a great power which arrogantly advanced from its base in the Atlantic Ocean to attack the cities of Europe and Asia." Even Atabranus's advice to Xerxes can be found in Plato's tale: "This dynasty," explains the priest, "gathering its whole power together, attempted to enslave, at a single stroke, your country and ours, and all the territory within the strait." (This is not to suggest that Plato cribbed from Herodotus; only that the idea of pride going before a fall is an ancient and honorable one. Herodotus died around 425, three years after Plato was born.)

When Plato first describes Atlantis in the *Timaeus,* he casts it in generally pejorative terms, but for ancient Athens, he has nothing but praise (Critias is the speaker):

You may remember only one deluge, though there have been many, and you do not know that the finest and best race of men that ever existed lived in your country; you and your fellow citizens are descended from the few survivors that remained, but you know nothing about it because so many succeeding generations left no record of it in writing. For before the greatest of all destructions by water, Solon, the city that is now Athens was preeminent in war and conspicuously the best governed in every way, its achievements and constitution being the finest of any in the world of which we have heard tell.

But when we get to the *Critias,* it is Atlantis about which he waxes euphoric. Even though this civilization (for which we might readily substitute the Persian invaders) "attempted to enslave, at a single stroke, your country and ours, and all the territory within the strait," his description of the land, city, and buildings of Atlantis is filled with encomia of the most fulsome sort. He praises the land ("a plain said to be the most beautiful and fertile of all plains"); the water ("hot and cold springs . . . that caused the earth to grow abundant produce of every kind"); and the fecundity of the soil, where "aromatic substances . . . cultivated crops . . . the fruits of trees . . . all these were produced by that sacred island, then still beneath the sun, in wonderful quantity and profusion." Why this reversal, this unrestrained glorification of the evil empire? So that he can bring it down, of course:

> This was the nature and extent of the power which existed then in those parts of the world and which god brought to attack our country. His reason, so the story goes, was this. For many generations, so long as the divine element in their nature survived, they obeyed the laws and loved the divine to which they were akin. They retained a certain greatness of mind, and treated the vagaries of fortune and one another with forbearance, as they reckoned that qualities of character were far more important than their present prosperity. . . . But when the divine element in them became weakened by frequent admixture with mortal stock, and their human traits became predominant, they ceased to be able to carry their prosperity with moderation. To the perceptive eye the depth of their degeneration was clear enough, but to those whose judgment is defective, they seemed, in their pursuit of unbridled ambition and power, to be at the height of their fame and fortune. And the god of gods, Zeus, who reigns by law, and whose eye can see such things, when he perceived the wretched state of this admirable stock, decided to punish them and reduce them to order by discipline.

Would that Plato had completed this dialogue. Save for an unfinished paragraph about Zeus summoning the gods to hear his address about the punishment, this is the end of the *Critias,* and therefore the conclusion of Plato's story about Atlantis. It appears obvious that he intended to have Zeus levy a punishment commensurate with the extent of the degeneration, and since we already know that the punishment consisted of the total destruction of their civilization, which was overwhelmed by earthquakes and sunk beneath the sea, we can imagine his impassioned speech.

The process whereby mythologists employ facts and then elaborate on them to support their own theories is known as "Euhemerism," after a third-century B.C. philosopher called Euhemerus of Messene, who wrote (in his *Sacred History,* around 300 B.C.) that heroes were glorified and their exploits exaggerated until they were transmogrified into gods. He also suggested that mythological events represented historical happenings. Although Euhemerism has generally been rejected as a factor in the mythmaking process, there were certainly contemporaneous elements that Plato could have incorporated into his story. There are enough common generalities to connect the story of Atlantis with the downfall of the Minoan civilization, such as the existence of a great and sumptuous palace and a proud, seafaring people who traded far and wide, but the differences between what we know of the Minoans and what Plato tells us about the Atlanteans is just too great.

Take, for example, the destruction of the palace at Knossos. It was indeed a large and luxurious structure, but as far as we can tell from its remains, it had no gold, silver, or ivory embellishments. The comparison disintegrates further when we realize that it was the island with the volcano that exploded, not the one with the luxurious palaces seventy miles away. There was no aspect of Crete (or Santorini) arrayed with a series of concentric canals—or, for that matter, with an 11,000-mile-long ditch. Even if we adjust the dates and chronologically relocate Plato's story to a point a mere nine hundred years before Critias tells it to Socrates, Timaeus, and Hermocrates, we are still at a loss to explain the "Athenians" of 1500 B.C., the military might of the Atlanteans, or the eastward migration of Atlantis into the Aegean after Plato said so specifically that it was in the Atlantic. Knossos and Akrotiri have revealed only evidence of a peaceful, nonaggressive people, not Plato's "great power which arrogantly advanced from its base in the Atlantic Ocean to attack the cities of Europe and Asia."

By the second half of the thirteenth century B.C., most of the Mycenaean settlements in Greece had vanished. There was probably no single cause, but a combination of civil war, social revolution, and foreign invasion. Some historians have suggested that the "Sea Peoples," mysterious pirates who were known to have assaulted Egypt around the twelfth century B.C., also initiated an invasion of Greece. The Egyptians defeated the Sea Peoples in 1187 off the western delta of the Nile, and again in 1180 off Cyprus, but their forces and governments were so depleted by the massive effort involved that they soon fell to the Philistines and the Assyrians. Only a single generation after the battles of the Delta and Cyprus, Mycenae was destroyed. We have evidence of earthquakes and volcanic eruptions for Crete and Thera, but there is nothing in the archaeological or geological record to account for the sudden abandonment of Myce-

nae, Dendra, Thebes, Tiryns, Pylos, and the other Mycenaean settlements.*
Furthermore, the excavations at Troy and Mycenae are hopelessly disfigured
by Schliemann's overenthusiastic archaeologizing, leaving what Michael
Wood (*In Search of the Trojan War*) called "a ruin of a ruin." (Even less generously,
Eberhard Zangger wrote that for Schliemann, "the term 'excavation' again
seems inappropriate, because he mainly *removed* most of the remains which
Bronze Age and Roman destruction had left.") Was Plato aware of the Sea Peoples? If he knew what became of the Mycenaeans, he has not told us—unless,
of course, they were destroyed by "earthquakes and floods of extraordinary
violence, and in a single dreadful day . . . [were] swallowed up by the sea and
vanished."

Although the Trojan War that Homer described in the eighth century
is believed to have occurred some four or five hundred years earlier, fifth-
century Greek historians thought that much of the *Iliad* and the *Odyssey* were
based on fact. There are many stock phrases in Homer's tale, but he describes
Troy as being "well-walled," and a "broad city" with "lofty gates" and "wide
towers." Homer's Troy, like Plato's Atlantis, was an imaginary city, far grander
than known settlements of the period. Wood wrote, "In some ways this is obviously a fairy-tale city, a place of the imagination, for it bears little relation to
excavated towns of Homer's day—but for what it is worth, it seems reasonable
to assume that Homer was imagining a city far bigger than the little Aeolian
colony of his own day, 200 yards across; even the great eighth-century Ionian
city of Smyrna was only 300 yards by 150." Around 413 B.C., in a eerily prescient
anticipation of modern archaeology, Thucydides wrote, "Mycenae was certainly a small place, and many of the towns of that period do not seem to us
today to be particularly imposing; yet that is not good evidence for rejecting
what the poets said and what general tradition has to say about the size of the
expedition. Suppose, for example, that the city of Sparta were to become deserted and that only the temples and foundations of buildings remained. I
think that future generations would, as time passed, find it difficult to believe
that the place had really been as powerful as it was represented to be."

Thucydides never mentions Herodotus by name, but Moses I. Finley, in his
introduction to the *History of the Peloponnesian War,* wrote, "There are enough
indirect indications that he read his predecessor with care," and Herodotus,

---

* The first artifacts that Carl Blegen found when he began what was to become the excavation of the
palace at Pylos were tablets that were written in Linear B, the same language that Evans had found on
the tablets at Knossos. Both sets of tablets were deciphered by Michael Ventris, who showed that they
were an early form of Greek. In other words, the same language was spoken—or at least written—in
Minoan Crete and in the Mycenaean settlements on the Peloponnese: Mycenae, Tiryns, and Pylos.

who lived from 485 to 425, certainly believed that the Trojan War had occurred. This is the story that was told to him by the Egyptian priests:

> I asked the priests if the Greek story of what happened at Troy had any truth in it, and they gave me in reply some information which they claimed to have had direct from Menelaus himself. This was, that after the abduction of Helen, the Greeks sent a strong force to the Troad in support of Menelaus' cause, and as soon as the men had landed and established themselves on Trojan soil, ambassadors, of whom Menalaus was one, were dispatched to Troy.

How could Plato, who lived only a generation after Thucydides, not have known of the historian's description of the Trojan War, which was transmitted to him by Egyptian priests? Is this not another element that could easily have been incorporated into Plato's story of Atlantis?

In the classic tale, the war ended with the famous Trojan Horse, left by the Greeks as a peace offering to the inhabitants of the walled city. When the wooden horse was taken into the city, the soldiers concealed inside it killed the Trojan sentries and opened the gates to the remainder of Agamemnon's army, who sacked and burned the city. It is a good story, but not likely to be true. Indeed, it is probable that Troy was destroyed by earthquake—not once but several times—in addition to fires, which may have been started by the quakes, but also may have been started by invaders.

The Trojan War, the sinking of Helice, Periclean Greece, the Parthenon, the Temple of Artemis at Ephesus, the Long Walls, the Peloponnesian War, the Plague of Athens, the Persian Wars, the collapse of the Mycenaean stongholds—surely this is more than enough grist for Plato's mill. These components could have been used to formulate the story of Atlantis, and attempts to juggle the facts to make them conform to one's preconceived notions about Knossos, Akrotiri, the Sahara Desert, Heligoland, Bimini, or Mars are a waste of time.

Even if no evidence of the Lost City is ever found—and I believe it will remain forever lost—the myth has shown a remarkable durability. What is it about the story of Atlantis that has enabled it to endure for more than two thousand years? Even though it contains many traditional elements, the story does not appear in Greek mythology. Indeed, Plato interweaves components of the mythology of his time into his tale, such as the long account of Poseidon and Cleito that he tells in the *Critias* to explain the founding of Atlantis:

> The story is a long one and begins like this. We have already mentioned how the gods distributed the whole earth between them in larger or smaller shares

and then established shrines and sacrifices for themselves. Poseidon's share was the island of Atlantis, and he settled the children born to him by a mortal woman in a particular district of it. At the center of the island, near the sea, was a plain. . . . Here there lived one of the original earth-born inhabitants called Evenor, with his wife Leucippe. They had an only child, a daughter called Cleito. She was just of marriageable age when her father and mother died, and Poseidon was attracted by her and had intercourse with her, and fortified the hill where she lived by enclosing it with concentric rings of sea and land. There were two rings of land, and three of sea, like cartwheels, with the island at their center and equidistant from each other, making the place inaccessible to man (for there were still no ships or sailing in those days). He equipped the central island with godlike lavishness; he made two springs flow, one of hot and one of cold water, and caused the earth to grow produce of every kind.

There follows an intricate genealogy of the children of Cleito and Poseidon (the five pairs of twins), a description of the fertile land, and a highly detailed picture of the city and buildings of Atlantis. We cannot know what Plato believed about Poseidon—indeed, we cannot know how much of the stories of the gods his contemporaries believed, either—but we do know that this Olympian god was described in the mythology of the Greeks of Plato's time. Shrines to Poseidon were erected at various locations, and numerous statues of the "earth-shaker" have been identified. He was the god of the sea and of earthquakes. Cleito seems to have been an invention of Plato's.

Plato never tells us if he actually believed in Poseidon, so we must assume that he included Poseidon and Cleito in his story of Atlantis in order to introduce a fictional parentage for the five pairs of twins. He gave them all names: the eldest he called Atlas, "the name from which the whole island and the surrounding ocean took their designation of 'Atlantic.' " (His twin was Eumelus.) The other pairs are Ampheres and Euaemon, Mneseus and Autochthon, Elasippus and Mestor, and Azaes and Diaprepes.

Is the Judeo-Christian story of the creation of the world in seven days a myth, a legend, or a fact? It depends upon whom you ask. This is not the forum in which to debate the "truth" of Christianity or Buddhism or New Guinea ancestor worship; it is sufficient to declare that at one time—and perhaps today—people believed in their mythologies as literal truths. Christian fundamentalists hold that every word of the Bible must be accepted as gospel, but most Christians are not prepared to argue that the texts of the Old and New Testaments are chronicles of fact. On the other hand, there are certain Muslim sects that believe that the Koran (also Qur'an) contains the true word of God, as revealed to the prophet Muhammad, and that as an uncreated and heavenly work, it is the ultimate authority in all legal and religious matters.

In many societies, the distinctions between mythology and religion— when there are distinctions—are cloudy and vague. Indeed, one often replaces the other. In her study of the world's myths, Edith Hamilton wrote:

> Greek mythology is largely made up of stories about gods and goddesses, but it must not be read as a kind of Greek Bible, an account of the Greek religion. According to the most modern idea [Hamilton wrote this in 1940], a real myth has nothing to do with religion. It is an explanation of something in nature; how, for instance, any and everything in the universe came into existence: men, animals, this or that tree or flower, the sun, the moon, the stars, storms, eruptions, earthquakes, all that is and all that happens.

We know little about the actual religious beliefs of the ancient Greeks, but their elaborate mythology has been revealed to us through the tales of Homer and the Roman poet Ovid, and also through contemporaneous Greek vase painting and sculpture. "The Greeks had no authoritative Sacred Book," wrote Hamilton, "no creed, no ten commandments, no dogmas. The very ideas of orthodoxy were unknown to them. They had no theologians to draw up sacrosanct definitions of the eternal and the infinite. They never tried to define it; only to express or suggest it. . . . Phidias' statue of Zeus at Olympia was his definition of Zeus, the greatest ever achieved in terms of beauty."

Did the average Athenian believe that Zeus assumed the form of a bull when he carried off Europa? That humans had fire because Prometheus stole it back from Zeus, or that women existed because Hephaestos fashioned the first one from clay? We do not know, but many Christians today believe that "God said, Let there be light: and there was light," and that from "the rib, which the Lord God had taken from man, made he a woman. . . ."

Just as today's Christians visit their churches and Muslims their mosques, the Greeks visited their temples. Although they built grand edifices to propitiate and house their gods, and furnished them with idols and shrines, the temples themselves were not meant to be filled with worshipers. Rather, the religious ceremonies were carried on in the great spaces outside, and sacrifices were offered on the altars, which were always in the open air. The temple was the dwelling place of the god, and the treasury where the gifts brought by the worshipers were stored.

If we examine historical Western mythology—as contrasted with religion—we see that very few of the myths have survived. Few Greeks nowadays believe in Zeus, Aphrodite, or Poseidon, but somehow, the myth of Atlantis has survived. Although its author was Greek, it is not a Greek myth—strictly speaking, it is not a myth at all. In *The Power of Myth*, Joseph Campbell says that "the dictionary definition of a myth would be stories about gods.... The myths are metaphorical of spiritual potentiality in the human being, and the same powers that animate our life animate the life of the world."

Only if we extend the definition of a myth, or try to fit it into our contemporary epistemology, can we call Plato's Atlantis story a myth. (*The Oxford English Dictionary*'s first definition of "myth" is: "A purely fictitious narrative, usually involving supernatural persons, actions or events, and embodying some popular idea concerning natural or historical phenomena. Often used vaguely to include any narrative having fictitious elements." Under this second definition, Plato's story of Atlantis would qualify as a myth, but then, so would *Gone with the Wind*.)

Even for a mythologist like Mircea Eliade, the definition of a myth is not a simple thing. In *Myth and Reality*, he wrote:

> Speaking for myself, the definition that seems the least inadequate because most embracing is this: Myth narrates a sacred history; it relates an event that took place in primordial time, the fabled time of the "beginnings." In other words, myth tells how, through the deeds of Supernatural Beings, a reality came into existence, be it the whole of reality, the Cosmos, or only a fragment of reality—an island, a species of plant, a particular kind of human behavior, an institution. Myth, then, is always an account of a "creation"; it relates how something was produced, began to *be*.

Employing this definition, we find that the "myth" of Atlantis does not conform at all; rather than explaining how something *began* to be, Plato tells us how something *ceased* to be. And since it had not existed in mythology before, except perhaps as a universal flood story, we cannot accurately place the Atlantis story in this category. Is it a legend, a "traditional story of unknown authorship"? Certainly this cannot be the case, since the author is hardly unknown. The safest definition is that it is a story, "the first essay in science fiction," as Desmond Lee characterized it.

The story of the destruction of a civilization by natural forces is not an uncommon theme. Eliade wrote:

> Myths of cosmic cataclysms are extremely widespread. They tell how the world was destroyed and mankind annihilated except for a single couple or a

few survivors. The myths of the Flood are the most numerous and are known nearly everywhere. In addition to the Flood myths, others recount the destruction of mankind by cataclysms of cosmic proportions—earthquakes, conflagrations, falling mountains, epidemics, and so forth. Clearly, this End of the World was not final; rather it was the end of one human race, followed by the appearance of another. But the total submergence of the Earth under the Waters, or its destruction by fire, followed by the emergence of a virgin Earth, symbolizes a return to chaos, followed by cosmogony.

Plato's depiction of Atlantis was of a rich and powerful society that was swallowed up by the sea in a great cataclysm, and every remnant of it destroyed. Like the *Iliad* and the *Odyssey,* it has managed to survive for more than two millennia. But unlike Homer's epic poems, Plato's tale—rarely considered an important part of his voluminous output—has not only survived as a demonstration of the storyteller's art, but also has become a part of our own mythology. It might be said that Plato's Atlantis has acquired a mythology of its own.

From the time he wrote the dialogues that contain the story of the origins and the downfall of Atlantis, the story has perdured, and indeed, it has been amended, interpreted, embellished, and modified to the point where it has become a standard. Not that everyone knows its origins; many believe that it was originally a Greek myth, or that Edgar Cayce heard of it while in a trance, or that Ignatius Donnelly discovered its origins in the Library of Congress.

Even without interpreting the dialogues in a subjective manner, it is possible to read Plato's description of Atlantis as a marvelous story. It has everything in it: wealth, war, floods, earthquakes, destruction, mystery, cataclysms, and the downfall of an entire civilization. We can accept Atlantis as fiction largely because there is no reliable evidence that any of the events that are described really occurred. In its scope it reminds us of a small-scale New Testament; it is not at all surprising that the tale has come down to us as one of the enduring legacies of the ancient world.

Regardless of how we read it, the story of Atlantis has passed through time as bright and new, as pertinent today as it was when Plato wrote it. Perhaps a myth has more to do with fantasy than with fact. The tenacity of the Atlantis story suggests that we need our fantasies; we have maintained the tale over time because it fills a need. It is an account of power and wealth, of greed and retribution, of natural disaster and mystery—everything that makes a good yarn.

The story of Atlantis has become a bridge to the past. It connects us directly to Plato—and, by extension, to an event that occurred nine thousand years before his birth—and then to the continuum of Western history. Everyone can try to make it fit his particular cosmography. But the tale of Atlantis will not be defined. Is it a true story, a myth, a parable, or science fiction? Does it matter? It means so much to so many; its strength lies in its universality. But all good stories—even the *Iliad* and the *Odyssey*—are not necessarily myths. As we have seen, Homer's poems incorporate contemporaneous mythology, but also descriptions of real places and real people. Atlantis, as far as we know, utilizes mythology, but no history unless we assume that Plato's personal experiences and recollections qualify as "history." It is Plato's story, and his alone, and no amount of mysticism, reinterpretation, scuba diving, or archaeology will ever change that.

APPENDIX

Dramatis Personae

T H E R E   A R E so many historians, archaeologists, writers, geologists, seismologists, volcanologists, mystics, and psychics associated with the story of Atlantis that I believe it will be instructive to review the cast of characters. Although many of these people are discussed at greater length in the text, some with annotations of their writings, the following brief entries will familiarize the reader with who they are—or were—what they did or wrote, and when they did it or wrote it.

AELIAN (170–230 A.D.)

Claudius Aelianus was born around 170 A.D. at Praeneste (Palestrina), south of Rome. Because he was an accomplished student of Attic Greek, he became a serious scholar and produced the fourteen-book *Varia historia* (Varied History), a collection of historical, biographical, and antiquarian anecdotes and narratives. He is probably best known, however, for *De natura animalium* (On the Characteristics of Animals), a mixed collection of fact, fancy, and legend, in no particular arrangement, but with the underlying motive that men might learn from the often selfless behavior of animals.

Francis Bacon (1561–1626)

An English essayist, lawyer, statesmen, and philosopher, Bacon entered Trinity College, Cambridge, at the age of twelve. He wrote treatises on inductive reasoning and scientific methodology, and essays on politics, economics, religion, love, and marriage, but he probably did not write the plays of Shakespeare. His utopian account of an ideal world in the essay *The New Atlantis* (published in London the year after his death) probably revealed more about what he believed was wrong with his own world than anything else.

Charles Berlitz (b. 1913)

From the jacket copy for *Atlantis: The Eighth Continent:* "Charles Berlitz was born in New York City. A graduate of Yale University and the grandson of Maximilian Berlitz, founder of the Berlitz language schools, he speaks twenty-five languages with varying degrees of fluency and is considered one of the fifteen most eminent linguists in the world. His interest in archaeology and underwater exploration led to his writing *The Bermuda Triangle.* Mr. Berlitz was awarded the Dag Hammarskjöld International Prize for Nonfiction in 1976."

Madame Blavatsky (1831–1891)

Born in Yekaterinoslav in the Ukraine, Helena Petrovna Hahn married a Russian military officer when she was seventeen, but left him after a few months to begin her travels. She claimed to have visited Istanbul, Cairo, Athens, New Orleans, Tokyo, and Calcutta, and to have spent seven years in Tibet studying with Hindu mahatmas, who taught her about the lost continents of Atlantis and Lemuria. She started the Theosophical movement in Russia in 1858 and brought it to New York in 1871. The movement was based largely on Madame Blavatsky's communications with dead Tibetan masters. Although the Indian press and the London Society for Psychical Research declared her a fraud, she persisted in her attempts to establish a spiritual connection between man and the universe.

Carl W. Blegen (1887–1971)

An American, educated at the University of Minnesota and Yale, Blegen was an archaeologist. From 1927 to 1957, he was professor of classical archaeology at the

University of Cincinnati. Regarded as one of the greatest of American archaeologists, he excavated at Korakou, Zygouries, and Prosymna, but he is best
known for his comprehensive and innovative work at the Mycenaean settlements at Troy, and at the palace of Pylos, in the southwestern Peloponnese.
The Carl W. Blegen Chair of Greek Archaeology at the University of Cincinnati was endowed in his name.

RHYS CARPENTER (1889–1980)

A Columbia University graduate, Carpenter established the School of Classical
Archaeology at Bryn Mawr College in 1916 and remained there until 1927, when
he was named director of the American School for Classical Studies in Athens.
He was appointed professor-in-charge of the Classical School of the American
Academy in Rome in 1940, returned to Bryn Mawr, and retired in 1955. After his
retirement, he lectured at many other universities, and in 1966 wrote *Beyond the
Pillars of Heracles,* an account of early exploration in and around the Medi-
terranean. His *Discontinuity in Greek Civilization* is a provocative study in which
he suggested that a widespread drought was responsible for the dissolution of
Mycenaean power and the subsequent Dark Age of Greek history.

RACHEL CARSON (1907–1964)

Communicating her abiding interest in wildlife, Rachel Carson taught at the
University of Maryland and Johns Hopkins University, and later worked as a
marine biologist for the U.S. Bureau of Fisheries. She was editor in chief of the
U.S. Fish and Wildlife Service. She is known as one of America's foremost
nature writers, having written four highly acclaimed books: *Under the Sea Wind,
The Edge of the Sea, Silent Spring,* and *The Sea Around Us,* which won the National
Book Award for 1951.

EDGAR CAYCE (1877–1945)

Although he aspired to the ministry, Edgar Cayce had to leave school in Kentucky in the seventh grade because of a throat ailment that reduced his voice
to a whisper. Hypnotized to cure this malady, "the sleeping prophet" found
that he had the ability to diagnose other people's ailments based on the color
of the energy cloud around them. Through other people's recollections and
dreams, Cayce could "see" into the past, and there he saw Atlantis, which he
believed would rise from the sea around 1968.

JOHN CHADWICK (B. 1920)

With Michael Ventris, philologist John Chadwick of Cambridge University deciphered Linear B, the ancient Greek language on the clay tablets found at Knossos by Arthur Evans, and at Pylos by Carl Blegen. Chadwick is the author of many technical discussions of early Greek philology, and in 1956, the year Ventris died at the age of thirty-four, the book they coauthored, *Documents in Mycenaean Greek,* was published. Chadwick also wrote *The Decipherment of Linear B,* published in 1958, and *The Mycenaean World,* which was published in 1976.

L. SPRAGUE DE CAMP (B. 1907)

Lyon Sprague de Camp is recognized as one of the foremost writers of science fiction in America. Born in California, de Camp received a master's degree in aeronautical engineering from the Stevens Institute of Technology in 1933. He wrote stories and novels that were collected into innumerable anthologies, and in 1978, he was awarded science fiction's highest award, the Nebula Grand Master Award. Although best known for his science and fantasy fiction, de Camp also wrote nonfiction, such as *Lost Continents: The Atlantis Theme in History, Science, and Literature,* one of the most useful, comprehensive, and intelligent books ever written on this subject.

IGNATIUS DONNELLY (1831–1901)

With the possible exception of Plato, who introduced the myth of Atlantis, Ignatius Donnelly was the most important Atlantean scholar of all time. Born in Philadelphia, he pursued a career in Minnesota politics, was elected to Congress from that state, and in 1882 wrote *Atlantis: The Antediluvian World.* This book, which has gone through many editions and is still in print, has served as an inspiration and guide for the legions of Atlantologists who followed Donnelly. He also wrote *Ragnarok: The Age of Fire and Gravel,* a book about the near collision of the earth with a comet; and several books in which he argued that Francis Bacon had written the plays of Shakespeare and Marlowe, as well as the essays of Montaigne.

CHRISTOS DOUMAS (B. 1933)

Having spent virtually all of his professional life studying the archaeology
of Greece, Doumas is now director of the dig at Akrotiri on the island of
Thera (Santorini). He was born in Patras and studied history and archaeology at the University of Athens before taking his doctorate at the University
of London. As a member of the Greek Archaeological Service, he was curator of antiquities in the Cyclades (the group that includes Santorini), and
then curator of the Acropolis in Athens. From 1968 to 1974, he was assistant to
Spyridon Marinatos at Akrotiri, and upon Marinatos's death, he was named
director.

ARTHUR CONAN DOYLE (1859–1930)

Born in Edinburgh and educated as a doctor, Conan Doyle practiced medicine until 1891, when he retired to devote himself to his writing. He is best
remembered for his novels and stories about the brilliant detective Sherlock
Holmes, but his writings also include *The Lost World,* several books on Spiritual-
ism, and the little-known—but pertinent—novel *The Maracot Deep,* about
adventurers discovering Atlantis. He was knighted in 1902 for his services during
the Boer War.

HAROLD EDGERTON (1903–1990)

"Doc" Edgerton was born in Nebraska and spent most of his professional life
at the Massachusetts Institute of Technology. Among other things, he was
the inventor of high-speed stroboscopic photography and side-scan sonar
and had a long-standing interest in underwater exploration. In 1954, he
deployed a remote-controlled underwater camera from Cousteau's *Calypso*
in the Mediterranean, obtaining some of the first shots of some of the rare
creatures of the depths. He initiated several expeditions to the Gulf of Corinth, seeking the lost city of Helice, and also participated in James Mavor's
1966 expedition to search for Atlantis on the island of Santorini. In 1984 he lent
his expertise and equipment to an expedition to try to film the Loch Ness
monster.

SIR ARTHUR EVANS (1851–1941)

Educated at Harrow and Oxford, Arthur John Evans is one of the towering figures in the history of archaeology. After travels and researches in the Balkans, he became keeper of the Ashmolean Museum at Oxford, a post he retained until 1908. He purchased the site of Knossos (from the Turks, who owned Crete at the time) and began excavating there in 1899. He uncovered a palace of a thousand rooms, which he believed to have been the home of the legendary King Minos, and he named the "Minoan" civilization. His four-volume *The Palace of Minos,* published from 1921 to 1936, is the highly subjective but definitive work on the subject. He was knighted in 1911.

ANGELOS GALANOPOULOS (B. 1910)

Born in Achaea, Greece, Galanopoulos graduated from the University of Athens and became a lecturer on seismology at the Athens Observatory. He became a professor in 1959 and published extensively on earthquakes, volcanoes, and tsunamis. In 1969, in collaboration with British writer Edward Bacon, he wrote the comprehensive *Atlantis: The Truth Behind the Legend,* in which he argued that although Plato got the dates wrong, he was actually describing the eruption of the volcano in Thera that destroyed most of that island, along with the Minoan civilization on Crete.

BRUCE HEEZEN (1923–1977)

Born and raised in Iowa, Heezen was planning a career in paleontology until a chance meeting with Maurice Ewing at Columbia University's Lamont Doherty Observatory redirected him to a career in oceanography. With oceanic cartographer Marie Tharp, Heezen documented the Mid-Atlantic Ridge, and together they made the first accurate maps of the floor of the Atlantic. On cruises aboard the R.V. *Vema* in the Aegean in 1956 and 1958, Heezen and fellow geologist Dragoslav Ninkovich found evidence of the eruption of Thera in deep-sea cores, and were among the first to recognize the magnitude of the fifteenth-century B.C. explosion.

HERODOTUS (C. 485–C. 425 B.C.)

Herodotus was born between 490 and 480 B.C., at Halicarnassus (now Bodrum) in what is now Turkey. As a young man, he traveled widely in Egypt, Africa, and other parts of the Greek world. He knew Athens well, and is said to have given a public reading of his *Historia* there in 446. His history of the Greco-Persian Wars also covers the customs, geography, and history of the Mediterranean peoples from the time of Croesus (c. 550 B.C.) to the Persian Wars of 500–448 B.C. The *Historia* incorporates tales he was told, firsthand observations, dreams, and superstitions, and it is considered the first great narrative history of the ancient world.

HOMER (NINTH–EIGHTH CENTURY B.C.)

Almost nothing is known of the life of this Greek poet, who is believed to have been an Ionian from the west coast of Asia Minor, not far from the Troy he wrote about. There is no evidence that he was blind, but the ancient Greeks thought he was, so it might be true. Probably relying on oral traditions, he wrote the *Iliad* and then the *Odyssey,* epic poems that the Greeks considered to be true accounts of events, but that later scholars thought were romantic story-telling. Because Heinrich Schliemann (q.v.) believed that Homer's poems were fact, he dug for the fabled city of Troy where Homer said it was—and found it.

MURRY HOPE (B. 1929)

On the jacket of *Atlantis: Myth or Reality?,* Murry Hope is described as a "journalist, teacher, lecturer, and a former professional classical singer . . . one of England's foremost authors on metaphysics, ancient magical religions, and parapsychology. She was co-founder of the Atlanteans in 1957, and served as the society's president, principal teacher, and healer for twenty years. In 1977 her psychic abilities were tested by Dr. Carl Sargent of Cambridge University under the auspices of the BBC, and she achieved an extraordinarily high percentage of accuracy. In 1988 she established the Institute of Transpersonal Sensitivity, the aims of which are to effect a bridge between the transpersonal experience and the more popularly accepted schools of psychology." She is also the author of *The Lion People* and *The 9 Lives of Tyo.*

SIR DESMOND LEE (1908–1993)

Translator of Plato's dialogues the *Timaeus* and the *Critias,* and also *The Republic,* Lee took a "double first" in classics at Corpus Christi College, Cambridge, and led a distinguished career in education as headmaster of two public schools, Clifton and Winchester, and as headmaster of Clifton College, Cambridge. His translations include careful analyses of the material, and for the Penguin edition of the *Timaeus* and the *Critias*—in which the Atlantis myth was first introduced—he provides an "Appendix on Atlantis," which is one of the most succinct and insightful discussions of the origins of the myth.

J. V. LUCE (B. 1920)

Educated in the classics at Trinity College, Dublin, J. V. Luce lectured in Greek at Glasgow University, then returned to Dublin, where he was elected fellow in the classics, then reader, tutor, and finally, senior tutor at Trinity College. His specialty is the relationship of classical sources to the story of Atlantis, and he discusses the connections in *Lost Atlantis: New Light on an Old Legend,* published in 1969 (in the same year, a paperback version, *The End of Atlantis,* was published).

NANNO MARINATOS (B. 1950)

The daughter of Professor Spyridon Marinatos, Ourania "Nanno" Marinatos earned her Ph.D. in classical archaeology in 1978 from the University of Colorado at Boulder. She worked with her father at Akrotiri until his untimely death, and went on to become a recognized expert on the history of ancient religion. She has also excavated in Boeotia (Greece) and Tell el Dab'a in Egypt. Her books include *Minoan Religion: Ritual Process, Image, and Symbol, Minoan Sacrifical Ritual,* and *Art and Religion in Thera.* She is the author of more than forty articles and has lectured on Minoan and Greek religion throughout the United States and Europe.

SPYRIDON MARINATOS (1901–1974)

The first to propose that the Minoan civilization had been destroyed by the volcano in Santorini (in the journal *Antiquity* in 1939), Marinatos was probably the most influential of all the archaeologists who studied the Minoans. In 1956,

Professor Marinatos was named director of antiquities and monuments of Greece, and in 1960, while he was at the Institute for Advanced Study at Princeton, he published *Crete and Mycenae,* a coffee-table art book on the treasures of these ancient civilizations. In 1967, he began the dig at Akrotiri in Santorini (Thera) which eventually revealed some of the most important archaeological and art finds of the Minoan period. Emily Vermeule (q.v.) described him as "Inspector General of the Antiquities Service, crack revolver shot, diplomat, astronomer, linguist, and portly wit. . . ." He suffered a stroke and died at his beloved Akrotiri on October 1, 1974, and is buried there.

JAMES W. MAVOR (B. 1923)

An oceanographic engineer at the Woods Hole Oceanographic Institution, Mavor worked on the design of the submersible *Alvin,* and in 1965 began investigating the riddle of Atlantis. He organized two expeditions to the Aegean, where he worked with seismologist Angelos Galanopoulos and also with Spyridon Marinatos. In his 1969 book, *Voyage to Atlantis,* he claimed that Thera was unquestionably Atlantis, and wrote that "Atlantis had lain exposed for centuries, for all to see, if they but knew what to look for."

KING MINOS

The son of Zeus and Europa, brother of Rhadamanthus, king and legislator of Crete, and, after his death, one of the judges of the shades in Hades. He was the husband of Pasiphaë (a daughter of Helios, the sun god), and the father of Deucalion, Androgeos, Ariadne, and Phaedra. After Minos's son Androgeos had been killed by a bull in Athens, Minos invaded Athens and declared he would raze it to the ground unless the Athenians sent him seven maidens and seven youths, whom he intended to sacrifice to the Minotaur, a half-man, half-bull monster that lived in the Labyrinth. Theseus, the son of King Aegeus of Athens, agreed to be one of the annual sacrifices, but he planned to kill the Minotaur rather than be killed by the beast. When Theseus arrived in Crete, Ariadne, the daughter of Minos, fell in love with him and arranged to have Daedalus, the architect of the Labyrinth, show him how to escape by taking a ball of twine with him. Theseus beat the Minotaur to death with his bare hands (he had no other weapons), and, with Ariadne, sailed for Athens. Theseus left Ariadne on the island of Naxos. On returning to Greece, he forgot to change the black sails of his ship to white. His father, Aegeus, seeing the black sails and thinking Theseus was dead, threw himself into the sea, which has been known as the Aegean ever since.

OTTO MUCK (1892–1956)

Otto Heinrich Muck, a Viennese, flew for the Germans in World War I. In 1921, he graduated with a degree in engineering from the Munich College of Advanced Technology and continued his studies in physics, geophysics, and early history—the ideal combination for an eventual study of Atlantis. In World War II, he invented the *Schnorchel* for U-boats and was a member of the research team at Peenemünde that developed the V-2 rocket—two of the more effective instruments in the Nazi arsenal. After the war, he worked for the Greek shipowner Stavros Niarchos, developing methane tankers. *The Secret of Atlantis* was published in English in 1978.

PAUSANIAS (SECOND CENTURY A.D.)

A Greek traveler and geographer whose *Description of Greece* is still an invaluable guide to ancient ruins. (Sir James Frazer, author of *The Golden Bough,* wrote that "without him the ruins of Greece would for the most part be a labyrinth without out a clue, a riddle without an answer.") His tour takes the form of a guidebook, describing daily life, ceremonial rites, and religious art and architecture throughout Greece. He is one of the few ancient writers to mention the disappearance of the Corinthian city of Helice in 373 B.C.

CHARLES PELLEGRINO (B. 1953)

Trained as a paleontologist (Ph.D., Victoria University, Wellington, New Zealand), Charles Pellegrino is a man of many talents. On the jacket of his *Unearthing Atlantis* (1991), he is described as working "simultaneously in crustaceology, paleontology, preliminary design of advanced rocket systems, and marine archaeology. . . . He is an award-winning painter . . . [and] a Fellow of the British Interplanetary Society, [and] in his spare time he builds sand cities on the beach, speaks at science fiction conventions, and smashes atoms." He is also the author of *Time Gate, Her Name, Titanic, Flying to Valhalla, Return to Sodom and Gomorrah,* and, with Jesse Stoff, *Chronic Fatigue Syndrome.*

J. D. S. PENDLEBURY (1904–1941)

A graduate of the Winchester School and Pembroke College, Cambridge, Pendlebury studied at the British School in Athens and excavated at Tell el-Amarna in Egypt. From 1928 to 1934, he was Arthur Evans's handpicked curator at Knossos, and published *The Archaeology of Crete* in 1939. As liaison officer for the British military mission in Crete during World War II, he was responsible for preparing the people for guerrilla warfare. He was killed by a German parachutist in 1941. *A Handbook to the Palace of Knossos* was published posthumously in 1954.

PLATO (C. 428–347 B.C.)

With Socrates and Aristotle, Plato is considered one of the founders of the philosophical foundations of Western culture. After the death of Socrates (399 B.C.), he traveled in Greece, Italy, Egypt, and Sicily, and when he returned to Athens (his birthplace), he founded an academy dedicated to the systematic pursuit of philosophical and scientific research. He is one of the greatest of all philosophical writers, and in addition to *The Republic,* the best-known and most influential of the dialogues, he wrote the *Timaeus* and the *Critias,* the dialogues in which the story of Atlantis first appears.

PLINY THE ELDER (23–79 A.D.)

Gaius Plinius Secundus was born at Novum Comum, in northern Italy. After a career in the Roman army, he served as procurator in Gaul, Africa, and Spain, and then returned to Rome to devote himself to writing. His *Natural History* is an encyclopedic collection reflecting the state of Roman scientific knowledge of the first century, and includes discussions of everything from astronomy and geography to zoology, botany, and medicine. The letters of his nephew, Pliny the Younger, describe his death during the eruption of the volcano Vesuvius in 79 A.D.

PLUTARCH (C. 46–120 A.D.)

Born during the reign of the Roman emperor Claudius (41 to 54 A.D.), Plutarch was an influential biographer, philosopher, and traveler whose best-known work is the *Lives,* from which much of our information about the great historical figures of Greece and Rome is derived. He was born and lived in the Greek city of Chaeronea, but he often visited Rome on official business and traveled to central Greece, Sparta, Corinth, Patrae, Sardis, and Alexandria. Since the first century, his works have almost always been in print, and have influenced such writers as Rabelais, Montaigne, Shakespeare, Izaak Walton, John Dryden, Goethe, Schiller, Nietzsche, Beethoven, and Ralph Waldo Emerson.

HEINRICH SCHLIEMANN (1822–1890)

After acquiring a large personal fortune as a military contractor in Amsterdam and St. Petersburg, Heinrich Schliemann of Germany retired at the age of thirty-six to become an archaeologist. Because he believed that Homer's *Iliad* and *Odyssey* were fact and not fiction, he excavated at Hissarlik in Turkey, where he found an immense treasure trove that he believed was the Gold of Troy. When he found another fabulous treasure at Mycenae on the Greek mainland, he cabled the king of Greece: "I have gazed upon the face of Agamemnon." As it turned out, it was not Agamemnon but a much earlier ruler, but Schliemann's successes brought him to the forefront of classical and prehistoric archaeological studies.

SOLON (630–560 B.C.)

Generally considered Athens' first great poet, Solon began with what we might call "light verse," but he soon progressed to more didactic poetry written to impart moral precepts and practical wisdom. This work so enhanced his reputation that he was soon regarded as one of the Seven Wise Men of Greece. He was a great reformer and legislator, and as *archon* (principal administrator) he relieved some of the worst sufferings of the poor, and also extended the influence of the wealthy aristocrats. After extracting a promise from the people of Athens to follow his laws for ten years, Solon traveled to Cyprus, Egypt (where Plato later said he had heard the story of Atlantis), and Lydia (Anatolia), where he is said to have visited with King Croesus. He returned to Athens after his travels and died there.

LEWIS SPENCE (1874–1955)

James Lewis Thomas Chalmers Spence was born in Forfarshire, Scotland, and attended the University of Edinburgh before commencing his journalistic career. He was editor of *The Scotsman,* the *Edinburgh Magazine,* and the *British Weekly,* and a prolific writer of books about mythology, folklore, and the occult. A lifetime advocate of the Atlantean myth, he wrote five books on the subject, edited a journal called *Atlantis Quarterly,* and advised Arthur Conan Doyle on Atlantis for *The Maracot Deep.*

STRABO (C. 63 B.C.–C. 24 A.D.)

A Greek geographer and historian whose *Geography* is the most complete work covering the peoples and lands of the ancient world. He wrote of Greece, Rome, Gaul, the European coasts of the Black Sea, the Caucasus, Italy, Arabia, Egypt, north Iran, Mesopotamia, Syria, Palestine, the Red Sea—virtually the known Western world in the first century B.C. He also wrote the forty-seven-volume *Historical Sketches,* which is lost. In volume I of *Geography,* Strabo mentions the city of Helice, on the southern shore of the Gulf of Corinth, which sank into the sea in 373 B.C. following an earthquake.

THESEUS

Like Hercules, Theseus was a great destroyer of monsters. His mother was Aethra, daughter of Pittheus, king of Troezen, but his paternity is in question. Aethra was visited at the same time by Aegeus, king of Athens, and by Poseidon. Theseus killed Sinis in the same way that Sinis killed others: by tying him to bent pine trees. He killed the wild sow of Crommyon, and also the giant Procrustes, who made his victims lie on a bed that was too short for them and then cut off whatever hung over. He journeyed to Knossos, where he killed the Minotaur in the Labyrinth of King Minos, and then made his way out by following the golden string that Ariadne gave him to trail behind him as he went in. He accompanied Hercules on his expedition against the Amazons, and sailed with the Argonauts.

THUCYDIDES (C. 460–C. 404 B.C.)

Born in Athens, Thucydides contracted the "Plague of Athens" around 428, but survived to write the most complete history of this mysterious epidemic. He served as a general in the Peloponnesian War, but his squadron of ships arrived too late to save the important colony of Amphipolis from the Spartans. For his failure he was exiled, and spent the next twenty years working on the *History of the Peloponnesian War,* which is regarded as the definitive work on the war, even though it was left unfinished. The circumstances of his death are not known, but he is believed to have met a violent end in the aftermath of the war.

THUTMOSE III (REIGNED 1504–1450 B.C.)

Probably the greatest of the ancient Egyptian pharaohs, Thutmose III ruled over the greatest epoch and the largest empire in the country's history. His father, Thutmose II, died in 1504 B.C., and at the age of ten, the boy was crowned king. His aunt, Hatshepsut, acted as regent. During his reign, he waged seventeen campaigns to enlarge and consolidate his kingdom, which included all of the Nile Valley, and maintained hegemony over islands in the Aegean—including Minoan Crete, from which he extracted tribute—as well as over Anatolia, Syria, and Mesopotamia. When he died, he was succeeded by his son Amenhotep II. The two obelisks known as "Cleopatra's Needles," one now in London, the other in New York, were erected at Karnak during his lifetime.

IMMANUEL VELIKOVSKY (1895–1979)

Born in Russia and educated in various disciplines at Edinburgh, Moscow (where he took a degree in medicine), Berlin, Zurich, and Vienna, Velikovsky moved to the United States in 1939 to escape the Nazis. In 1950, he published the controversial *Worlds in Collision,* in which he argued that the arrival of the planet Venus as a comet changed the configuration of the solar system in historical times and resulted in cataclysmic upheavals on Earth, many of which are documented in ancient texts. Although most scientists greeted his theories with derision (Macmillan, his original publisher, had to transfer the rights to Doubleday after only two months, because Macmillan's textbook business was threatened by a boycott from scientists), some of his wilder ideas—such as the unexplained high temperature of Venus, and the arrival of a large comet that initiated the decline and fall of the dinosaurs—have now gained scientific respectability.

MICHAEL VENTRIS (1922–1956)

In 1936, fourteen-year-old Michael Ventris heard Sir Arthur Evans lecture in London. He became fascinated by Evans's description of the then undeciphered "Linear B" and vowed to solve the puzzle. He flew as a navigator in the

Royal Air Force in World War II, and after the war, resumed his study of architecture. With the classicist John Chadwick, he deciphered Linear B, recognizing it as an early form of Greek, thereby altering the historical interpretation of the Minoan civilization. Shortly after being awarded an O.B.E. for his contributions to paleogeography, he was killed in an automobile accident in 1956, at the age of thirty-four.

EMILY VERMEULE (B. 1928)

Trained in classics at Bryn Mawr College, Emily Vermeule taught at her alma mater, then at Boston University, and at Wellesley College, where she was professor of Greek. Since 1970, she has been a professor of classical studies at Harvard. She has translated several important Greek plays and has participated in various archaeological digs in Greece and Turkey. Her *Greece in the Bronze Age* (1964) is considered one of the most important and authoritative books on the early Aegean. In 1967, she joined James Mavor on Thera (Santorini), where Professor Spyridon Marinatos discovered the buried Minoan settlement at Akrotiri.

JULES VERNE (1828–1905)

Jules Verne was born in Nantes, France, and originally studied law but later turned to writing. He is regarded as the father of science fiction, having written *Five Weeks in a Balloon* (1863), *Journey to the Center of the Earth* (1864), *The Mysterious Island* (1874), and probably his best-known work, *Twenty Thousand Leagues Under the Sea* (1870), which Walt Disney Studios made into a popular movie in 1954, and which contains, among other things, an undersea walking tour of the Lost City of Atlantis.

DOROTHY VITALIANO (B. 1916)

A graduate of Barnard College (class of '36) and a geologist by training, Dorothy Vitaliano is also a professional translator. Her specialty is volcanology, and she has written extensively on the eruption of Santorini. She has participated in sessions of the International Scientific Congress on the Volcano of Thera (held in Athens and, more recently, in Santorini), and for the *Journal of the Folklore Institute,* she composed an essay on Atlantis. In Ramage's *Atlantis: Fact or Fiction?,* Vitaliano wrote the chapter on "The Geological Perspective," and her own book, *Legends of the Earth*, includes important discussions of the Minoan eruption of Santorini and "Lost Atlantis."

A. J. B. Wace (1879–1957)

Alan John Bayard Wace, a Cambridge-educated classical archaeologist, excavated at Mycenae, Sparta, Troy, and Thessaly, and was director of the British School in Athens from 1914 to 1923.

David Zink

Described (on the flap copy for *The Stones of Atlantis*) as a "historian, explorer, lecturer, mountaineer, blue-water sailor, scuba diver and underwater photographer," and also a professor of English literature at Lamar University in Texas, David Zink initiated the "Poseidia" expeditions to the island of Bimini, where he found "stupendously ancient submarine ruins [that] not only seem to confirm the historical existence of the lost continent of Atlantis, but also contain unmistakable extra-terrestrial references."

BIBLIOGRAPHY

AELIAN. N.d. *On the Characteristics of Animals.* 3 vols. Translated by A. F. Scholfield. Harvard University Press, Loeb Classical Library, 1958.

ALEXANDER, C. 1996. Troy's Prodigious Ruin. *Natural History* 105(4):42–51.

ALEXIOU, S. 1969. *Minoan Civilization.* Spyros Alexiou.

ALSOP, J. 1964. *From the Silent Earth: A Report on the Greek Bronze Age.* Harper & Row.

ALVAREZ, W., F. ASARO, H. V. MICHEL, and L. W. ALVAREZ. 1984. Evidence for a Major Meteorite Impact on the Earth 34 Million Years Ago: Implication for Eocene Extinctions. *Science* 216:474–89.

ANON. 1866a. A New Volcanic Island. *Illustrated London News,* March 17, p. 256.

ANON. 1866b. The New Submarine Volcano at Santorin, Greek Archipelago. *Illustrated London News,* March 31, p. 318.

ANON. 1870. The Isles of Santorin. *Illustrated London News,* July 23, p. 80.

ANON. 1966. Atlantis Search Shifts to Aegean. *New York Times,* August 21, p. 14.

ANON. 1966. Moat Believed to Be Part of Atlantis Is Found in Aegean Sea. *New York Times,* sec. 1, p. 8.

ANON. 1967. Quest for Atlantis. Editorial. *New York Times,* July 23, sec. 4, p. 10.

ANON. 1967. Economy-Size Atlantis. *Time* 90(4):68–69.

APOLLONIUS OF RHODES. N.d. *The Voyage of the Argo.* Translated by E. V. Rieu. Penguin Classics, 1959.

ARMAKI, S. 1990. The 1783 Eruption of Asama Volcano, Japan. In D. Hardy, ed., *Thera and the Aegean World III,* vol. 2, *Earth Sciences,* pp. 453–54. Thera Foundation.

ASHE, G. 1992. *Atlantis: Lost Lands, Ancient Wisdom.* Thames & Hudson.

ASIMENOS, K. 1978. Technological Observations on the Thera Wall-Paintings. In C. Doumas, ed., *Thera and the Aegean World I*, pp. 571–78. Thera Foundation.

ASTON, M. A., and P. G. HARDY. 1990. The Pre-Minoan Landscape of Thera: A Preliminary Statement. In D. Hardy, ed., *Thera and the Aegean World III*, vol. 2, *Earth Sciences*, pp. 348–61. Thera Foundation.

ÅSTRÖM, P. 1978. Traces of the Eruption of Thera in Cyprus? In C. Doumas, ed., *Thera and the Aegean World I*, pp. 231–34. Thera Foundation.

BABCOCK, W. H. 1922. *Legendary Islands of the Atlantic.* American Geographic Society.

BACON, E., ed. 1976. *The Great Archaeologists.* Bobbs-Merrill.

BACON, F. 1627. *The New Atlantis.* London. In G. S. Haight, ed., *Essays and New Atlantis*, pp. 245–302. Van Nostrand, 1942.

BAILEY, H. S. 1953. The Voyage of the Challenger. *Scientific American* 188(5):88–94.

BALCH, E. S. 1917. Atlantis or Minoan Crete. *Geographical Review* 3(5):388–92.

BARBER, R. L. N. 1987. *The Cyclades in the Bronze Age.* University of Iowa Press.

BARWOOD, H., and N. FALSTEIN. 1992. *Indiana Jones and the Fate of Atlantis.* Dark Horse Comics.

BASCOM, W. 1964. *Waves and Beaches: The Dynamics of the Ocean Surface.* Doubleday.

BASS, G. F. 1966. *Archaeology Under Water.* Praeger.

————, ed. 1972. *A History of Seafaring, Based on Underwater Archaeology.* Thames & Hudson.

————. 1987. Oldest Known Shipwreck Reveals Splendors of the Bronze Age. *National Geographic* 172(6):692–733.

BATE, D. M. A. 1903. Preliminary Note on the Discovery of a Pigmy Elephant in the Pleistocene of Cyprus. *Proc. Royal Soc.* 73:498–500.

————. 1904a. On the Ossiferous Cave-Deposits of Cyprus. *Geological Magazine* 4(1):324–25.

————. 1904b. Further Note on the Remains of *Elephas cypriotes* Bate, from a Cave-Deposit in Cyprus. *Geological Magazine* 4(1):325.

————. 1905. Four and a Half Months in Crete in Search of Pleistocene Mammalian Remains. *Geological Magazine* 5(2):193–203.

————. 1906. The Pigmy Hippopotamus of Cyprus. *Geological Magazine* 5(3):241–45.

BAUMANN, H. 1967. *Lion Gate and Labyrinth: The World of Troy, Crete, and Mycenae.* Pantheon.

BEHRMAN, D. 1969. *The New World of the Oceans.* Little, Brown.

BENNETT, J. C. 1963. Geo-Physics and Human History: New Light on Plato's Atlantis and the Exodus. *Systematics* 1:127–56.

BENOÎT, P. 1920. *L'Atlantide.* Michel.

BERLITZ, C. 1969. *The Mystery of Atlantis.* Grossett & Dunlap.

————. 1972. *Mysteries from Forgotten Worlds.* Doubleday.

————. 1974. *The Bermuda Triangle.* Doubleday.

————. 1977. *Without a Trace.* Doubleday.

————. 1984. *Atlantis: The Eighth Continent.* Putnam's.

BERNSTEIN, J. 1954. Tsunamis. *Scientific American* 190(2):60–64.

BETANCOURT, P. P. 1990. High Chronology or Low Chronology: The Archaeological Evidence. In D. Hardy and A. C. Renfrew, eds., *Thera and the Aegean World III*, vol. 3, *Chronology*, pp. 19–23. Thera Foundation.

BETANCOURT, P. P., and C. DAVARAS. 1991. Haven for Minoan Mariners. *Archaeology* 44(3):32–35.

BETANCOURT, P. P., P. GOLDBERG, R. HOPE SIMPSON, and C. J. VITALIANO. 1990. Excavations at Pseria: The Evidence for the Theran Eruption. In D. Hardy and A. C. Renfrew, eds., *Thera and the Aegean World III*, vol. 3, *Chronology*, pp. 96–99. Thera Foundation.

BIBBY, G. 1961. *Four Thousand Years Ago: A World Panorama of Life in the Second Millennium B.C.* Knopf.

BIDDLE, M., and E. K. RALPH. 1980. Radiocarbon Dates from Akrotiri: Problems and a Strategy. In C. Doumas, ed., *Thera and the Aegean World II*, pp. 247–52. Thera Foundation.

BJORKMAN, E. 1927. *The Search for Atlantis.* Knopf.

BLEGEN, C. W. 1963. *Troy and the Trojans.* Praeger.

BLEGEN, C. W., and M. RAWSON. 1966. *The Palace of Nestor in Pylos in Western Messinia.* Princeton University Press.

BLONG, R. J. 1980. The Possible Effects of Santorini Tephra Fall on Minoan Crete. In C. Doumas, ed., *Thera and the Aegean World II*, pp. 217–26. Thera Foundation.

BOEKSCHOETEN, G. J., and P. Y. SONDAAR. 1972. On the Fossil Mammalia of Cyprus. *Proc. Kon. Ned. Akad. Wetensch.* 75B:306–38.

BOLT, B. A. 1993. *Earthquakes.* Freeman.

BOND, A., and R. S. J. SPARKS. 1976. The Minoan Eruption of Santorini, Greece. *Jour. Geol. Soc. London* 132:1–16.

BORCHARDT, P. 1927a. Platos Insel Atlantis. *Petermanns Geographische Mitteilungen* 73:19–31.

————. 1927b. Nordafrika und die Metallreichtümer von Atlantis. *Petermanns Geographische Mitteilungen* 73:280–82.

BRAGHINE, A. P. 1940. *The Shadow of Atlantis.* Dutton.

BRAMWELL, J. 1938. *Lost Atlantis.* Harper & Bros.

BRAYMER, M. 1983. *Atlantis: The Biography of a Legend.* Atheneum.

BROWN, A. 1994. *Arthur Evans and the Palace of Minos.* Ashmolean Museum, Oxford.

BROWN, L. M. 1978. The Ship Procession in the Miniature Fresco. In C. Doumas, ed., *Thera and the Aegean World I*, pp. 629–44. Thera Foundation.

BRUGG, A. 1996. Ancient Ebola Virus? *Archaeology* 49(6):28.

BRYAN, W. B. 1992. From Pillow Lava to Sheet Flow: Evolution of Deep-Sea Volcanology. *Oceanus* 34(4):42–50.

BUCHHOLZ, H.-G. 1980. Some Observations Concerning Thera's Contacts Overseas During the Bronze Age. In C. Doumas, ed., *Thera and the Aegean World II*, pp. 227–40. Thera Foundation.

BULFINCH, T. 1855. *The Age of Fable.* Modern Library.

BULLARD, E. C. 1969. The Origin of the Oceans. *Scientific American* 221(3):68–75.

BULLARD, E. C., J. E. EVERETT, and A. G. SMITH. 1965. The Fit of the Continents Around the Atlantic. *Phil. Trans. Royal Soc. London* 258:41–51.

BULLARD, F. 1962. *Volcanoes in History, in Theory, in Eruption.* University of Texas Press.

————. 1984. *Volcanoes of the Earth.* University of Texas Press.

BURKE, E., and J. WILSON. 1976. Hot Spots on the Earth's Surface. *Scientific American* 235(3): 46–57.

CADOGAN, G. 1990. Thera's Eruption into Our Understanding of the Minoans. In D. Hardy, ed., *Thera and the Aegean World III,* vol. 1, *Archaeology,* pp. 93–97. Thera Foundation.

CADOGAN, G., R. K. HARRISON, and G. E. STRONG. 1972. Volcanic Glass Shards in Late Minoan I, Crete. *Antiquity* 46(184):310–13.

CALDER, N. 1972. *The Restless Earth: A Report on the New Geology.* Viking.

CAMERON, M. A. S. 1971. The Lady in Red: A Complementary Figure to the Ladies in Blue. *Archaeology* 24(1):35–43.

————. 1978. Theoretical Interrelations Among Theran, Cretan and Mainland Frescoes. In C. Doumas, ed., *Thera and the Aegean World I,* pp. 579–92. Thera Foundation.

CAMPBELL, J. 1988. *The Power of Myth.* Anchor.

CARPENTER, R. 1966a. *Beyond the Pillars of Heracles.* Delacorte.

————. 1966b. *Discontinuity in Greek Civilization.* Cambridge University Press.

CARRINGTON, R. 1960. *A Biography of the Sea.* Basic Books.

CARSON, R. 1951. *The Sea Around Us.* Oxford University Press.

————. 1955. *The Edge of the Sea.* Houghton Mifflin.

CASKEY, J. L. 1969. Crisis in the Minoan-Mycenaean World. *Proc. Amer. Phil. Soc.* 113:433–49.

CASTLEDEN, R. 1994. *Minoans: Life in Bronze Age Crete.* Routledge.

CAVENDISH, R. 1982. *Legends of the World.* Little, Brown U.K.

CAYCE, E. 1962. *Edgar Cayce on Atlantis.* Warner.

CERAM, C. W. (KURT W. MAREK). 1951. *Gods, Graves, and Scholars.* Knopf. Vintage, 1986.

————. 1966. *Hands on the Past.* Knopf.

CHADWICK, J. 1958. *The Decipherment of Linear B.* Cambridge University Press.

————. 1976. *The Mycenaean World.* Cambridge University Press.

CHAPIN, H. 1968. *The Search for Atlantis.* Macmillan.

CHAPIN, H., and F. G. WALTON SMITH. 1952. *The Ocean River: The Story of the Gulf Stream.* Scribner's.

CHARLIER, R. H., and A. M. GESSMAN. 1972. Perennial Atlantis. *Sea Frontiers* 18(1):40–49.

CHAUVET, J.-M., E. B. DESCHAMPS, and C. HILLAIRE. 1996. *Dawn of Art: The Chauvet Cave.* Abrams.

CHESTER, D. K., A. M. DUNCAN, J. E. GUEST, and C. R. J. KILBURN. 1985. *Mount Etna: The Anatomy of a Volcano.* Stanford University Press.

CHURCHWARD, J. 1926. *The Lost Continent of Mu.* Washburn.

———. 1931. *The Children of Mu.* Washburn.

———. 1933. *The Sacred Symbols of Mu.* Washburn.

CLARKE, A. C. 1966. *The Challenge of the Sea.* Dell.

———. 1990. *Astounding Days.* Bantam.

CLARK, K. 1977. *Animals and Men.* Morrow.

CLAYTON, P., and M. J. PRICE, eds. 1988. *The Seven Wonders of the Ancient World.* Routledge.

CLUTE, J., and P. NICHOLS. 1995. *Encyclopedia of Science Fiction.* St. Martin's, Griffin.

COHEN, I. B. 1955. An Interview with Einstein. *Scientific American* 193(1):68–73.

CONNELL, E. S. 1988. Aristokles' Atlantis. In *A Long Desire,* pp. 45–57. North Point Press.

CONRAD, J. R. 1957. *The Horn and the Sword: The History of the Bull as Symbol of Power and Fertility.* Dutton.

CORNELL, J. 1982. *The Great International Disaster Book.* Scribner's.

COTTERELL, A. 1979. *The Minoan World.* Scribner's.

COTTRELL, L. 1957. *Lost Cities.* Rinehart & Co.

———. 1958. *The Bull of Minos.* Rinehart & Co.

———. 1962a. *The Anvil of Civilization.* Mentor.

———. 1962b. *The Horizon Book of Lost Worlds.* American Heritage.

———. 1963. *Realms of Gold: A Journey in Search of the Mycenaeans.* New York Graphic Society.

———. 1971. *Reading the Past: The Story of Deciphering Ancient Languages.* Crowell-Collier.

COUSTEAU, J.-Y., and J. DUGAN. 1963. *The Living Sea.* Harper & Bros.

COUSTEAU, J.-Y., and Y. PICCALET. 1981. *A la recherche de L'Atlantide.* Flammarion.

COWEN, R. C. 1960. *Frontiers of the Sea: The Story of Oceanographic Exploration.* Doubleday.

CREMO, M. A., and R. L. THOMPSON. 1994. *The Hidden History of the Human Race.* Govardhan Hill.

DALY, R. A. 1936. The Origin of Submarine Canyons. *Amer. Jour. Sci.* 31:401–20.

DAUGHERTY, C. M. 1961. *Searchers of the Sea: Pioneers in Oceanography.* Viking.

DAVARAS, C. 1976. *Guide to Cretan Antiquities.* Eptalofos.

———. N.d. *Knossos and the Herakleion Museum.* Hannibal.

———. N.d. *Phaistos, Hagia Triada, Gortyn.* Hannibal.

DAVIDSON, K., and A. R. WILLIAMS. 1995. Under Our Skin: Hot Theories on the Center of the Earth. *National Geographic* 189(1):100–11.

DAVIES, N. 1979. *Voyages to the New World.* Morrow.

DAVIS, E. N. 1990a. The Cycladic Style of the Theran Frescoes. In D. Hardy, ed., *Thera and the Aegean World III*, vol. 1, *Archaeology*, pp. 214–28. Thera Foundation.

——. 1990b. A Storm in Egypt During the Reign of Ahmose. In D. Hardy and A. C. Renfrew, eds., *Thera and the Aegean World III*, vol. 3, *Chronology*, pp. 232–35. Thera Foundation.

DAVIS, J. S., and J. A. DAY. 1961. *Water, the Mirror of Science.* Doubleday Anchor.

DAVIS, L. 1992. *Natural Disasters from the Black Plague to the Eruption of Mount Pinatubo.* Facts on File.

DAVISON, C. 1929. The Atlantic Earthquake of November 18, 1929. *Nature* 124:859.

DEACON, G. E. R. 1958. Deep Ocean Currents. *Discovery* 18(9):386–87.

——, ed. 1962. *Seas, Maps, and Men: An Atlas-History of Man's Exploration of the Oceans.* Doubleday.

DE BLIJ, H. J., ed. 1994. *Nature on the Rampage.* Smithsonian Books.

DE CAMP, L. S. 1954. *Lost Continents: The Atlantis Theme in History, Science, and Literature.* Gnome Press. Dover, 1970.

——. 1964a. *Citadels of Mystery.* Ballantine.

——. 1964b. *Elephant.* Pyramid.

DECKER, R. W. 1990. How Often Does a Minoan Eruption Occur? In D. Hardy, ed., *Thera and the Aegean World III*, vol. 2, *Earth Sciences*, pp. 444–52. Thera Foundation.

DECKER, R. W., and B. B. DECKER. 1981. *Volcanoes.* Freeman.

——. 1991. *Mountains of Fire.* Cambridge University Press.

DEISS, J. J. 1985. *Herculaneum: Italy's Buried Treasure.* Harper & Row.

DE LA HABA, L. 1979. Roots of the City: Jericho and Çatal Hüyük. In *Mysteries of the Ancient World*, pp. 30–53. National Geographic Society.

DE LATIL, P., and J. RIVOIRE. 1956. *Man and the Underwater World.* Putnam's.

DE PROROK, B. K. 1929. *Mysterious Sahara: The Land of Gold, of Sand and of Ruin.* Reilly & Lee.

DE ROY, T. 1995. The Day the Earth Blew. *International Wildlife* 25(5):4–11.

DIETZ, R. S. 1961. Continent and Ocean Basin Evolution by Spreading of Sea Floor. *Nature* 190:854–57.

——. 1969. Ocean Basins and Lunar Seas. *Oceanus* 2(1):7–15.

DIETZ, R. S., and J. HOLDEN. 1970a. The Breakup of Pangaea. *Scientific American* 223(4):30–41.

——. 1970b. Reconstruction of Pangaea: Breakup and Dispersion of Continents, Permian to Present. *Jour. Geophys. Res.* 75:4939–56.

DIOLÉ, P. 1954. *The Undersea Adventure.* Julian Messner.

DIVINE, D. 1973. *The Opening of the World: The Great Maritime Exploration.* Putnam's.

DONNELLY, I. 1882. *Atlantis: The Antediluvian World.* Harper & Bros. Dover, 1976.

DORST, J., and P. DANDELOT. 1970. *Field Guide to the Larger Mammals of Africa.* Houghton Mifflin.

DOUMAS, C. 1974. The Minoan Eruption of Santorin Volcano. *Antiquity* 48:110–15.

——. 1978. The Stratigraphy of Akrotiri. In C. Doumas, ed., *Thera and the Aegean World I*, pp. 777–82. Thera Foundation.

———. 1983. *Thera: Pompeii of the Ancient Aegean.* Thames & Hudson.

———. 1990. Archaeological Observations at Akrotiri Relating to Volcanic Destruction. In D. Hardy and A. C. Renfrew, eds., *Thera and the Aegean World III,* vol. 3, *Chronology,* pp. 48–50. Thera Foundation.

———. 1992. *The Wall Pantings of Thera.* Thera Foundation.

———. 1994. *Santorini: A Guide to the Island and Its Archaeological Treasures.* Ekdotike Athenon.

DOYLE, A. CONAN 1912. *The Lost World.* Puffin, 1981.

———. 1929. *The Maracot Deep.* Doubleday, Doran.

DREWS, R. 1989. *The Coming of the Greeks: Indo-European Conquests in the Aegean and the Near East.* Princeton University Press.

DRUITT, T. H. 1990. The Pyroclastic Stratigraphy and Volcanology of Santorini. Abstract. In D. Hardy, ed., *Thera and the Aegean World III,* vol. 2, *Earth Sciences,* pp. 27–28. Thera Foundation.

DRUITT, T. H., and FRANCAVIGLIA, V. 1992. Caldera Formation on Santorini and the Physiography of the Islands in the Late Bronze Age. *Bull. Volc.* 54:484–93.

DRUITT, T. H., R. A. MELLORS, D. M. PYLE, and R. S. J. SPARKS. 1989. Explosive Volcanism in Santorini, Greece. *Geol. Mag.* 126:95–126.

DUDLEY, W. C., and M. LEE. 1988. *Tsunami!* University of Hawaii Press.

DUGAN, J. 1956. *Man Under the Sea.* Harper & Bros.

———. 1967. *World Beneath the Sea.* National Geographic Society.

DUNN, J. C. 1994. Secrets in the Dust. *Islands* 14(4):94–105.

DU TOIT, A. L. 1927. A Geological Comparison of South America with South Africa. *Carnegie Inst. Wash. Publ.* 381:1–157.

———. 1937. *Our Wandering Continents: An Hypothesis of Continental Drifting.* Oliver & Boyd.

EASTON, S. 1980. *Rudolf Steiner: Herald of a New Epoch.* Anthroposophic Press.

ECKSTROM, C. K. 1979. Minoans: A Joyous People Vanishes in Myth. In *Mysteries of the Ancient World,* pp. 124–43. National Geographic Society.

EDGERTON, H. E. 1955. Photographing the Sea's Dark Underworld. *National Geographic* 107(4):523–37.

EINARSSON, T. 1965. *The Surtsey Eruption.* Heimskringla.

ELIADE, M. 1963. *Myth and Reality.* Harper & Row.

ELLIS, R. 1996. *Deep Atlantic.* Knopf.

ERICKSON, J. 1994. *Quakes, Eruptions, and Other Geologic Cataclysms.* Facts on File.

ERICKSON, U., W. J. FRIEDRICH, B. BURCHARDT, H. TAUBER, and M. S. THOMSEN. 1990. The Stronghyle Caldera: Geological, Paleontological and Stable Isotope Evidence from Radiocarbon Dated Stromatolites from Santorini. In D. Hardy, ed., *Thera and the Aegean World III,* vol. 2, *Earth Sciences,* pp. 139–50. Thera Foundation.

EVANS, A. 1921–36. *The Palace of Minos.* 4 vols. Macmillan.

———. 1929. *The Shaft Graves and Beehive Tombs of Mycenae and Their Interrelation.* Macmillan.

EWING, M. 1948. Exploring the Mid-Atlantic Ridge. *National Geographic* 94(3):275–94.

———. 1949. New Discoveries on the Mid-Atlantic Ridge. *National Geographic* 96(5):611–40.

FACAROS, D. 1994. *The Cyclades.* Cadogan Island Guides.

FEARS, J. R. 1978. Atlantis and the Minoan Thalassocracy: A Study in Modern Mythopoeism. In E. S. Ramage, ed., *Atlantis: Fact or Fiction?*, pp. 49–78. Indiana University Press.

FENTON, J. H. 1966. A Minoan City, Found After 3,400 Years, Is Linked to Atlantis. *New York Times*, July 19, pp. 1, 8.

FERNANDEZ-ARMESTO, F. 1987. *Before Columbus: Exploration and Colonisation from the Mediterranean to the Atlantic, 1229–1492.* Macmillan Education.

FERRO, R., and M. GRUMLEY. 1970. *Atlantis: The Autobiography of a Search. A Psychic and a Real Journey to Find the Lost Continent as Prophesied by Edgar Cayce.* Bell.

FINDLEY, R. 1981. The Mountain That Was—and Will Be. *National Geographic* 160(6):710–33.

FINLEY, M. I. 1963. *The Ancient Greeks: An Introduction to Their Life and Thought.* Viking.

———. 1965. The Rediscovery of Crete. *Horizon* 7(3):66–75.

———. 1969. Atlantis or Bust. Review of *Voyage to Atlantis*, by J. W. Mavor. *New York Review of Books* 12(10):38–40.

———. 1981. *Early Greece: The Bronze and Archaic Ages.* Norton.

FISCHER, S. R. 1997. *Glyphbreaker.* Copernicus.

FISHER, J. 1956. *Rockall.* Geoffrey Bles.

FLEM-ATH, R., and R. FLEM-ATH. 1995. *When the Sky Fell: In Search of Atlantis.* St. Martin's.

FORSYTH, P. Y. 1980. *Atlantis: The Making of a Myth.* McGill-Queen's University Press.

FORTUNE, D. 1978. *The Sea Priestess.* Weiser. Originally published privately in 1938.

FOUQUÉ, F. 1869. Une Pompéi antéhistorique. *Rev. Deux Mondes* 39:923–43.

———. 1879. *Santorini et ses éruptions.* Paris.

FOX, P. J. 1992. Bruce C. Heezen: A Profile. *Oceanus* 34(4):100–107.

FRANCAVIGLIA, V., and B. DI SABATINO. 1990. Statistical Study on Santorini Pumice Falls. In D. Hardy, ed., *Thera and the Aegean World III*, vol. 2, *Earth Sciences*, pp. 29–52. Thera Foundation.

FRANCIS, P. 1976. *Volcanoes.* Penguin.

FRANKLIN, B. 1786. On the Gulf Stream. *Trans. Amer. Phil. Soc.* 2:314–17.

FRASER, F. C. 1977. Royal Fishes: The Importance of the Dolphin. In R. H. Harrison, ed., *Functional Anatomy of Marine Mammals*, pp. 1–44. Academic Press.

FREDERICKS, S. C. 1978. Plato's Atlantis: A Mythologist Looks at Myth. In E. S. Ramage, ed., *Atlantis: Fact or Fiction?*, pp. 81–99. Indiana University Press.

FREUCHEN, P. 1957. *Peter Freuchen's Book of the Seven Seas.* Julian Messner.

FRIEDRICH, W. L., U. ERICKSON, H. TAUBER, J. HEINEMIER, N. RUD, M. S. THOMSEN, and B. BURCHARDT. 1988. Existence of a Water-Filled Caldera Prior to the Eruption of Santorini, Greece. *Naturwissenschaften* 75:567–69.

FRIEDRICH, W. L., R. FRIBORG, and H. TAUBER. 1980. Two Radiocarbon Dates of the Minoan Eruption of Santorini (Greece). In C. Doumas, ed., *Thera and the Aegean World II*, pp. 241–43. Thera Foundation.

FROST, K. T. 1909. The Lost Continent. London *Times*, February 19, p. 10.

———. 1913. The *Critias* and Minoan Crete. *Journal of Hellenic Studies* 33:189–206.

FRYER, G. 1995. The Most Dangerous Wave. *The Sciences.* 35(4):38–43.

FURNEAUX, R. 1964. *Krakatoa.* Prentice-Hall.

FURUMARK, A. 1978. The Thera Catastrophe—Consequences for European Civilization. In C. Doumas, ed., *Thera and the Aegean World I*, pp. 667–74. Thera Foundation.

FYTIKAS, M., N. KOLIOS, and G. VOUGIOUKALAKIS. 1990. Post-Minoan Volcanic Activity of the Santorini Volcano. Volcanic Hazard and Risk, Forecasting Possibilities. In D. Hardy, ed., *Thera and the Aegean World III*, vol. 2, *Earth Sciences*, pp. 183–98. Thera Foundation.

GALANOPOULOS, A. G. 1958. Zur Bestimmung des Alters der Santorin-Kaldera. *Annales Géologiques Pays Helléniques* 9:185–86.

———. 1960a. On the Origin of the Deluge of Deucalion and the Myth of Atlantis. *Greek Arch. Soc.* 3:226–31.

———. 1960b. On the Location and Size of Atlantis. *Prakt. Akad. Athens* 35:401–18.

———. 1960c. Tsunamis Observed on the Coasts of Greece from Antiquity to the Present Time. *Ann. Geofis.* 13:369–86.

———. 1963. On the Mapping of Seismic Activity in Greece. *Ann. Geofis.* 16:177–84.

GALANOPOULOS, A. G., and E. BACON. 1969. *Atlantis: The Truth Behind the Legend.* Bobbs-Merrill.

GAMOW, G. 1941. *Biography of the Earth: Its Past, Present, and Future.* Viking.

GARDNER, M. 1952. *In the Name of Science.* Putnam's.

GASKELL, T. F. 1960. *Deep Under the Oceans.* Eyre & Spottiswoode.

GATTEFOSSÉ, J., and C. ROUX. 1926. *Bibliographie de L'Atlantide et des questions connexes.* Caen.

GEORGALAS, G. C. 1962. Greece. *Catalogue of the Active Volcanoes of the World Including Solfatara Fields* 12:40. Napoli.

GIDON, F. 1934. Les Submersions atlantiques (irlando-armoricaines) de l'âge du bronze et la question de L'Atlantide. *Mémoires de l'Académie des Sciences, Arts et Belles-Lettres de Caen* 8:91–114.

GILLMER, T. C. 1975. Ships of Atlantis. *Sea Frontiers* 21(6):351–58.

GORDON, C. H. 1963. The Decipherment of Minoan. *Natural History* 72(9):22–31.

GORE, R. 1982. The Mediterranean: Sea of Man's Fate. *National Geographic* 162(6):694–737.

———. 1984. A Prayer for Pozzuoli. *National Geographic* 165(5):614–25.

GOULD, S. J. 1996. Up Against a Wall. *Natural History* 105(7):16–22, 70–73.

GRAHAM, J. W. 1962. *The Palaces of Crete.* Princeton University Press.

GRANT, L. 1994. *The Coming Plague.* Farrar, Straus & Giroux.

GRANT, M. 1971. *Cities of Vesuvius: Pompeii and Herculaneum.* Macmillan.

GRIBBIN, J. 1978. *This Shaking Earth.* Putnam's.

GROVE, N. 1992. Volcanoes: Crucibles of Creation. *National Geographic* 182(6):5–41.

GRUBE, G. M. A. 1935. *Plato's Thought.* Beacon.

GUTENBERG, B. 1939. Tsunamis and Earthquakes. *Bull. Seismol. Soc. Amer.* 29:517–26.

GUTENBERG, B., and C. F. RICHTER. 1936. Materials for the Study of Deep-focus Earthquakes. *Bull. Seismol. Soc. Amer.* 26:375–92.

———. 1942. Earthquake Magnitude, Intensity, Energy and Acceleration. *Bull. Seismol. Soc. Amer.* 32:163–91.

———. 1954. *Seismicity of the Earth and Associated Phenomena.* Princeton University Press.

HACKFORTH, R. 1944. The Story of Atlantis: Its Purpose and Moral. *Classical Review* 58:7–9.

HALLAM, A. 1972. Continental Drift and the Fossil Record. *Scientific American* 227(11):56–66.

———. 1973. *A Revolution in Earth Sciences: From Continental Drift to Plate Tectonics.* Oxford University Press.

HALLIWELL, L. 1989. *Halliwell's Film Guide.* Harper & Row.

HAMILTON, E. 1932. *The Greek Way.* Norton.

———. 1940. *Mythology.* Signet.

———. 1944. The Greek Way. *National Geographic* 85(3):257–351.

———. *The Echo of Greece.* Norton.

HAMMER, C. U., H. B. CLAUSEN, W. L. FRIEDRICH, and H. TAUBER. 1987. The Minoan Eruption of Santorini in Greece Dated to 1645 B.C.? *Nature* 328:517–19.

HANSEN, L. T. 1969. *The Ancient Atlantic.* Palmer Publications.

HAPGOOD, C. H. 1958. *Earth's Shifting Crust—A Key to Some Basic Problems of Earth Science.* Foreword by Albert Einstein. Pantheon.

———. 1966. *Maps of the Ancient Sea Kings: Evidence of an Advanced Civilization in the Ice Age.* Chilton.

———. 1970. *The Path of the Pole.* Chilton.

HARPUR, J., and J. WESTWOOD. 1989. *The Atlas of Legendary Places.* Grove Press.

HARTMANN, N. 1987. Atlantis Lost and Found. *Expedition* 29(2):19–22.

HARTT, F. 1976. *Art: A History of Painting, Sculpture, Architecture.* Prentice-Hall and Abrams.

HAWKES, J. 1968. *Dawn of the Gods: Minoan and Mycenaean Origins of Greece.* Random House.

HECK, N. H. 1947. List of Seismic Sea Waves. *Bull. Seismol. Soc. Amer.* 37:269–86.

HÉDERVÁRI, P. 1967. Volcanophysical Investigations Concerning the Energies of the Minoan Eruption of Volcano Santorin. *Bull. Volc.* 32:439–61.

———. 1978. Geonomic Notes on the Bronze Age Eruption of Santorini. In C. Doumas, ed., *Thera and the Aegean World I,* pp. 153–62. Thera Foundation.

HEEZEN, B. C. 1956. The Origin of Submarine Canyons. *Scientific American* 195(8):36–41.

———. 1960. The Rift in the Ocean Floor. *Scientific American* 203(4):98–110.

———. 1969. A Time Clock for History. *Saturday Review* 52(49):87–90.

———. 1973. On Tracing Thera's Tephra to Crete. Abstract. *Report Given at ACTA, 1st Annual Scientific Congress on the Volcano of Thera.* Athens.

HEEZEN, B. C., and M. EWING. 1952. Turbidity Currents and Submarine Slumps, and the 1929 Grand Banks Earthquake. *Amer. Jour. Sci.* 250:849–73.

———. 1963. The Mid-Oceanic Ridge. In M. N. Hill, ed., *The Sea,* vol. 3, *The Earth Beneath the Sea,* pp. 388–409. Wiley Interscience.

HEEZEN, B. C., M. EWING, and D. B. ERICSON. 1951. Submarine Topography in the North Atlantic. *Bull. Amer. Geol. Soc.* 62:1407–9.

HEEZEN, B. C., and C. D. HOLLISTER. 1971. *The Face of the Deep.* Oxford University Press.

HEEZEN, B. C., and A. S. LAUGHTON. 1963. Abyssal Plains. In M. N. Hill, ed., *The Sea,* vol. 3, *The Earth Beneath the Sea,* pp. 281–311. Wiley Interscience.

HEEZEN, B. C., and H. W. MENARD. 1963. Topography of the Deep-Sea Floor. In M. N. Hill, ed., *The Sea,* vol. 3, *The Earth Beneath the Sea,* pp. 233–80. Wiley Interscience.

HEEZEN, B. C., M. THARP, and M. EWING. 1959. The Floors of the Oceans. *Geological Society of America.* Special Paper 65:1–122.

HEIDEL, W. A. 1933. A Suggestion Concerning Plato's Atlantis. *Proc. Amer. Acad. Arts and Sci.* 68:189–228.

HEIKEN, G. 1947. Origin and Development of Craters. *Geol. Soc. Amer. Mem.* 21:1–508.

HEIKEN, G., and F. MCCOY. 1984. Caldera Development During the Minoan Eruption, Thira, Cyclades, Greece. *Jour. Geophys. Res.* 89:8441–62.

———. 1990. Precursory Activity to the Minoan Eruption, Thera, Greece. In D. Hardy, ed., *Thera and the Aegean World III,* vol. 2, *Earth Sciences,* pp. 79–88. Thera Foundation.

HEIKEN, G., F. MCCOY, and M. SHERIDAN. 1990. Paleotopographic and Paleographic Reconstruction of Minoan Thera. In D. Hardy, ed., *Thera and the Aegean World III,* vol. 2, *Earth Sciences,* pp. 370–76. Thera Foundation.

HEILPRIN, A. 1906. The Shattered Obelisk of Mt. Pelée. *National Geographic* 17(8):465–74.

HEINBERG, R. 1989. *Memories and Visions of Paradise: Exploring the Universal Myth of a Lost Golden Age.* Theosophical Publishing House.

———. 1996a. The Lost History of Humankind, part 1, Plato to 1980. *Venture Inward* 12(2):20–24.

———. 1996b. The Lost History of Humankind, part 2, 1980 to the Present. *Venture Inward* 12(3):30–34.

HEIRTZLER, J. R. 1968. Sea-Floor Spreading. *Scientific American* 219(6):60–70.

———. 1975. Project FAMOUS—Man's First Voyage Down to the Mid-Atlantic Ridge; Where the Earth Turns Inside Out. *National Geographic* 147(5):587–615.

HEIRTZLER, J. R., and W. B. BRYAN. 1975. The Floor of the Mid-Atlantic Rift. *Scientific American* 233(2):78–90.

HENDERSON, J. L. 1972. Ancient Myths and Modern Man. In C. G. Jung, ed., *Man and His Symbols*, pp. 97–156. Dell.

HERMANN, P. 1954. *Conquest by Man*. Harper & Bros.

HERODOTUS. N.d. *The Histories*. Translation by Aubrey de Sélincourt. Penguin Books, 1954.

HERSEY, J. B. 1962. The Puerto Rico Trench: A Geophysical Laboratory. *Oceanus* 8(3):14–21.

HEYERDAHL, T. 1979. *Early Man and the Ocean*. Doubleday.

HIGGINS, R. 1974. *Minoan and Mycenaean Art*. Praeger.

HILDRETH, W. 1990. The Katmai Eruption of 1912: A Comparison with the Minoan Eruption of Santorini. In D. Hardy, ed., *Thera and the Aegean World III*, vol. 2, *Earth Sciences*, pp. 455–62. Thera Foundation.

HILL, R. T. 1902. Report on the Volcanic Disturbances in the West Indies. *National Geographic* 13(6):223–67.

HILLER, S. 1990. The Miniature Frieze in the West House—Evidence for Minoan Poetry? In D. Hardy, ed., *Thera and the Aegean World III*, vol. 1, *Archaeology*, pp. 229–36. Thera Foundation.

HÖCKMANN, O. 1978. Theran Floral Style in Relation to That of Crete. In C. Doumas, ed., *Thera and the Aegean World I*, pp. 605–16. Thera Foundation.

HOLBROOK, S. 1944. A Congressman Rediscovers Atlantis. [Donnelly's life.] *New York Times Book Review*, July 30, p. 2.

HOLDEN, C. 1996a. Ebola: Ancient History of "New" Disease? *Science* 272:1591.

HOLLISTER, C. D., R. FLOOD, and I. N. MCCAVE. 1978. Plastering and Decorating [Sediment Drifts] in the North Atlantic. *Oceanus* 21(1):5–13.

HOLLISTER, C. D., A. R. M. NOWELL, and P. A. JUMARS. 1984. The Dynamic Abyss. *Scientific American* 250(3):42–53.

HOMER. N.d. *The Iliad*. Translation by E. V. Rieu. Penguin Classics, 1950.

———. N.d. *The Odyssey*. Translation by Robert Fitzgerald. Doubleday Anchor, 1963.

HOOD, S. 1971. *The Minoans: The Story of Bronze Age Crete*. Praeger.

———. 1978a. *The Arts in Prehistoric Greece*. Penguin.

———. 1978b. Traces of the Eruption Outside of Thera. In C. Doumas, ed., *Thera and the Aegean World I*, pp. 683–90. Thera Foundation.

———. 1990. The Cretan Element on Thera in Late Minoan IA. In D. Hardy, ed., *Thera and the Aegean World III*, vol. 1, *Archaeology*, pp. 118–23. Thera Foundation.

HOPE, M. 1991. *Atlantis: Myth or Reality?* Arkana.

HOPPER, R. J. 1977. *The Early Greeks*. Harper & Row.

HORWITZ, S. L. 1981. *The Find of a Lifetime: Sir Arthur Evans and the Discovery of Knossos*. Viking.

HOSEA, L. M. 1875. Atlantis: A Statement of the "Atlantic" Theory Respecting Aboriginal Civilization. *Cincinnati Quar. Jour. Sci.* 2(3):193–211.

HOVEY, E. O. 1902. The Eruptions of La Soufrière, St. Vincent, in May, 1902. *National Geographic* 13(6):444–59.

HURLEY, P. M. 1968. The Confirmation of Continental Drift. *Scientific American* 218(4):52–64.

HUTCHINSON, R. W. 1962. *Prehistoric Crete.* Penguin.

HUYGHE, P. 1986. Seafloor Mapping. *Oceans* 19(6):22–29.

HYNE, C. J. C. 1900. *The Lost Continent.* Harper.

IDYLL, C. P. 1964. *The Abyss: The Deep Sea and the Creatures That Live in It.* Crowell.

————, ed. 1969. *Exploring the Ocean World: A History of Oceanography.* Crowell.

ILIAKIS, K. 1978. Morphological Analysis of the Akrotiri Wall-Paintings of Santorini. In C. Doumas, ed., *Thera and the Aegean World I,* pp. 617–28. Thera Foundation.

IMMERWAHR, S. A. 1990. Swallows and Dolphins at Akrotiri: Some Thoughts on the Relationship of Vase-Painting to Wall-Painting. In D. Hardy, ed., *Thera and the Aegean World III,* vol. 1, *Archaeology,* pp. 237–45. Thera Foundation.

JACOBSEN, T. W. 1976. 17,000 Years of Greek Prehistory. *Scientific American* 234(6):76–87.

JAMES, P. 1995. *The Sunken Kingdom: The Atlantis Mystery Solved.* Jonathan Cape.

JANSON, H. W. 1962. *History of Art.* Prentice-Hall and Abrams.

JENKYNS, H. C. 1994. Early History of the Oceans. *Oceanus* 36(4):49–52.

JOHNSON, D. L. 1978. The Origin of Island Mammoths and the Quaternary Land Bridge History of the Northern Channel Islands, California. *Quaternary Research* 10(4):204–25.

————. 1980. Problems in the Land Vertebrate Zoogeography of Certain Islands and the Swimming Powers of Elephants. *Journal of Biogeography* 7(4):383–98.

JOHNSON, D. S. 1994. *Phantom Islands of the Atlantic.* Goose Lane.

KALOGEROPOULOS, S., and S. PARITSIS. 1990. Geological and Geochemical Evolution of the Santorini Volcano: A Review. In D. Hardy, ed., *Thera and the Aegean World III,* vol. 2, *Earth Sciences,* pp. 164–71. Thera Foundation.

KAMPION, D. 1989. *The Book of Waves.* Arpel Graphics and Surfer Publications.

KARAGEORGHIS, V. 1990. Rites de Passage at Thera: Some Oriental Comparanda. In D. Hardy, ed., *Thera and the Aegean World III,* vol. 1, *Archaeology,* pp. 67–71. Thera Foundation.

KATZ, E. 1994. *The Film Encyclopedia.* HarperCollins.

KAY, F. G. 1954. *The Atlantic Ocean: Bridge Between Two Worlds.* Museum Press, London.

KEAN, V. J. 1985. *The Disk from Phaistos.* Efstathiadis.

KELLER, J. 1990. Summary of the Progress in Volcanology. In D. Hardy, ed., *Thera and the Aegean World III.* vol. 2, *Earth Sciences,* pp. 486–87. Thera Foundation.

KELLER, J., T. REHREN, and E. STADLBAUER. 1990. Explosive Volcanism in the Hellenic Arc: A Summary and Review. In D. Hardy, ed., *Thera and the Aegean World III,* vol. 2, *Earth Sciences,* pp. 13–26. Thera Foundation.

KENNEDY, W. Q., and H. E. RICHEY. 1947. Catalog of the Active Volcanoes of the World. *Bull. Volc.* 7:1–11.

KISKYRAS, D. A. 1978. The Geotectonic State of the Greek Area: Volcanism, Intermediate Earthquakes, and Plate Tectonics. In C. Doumas, ed., *Thera and the Aegean World I,* pp. 85–96. Thera Foundation.

KITTO, H. D. F. 1957. *The Greeks.* Penguin.

KOMLÓS, G., P. HÉDEVÁRI, and S. MÉSZÁROS. 1978. A Brief Note on Tectonic Earthquakes Related to the Activity of Santorini from Antiquity to the Present. In C. Doumas, ed., *Thera and the Aegean World I,* pp. 97–108. Thera Foundation.

KOSTER, A. L. 1956. City of the Dead [St. Pierre]. *Natural History* 65(8):412–15.

KOUFOU, A. 1992. *Crete: All the Museums and Archaeological Sites.* Ekdotike Athenon.

KRAFFT, M. 1993. *Volcanoes: Fires from the Earth.* Abrams.

KRONTIRA, L. 1987. *In the Days of King Minos.* Ekdotike Athenon.

KUNIHOLM, P. I. 1990. Overview and Assessment of the Evidence for the Date of the Eruption of Thera. In D. Hardy and A. C. Renfrew, eds., *Thera and the Aegean World III,* vol. 3, *Chronology,* pp. 13–18. Thera Foundation.

KURTEN, B. 1969. Continental Drift and Evolution. *Scientific American* 220(3):54–64.

LAFFINEUR, R. 1990. Composition and Perspective in Theran Wall-Paintings. In D. Hardy, ed., *Thera and the Aegean World III,* vol. 1, *Archaeology,* pp. 246–51. Thera Foundation.

LAMBROU-PHILLIPSON, C. 1995. Thera in the Mythology of the Classical Tradition: An Archaeological Approach. In D. Hardy, ed., *Thera and the Aegean World III,* vol. 1, *Archaeology,* pp. 128–61. Thera Foundation.

LANE, F. W. 1965. *The Elements Rage.* Chilton.

LANGMUIR, A. D. 1994. Invited Commentary: "Thucydides Syndrome" Reconsidered. *Amer. Jour. Epidemiol.* 140(7):629–30.

LANGMUIR, A. D., T. D. WORTHEN, J. SOLOMON, C. G. RAY, and E. PETERSEN. 1985. The Thucydides Syndrome: A New Hypothesis for the Cause of the Plague of Athens. *N.E. Jour. Med.* 313(16):1027–30.

LATTER, J. H. 1981. Tsunamis of Volcanic Origin: Summary of Causes, with Particular Reference to Krakatoa. *Bull. Volc.* 44:467–90.

LEE, D. 1965. Appendix on Atlantis. In Plato, *Timaeus and Critias.* Pp. 146–67. Penguin.

LEET, L. D. 1948. *Causes of Catastrophe: Earthquakes, Volcanoes, Tidal Waves, and Hurricanes.* McGraw-Hill.

LEIP, H. 1957. *The Gulf Stream Story.* Jarrolds.

LE PLONGEON, A. 1886. *Sacred Mysteries Among the Mayas and Quiches 11,000 Years Ago.* Macoy.

————. 1896. *Queen Móo and the Egyptian Sphinx.* Kegan, Paul, Trench, Tribner.

LEY, W. 1969. *Another Look at Atlantis, and Fifteen Other Essays.* Doubleday.

LIN, J. 1992. The Segmented Mid-Atlantic Ridge. *Oceanus* 34(4):11–18.

LISSAU, S. 1975. Ocean Waves. *Oceans* 8(5):12–24.

LOLOS, Y. G. 1990. On the Late Helladic I of Akrotiri, Thera. In D. Hardy and A. C. Renfrew, eds., *Thera and the Aegean World III*, vol. 3, *Chronology*, pp. 51–56. Thera Foundation.

LUCE, J. V. 1969. *Lost Atlantis: New Light on an Old Legend.* Thames & Hudson.

———. 1978a. The Sources and Literary Form of Plato's Atlantis. In E. S. Ramage, ed., *Atlantis: Fact or Fiction?*, pp. 49–78. Indiana University Press.

———. 1978b. The Chronology of the LM I Destruction Horizons on Thera and Crete. In C. Doumas, ed., *Thera and the Aegean World I*, pp. 785–90. Thera Foundation.

MACDONALD, C. 1990. Destruction and Construction in the Palace at Knossos: LM IA–B. In D. Hardy and A. C. Renfrew, eds., *Thera and the Aegean World III*, vol. 3, *Chronology*, pp. 83–88. Thera Foundation.

MACDONALD, G. A., A. T. ABBOTT, and F. L. PETERSON. 1983. *Volcanoes in the Sea.* University of Hawaii Press.

MACKENZIE, D. A. 1917. *Myths of Crete and Pre-Hellenic Europe.* Gresham.

MACLAREN, C. 1822. *A Dissertation on the Topography of the Plains of Troy—Including an Examination of the Opinion of Demetrius, Chevalier, Dr. Clarke, and Major Rennell.* Edinburgh.

MACLIESH, W. 1989. *The Gulf Stream: Encounters with the Blue God.* Houghton Mifflin.

MANNING, S. W. 1990. The Eruption of Thera: Date and Implications. In D. Hardy and A. C. Renfrew, eds., *Thera and the Aegean World III*, vol. 3, *Chronology*, pp. 29–40. Thera Foundation.

MARCUS, J. G. 1981. *The Discovery of the North Atlantic.* Oxford University Press.

MARINATOS, N. 1980. Atlantis: Fact or Fiction? Book review. *Classical Journal* 75:362–64.

———. 1985. *Art and Religion in Thera: Reconstructing a Bronze Age Society.* Andromedas.

———. 1990. Minoan-Cycladic Syncretism. In D. Hardy, ed., *Thera and the Aegean World III*, vol. 1, *Archaeology*, pp. 370–77. Thera Foundation.

MARINATOS, S. 1939. The Volcanic Destruction of Minoan Crete. *Antiquity* 13:425–39.

———. 1950. On the Legend of Atlantis. *Cretica Chronicles* 4:195–213. Reprinted in 1969 as "Some Words About the Legend of Atlantis" by the Athens Museum.

———. 1960b. *Crete and Mycenae.* Abrams.

———. 1960a. Helice: A Submerged Town in Classical Greece. *Archaeology* 13(3):186–93.

———. 1968b. *Excavations at Thera I.* Athens.

———. 1968a. Helike—Thera—Thebai. *Athens Annals of Archaeology* 1:12–17.

———. 1969. *Excavations at Thera II.* Athens.

———. 1970a. *Excavations at Thera III.* Athens.

———. 1970b. Investigations in Helice. *Acta Acad. Athens* 41:511–18.

———. 1971. *Excavations at Thera IV.* Athens.

———. 1972a. *Excavations at Thera V.* Athens.

———. 1972b. Thera: Key to the Riddle of Minos. *National Geographic* 141(5):702–26.

————. 1974b. Ethnic Problems Raised by Recent Discoveries on Thera. In R. A. Crossland and A. Birchell, eds., *Bronze Age Migrations in the Aegean,* pp. 199–202. Rutgers University Press.

————. 1974a. *Excavations at Thera VI.* Athens.

————. 1976. *Excavations at Thera VII.* Athens.

MARINO, G. 1994. Back to the Jurassic in Space Age Subs: Deep Ocean Exploration for the Next Millennium. *Science News* 146(8):122–26.

MARINOS, G., and N. MELIDONIS. 1959. About the Size of the Sea Wave (Tsunami) During the Prehistoric Eruption of Santorin. *Bull. Geol. Soc. Greece* 4:210–18.

MARKETOU, T. 1990. Santorini Tephra from Rhodes and Kos: Some Chronological Remarks Based on the Stratigraphy. In D. Hardy and A. C. Renfrew, eds., *Thera and the Aegean World III,* vol. 3, *Chronology,* pp. 100–13. Thera Foundation.

MARSHACK, A. 1995. Images of the Ice Age. *Archaeology* 48(4):28–39.

MARTHARI, M. 1990. The Chronology of the Last Phases of Occupation at Akrotiri in the Light of the Evidence from the West House Pottery Groups. In D. Hardy and A. C. Renfrew, eds., *Thera and the Aegean World III,* vol. 3, *Chronology,* pp. 57–70. Thera Foundation.

MARTIN, T. H. 1841. *Etudes sur le Timée de Platon.* Ladrange.

MASOOD, E. 1995. Row Erupts over Evacuation Plans for Mount Vesuvius. *Nature* 377(6549):471.

MATTHEW, W. D. 1920. Plato's Atlantis in Paleogeography. *Proc. Nat. Acad. Sci.* 6:17–18.

MATZ, F. 1962. *The Art of Crete and Early Greece.* Greystone.

MAVOR, J. W. 1966a. A Mighty Bronze Age Explosion. *Oceanus* 12(3):8–13.

————. 1966b. Volcanoes and History; or, "Atlantis" Revisited. *Oceanus* 13(1):14–22.

————. 1969. *Voyage to Atlantis.* Putnam's.

————. 1984. Atlantis and Catastrophe Theory. *Oceanus* 28(1):44–51.

MCBIRNEY, A. R. 1963. Factors Governing the Nature of Submarine Volcanoes. *Bull. Volc.* 26:55–69.

MCCLELLAND, E., and R. THOMAS. 1990. A Paleomagnetic Study of Minoan Tephra from Thera. In D. Hardy, ed., *Thera and the Aegean World III,* vol. 2, *Earth Sciences,* pp. 129–38. Thera Foundation.

MCCOY, F. W. 1980a. Climatic Change in the Eastern Mediterranean Area During the Past 240,000 Years. In C. Doumas, ed., *Thera and the Aegean World II,* pp. 57–78. Thera Foundation.

————. 1980b. The Upper Thera (Minoan) Ash in Deep-Sea Sediments: Distribution and Comparison with Other Ash Layers. In C. Doumas, ed., *Thera and the Aegean World II,* pp. 57–78. Thera Foundation.

MELLAART, J. 1965. *Earliest Civilizations of the Near East.* McGraw-Hill.

————. 1967. *Çatal Hüyük: A Neolithic Town in Anatolia.* McGraw-Hill.

MELLERSH, H. E. L. 1970. *The Destruction of Knossos: The Rise and Fall of Minoan Crete.* Barnes & Noble.

————. 1976. *Chronology of the Ancient World: 10,000 B.C. to A.D. 799.* Helicon.

MENARD, H. W. 1969. The Deep Ocean Floor. *Scientific American* 221(3):126–42.

MÉSZÁROS, S. 1978. Some Words on the Minoan Tsunami of Santorini. In C. Doumas, ed., *Thera and the Aegean World I,* pp. 257–62. Thera Foundation.

METZGER, E. 1884. Gleanings from the Reports Concerning the Eruption of Krakatoa. *Nature* 29:240–44.

MEYER, K. D. 1995. Who Owns the Spoils of War? *Archaeology* 48(4):46–52.

MICHAEL, H. N. 1978. Radiocarbon Dates from the Site of Akrotiri, Thera, 1967–1977. In C. Doumas, ed., *Thera and the Aegean World I,* pp. 791–96. Thera Foundation.

————. 1980. Addendum to Radiocarbon Dates from the Site of Akrotiri. In C. Doumas, ed., *Thera and the Aegean World II,* pp. 245–46. Thera Foundation.

MILIADIS, J. 1965. *The Acropolis.* Atlantis Ltd.

MILLER, D. J. 1960. The Alaska Earthquake of July 10, 1958: Giant Wave in Lituya Bay. *Bull. Seismol. Soc. Amer.* 50:253–66.

MILLER, R. 1983. *Continents in Collision.* Time-Life Books.

MILLER, W. J. 1976. *The Annotated Jules Verne: Twenty Thousand Leagues Under the Sea.* Crowell.

MILTNER, F. 1958. Two New Statues of Diana of the Ephesians. *Illustrated London News,* February 8, p. 3.

MITCHELL, J. 1969. *The View over Atlantis.* Ballantine.

MONEY, J. 1973. The Destruction of Acrotiri. *Antiquity* 47:50–3.

MONTSERRAT VOLCANO OBSERVATORY TEAM. 1997. The Ongoing Eruption in Montserrat. *Science* 276:371–72.

MOONEY, M. J. 1975. Tsunami Coming! *Oceans* 8(5):26–33.

MOORE, T. D. 1979. Rivers of Lava. *Oceans* 12(4):50–56.

MOOREHEAD, C. 1996. *Lost and Found: The 9,000 Treasures of Troy.* Viking.

MORENS, D. M., and R. J. LITTMAN. 1994a. The Thucydides Syndrome Reconsidered: New Thoughts on the Plague of Athens. *Amer. Jour. Epidemiol.* 140(7):621–27.

————. 1994b. Morens and Littman Reply to Langmuir. *Amer. Jour. Epidemiol.* 140(7):631.

MORGAN, L. 1990. Island Iconography: Thera, Kea, Milos. In D. Hardy, ed., *Thera and the Aegean World III,* vol. 1, *Archaeology,* pp. 252–66. Thera Foundation.

MORGAN, W. J. 1968. Rises, Trenches, Great Faults and Crustal Blocks. *Jour. Geophys. Res.* 73:1959–82.

————. 1972. Deep Mantle Convection Plumes and Plate Motions. *Bull. Amer. Assoc. Petrol. Geol.* 56:203–13.

MORISON, S. E. 1971. *The European Discovery of America: The Northern Voyages, A.D. 500–1600.* Oxford University Press.

MORSE, R. 1972. The Frescoes of Thera: Spectacular Finds in Ancient Aegean Rubble. *Smithsonian* 2(10):15–23.

MOSER, D. 1976. The Azores, Nine Islands in Search of a Future. *National Geographic* 149(2):261–88.

MOUNDREA-AGRAFIOTI, A. 1990. Akrotiri, the Chipped Stone Industry: Reduction Techniques and Tools of the LC I Phase. In D. Hardy, ed., *Thera and the Aegean World III*, vol. 1, *Archaeology*, pp. 390–406. Thera Foundation.

MUCK, O. 1978. *The Secret of Atlantis*. Collins.

MULLER, E., W. JUHLE, and H. COULTER. 1954. Current Volcanic Activity in Katmai National Monument. *Science* 119:319–21.

MURRAY, J., and J. HJORT. 1912. *The Depths of the Sea*. Macmillan, London. Reprinted in 1965, Stechert & Hafner, New York.

MYLES, D. 1985. *The Great Waves: Tsunamis*. McGraw-Hill.

NAPPI, G. 1976. Recent Activity of Stromboli. *Nature* 261:119–20.

NATIONAL GEOGRAPHIC SOCIETY. 1990. Map. World Ocean Floors: Atlantic Ocean. *National Geographic* 149(2):261–88.

NICHOLS, M. 1975. *Man, Myth, and Monument*. Morrow.

NIEMEIER, W.-D. 1990. Mycenaean Elements in the Miniature Fresco from Thera? In D. Hardy, ed., *Thera and the Aegean World III*, vol. 1, *Archaeology*, pp. 267–84. Thera Foundation.

NINKOVICH, D., and B. C. HEEZEN. 1965. Santorini Tephra. In W. F. Whittard and R. Bradshaw, eds., *Submarine Geology and Geophysics*, pp. 413–52. Butterworth.

OBEE, B. 1989. Tsunami! *Canadian Geographic* 109(1):46–53.

OLIVER, J. 1959. Long Earthquake Waves. *Scientific American* 200(3):131–43.

OLSEN, P. E., C. S. HAMES, A. S. BENESON, and E. N. GENOVESE. 1996. The Thucydides Syndrome: Ebola Déjà Vu? (or Ebola Reemergent?). *Emerging Infectious Diseases* 2(2):19–20.

OROWAN, E. 1969. The Origin of Oceanic Ridges. *Scientific American* 221(5):102–18.

O'TOOLE, T. 1966. Sonar to Hunt for Two Lost Cities. *New York Times*, February 7, p. 21.

OUTHWAITE, L. 1957. *The Atlantic: History of an Ocean*. Coward-McCann.

PAGE, D. L. 1970. *The Santorini Volcano and the Destruction of Minoan Crete*. Society for Promotion of Hellenic Studies.

————. 1978. On the Relation Between the Thera Eruption and the Desolation of Eastern Crete, c. 1450 B.C. In C. Doumas, ed., *Thera and the Aegean World I*, pp. 691–98. Thera Foundation.

PALMER, L. R. 1965. *Mycenaeans and Minoans*. Knopf.

————. 1969. *A New Guide to the Palace of Knossos*. Praeger.

PALYVOU, C. 1990. Architectural Design at Late Cycladic Akrotiri. In D. Hardy, ed., *Thera and the Aegean World III*, vol. 1, *Archaeology*, pp. 44–56. Thera Foundation.

PAPAPASTOLOU, J. A. 1981. *Crete*. Clio Editions.

PAPAZACHOS, B. C., and P. E. COMNINAKIS. 1978. Geotectonic Significance of the Deep Seismic Zones in the Aegean Area. In C. Doumas, ed., *Thera and the Aegean World I,* pp. 121–30. Thera Foundation.

PAUSANIAS. N.d. *Description of Greece.* Translation and commentary by J. G. Frazer. Bilbo & Tannen, 1965.

———. N.d. *Guide to Greece,* vol. 1, *Central Greece.* Translated and with an introduction by Peter Levi. Penguin, 1971.

PAYNE, R. 1959. *The Gold of Troy.* Funk & Wagnalls.

PELLEGRINO, C. 1991. *Unearthing Atlantis.* Random House.

———. 1994. *Return to Sodom and Gomorrah.* Avon.

PENDLEBURY, J. D. S. 1939. *The Archaeology of Crete.* London. Norton Library, New York, 1965.

———. 1954. *A Handbook to the Palace of Minos at Knossos.* Max Parrish.

PERRY, R. 1972. *The Unknown Ocean.* Taplinger.

PICHLER, H., and W. L. FRIEDRICH. 1980. Mechanism of the Minoan Eruption of Santorini. In C. Doumas, ed., *Thera and the Aegean World II,* pp. 15–30. Thera Foundation.

PIGGOTT, S. 1965. *Ancient Europe: From the Beginnings of Agriculture to Classical Antiquity.* Aldine.

PITMAN, W. C., and M. TALWANI. 1972. Sea Floor Spreading in the North Atlantic. *Bull. Geol. Soc. Amer.* 83:619–46.

PLATO. N.d. *The Collected Dialogues of Plato.* Bollingen edn. Edited by E. Hamilton and H. Cairns. Princeton University Press, 1961.

PLATON, N. 1965. Kato Zakro: A Rediscovered Palace. *Horizon* 7(3):76–79.

———. 1971. *Zakros: The Discovery of a Lost Palace of Ancient Crete.* Scribner's.

PLINY. N.d. *Natural History.* 10 vols. Harvard University Press, Loeb Classical Library.

———. N.d. *Letters.* Book 4, 16 and 20. Macmillan.

PLUTARCH. N.d. *Lives.* Translation by Bernadotte Perrin. Harvard University Press, Loeb Classical Library, 1914.

POLLITT, J. J. 1972. *Art and Experience in Ancient Greece.* Cambridge University Press.

POMERANCE, L. 1970. The Final Collapse of Santorini (Thera): 1400 B.C. or 1200 B.C.? *Studies in Mediterranean Archaeology* 26.

———. 1978. Improbability of a Theran Collapse During the New Kingdom, 1503–1447 B.C. In C. Doumas, ed., *Thera and the Aegean World I,* pp. 797–803. Thera Foundation.

POPHAM, M. R. 1990. Pottery Styles and Chronology. In D. Hardy and A. C. Renfrew, eds., *Thera and the Aegean World III,* vol. 3, *Chronology,* pp. 27–28. Thera Foundation.

POUGH, F. H. 1933. The Volcano Museum on Mt. Pelée. *Natural History* 33:31–40.

POULIANOS, A. N. 1972. The Discovery of the First Known Victim of Thera's Bronze Age Eruption. *Archaeology* 25:229–30.

POURSAT, J.-C. 1990. Craftsmen and Traders at Thera: A View from Crete. In D. Hardy, ed., *Thera and the Aegean World III*, vol. 1, *Archaeology*, pp. 124–27. Thera Foundation.

PRATT, R. M. 1964. The Mid-Atlantic Ridge: Youthful Key to an Old Ocean. *Oceanus* 11(2): 8–15.

PUCHELT, H. 1978. Evolution of the Volcanic Rocks of Santorini. In C. Doumas, ed., *Thera and the Aegean World I*, pp. 131–46. Thera Foundation.

PULAK, C., and D. A. FREY. 1985. The Search for a Bronze Age Shipwreck. *Archaeology* 38(4):18–24.

PYLE, D. M. 1990. New Estimates for the Volume of the Minoan Eruption. In D. Hardy, ed., *Thera and the Aegean World III*, vol. 2, *Earth Sciences*, pp. 113–21. Thera Foundation.

RACKHAM, O. 1990. Observations on the Historical Ecology of Santorini. In D. Hardy, ed., *Thera and the Aegean World III*, vol. 2, *Earth Sciences*, pp. 384–91. Thera Foundation.

RADICE, B. 1973. *Who's Who in the Ancient World.* Penguin.

RAMAGE, E. S., ed. 1978a. *Atlantis: Fact or Fiction?* Indiana University Press.

———. 1978b. Perspectives Ancient and Modern. In E. S. Ramage, ed., *Atlantis: Fact or Fiction?* Pp. 3–45. Indiana University Press.

RAMSAY, C. R. 1979. Mycenaeans: Warrior-Merchants of Greece. In *Mysteries of the Ancient World*, pp. 144–67. National Geographic Society.

RANDI, J. 1982. *Flim-Flam!: Psychics, ESP, Unicorns and Other Delusions.* Prometheus Books.

RAPP, G., S. R. B. COOKE, and E. HENRICKSON. 1972. Pumice from Thera (Santorini) Identified from a Greek Mainland Archaeological Excavation. *Science* 179:471–73.

REEDS, C. A. 1928. Volcanoes in Action. *Natural History* 28:302–17.

REID, H. F. 1914. The Lisbon Earthquake of November 1, 1755. *Bull. Seismol. Soc. Amer.* 4:53.

RENAULT, M. 1958. *The King Must Die.* Pantheon.

REVELLE, R. 1969. The Ocean. *Scientific American* 221(3):55–65.

REVERDIN, O. 1961. *Crete and Its Treasures.* Viking.

REXINE, J. 1974. Atlantis: Fact or Fantasy? *Classical Bulletin* 51:49–53.

RICHTER, C. F. 1935. An Instrumental Earthquake Magnitude Scale. *Bull. Seismol. Soc. Amer.* 25:1–32.

RITCHIE, D. 1981. *The Ring of Fire.* Atheneum.

———. 1994. *The Encyclopedia of Earthquakes and Volcanoes.* Facts on File.

ROBERTS, C., and S. V. ROBERTS. 1976. Atlantis Recaptured. *New York Times Magazine*, September 5, pp. 12–13, 34–37.

ROBERTS, E. B. 1961. History of a Tsunami [Alaskan tsunami of July 9, 1958]. *Rep. Smithson. Inst.* 1960:237–40.

———. 1967. The Santorini Volcano. Letter to the Editor. *Saturday Review*, February 4, p. 16.

ROBINSON, L. 1972. *Edgar Cayce's Story of the Origin and Destiny of Man.* Berkeley.

ROMM, J. S. 1992. *The Edges of the Earth in Ancient Thought.* Princeton University Press.

RONA, P. A. 1973. Plate Tectonics and Mineral Resources. *Scientific American* 229(1):86–95.

———. 1985. Black Smokers on the Mid-Atlantic Ridge. *Eos* 66(40):682–83.

RUSSELL, F. 1980. Mysterious Voyages Through Atlantic Mists. In J. J. Thorndike, ed., *Mysteries of the Deep,* pp. 168–77. American Heritage.

RUSSELL, I. C. 1902. The Recent Volcanic Eruptions in the West Indies. *National Geographic* 13(12):267–85.

RUX, B. 1996. *Architects of the Underworld: Unriddling Atlantis, Anomalies of Mars, and the Mystery of the Sphinx.* Frog, Ltd.

RYTHER, J. H. 1956. The Sargasso Sea. *Scientific American* 194(1):98–104.

SACHS, P. L. 1963. A Visit to St. Peter and St. Paul Rocks. *Oceanus* 9(4):2–5.

SAKELLARAKIS, J. A. 1967. Minoan Cemeteries at Arkhanes. *Archaeology* 20(4):276–81.

———. 1990. Fashioning of Ostrich-Egg Rhyta in the Creto-Mycenaean Aegean. In D. Hardy, ed., *Thera and the Aegean World III,* vol. 1, *Archaeology,* pp. 285–308. Thera Foundation.

———. 1994. *Herakleion Museum.* Ekdotike Athenon.

SAKELLARIOU, A. 1980. The West House Miniature Frescoes. In C. Doumas, ed., *Thera and the Aegean World II,* pp. 147–54. Thera Foundation.

SATAKE, K. 1994. Study of Recent Tsunamis Sheds Light on Earthquakes. *Eos* 75(13):135–37.

SCARTH, A. 1994. *Volcanoes.* Texas A&M University Press.

SCHACHERMEYR, F. 1978. Akrotiri—First Maritime Republic? In C. Doumas, ed., *Thera and the Aegean World I,* pp. 423–36. Thera Foundation.

SCHERMAN, K. 1976. *Daughter of Fire: A Portrait of Iceland.* Little, Brown.

SCHIERING, W. 1978. The Eruption of the Volcano on Thera and the Destructions on Crete. In C. Doumas, ed., *Thera and the Aegean World I,* pp. 699–701. Thera Foundation.

SCHLEE, S. 1973. *The Edge of an Unfamiliar World: A History of Oceanography.* Dutton.

SCHLIEMANN, H. 1875. *Troy and Its Remains.* John Murray. Dover, 1994.

SCHMIDT, J. F. J. 1875. *Studien über Erdbeben.* Leipzig.

SCHNEIDER, D. 1996. Pot Luck: Linear A, an Ancient Script, Is Unearthed in Turkey. *Scientific American* 275(1):20.

SCHUCHERT, C. 1917a. Atlantis, the "Lost" Continent. *Geog. Rev.* 3(1):64–66.

———. 1917b. Atlantis and the Permanency of the North Atlantic Ocean Bottom. *Proc. Nat. Acad. Sci.* 3:65–72.

SCHUESSLER, R. 1975. Wave Energy. *Oceans* 8(5):34–37.

SCHULLER, R. 1917. Atlantis, the "Lost" Continent. *Geog. Rev.* 3(1):61–64.

SCHULTEN, A. 1927. Tartessos and Atlantis. *Petermanns Geographische Mitteilungen* 73:284–88.

———. 1939. Atlantis. *Rheinisches Museum für Philologie* 88:326–46.

SCOTT-ELLIOT, W. 1925. *Legends of Atlantis and Lost Lemuria.* Theosophical Publication Society.

SELF, S., and M. R. RAMPINO. 1980. Krakatau, West of Java: A Reappraisal of the 1883 Eruption. *Eos* 61(46):1141.

——. 1981. The 1883 Eruption of Krakatau. *Nature* 294:699–704.

SELF, S., M. R. RAMPINO, M. S. NEWTON, and J. A. WOLFF. 1984. Volcanological Study of the Great Tambora Eruption of 1815. *Geology* 12(11):659–63.

SETTEGAST, M. 1990. *Plato Prehistorian.* Lindisfarne.

SEVERIN, T. 1977. The Voyage of the Brendan. *National Geographic* 152(6):769–97.

——. 1978. *The Brendan Voyage.* McGraw-Hill.

SHACKELTON, J. C., and T. H. VAN ANDEL. 1980. Prehistoric Shell Assemblages from Franchthi Cave and Evolution of the Adjacent Coastal Zone. *Nature* 288:357–59.

SHAW, J. W. 1978. Consideration of the Site of Akrotiri as a Minoan Settlement. In C. Doumas, ed., *Thera and the Aegean World I,* pp. 429–36. Thera Foundation.

SHEPARD, F. P. 1959. *The Earth Beneath the Sea.* Johns Hopkins University Press.

——. 1961. Submarine Erosion: A Discussion of Recent Papers. *Bull. Geol. Soc. Amer.* 62: 1413–17.

SHEPARD, F. P., and R. F. DILL. 1966. *Submarine Canyons.* Rand McNally.

SIGURDSSON, H., S. N. CAREY, W. CORNELL, and T. PESCATORE. 1985. The Eruption of Vesuvius in 79 A.D. *Nat. Geog. Res.* 1:332–87.

SIGURDSSON, H., S. CAREY, and J. D. DEVINE. 1990. Assessment of Mass, Dynamics and Environmental Effects of the Minoan Eruption of Santorini Volcano. In D. Hardy, ed., *Thera and the Aegean World III,* vol. 2, *Earth Sciences,* pp. 100–12. Thera Foundation.

SIGURDSSON, H., S. CASHDOLLAR, and S. R. J. SPARKS. 1982. The Eruption of Vesuvius in A.D. 79: Reconstruction from Historical and Volcanological Evidence. *Amer. Jour. Archaeol.* 86:133–54.

SILBERMANN, O. 1930. *Un Continent perdu: L'Atlantide.* Genet.

SIMKIN, T., and R. S. FISKE. 1983. *Krakatau 1883: The Volcanic Eruption and Its Effects.* Smithsonian Institution Press.

SIMKIN, T., and K. A. HOWARD. 1970. Caldera Collapse in the Galápagos Islands, 1968. *Science* 169(3944):429–37.

SIMPKIN, T., and L. SIEBERT. 1994. *Volcanoes of the World.* Geoscience Press and Smithsonian Institution Press.

SOLES, J. S., and C. DARVAS. 1990. Theran Ash in Minoan Crete: New Excavations on Mochlos. In D. Hardy and A. C. Renfrew, eds., *Thera and the Aegean World III,* vol. 3, *Chronology,* pp. 89–95. Thera Foundation.

SONDAAR, P. Y. 1986. The Island Sweepstakes: Dwarf Animals—Now Extinct—Once Populated Many Mediterranean Islands. Why? *Natural History* 95(9):50–57.

SONDAAR, P. Y., and G. J. BOEKSCHOETEN. 1967. Quaternary Mammals in the South Aegean Island Arc. *Proc. Kon. Ned. Akad. Wetensch.* 70B:556–76.

SONG, X., and P. G. RICHARDS. 1996. Seismological Evidence for Differential Rotation of the Earth's Core. *Nature* 382(6588):221–24.

SOTIRAKOPOULOU, P. 1990. The Earliest History of Akrotiri: The Late Neolithic and Early Bronze Age Phases. In D. Hardy and A. C. Renfrew, eds., *Thera and the Aegean World III*, vol. 3, *Chronology*, pp. 41–47. Thera Foundation.

SPANUTH, J. 1979. *Atlantis of the North*. Van Nostrand Reinhold.

SPARKS, R. S. J., and C. J. N. WILSON. 1990. The Minoan Deposits: A Review of Their Characteristics and Interpretation. In D. Hardy, ed., *Thera and the Aegean World III*, vol. 2, *Earth Sciences*, pp. 89–99. Thera Foundation.

SPARKS, S., and H. SIGURDSSON. 1978. The Big Blast at Santorini. *Natural History* 87(4): 70–77.

SPENCE, L. 1924. *The Problem of Atlantis*. Republished in 1974 as *Atlantis Discovered* by Causeway Books, New York.

———. 1925. *Atlantis in America*. Brentano's.

———. 1942. *Will Europe Follow Atlantis?* Rider.

———. 1943. *The Occult Sciences in Atlantis*. Rider.

———. 1968. *The History of Atlantis*. Bell.

SPIVEY, N. 1995. The Mystery That Isn't. Review of *The Sunken Kingdom: The Atlantis Mystery Solved*, by Peter James. London *Times Literary Supplement*, December 8, p. 11.

STAMATOPOULOS, A. C., and P. C. KOTZIAS. 1990. Volcanic Ash in Ancient and Modern Construction. In D. Hardy, ed., *Thera and the Aegean World III*, vol. 1, *Archaeology*, pp. 491–501. Thera Foundation.

STEARN, J. 1967. *Edgar Cayce: The Sleeping Prophet*. Doubleday.

STEIGER, B. 1973. *Atlantis Rising*. Dell.

———. 1989. *Overlords of Atlantis and the Great Pyramid*. Inner Light.

STEINER, R. 1923. *Atlantis and Lemuria*. Anthroposophical Publishing Co.

———. 1959. *Cosmic Memory: Prehistory of Earth and Man*. Steinerbooks.

STEWART, J. A. 1905. *The Myths of Plato*. Macmillan.

STILLE, A. 1997. Perils of the Sphinx. *New Yorker* 72(46):54–66.

STOCKING, H. E. 1943. The Greatest Explosion of All Time. *Natural History* 51:236–39, 244.

STOMMEL, H., and E. STOMMEL. 1979. The Year Without a Summer. *Scientific American* 240(6):176–80.

STOS-GALE, Z. A., and N. H. GALE. 1990. The Role of Thera in the Bronze Age Trade in Metals. In D. Hardy, ed., *Thera and the Aegean World III*, vol. 1, *Archaeology*, pp. 72–91. Thera Foundation.

STOTHERS, R. B. 1984. The Great Tambora Eruption in 1815 and Its Aftermath. *Science* 224:1191–98.

STOTHERS, R. B., and M. R. RAMPINO. 1983. Volcanic Eruptions in the Mediterranean Before A.D. 630 from Written and Archaeological Sources. *Jour. Geophys. Res.* 88:6357–71.

STRABO. N.d. *Geography*. Translation by Horace L. Jones. Harvard University Press, Loeb Classical Library, 1917.

STUART, G. S. 1979. Ice Age Hunters: Artists in Hidden Caves. In *Mysteries of the Ancient World,* pp. 8–29. National Geographic Society.

SULLIVAN, D. G. 1988. The Discovery of Santorini (Thera) Tephra in Western Turkey. *Nature* 333:552–54.

————. 1990. Minoan Tephra in Lake Sediments in Western Turkey: Dating the Eruption and Accessing the Atmospheric Dispersal of the Ash. In D. Hardy and A. C. Renfrew, eds., *Thera and the Aegean World III,* vol. 3, *Chronology,* pp. 114–19. Thera Foundation.

SULLIVAN, W. 1967. Light on an Old Mystery. *New York Times,* July 23, sec. 4, p. 8.

————. 1974. *Continents in Motion: The New Earth Debate.* McGraw-Hill.

————. 1986. Deep Seeing. *Oceans* 19(1):19–23.

SYKES, E. 1945. *Bibliography of Classical References to Atlantis.* Rome.

SYNOLAKIS, C., F. IMAMURA, Y. TSUJI, H. MATSUTOMI, S. TINTI, B. COOK, Y. P. CHANDRA, and M. USMAN. 1995. Damage Conditions of East Java Tsunami of 1994 Analyzed. *Eos* 76(26):257–62.

TAKASHI, T., and W. A. BASSETT. 1965. The Structure of the Earth's Interior. *Scientific American* 212:100–108.

TAYLOR, A. E. 1922. *The Mind of Plato.* Constable & Co. Republished in 1960 by University of Michigan Press.

————. 1928. *A Commentary on Plato's* Timaeus. Oxford University Press, Clarendon Press.

TAYLOR, S. R., and S. M. MCLENNAN. 1996. The Evolution of Continental Crust. *Scientific American* 274(1):76–81.

TAYLOUR, W. 1964. *The Mycenaeans.* Praeger.

TAZIEFF, H. 1952. *Craters of Fire.* Harper & Bros.

————. 1961. *The Orion Book of Volcanoes.* Orion.

————. 1964. *When the Earth Trembles.* Harcourt, Brace & World.

TEAL, J., and M. TEAL. 1975. *The Sargasso Sea.* Little, Brown.

TEDLOCK, D., trans. 1985. *Popul Vuh.* Simon & Schuster.

TELEVANTOU, C. A. 1990. New Light on the West House Wall-Paintings. In D. Hardy, ed., *Thera and the Aegean World III,* vol. 1, *Archaeology,* pp. 309–26. Thera Foundation.

TERMIER, P. 1916. Atlantis. *Ann. Rep. Smithsonian Inst.* 1915:219–34.

THARP, M., and H. FRANKEL. 1986. Mappers of the Deep. *Natural History* 10/86:49–62.

THOMAS, G., and M. M. WITTS. 1976. *The Day the World Ended.* Stein & Day.

THOMPSON, C. W. 1873. *The Depths of the Sea.* Macmillan.

————. 1878. *The Atlantic: A Preliminary Account of the General Results of the Exploring Voyage of H.M.S. Challenger.* Macmillan.

THORARINSSON, S. 1965. Surtsey: Island Born of Fire. *National Geographic* 127(5):713–26.

————. 1978. Some Comments on the Minoan Eruption of Santorini. In C. Doumas, ed., *Thera and the Aegean World I,* pp. 263–76. Thera Foundation.

THORNDIKE, J. J., ed. 1980. *Mysteries of the Sea.* American Heritage.

THORPE-SCHOLES, K. 1978. Akrotiri: Genesis, Life and Death. In C. Doumas, ed., *Thera and the Aegean World I,* pp. 437–47. Thera Foundation.

THROCKMORTON, P. 1980. "Under Ancient Seas." In J. J. Thorndike, ed., *Mysteries of the Deep,* pp. 62–111. American Heritage.

———. 1984. Underwater Archaeology. *Oceanus* 28(1):3–12.

THUBRON, C. 1981. *The Ancient Mariners.* Time-Life Books.

THUCYDIDES. N.d. *History of the Peloponnesian War.* Translation by Rex Warner. Penguin, 1972.

TIME-LIFE BOOKS. 1982. *Volcano.* Time Inc.

———. 1987. *Mystic Places.* Time Inc.

TOKSÖZ. C. 1964. *Ephesus: Legends and Facts.* Ayyildiz Matbaasi, Ankara.

TOMAS, A. 1972. *Atlantis: From Legend to Discovery.* Robert Hale.

TOMPKINS, P. 1997. Lost Atlantis: Nude Scientists, Giant Sharks, Bad Vibes, and Me. *Harper's* 294(760):76–83.

TRAILL, D. A. 1995. *Schliemann of Troy: Treasure and Deceit.* St. Martin's.

TREISTER, M. 1995. First Report on Priam's Treasure. *Archaeology* 48(5):64–66.

TRELL, B. L. 1988. The Temple of Artemis at Ephesos. In P. Clayton and M. Price, eds., *The Seven Wonders of the Ancient World,* pp. 78–99. Routledge.

TRUBY, J. D. 1979. The Blast That Shook the World. *Oceans* 12(2):54–56.

VAN ANDEL, T. 1977. *Tales of an Old Ocean.* Norton.

VAN ANDEL, T., and J. C. SCHACKLETON. 1982. Late Paleolithic and Mesolithic Coastlines of Greece and the Aegean. *Jour. Field Arch.* 9:445–54.

VAN HORN, L. R. 1923. *Greek Life and Thought.* Columbia University Press.

VANSCHOONWINKEL, J. 1990. Animal Representations in Theran and Other Aegean Arts. In D. Hardy, ed., *Thera and the Aegean World III,* vol. 1, *Archaeology,* pp. 327–47. Thera Foundation.

VAUGHAN, A. 1996. Early Prophecies of Earth Changes and Atlantis. *Venture Inward* 12(1): 16–18, 36.

VAUGHAN, A. C. 1959. *The House of the Double Axe: The Palace at Knossos.* Doubleday.

VELIKOVSKY, I. 1950. *Worlds in Collision.* Macmillan.

VENTRIS, M., and J. CHADWICK. 1956. *Documents in Mycenaean Greek.* Cambridge University Press.

VERBEEK, R. D. M. 1884. The Krakatoa Eruption. *Nature* 30:10–15.

VERMEULE, E. 1964. *Greece in the Bronze Age.* University of Chicago Press.

———. 1967. The Promise of Thera: A Bronze Age Pompeii. *Atlantic Monthly* 220(6):83–94.

VERNE, J. 1864. *Voyage au centre de la Terre (Journey to the Center of the Earth).* Paris.

———. 1870. *Vingt mille lieues sous les mers. (Twenty Thousand Leagues Under the Sea).* Paris.

VIGGERS, D. 1944. *Atlantis Rising.* Andrew Dakers.

VINE, F. J. 1966. Spreading of the Ocean Floor: New Evidence. *Science* 154:1405–15.

VINE, F. J., and D. H. MATTHEWS. 1963. The Magnetic Anomalies over Ocean Ridges. *Nature* 199:947–49.

VITALIANO, C. J., S. R. TAYLOR, M. D. NORMAN, M. T. MCCULLOCH, and I. A. NICHOLS. 1990. Ash Layers of the Thera Volcanic Series: Stratigraphy, Petrology and Geochemistry. In D. Hardy, ed., *Thera and the Aegean World III,* vol. 2, *Earth Sciences,* pp. 53–78. Thera Foundation.

VITALIANO, D. B. 1971. Atlantis: A Review Essay. *Journal of the Folklore Inst.* 8:68–76.

——————. 1973. *Legends of the Earth: Their Geologic Origins.* Indiana University Press.

——————. 1978. Atlantis from the Geological Point of View. In E. S. Ramage, ed., *Atlantis: Fact or Fiction?,* pp. 137–60. Indiana University Press.

VOLTAIRE (F.-M. ARQUET). 1759a. *Candide.* Limited Editions Club, 1973.

——————. 1759b. The Lisbon Earthquake. In B. R. Redman, ed., *The Portable Voltaire,* pp. 556–69. Penguin, 1968.

WACE, A. J. B. 1949. *Mycenae: An Archaeological History and Guide.* Princeton University Press.

WAGSTAFF, J. M. 1978. The Reconstruction of Settlement Patterns on Thera in Relation to the Cyclades. In C. Doumas, ed., *Thera and the Aegean World I,* pp. 449–56. Thera Foundation.

WALKER, B. 1982. *Earthquake.* Time-Life Books.

WALLACE, J. 1987. *The Deep Sea.* Gallery Books.

WARD, A. G. 1970. *The Quest for Theseus.* Praeger.

WARREN, P. 1975. *The Aegean Civilizations.* Elsevier Phaidon.

WARREN, P. M. 1978. The Unfinished Red Marble Jar at Akrotiri, Thera. In C. Doumas, ed., *Thera and the Aegean World I,* pp. 555–68. Thera Foundation.

——————. 1990. Summary of Evidence for the Absolute Chronology of the Early Part of the Aegean Late Bronze Age Derived from Historical Egyptian Sources. In D. Hardy and A. C. Renfrew, eds., *Thera and the Aegean World III,* vol. 3, *Chronology,* pp. 24–26. Thera Foundation.

WARREN, P. M., and H. PUCHELT. 1990. Stratified Pumice from Bronze Age Knossos. In D. Hardy and A. C. Renfrew, eds., *Thera and the Aegean World III,* vol. 3, *Chronology,* pp. 71–81. Thera Foundation.

WASHINGTON, H. S. 1926. Santorini Eruption of 1925. *Bull. Geol. Soc. Amer.* 37:349–84.

WATKINS, N. D., R. S. J. SPARKS, J. SIGURDSSON, T. C. HUANG, A. FEDERMAN, S. CAREY, and D. NINKOVICH. 1978. Volume and Extent of the Minoan Tephra from Santorini Volcano: New Evidence from Deep-Sea Sediment Cores. *Nature* 271:122–26.

WEGENER, A. 1915. *The Origin of Continents and Oceans.* Dover, New York, 1966.

WEINER, J. 1986. *Planet Earth.* Bantam.

WERTENBAKER, W. 1974. *The Floor of the Sea: Maurice Ewing and the Search to Understand the Earth.* Little, Brown.

————. 1980. Land Below, Sea Above. In J. J. Thorndike, ed., *Mysteries of the Deep,* pp. 294–341. American Heritage.

WEXLER, H. 1952. Volcanoes and World Climate. *Scientific American* 186(4):74–81.

WHELAN, M. 1994. The Night the Sea Smashed Lord's Cove. *Canadian Geographic* 114(6):70–73.

WHITSHAW, E. M. 1928. *Atlantis in Andalucia.* Rider. Reissued in 1994 as *Atlantis in Spain* by Adventures Unlimited.

WIENER, M. H. 1984. Crete and the Cyclades in LM I: The Tale of the Conical Cups. In R. Hägg and N. Marinatos, eds., *The Minoan Thalassocracy: Myth and Reality,* pp. 17–26. Proc. Third Int. Symp. Swedish Inst. in Athens. Stockholm.

————. 1987. Trade and Rule in Palatial Crete. In R. Hägg and N. Marinatos, eds., *The Function of Minoan Palaces,* pp. 262–68. Proc. Fourth Int. Symp. Swedish Inst. in Athens. Stockholm.

————. 1990. The Isles of Crete? The Minoan Thalassocracy Revisited. In D. Hardy, ed., *Thera and the Aegean World III,* vol. 1, *Archaeology,* pp. 128–61. Thera Foundation.

————. 1991. Bronze Age Trade in the Mediterranean. In N. H. Gale, ed., *Studies in Mediterranean Archaeology,* vol. 90, pp. 325–50. Paul Åströms Förlag.

WILCOXSON, K. H. 1966. *Chains of Fire: The Story of Volcanoes.* Chilton.

WILLETS, R. F. 1969. *Everyday Life in Ancient Crete.* Batsford.

WILLIAMS, A. R. 1997. Under the Volcano Montserrat. *National Geographic* 192(1):59–75.

WILLIAMS, F. L. 1963. *Matthew Fontaine Maury, Scientist of the Sea.* Rutgers University Press.

WILLIAMS, M. O. 1953. Crete, Cradle of Western Civilization. *National Geographic* 104(5):693–706.

WILSON, C. J. N., and B. F. HOUGHTON. 1990. Eruptive Mechanisms in the Minoan Eruption: Evidence from Pumice Vescularity. In D. Hardy, ed., *Thera and the Aegean World III,* vol. 2, *Earth Sciences,* pp. 122–28. Thera Foundation.

WILSON, J. T. 1963. Continental Drift. *Scientific American* 208(4):86–100.

————. 1965. A New Class of Faults and Their Bearing on Continental Drift. *Nature* 207:343–47.

————. 1966. Did the Atlantic Close and Then Reopen? *Nature* 211:676–81.

WILSON, L. 1978. Energetics of the Minoan Eruption. In C. Doumas, ed., *Thera and the Aegean World I,* pp. 221–30. Thera Foundation.

————. 1980. Energetics of the Minoan Eruption: Some Revisions. In C. Doumas, ed., *Thera and the Aegean World II,* pp. 31–35. Thera Foundation.

WOOD, M. 1985. *In Search of the Trojan War.* Facts on File.

WUNDERLICH, H. G. 1974. *The Secret of Crete.* Macmillan.

WYSESSION, M. 1995. The Inner Workings of the Earth. *American Scientist* 83(2):134–47.

YEH, H., F. IMAMURA, C. SYNOLAKIS, Y. TSUJI, P. LIU, and S. SHI. 1993. The Flores Island Tsunamis. *Eos* 74(33):369, 371–73.

YOKOYAMA, I. 1978. The Tsunami Caused by the Prehistoric Eruption of Thera. In C. Doumas, ed., *Thera and the Aegean World I,* pp. 277–83. Thera Foundation.

YOKOYAMA, I., and V. BONASIA. 1978. Gravity Anomalies on the Thera Islands. In C. Doumas, ed., *Thera and the Aegean World I,* pp. 147–52. Thera Foundation.

ZANGGER, E. 1992. *The Flood from Heaven: Deciphering the Atlantis Legend.* Morrow.

ZINK, D. 1978. *The Stones of Atlantis.* Prentice-Hall.

ZWINGLE, E. 1987. "Doc" Edgerton: The Man Who Made Time Stand Still. *National Geographic* 172(4):464–83.

INDEX

Page numbers in *italics* indicate illustrations.

ILLUSTRATION CREDITS